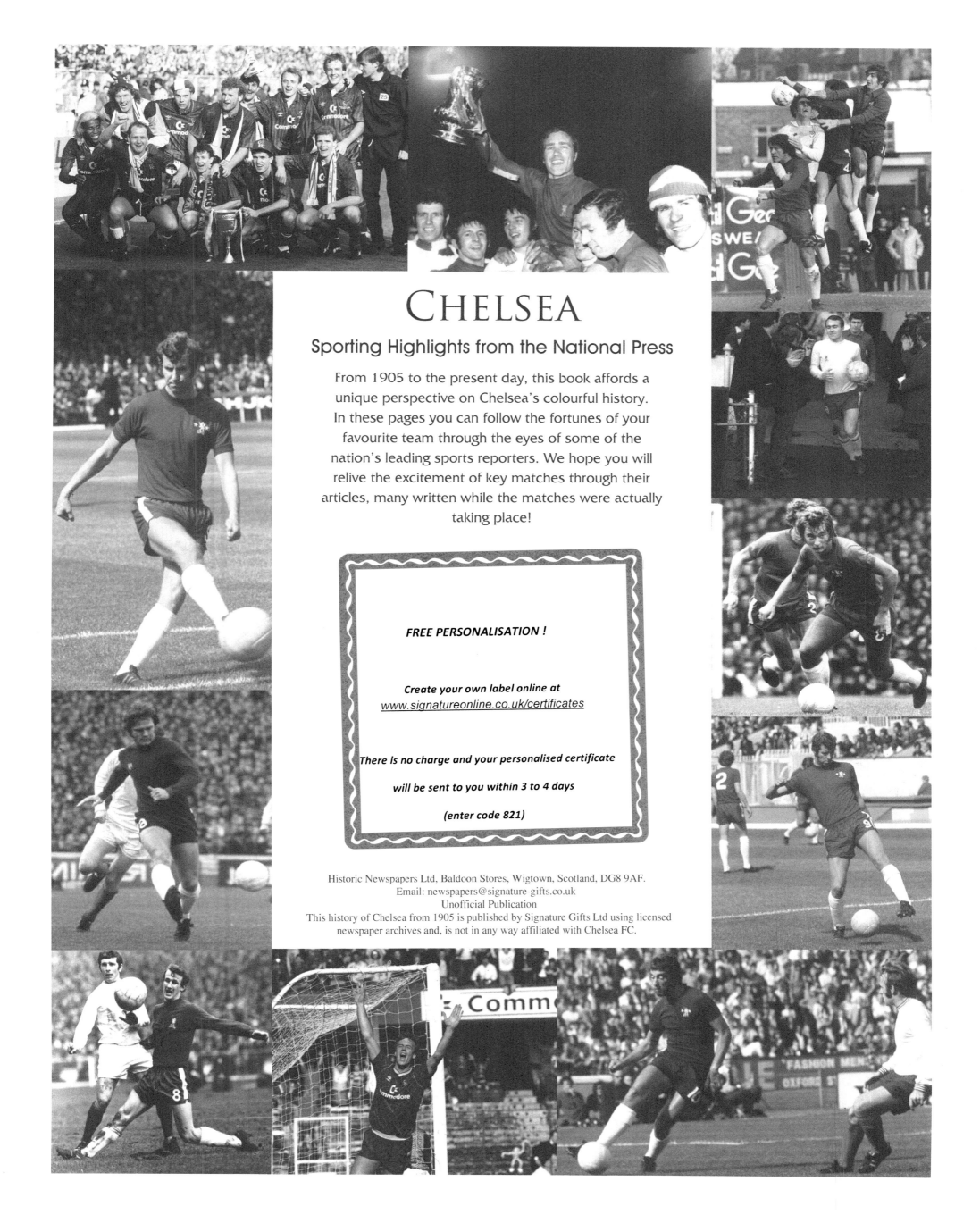

CHELSEA

Sporting Highlights from the National Press

From 1905 to the present day, this book affords a unique perspective on Chelsea's colourful history. In these pages you can follow the fortunes of your favourite team through the eyes of some of the nation's leading sports reporters. We hope you will relive the excitement of key matches through their articles, many written while the matches were actually taking place!

FREE PERSONALISATION !

Create your own label online at
www.signatureonline.co.uk/certificates

There is no charge and your personalised certificate

will be sent to you within 3 to 4 days

(enter code 821)

Historic Newspapers Ltd, Baldoon Stores, Wigtown, Scotland, DG8 9AF.
Email: newspapers@signature-gifts.co.uk
Unofficial Publication
This history of Chelsea from 1905 is published by Signature Gifts Ltd using licensed newspaper archives and, is not in any way affiliated with Chelsea FC.

Published by Historic Newspapers
PO Box 453
Harpenden
AL5 9AL

ISBN-13: 978-0-9552803-4-4

CRICKET SNAPSHOTS.

Exciting Cricket at Nottingham —Cotter's Bowling—Scores in Other Matches.

(A special description of the Test match at Nottingham by Mr. F. B. Wilson appears on page 5.)

The first day's play in the first Test match went all against England, and it will need a long pull, a strong pull, and a pull altogether in the later stages to straighten matters out.

* * *

Jackson 0, MacLaren 2, Jessop 0 is awful from the English point of view. Moreover, the disasters were not owing to a bad wicket, but rather to bad batting.

* * *

Cotter has never bowled so fast in this country, but he was very erratic, and wanted a deal of watching. It is a trifle disconcerting to hear a ball whistle through the air within an inch of one's ear, and probably the English batsmen were a bit unnerved by his great pace.

* * *

Laver's bowling was a great contrast to Cotter's. He kept a perfect length, made the ball swing away with his arm, and altogether gave a magnificent display of scientific trundling.

* * *

Hayward played altogether too late at the yorker which bowled him.

* * *

C. B. Fry was at Nottingham, but his hand was swathed in bandages, and he was always a certain non-starter. Lees was the other man to stand down.

* * *

Byes were numerous during the day. Every now and then Cotter sent the ball high over Kelly's head to the boundary.

* * *

Cotter rather disproved the theory that a fast bowler was not wanted for Nottingham owing to the perfect state of the wicket. He, at any rate, could make the ball bump.

* * *

The four men who stood out head and shoulders above their fellows on the England side were Tyldesley, Bosanquet, Rhodes, and Lilley, and of these the best was Bosanquet.

* * *

Australia made a bad start by losing Duff with only 1 on the board. He was caught at square leg by Hayward, off John Gunn's first ball.

* * *

Then Trumper strained himself. But Noble and Hill made a splendid stand, and for a time the English bowlers were held cheaply.

* * *

The crowd acted in a most sportsmanlike manner, and cheered Noble and Hill with the utmost impartiality whilst making their grand stand.

* * *

Jessop was called upon to bowl fast for England, but met with no success.

* * *

Jackson dismissed Noble, Hill, and Darling in one over.

* * *

Yorkshire, without Lord Hawke, F. S. Jackson, Hirst, and Rhodes, took the field against Worcester at Leeds yesterday. It did not make much difference, as the Tykes hit up 323, Denton and H. Wilkinson being scorers-in-chief.

* * *

Brighton wickets are not providing such crops of runs as in some previous seasons. Northampton were put out for 230 yesterday, and then Sussex lost two wickets for 54 before the close.

* * *

The Cantabs made a lot of runs against Surrey. M. W. Payne hit up a brilliant century, and R. P. Keigwin only just missed one.

* * *

Gold medals will be presented to the Northamptonshire cricket team next week by Lord Lilford, the president, in commemoration of the club's promotion to first-class honours.

CITIZEN.

MODERATE SCORING AT BRIGHTON.

NORTHAMPTONSHIRE.

W. H. Kingston c Smith, b Vine	24	T. Horton, c Leach, b Killick	3
Cox, c Goldie, b Cox	0	H. E. Kingston, c Butt, b Leach	29
Thompson, c Cox, b Relf	0	H. Hawkins b Killick	2
East, st Butt, b Relf	27	B. C. Smith, c Goldie, b Killick	0
C. J. T. Pool, c Vine, b Killick	91	Extras	10
F. M. Crosse, c Goldie, b Cox	34		
Knight, not out	10	Total	230

SUSSEX.

Vine c Hawkins, b Thompson	0	W. L. Knowles, not out	3
K. O. Goldie, b Thompson	13	Extras	3
Killick, not out	35	Total (2 wkts)	54

P. B. Chapman, C. L. A. Smith, Relf, Cox, Leach, Butt, and Tate to bat.

BOWLING ANALYSIS.

NORTHAMPTONSHIRE.—First Innings.

	o.	m.	r.	w.		o.	m.	r.	w.
Cox	25	6	78	2	Goldie	10	3	22	0
Relf	24	9	39	2	Killick	11.4	0	31	4
Tate	9	2	19	0	Leach	5	1	11	1
Vine	9	2	20	1					

DARK BLUES OPPOSE KENT.

KENT.

Seymour, b Martin	10	A. P. Day, b Martin	0
Humphreys, st Wright, b Burn	85	Huish, c Henley, b Martin	36
F. Penn, c Norris, b Martin	43	Fairservice, c Foster, b Martin	9
Hearne (A.), c Carlisle, b Martin	46	Fielder, c Wright, b Martin	0
F. B. Leney, c Branston, b Henley	30	Blythe, not out	14
F. H. B. Marsham, b Henley	1	Extras	13
		Total	287

OXFORD UNIVERSITY.

First Innings: F. A. Henley, b Fielder, 0; R. C. Burn, not out, 1; G. G. Bennett, not out, 3; total (for 1 wkt.), 4.

E. L. Wright, G. T. Branston, K. M. Carlisle, A. E. Worsley, O. T. Norris, W. S. Bird, E. G. Martin, and G. N. Foster to bat.

LEICESTER AT LORD'S.

LEICESTERSHIRE.

C. E. de Trafford, lbw, b Tarrant	38	R. T. Crawford, c Board, b Tarrant	20
C. J. B. Wood, b Dennett	54	Jayes, c Wynyard, b Hartley	4
Whitehead, run out	3	Allsopp, b Vogler	4
Knight, b Hartley	24	Whiteside, not out	5
Coe, c Hartley, b Dennett	19	Extras	7
V. F. S. Crawford, b Tarrant	43		
W. W. Odell, b Tarrant	27	Total	248

ROBERTS STILL GAINING.

Veteran Champion Now Only 122 Behind His Opponent.

Another wonderful gathering of billiards enthusiasts filled the Caxton Hall, Westminster, yesterday afternoon, when the big billiards match was resumed.

By the conditions of the match each half of the 18,000 up is played with a set of balls of either player's choosing. Last week Stevenson had the privilege. This week it is left to Roberts to provide the ivories.

There is more in this than will probably be at first recognised by the ordinary player. It is worth many hundreds of points to the player who is using the set of balls to which he is accustomed. Therefore Roberts's performance of scoring no fewer than 1,233 in excess of his opponent's total last week is even more creditable than it appears to be.

At first Roberts, who recommenced with his score at 9,000 to Stevenson's 9,767, was not seen at his best. In fifteen innings the best things he accomplished were paltry moves of 21 and 20. There was an abundance of safety exchanges, these closing up the game always to the big man's disadvantage. He could not get a favourable opening. All the time Stevenson was scoring usefully.

At one time the leader, playing in beautiful style, scored 58, 123, 77, and 39 in four consecutive innings. During their course he regained a four-figure lead, to a big round of cheering.

It was quite a breezy afternoon's sitting, the opposing partisans more than once letting their feelings get the better of them, and some ironical applause and exchange of remarks cropped up.

Stevenson Out of Luck.

These interruptions seemed to act as an incentive to Roberts, who from that time forward displayed great improvement. Some of his cannons, after losing position, were simply marvellous. A big five shot was the leading feature in a fine effort of 168. A rasping kiss-back cannon was seen in a break of 136.

Backing up these valuable moves by such useful runs as 109, 53, 40, and 84, John regained all his lost ground of the first hour.

In the evening, among many other notables present, was Lord Alverstone, the Lord Chief Justice. He proved a very observant spectator, watching every stroke with keen interest: Lord Cadogan was none the less enthusiastic.

It proved to be a very one-sided session from a scoring point of view. Roberts had all the best of the deal, and, after running his unfinished break into 63, improved his position by the aid of such items as 169, 68, 89 in succession, 107, 149, and 87, also in following order.

There seemed to be no cessation to his rapid progress, until within 16 of his specified number for the stage. He then let in Stevenson, who gave a meritorious display while subscribing 95, which terminated over a difficult run-through loser.

Closing scores:

Stevenson (receives 2,000)	10,623
Roberts (in play)	10,501

LADIES' GOLF.

Miss Campbell Wins the Stroke Contest at the Championship Meeting.

At Cromer yesterday the thirteenth annual championship meeting of the Ladies' Golf Union was begun with the customary eighteen holes stroke competition. Nearly all the entrants for the championship took out cards, and Miss Dorothy Campbell, of North Berwick, won with the splendid score of 82.

A strong south-westerly wind made the golf difficult. The men's scratch score for the links is 78. Miss F. Hezlet, 86, and Miss Glover, 86, tied for second place.

On playing off the tie for second prize Miss F. Hezlet beat Miss Glover by a putt on the last green.

Miss H. Curtis was the only American competitor to get into the first twelve. Miss Bertha Thompson reached the turn in the remarkably fine score of 37—one under scratch—but coming home her driving was erratic, and the last nine holes cost her 51 strokes.

M.C.C. AND GROUND.

G. J. V. Weigall, c R. Crawford, b Coe	39	Board, not out	26
Vogler, b Jayes	22	Extras	5
Hulton, not out	33	Total (2 wkts)	125

Capt. E. G. Wynyard, Tarrant, J. C. Hartley, Major H. C. Moorhouse, A. Butcher, F. H. Liebenrood jun., and Dennett to bat.

BOWLING ANALYSIS.

LEICESTERSHIRE.—First Innings.

	o.	m.	r.	w.		o.	m.	r.	w.
Dennett	26	2	79	2	Hartley	19	2	55	2
Vogler	8	2	27	1	Liebenrood	2	0	8	0
Tarrant	24.4	6	72	4					

YORKSHIRE'S FINE SCORE.

YORKSHIRE.

Grimshaw, c and b Cuffe	43	Myers, c Gaukrodger, b Keene	23
Rothery, c Gaukrodger, b Wilson	4	H. Wilkinson, run out	78
Denton, b Pearson	91	Higgins, c Cuffe, b Keene	2
Tunnicliffe, b Burrows	0	Ringrose, b Bird	15
Wilkinson (W.H.), b Wilson	16	Oyston, not out	2
Haigh, b Pearson	34	Extras	15
		Total	323

WORCESTERSHIRE.

Bowley, b Myers	1	Cuffe, not out	14
W. B. Burns, c Ringrose, b Myers	18	Pearson, not out	0
		Total (2 wkts)	33

R. S. Brinton, Bird, Gaukrodger, Wilson, Burrows, Wheldon, and Keene to bat.

BOWLING ANALYSIS.

YORKSHIRE.—First Innings.

	o.	m.	r.	w.		o.	m.	r.	w.
Wilson	22	1	102	2	Pearson	16	4	52	2
Bird	20.5	3	48	1	Cuffe	13	3	35	1
Burrows	14	4	43	1	Keene	10	2	28	2

Pearson bowled one no-ball.

CENTURY BY M. W. PAYNE.

CAMBRIDGE UNIVERSITY.

M. W. Payne, b Gooder	178	H. C. McDonell, c Strudwick, b Gooder	19
R. A. Young, c Holland, b Nice	3	F. J. V. Hopley, b Gooder	12
E. W. Mann, c and b Hayes	14	A. F. Morcom, not out	10
C. C. Page, c and b Smith	22	P. R. May, c Strudwick, b Nice	14
W. P. Harrison, b Smith	0	G. G. Napier, b Nice	0
R. P. Keigwin, lbw, b Gooder	89	Extras	4
		Total	365

SURREY.

Hobbs, c Payne, b Napier	0	Baker, not out	9
Holland, not out	8		
Davis, lbw, b McDonell	11	Total (2 wkts)	28

N. A. Knox, R. E. H. Baily, Hayes, Nice, Gooder, Smith (W. C.), and Strudwick to bat.

DERBY MEETING OPENS.

Promise of Excellent Sport—Rain Badly Wanted to Soften Epsom Downs.

(A Special Article on the Derby by "Grey Friars" appears on page 6.)

Lovely weather makes the countryside a delight just now, and none more picturesque than the Epsom district will be seen this week. Lord Rosebery's charming place, The Durdans, is a leafy paradise to-day in the flush of early summer.

* * *

Will that noble owner have occasion to build another entrance, following the example of the "Ladas Gate" by one named after Cicero, is a pretty question. The Derby seems a certainty for Cicero, and for the third time—a most remarkable record—Lord Rosebery will lead back to the weighing-room the winner of the great classic race.

* * *

One of the most interesting races to-day will be that for the Woodcote Stakes. It is the first six furlong race of the season, and on all reasoning from recent form we may expect to see this prize of 1,000 sovs won by Alcanzor.

* * *

There should be an interesting contest for the Norbury Handicap. Henley's runaway win at Kempton Park indicated him as probable winner of subsequent races. But Henley dropped into the Derby fashion, fell a-coughing, and was obliged to let slide his recent engagement in the north. Henley has, however, quite recovered, and may make a bold bid to-day.

* * *

The going at Epsom is harder than for years past, and rain is badly wanted to make the galloping good.

SELECTIONS FOR TO-DAY.

EPSOM.

1.30.—Craven Stakes—PURE CRYSTAL.
2. 5.—Wallington Plate—SWEET MARY.
2.40.—Norbury Handicap—CARO.
3.15.—Woodcote Stakes—ALCANZOR.
3.50.—Ashstead Plate—PRINCESS SAGAN.
4.25.—Egmont Plate—DIVORCE COURT.
5. 0.—Epsom Handicap—EXTRADITION.

SPECIAL SELECTION.

ALCANZOR.

GREY FRIARS.

TO-DAY'S PROGRAMME.

EPSOM.

1.30—CRAVEN STAKES of 200 sovs. The last mile of the Derby Course.

	yrs	st	lb		yrs	st	lb
His Lordship	6	10	1	Dispute	3	7	0
Aggressor	6	8	8	Marsuma	3	7	0
aSir Dennis	4	8	6	Camoens	3	6	10
El Maestro	4	8	6	a Hairdress c	3	6	10
Park Ranger	4	8	6	a Pure Crystal	3	6	10
American Boy	6	8	5	Coldstream	3	6	10
Capot	5	8	5	Leopold	3	6	10
St. Kilda	4	7	13	aFiesta	3	6	7
a Laughing Gull	5	7	3	Commune	3	6	7
aMaria	3	7	0	Controversy	3	6	7

2.5—WALLINGTON PLATE of 200 sovs. Five furlongs.

	st	lb		st	lb
aNinias	9	0	a Nell H.	8	11
a Crusader	9	0	a Evie	8	11
Peter Jackson	9	0	Only	8	11
Wild Ride	9	0	St. Ives	8	11
Republican	9	0	Sybil Primrose	8	11
a Sophron	9	0	Holmhurst f	8	11
Stavordale	9	0	Cambaan	8	11
Gliming	9	0	a Charlotte f	8	11
Nero	9	0	Gold Benella f	8	11
Gone By	9	0	a Lady Ursuline	8	11
Bramble c	9	0	The Rouken f	8	1
a Preparation	8	11	Aziz	8	1
Sweet Mary	8	11	aMaddalena f	8	1

2.40—NORBURY PLATE (handicap) of 300 sovs. The Derby Course, about one mile and a half.

	yrs	st	lb		yrs	st	lb
Colonel Wozac	6	9	3	a Queen of the Earth	3	8	1
Love Charm	5	9	2	McYardley	a	8	1
Harmony Hall	5	9	0	Brownist	5	8	0
Aralia	a	8	12	a Filbert	3	8	0
Sun Bonnet	a	8	12	Lychnobite	6	7	13
Wet Paint	6	8	11	Fonbio	3	7	11
aCaro	6	8	5	Song Thrush	3	7	10
Stephanas	5	8	5	Cortona	4	7	8
aHenley	4	8	4	Fraxinus	3	7	6
aBroke	5	8	2	aLiza Johnson	5	7	5
aIslesman	4	8	2	aMaria	3	7	1
a Winkfield's Charm	6	8	2	aDarwinian	3	7	0
Orbel	a	8	2	Horn Head	3	7	0
a Hong Kong	4	8	2	Premiere Marche	3	7	0

3.15—WOODCOTE STAKES of 1000 sovs, by subscription of 20 sovs each, for two-year-olds. The last six furlongs of the Derby Course.

	st	lb		st	lb
aAlcanzor	9	3	Flair	8	9
aBlack Auster	8	12	Ramrod	8	9
Dame Agneta c	8	12	Rosewater	8	9
Ormeton	8	12	Applemint f	8	9
Adamas	8	12	Blare f	8	9
Burnisher	8	12	Musley Maid f	8	9
St. Swithin	8	12	Serenata	8	9
a Gals' Gossip	8	12	Ishallah	8	9
Rocketter	8	12	Nurang	8	9
Muscar	8	12	a Glucose	8	9
Mona Cross c	8	12	Turkish Princess	8	6
Enfant de Miracle	8	12	Victoria May f	8	6
aMerry Miser f	8	9	Mandorla f	8	6
aNorman Mint	8	9	Peloria	8	6
Ella Tweed f	8	9			

3.50—ASHSTEAD PLATE of 200 sovs; winner to be sold for 200 sovs. Six furlongs, on the New Course.

	yrs	st	lb		yrs	st	lb
aRetrieve	4	9	7	aCraigellachie	3	8	4
aNahlband	a	9	7	aAmychen	3	8	4
aCountry Boy	5	9	7	aAbelard	3	8	4
aTickets	5	9	7	aPrincess Sagan	3	8	4
aAkbar	5	9	4	aMinikin	3	8	4
aPoppits	6	9	4	aChevening Belle	3	8	4
aNeutrality	3	8	4				

4.25—EGMONT PLATE (handicap) of 300 sovs. Five furlongs.

	yrs	st	lb		yrs	st	lb
aSermon	5	9	0	Laughter	3	8	0
aDivorce Court	4	8	11	aRaven's Pride	3	7	12
aPansy Masters	5	8	10	Scuttler	4	7	11
Be Very Wise	5	8	10	St. Trumpet	3	7	9
a Gun Club	5	8	7	Lady Burgoyne	5	7	9
a Blowing Stone	5	8	5	Eurotas	3	7	4
a Simonstown	3	8	1	Economical	3	7	4
aHellene	3	8	0				

5.0—EPSOM PLATE (handicap) of 500 sovs. Seven furlongs.

	yrs	st	lb		yrs	st	lb
William's Hill	4	9	3	aThe Warrior	4	8	1
aCharcot	a	9	0	aBoycot	4	7	11
Otherwise	4	8	10	El Maestro	4	7	11
aExtradition	4	8	9	a Shanid Aboo	3	7	11
Earls Mor	4	8	8	Ticket o' Leave	4	7	10
St. Kilda	4	8	4	a Hackenschmidt	4	7	10
Mandelay	a	8	4	aTopstone	4	7	9
Semper Vivent	6	8	2				

FOOTBALL MAY MEETINGS.

Association's Annual Gathering—Cup Tie Profits Divided.

The council of the F.A. met at the Holborn offices yesterday prior to the annual general meeting.

The Finance Committee reported that the profits on the semi-final and final ties of the Cup would be divided as under:—Aston Villa, £3,362 13s. 5d.; Newcastle United, £2,068 10s.; Everton, £1,257 14s. 3d.; Sheffield Wednesday, £563 10s. 11d. Amateur Cup: West Hartlepool, £63 8s. 2d.; Bishop Auckland, £58 2s. 2d.; Clapton, £27 13s. 10d.; Ilford, £20 7s. 10d.

Letters were read from the London, Surrey, Middlesex, and Berks and Bucks Associations on the subject of admitting professional clubs to membership, and it was decided to arrange a conference between representatives of the F.A. and these associations.

Sanction was given for the enlargement of the Football League to forty clubs. Permission was given for Aston Villa to present gold watches and chains to the players who represented the club in the F.A. Cup final, and for Bolton Wanderers to present gold medals to their players to commemorate the return of the club to the first division of the League.

It was decided to present S. Bloomer with a special framed portrait of himself to commemorate his unique record of playing for England in twenty-one matches.

The report of the commission which inquired into the Brighton and Hove Albion F.C. was received and adopted. The report stated that illegal payments were made to an amateur player, and that the books of the club were in a state of chaos. The directors of the club holding office at the time were suspended for periods of from three to six months.

ANNUAL GENERAL MEETING.

Lord Kinnaird presided over a large attendance at the annual general meeting at the Holborn Restaurant last night.

The whole of the alterations in the rules of the Association submitted by the Council were passed. The chief alterations provided for the election of the Council in the month of June, instead of August; and the limitation of the fee paid for the transfer of a player to £350.

Mr. Pinder, for Aston Villa, moved that all reference to financial arrangements between clubs and players be deleted from the rules of the Association, and that the necessary alterations be made in the rules to carry this into effect. Mr. T. Maley (Manchester City) seconded in an excellent speech. Messrs. T. Houghton (Preston North End) and Lythaby (Queen's Park Rangers) were the chief speakers against the proposal, and on a vote it was defeated, 85 voting for, and 66 against. Mr. Pinder withdrew his request for a poll.

The alterations in the laws of the game submitted by the Council were approved. The chief alteration referred to the penalty-kick, and provided that when the kick is taken the goalkeeper must not advance beyond his own goal line.

LONDON AND THE LEAGUE.

Two Metropolitan Clubs in Division II —Membership Extended.

The annual general meeting of the English Football League was held at the Tavistock Hotel yesterday morning, Mr. J. J. Bentley presiding.

There were eight applicants for the three places in the Second Division—Burslem Port Vale, Burton United, Doncaster Rovers, Chelsea, Clapton Orient, Hull City, Leeds City, and Stockport County.

Leeds, Burslem, and Chelsea were elected.

The proposition before the meeting that the League should be extended to forty clubs, twenty for the First and twenty for the Second Division, was carried with a three-fourths majority. Four more clubs were thus eligible for election, and the favoured lot were Burton United, Hull City, Clapton Orient, and Stockport County. Doncaster Rovers were not elected.

Applications for entrance into the First Division were made by Notts County, Bury, Bristol City, Manchester United, and West Bromwich Albion. Bury and Notts County were elected.

The proposal of Bradford City, that in the event of an extension to forty clubs being granted "the three highest clubs in Division II. shall take the places of the three lowest in Division I., and the three lowest in Division I. shall go into Division II.," was lost.

The balance-sheet showed a loss of £7 16s. 5d. on the year's working.

LATEST LONDON BETTING.

THE DERBY.

3 ¼ on Cicero (laid) ....P. P
4 — agst Jardy (offered; 5 to 1 t) .Jr
100 any other (offered).

LATEST SCRATCHINGS.

Derby Stakes.—Jannaway, Coldstream, Dionard, Acropolis, Gallinago, The King, Costly Lady, Roe di Navarre, Kazbeck, Standon, Kama, Illuminata colt.

Oaks Stakes.—Sweet Briar filly, Munera, Etui, Kilblair, The Dhow, Carita.

Coronation Cup.—Flower Seller, St. Emilion.

OXFORD SUMMER EIGHTS.

The summer eight-oar races were continued at Oxford yesterday under almost tropical conditions before a very large crowd of spectators. In the second division Hertford bumped Oriel at the Long Bridges. A grand race along the barges also took place between St. Catherine's and Wadham, the former, sticking well to their work, getting home by a few feet.

In the first division Magdalen had to row hard to keep away from University, the latter gaining considerably after passing the Long Bridges. One bump only took place, St. John's falling to Keble before reaching the Gut.

SPORTING NEWS ITEMS.

Union Jack, after taking part in a mile gallop at Newmarket, yesterday morning, pulled up very lame.

At Newmarket yesterday morning P. Peck sent Colonel Wozac and Cicero a mile and a half at a capital pace.

The annual general meeting of the South-Eastern Football League will be held at the George Hotel, Strand, on Thursday, June 10.

At a meeting of the Ladies' Golf Union, held at Cromer in the evening, it was decided to hold next year's championship at Burnham (Somerset).

The vacancy on the committee of the Surrey County C.C., caused by the death of Sir Reginald Hanson, Bart., has been filled by the election of Lord Dalmeny.

EXCITING PLAY IN LEAGUE TOURNAMENTS

Great Games at Liverpool, Wolverhampton, and Birmingham —Villa Player's Bad Luck.

FULHAM DRAW AGAIN.

By S. B. ASHWORTH (League International).

After the excitement created by the first round of the English Cup last week, the League games seemed somewhat tame on Saturday, although they furnished one or two noteworthy performances. Liverpool, still going strongly, strengthened their position as leaders by a two goals win over Sunderland, and they were always winning, notwithstanding the fact that two of their cleverest forwards—Raybould and Cox—were missing. The proceeds were for the benefit of Morris Parry, a well-earned reward for long and faithful service in the ranks of the Liverpool Club.

* * *

Manchester City, thus early in the season free from anxiety as far as the Cup is concerned, have jumped into second place through their victory at Wolverhampton, and will certainly have a say in the championship. The victory was only by the narrowest of margins, and the Wolves held a lead at one time and looked likely winners. There was a "do or die" style about them which gave one the impression that they were making a last despairing attempt to improve their melancholy record.

* * *

Another "dark horse" for honours, Blackburn Rovers accomplished a feat of exceptional merit by defeating United in Sheffield. From all accounts the fine footwork of the Rovers, backed up by superb defence, created a deep impression on the people of the cutlery town, and the sturdy Blades were absolutely routed. Arnold Whittaker was the star of the game. Birmingham would doubtless rejoice greatly at their success over their neighbours at Aston Park, but the game only went their way after a deplorable accident to Evans, who broke his leg. He is one of the most unfortunate fellows who ever toed a ball. It is regrettable, too, to hear that some of the players allowed their tempers to run riot, for the game is not improved thereby. Howard Spencer was a much-missed man, and altogether it was not an "at home" day for the Villa.

* * *

Bolton Wanderers stole a march on Stoke, and returned the "compliment" paid by the Potters at Burnden Park early in the present campaign. It was one of those days when everything went wrong for one team, and that happened to be Stoke. Excepting for the opening twenty minutes, during which the home side got a "gift" goal, the Trotters were always the superior party, and played "ducks and drakes" with the opposition. A curious incident marked the game, as David Stokes got in a shot which reached the net without Roose making any effort to arrest it. The referee gave a goal, but Roose, in a virulent manner, disputed the decision, and eventually persuaded the officials that the ball had been shot through a rent in the side of the net—a fact admitted, I believe, by the marksman.

* * *

Everton failed to hold Newcastle in the North, and were somewhat lucky to get off with 4—2 against. United played their usual pattern-weaving game with success, and gave the opposing defence little rest. Middlesbrough continued their fine form, and deserved to beat Sheffield Wednesday, although the latter made a grand recovery after being two behind. I think the Northerners will soon escape the danger zone. Bury took a mild sort of revenge out of Notts Forest, although it was as much as they could do to get two past the watchful Linacre, who seems very much at home at Gigg-lane. The Shakers have done uncommonly well in the tournament considering their wretched start.

* * *

Woolwich Arsenal failed at Nottingham, although the margin was very narrow. The County played smart football with a dash of "devil," an element wanting in the opposition. With the men at their command the Gunners are in a wrong position, and must improve quickly or disaster faces them. North End revenged themselves on Derby County, and their robust methods, rough when it came to tackling Bloomer, pulled them through. I believe they, too, have one eye on the championship.

NECK AND NECK IN THE SOUTH.

BY F. B. WILSON.

By only managing to draw with Millwall on Saturday Fulham dropped a point in the fight for the championship of the Southern League on Tottenham, who picked up 2 points by beating Brighton and Hove Albion at Tottenham. Fulham still keep their position at the head of the Southern League; but should the 'Spurs win their next match they bump the Cottagers, as the latter have played one more game than the Tottenham men.

Southampton are third on the list, and still dangerous. They have played the same number of matches as the 'Spurs—nineteen—and are only 2 points behind them. Now that the Cup-tie season has come on the Saints are especially dangerous. A win puts them a point behind Fulham, and equal with the 'Spurs, should the 'Spurs lose their next game.

Fulham seem to have lost their dash forward, and only their fine defence saved them from a beating at North Greenwich. Millwall, on the other hand, played a fine, free game forward and were always dangerous. The Bristol Rovers went down before Portsmouth on the latter's ground, after leading by one goal to none. Portsmouth did really well all round, but the great hero of the match was Harris, who gave one of the best performances of the year in goal.

West Ham did very well to draw with Luton, at Luton. The home side did best in the first half, and crossed over one up, through Brown. In the second half West Ham did better, and Stapley equalised; West Ham were unlucky not to win on the day's play. Queen's Park Rangers were just too good for Swindon, at Swindon, and won by 2 goals to 1. The Rangers have been disappointing at times this season, but the team seems likely to do better before the end.

The New Boys (Norwich City) experienced their first defeat at Norwich, at the hands of Reading. The visitors scored twice before the opposition, but Norwich equalised, only to lose, rather unluckily, by the odd goal. New Brompton just got home against Northampton by 1 goal to nil, at Northampton. New Brompton quite deserved their victory, and thus demonstrated that their Cup-tie victory last week was no fluke.

Watford, who are at the bottom of the table, experienced another reverse at Brentford, and went down by the margin of 3 goals to 1. Brentford played a fast, clever game, and they are a formidable side on present form.

VIGOROUS PLAY AT TOTTENHAM.

BY CITIZEN.

Tottenham Hotspur beat Brighton and Hove Albion at Tottenham on Saturday by 3 to 1, and avenged the defeat they sustained at Brighton in September at the hands of the Albion.

The play was vigorous, not to say rough, and there were a good many fouls, but Mr. Ward, the referee, kept the men well in hand.

It was a capital match to watch, the game going with a swing from start to finish. Brighton led by a goal for nearly half the time, and defended so splendidly that it was only in the concluding stages that the Hotspur forwards wore their opponents down.

Mellors, in the Brighton goal, was the hero of the match, but Hulme and Turner, the backs, both played in capital style, and, well as the Hotspur line played, it really looked at one time as if the Albion would win.

Walton, at outside right, was the best of the Hotspur forwards, his pace and cleverness having an important bearing on the result. Bull, at centre-half, was the other outstanding player on the side.

Joynes scored for Brighton half-way through the first half. Bull, Walton, and Woodward scored Tottenham's goals in the concluding stages.

BRIGHT GAME AT CHELSEA.

BY ALFRED DAVIS.

Chelsea led Bradford City 4—0 midway through the second half of the game at Stamford Bridge on Saturday, and it looked as if that substantial lead would be added to before the finish. But a temporary easing-up by Chelsea and a praiseworthy rally by the visitors saw the latter improve their position by scoring twice, and at the finish Chelsea had to be content with a 4—2 win.

The game was a fairly interesting one to watch, and Bradford, who came to town without their best half-back, created a favourable impression. For some time they fully held their own, Foulke being called upon to negotiate one or two awkward shots. Then Chelsea came with a rush, and goals from James Robertson and McDermott enabled them to claim a 2—0 lead on crossing over.

Bradford met with further disaster when the second half opened, for Copeland and Kirwan added to the total, and the Yorkshiremen looked a badly-beaten team.

Then a change came over the scene. A magnificent volley into the net by McMillan from a corner-kick put fresh life into the visitors, and Clarke scored a second goal before the finish.

The Chelsea forwards played very pretty football, with a tendency to overdo the short passing. The halves were sound, and Foulke delighted the crowd by some agile feats. Bradford have a very fast and clever outside left in Conlin, and their backs kicked strongly and well.

On Saturday Bristol City, the leaders, won again, beating Stockport County by no fewer than 7 goals to love. Manchester United beat Glossop by 5 goals to 2. Manchester have a lead of two points from Chelsea, but they have played one more game. West Bromwich Albion, although they only drew with Burton on Saturday, are in the same position to Chelsea as Chelsea are to Manchester United—two points behind, with a game in hand—so the fight for promotion remains as keen as ever, with Bristol well ahead of the others.

ASSOCIATION RESULTS.

THE LEAGUE.—Division I.			
Notts County (h)	1	Woolwich Arsenal	0
Liverpool (h)	2	Sunderland	0
Birmingham	3	Aston Villa (h)	1
Blackburn Rovers	2	Sheffield United (h)	0
Bolton Wanderers	2	Stoke (h)	1
Middlesbrough (h)	2	Sheffield Wednesday	2
Manchester City	3	Wolverhampton Wdrs (h)	2
Bury (h)	2	Notts Forest	1
Preston North End (h)	3	Derby County	1
Newcastle United (h)	4	Everton	2
Division II.			
Chelsea (h)	4	Bradford City	2
Clapton Orient (h)	3	Lincoln City	0
Bristol City (h)	7	Stockport County	0
Manchester United (h)	5	Glossop	2
Burton United (h)	2	West Bromwich Albion	2
Barnsley (h)	8	Chesterfield	1
Grimsby Town (h)	5	Burslem Port Vale	0
Leeds City (h)	4	Leicester Fosse	1
Blackpool	1	Gainsborough Trinity (h)	0
Hull City	3	Burnley (h)	1
SOUTHERN LEAGUE.			
Tottenham Hotspur (h)	3	Brighton and H. Albion	1
Millwall (h)	1	Fulham	1
Brentford (h)	3	Watford	0
New Brompton	1	Northampton (h)	0
Luton (h)	1	West Ham	1
Queen's Park Rangers	2	Swindon (h)	1
Reading	3	Norwich City (h)	2
Portsmouth (h)	2	Bristol Rovers	1
Division II.			
Watford Reserves (h)	8	Grays United	1
Crystal Palace (h)	3	St. Leonards	1
WESTERN LEAGUE.			
Plymouth Argyle (h)	2	Southampton	1
SOUTH-EASTERN LEAGUE.			
Tottenham Hotspur R.	2	Brighton and Hove R. (h)	0
Southern United (h)	5	Chesham Town	0
LONDON LEAGUE.			
Fulham Reserves (h)	4	Clapton Orient Reserves	0
Leyton Reserves	3	West Ham Reserves (h)	1
SCOTTISH LEAGUE.			
Dundee (h)	2	Motherwell	0
Glasgow Rangers (h)	4	Port Glasgow	0
Kilmarnock (h)	2	Third Lanark	0
Falkirk (h)	2	Heart of Midlothian	2
Celtic (h)	4	Partick Thistle	1
Airdrieonians	4	Hibernians (h)	0
Queen's Park (h)	3	Aberdeen	0
Greenock Morton (h)	1	St. Mirren	0
AMATEUR CUP.			
New Crusaders (h)	6	Townley Park	2
Clapton (h)	3	Civil Service	0
Ealing (h)	2	Gosport United	1
Cheshunt	3	Ilford (h)	0
Uxbridge (h)	4	Tunbridge Wells	2
Romford (h)	4	Ipswich	2
Oxford City (h)	4	Dulwich Hamlet	0
ARTHUR DUNN CUP.			
Old Carthusians (h)	3	Old Westminsters	3
Old Aldenhamians (h)	6	Old Wykehamists	0

TO-DAY'S MATCHES.

The game between the North and South at Leeds to-day should prove one of the best ever contested by representative teams. Both sides are as chosen, except for the substitution of Riley for Herbert Smith in the South team.

Aston: Blackpool v. Crystal Palace (F.A. Cup).

Park Royal: Queen's Park Rangers v. West Ham (Western League).

Oxford: University v. Woolwich Arsenal.

Mr. E. Gwyn Nicholls's article on Welsh football appears on page 6.

ENGLISH RUGBY MATCHES

Blackheath Beat Richmond After a Strenuous Game.

By TOUCH JUDGE.

We had quite a nice game at Richmond on Saturday. The football all round was quite of as good quality as could be expected, and, what was of equal importance, the struggle was a close one. Blackheath did not repeat their Rectory Field performance when they ran over Richmond, and indeed had hard work to win by a try to nothing. The Kent club should perhaps have got home by a larger margin, and they quite deserved their win.

Blackheath owed their success mainly to better work outside the scrummage. Robson, who has come on a good deal lately, was excellent as the half-back standing off, and he played up very smartly to Basil MacLear. The burly Irish three-quarter was well marked by Godfray and Lawson, but he gave the opposition a lot of trouble. When the ball was in the open he always seemed to be in the thick of the fray. He tackled in his usual robust manner, being on to his man promptly, and he ran very strongly.

The solitary score in the match was the outcome of a blunder by Glover, the Richmond full-back, who kicked across in front of his own goal. MacLear was on the ball in a trice, and, making full use of his pace and strength, literally forced his way over. In the circumstances the try would hardly have been possible to anyone else on the side.

The winning point did not come until late in the game, and a little later Palmer lost a glorious chance of scoring for Richmond. Lawson ran right through, and threw out to Palmer, who only had to catch the ball to score. But last year's English international did not catch it, though it went straight to him.

The Richmond forwards played very well, being smart in their heeling, and they held up even after losing Fraser at half-time. The Richmond halves had the ball pretty often, but they generally passed out before getting their three-quarters on the run. Bennetts, on the right, was dangerous once or twice, but, with MacLear and Curl on top of them before they could get going, the Richmond centres had to resort to much kicking.

The Old Alleynians were outplayed by the Marlborough Nomads; the Old Merchant Taylors had a warm time at Northampton; but the London Scottish won their return with Cambridge University. The Light Blues, however, were playing their first match since vacation. Leicester just managed to beat Devonport Albion, and, as they drew down in the West, the Tigers will be pleased with themselves. It will help to console them for their two lickings from Northampton.

On the Old Deer Park, Rosslyn Park and the Harlequins had a tough match, and, thanks mainly to the fine work of their forwards, the latter managed to avenge the defeat they sustained earlier in the season at the hands of Rosslyn Park. The London Welsh wiped out Guy's to the tune of 5 goals (one penalty) and 5 tries to nothing. Qualified for both sides, Teddy Morgan very properly stood out of the match, but otherwise Guy's trotted out their best side. With the Hospital Cup-ties starting this week, Guy's are not to be envied their Saturday's experience.

Thanks to a succesful place-kick, Cheshire beat Yorkshire; and Northumberland defeated Lancashire. This clears the air a little in the Northern division. If Northumberland can overcome or even draw with Durham next Saturday they will be practically assured of the championship of the North.

TROJANS TO BE REVIVED.

One result of the visit of the New Zealand footballers is likely to be the revival of a once-famous Rugby club, the Trojans, at Southampton.

Speaking at a luncheon given on the St. Louis after the departure of the team, Dr. Adking, of Southampton, said that steps were being taken to revive the game under Rugby rules in the city.

It is likely, therefore, that next season will see the once-famous colours again sported by a team of Southern enthusiasts.

RUGBY RESULTS.

	Pts.		Pts.
COUNTY CHAMPIONSHIP.			
Northumberland	8	Lancashire	3
Cheshire	8	Yorkshire	6
OTHER MATCHES.			
Blackheath	3	Richmond (h)	0
Harlequins	14	Rosslyn Park (h)	9
London Welsh (h)	38	Guy's Hospital	0
Marlboro' Nomads (h)	28	Old Alleynians	3
St. Bartholomew's H.	12	London Irish (h)	0
London Scottish	30	Cambridge University (h)	8
Exeter (h)	9	Stroud	0
Cheltenham (h)	3	Cinderford	0
Leinster (h)	14	Connaught	8
Leinster	17	Munster (h)	8

SATURDAY'S HOCKEY.

The second of this season's English international trials was played at Bromsgrove, on Saturday, between teams representing the Midland and Western Counties. After an evenly-contested first-half, the Westerners deteriorated to such an extent that they had no fewer than eight goals scored against them in the second moiety, and the match ended in a decisive victory for the Midland team by 9 goals to nil.

Both University hockey elevens were engaged on Saturday. Cambridge, after leading by one to nothing at half-time, beat Beckenham, at Beckenham, by 3 goals to 0.

Oxford, who were not at full strength, lost on their own ground to Blackheath. Oxford scored the first two goals of the match, but then lost four in succession, and Blackheath eventually won by 6 goals to 5.

Most of the leading London clubs won their matches on Saturday. Bromley, however, gave the unbeaten Southgate team a hard game, the latter only winning by 2 goals to nil. Hampstead, whose forwards combined well, defeated East Sheen by 6 to 2, and Staines found their form at the expense of Wimbledon, whose defence was penetrated five times. Teddington defeated Surbiton by 5 to nothing. A creditable performance was the victory of Norwood over Willesden by 2 to 1.

The M.C.C. commenced a return match with Natal at Pietermaritzburg on Saturday, states Reuter. Warner won the toss and put Natal in, who were all out for 117. At the close the M.C.C. had scored 121 for five wickets.

Neither the Blackheath Harriers nor the United Hospitals Hare and Hounds had their strongest team for an eight miles match at Blackheath. With the lower score of twenty-five points to thirty, the Blackheath Harriers won an interesting contest by five points.

With the low score of twenty-two points, the Leeds West Riding Harriers won the annual championship at Headingley of the Leeds and District Cross-Country Association, and, in J. Brow, who covered the five miles course in 28min. 32 4-5sec., supplied the first man home.

HURST PARK FIASCO.

Horses Take the Wrong Course and Charge Into the Crowd.

LORD OF THE LEVEL'S SUCCESS.

There was a curious fiasco at Hurst Park Steeplechases on Saturday. One of the riders in the Weir Hurdle race mistook the steeplechase course for the hurdle race course at the stand turn. As this part was crowded with people there was a big scramble to get out of the way, but fortunately no serious harm was done, although one or two people were bowled over, and in one case a man had to be attended by the ambulance brigade.

* * *

The stupidity of the jockeys who followed Parvin, the rider of Melia, into the wrong course cannot be too strongly commented on. Men who have ridden for years at Hurst Park, one would think, must have known they were going wrong, even though the "dolls" were not in position across the course. "It's an ill wind that blows nobody good," and Sunburnt, who was toiling along in the rear, and whistling like a railway engine, profited by the mistake, as Taylor secured 300 yards lead before the others could turn and get into the right course, and leisurely cantered home. Yalu slipped up and broke a blood-vessel, and Gollanfield upset a spectator and afterwards broke down badly.

* * *

Oasis, who was purchased by his present owner after defeating a large field here in February last, enlisted a big following, and it was to the consternation of his supporters, that he was one of the lot that went into the wrong course. It was W. Taylor's first mount since he fractured his collar-bone through the falling of Helter Skelter at Windsor at the close of last year.

* * *

The afternoon's entertainment at Hurst Park was favoured with beautifully fine weather for the time of the year, and another very large company assisted at the proceedings, which aroused plenty of interest from beginning to end. Armoy was the only absentee for the Richmond Selling Steeplechase, for which George Fordham, who disappointed his owner in the race won by Kolian at Lingfield, was again trusted by the stable. He failed to improve on his previous running—indeed, he was last throughout, and, after Zampieri had looked formidable entering the straight, he was overtaken at the final fence by his stable companion, Coroun, who won comfortably. The backers of Mr. Schomberg must be condoled with, as when playing a conspicuous part in the race he was accidentally carried out of the course by Zampieri at the top turn.

* * *

Some close wagering was seen in connection with the Middlesex Handicap Steeplechase, Lord of the Level eventually settling down with a point advantage of Springbok. He, moreover, justified his market status by gaining a clever victor, Mason being seen to great advantage in a close finish with Mr. R. Payne.

* * *

Aspendale was not sent to compete for the Novices' Hurdle Race, and in his absence there was very little to choose between Crepuscule and Gold Lock. Both were confidently befriended by their connections, but the success of Lord Dalmeny's colours was entirely due to the erratic course pursued by Gold Lock, who swerved right across the track after clearing the last hurdles.

* * *

The Open Steeplechase was reduced to a match between Cossack Post and Countenance. The former, upon whom substantial odds were laid, made a bad blunder at the water, but he had his opponent beaten three fences from home, and finally won pulling up. Eight tried conclusions in the January Handicap Hurdle, which fell to the favourite, Little Sprout.

WINNERS AND PRICES AT HURST PARK.

Race.	Winner.	Rider.	Price.
Richmond (7)	Coroun	Mr. Payne	6 to 1
Weir (7)	Sunburnt	W. Taylor	4 — 1
Middlesex (6)	Lord of the Level	F. Mason	2 — 1
Novices (8)	Crepuscule	J. Nightingall	9 — 4
Open (2)	Cossack Post	W. Morgan	1 — 4
January (8)	Little Sprout	F. Mason	9 — 4

The above are both "Sporting Life" and "Sportsman" prices. (The figures in parentheses indicate the number of starters.)

SHRUBB A PROFESSIONAL.

Among other business of the general committee of the Amateur Athletic Association at Anderton's Hotel on Saturday was the appeal of A. A. Shrubb against his suspension for "malpractices in connection with athletic sports." After hearing Shrubb's explanation, the committee disallowed his appeal.

As a professional, Shrubb will run at Olympia every Monday, Thursday, and Saturday, commencing to-day. During his stay he will endeavour to lower the record for one mile, made by W. G. George.

Next year's amateur athletic championships will be held in the South of England.

ENGLISH GOLFERS IN MEXICO.

Mexico City, Saturday.—The second annual tournament for the open golf championship of Mexico was brought to a close to-day on the links of the Mexico Country Club, at San Pedro de los Pinos. Victory rested with Willie Smith, a native of Carnoustie, near Dundee, who settled in America some years ago, and who has recently been attached to the Mexico Country Club.

Unfortunately not one of the British entrants did himself justice. Herd finished third; his score of 312 for the 72 holes was 23 strokes worse than that of the winner, Willie Smith, who totalled only 289. Kirkaldy and White, with 319 each, tied for eighth place, and Jones, with 323, could only finish thirteenth.

Willie Anderson, an old North Berwick player and winner of the United States open championship in 1901, 1903, 1904, and 1905, was second with 301.

The Stade Française yesterday beat the Clifton Football Club, at Paris, states Reuter, by 10 points to 9.

The fifth annual automobile show at the Crystal Palace will open on Friday next. It promises to be one of the most interesting shows that have ever taken place at the Palace.

Highgate Harriers beat the Societe Athletique de Montrouge in a cross-country race at Montrouge by 11 points, states Reuter. Ragenau, a Frenchman, was first man home.

Peter Latham returned from America yesterday by the Carmania, after playing a series of racquets matches in America. He was defeated by George Standing, an American, but, on again meeting the same player, he won in the most decisive fashion.

Diggle (receives 1,250) beat Reece (receives 2,500) in the billiard tournament, at Soho-square, on Saturday, by 735. The game of 16,000, between Mitchell and Weiss, at Leicester-square, was not finished. The scores at the close were: Mitchell, 15,883; Weiss, 15,832.

THOUSANDS OF SPECTATORS WATCH HOLIDAY FOOTBALL MATCH AT STAMFORD BRIDGE YESTERDAY.

An enormous crowd invaded Stamford Bridge yesterday, where Chelsea defeated Newcastle United by two goals to one. So great was the crowd that a number of people broke through the gateways and obtained places for nothing. (1) Crowd entering the ground. Note the people going through the gateway without payment. (2) The crowd on the track.—(*Daily Mirror* and Half-Tones.)

PRINCESS MARY EIGHTEEN TO-DAY.

BRAVE FRENCH OFFICERS DECORATED.

The latest portrait of Princess Mary, who, but for the war, would have "come out" this month. Her Royal Highness, who is their Majesties' only daughter and third child, is eighteen years old to-day.—(Campbell Gray.)

General Galopin decorates officers at the Invalides, Paris, after reviewing 5,000 territorial troops. The General, who is in command of the Paris garrison, is about to embrace a brave cuirassier who has lost an arm.

SHEFFIELD UNITED WON THE CUP AT MANCHESTER · CHELSEA BEATEN BY 3-0.

Play in midfield in the gloom.

The captains, Utley and Taylor shake.

Bernard collected over £100 for Red Cross.

The wounded soldiers made the most of the day.

How the spectators "enjoyed" the game in the wet—especially those behind the umbrellas.

Some 60,000 people watched the Cup final, played in disagreeable weather, at Manchester yesterday. Sheffield United defeated Chelsea by 3-0.

HOW SHEFFIELD UNITED WON THE ENGLISH CUP.

Chelsea Beaten by 3 Clear Goals at Manchester.

WOODWARD MISSED.

Over 60,000 People See Southern Hopes Destroyed.

("SUNDAY PICTORIAL" SPECIAL.)

MANCHESTER, Saturday.

Sheffield United won the English Cup for the third time in their history by beating Chelsea on the Manchester United Club ground by three goals to none. It was a clean-cut, decisive victory, and in all departments of the game the winners were far and away the better team. At back Cook and English played superbly, but their work was rendered comparatively easy by the determination of the three half-backs—Sturgess, Brelsford and Utley. They scarcely made a mistake between them, and never gave the Chelsea forwards the slightest chance of settling down to play their game, with the result that the Chelsea half-backs were over-run by the opposing forwards.

In the first half particularly Sheffield United played fast, robust football, keeping the ball always on the move and, as a matter of fact, showing considerably more combination than the Londoners front line. Evans and Simmons, the two wingers, made many glorious openings for their inside men, but they were met by a fine defence.

Fighting a forlorn hope, Bettridge and Harrow, hard as they were worked, were never really run off their legs until the last ten minutes or a very strenuous game. Then the inevitable happened and Sheffield got their second and third goals, which they were clearly entitled to on the run of the play. Molyneux has never kept goal better. He made many wonderful saves from all sorts of ranges, but he might have been off the field for what earthly chance he had of stopping either of the shots which scored. To him Chelsea can in no wise attribute their defeat.

Where Chelsea Failed.

As a matter of fact, Chelsea failed just where they were expected to prove strongest. Fine line as the forwards undoubtedly are, they lacked just that touch of genius which would have enabled them to rise to a great occasion. There was a lack of a guiding hand to control their movements. They were spasmodic and fitful in their attacks, and they gradually accepted the inevitable. Thomson, who played at centre forward, was not often seen in the picture. Croal and MacNeil occasionally showed glimpses of their real form, their inter-passing was extremely pretty, but they lacked finish and were not often very dangerous.

Ford made a few good runs on the right wing, and Halse at times seemed to try to pull the match out of the fire on his own. Against a less daring and less resourceful defence he might have been successful, but on the day's play I think Vivian Woodward would have improved matters, although even then I don't think it would have affected the issue. Taylor, Logan and Walker—especially Walker—were much better in defence than attack, but probably they played as well as they were allowed to. They were always too far in front with their passes to their forwards. Perhaps this was due to the fact that those very passes were more often than not clearances from the Sheffield attacks. Had the Chelsea forwards been able to take the game more in their own hands doubtless the intermediate line would have been more effective. It was by no stretch of imagination a great match—it was like the day.

It was a dull, drizzling morning, and in the city there was nothing like the arrival scenes so common in the Euston-road when the Cup final invades on of London takes place. Few, if any, of the people in the streets wore favours, and it was to Manchester and its environs that the greater part of the crowd, which early on began to travel Old Trafford-wards, belonged.

Naturally there was a lot of khaki to be seen, but not so much as might have been expected. Still, the good folk of Manchester are enthusiastic for their lads in the King's uniform, and as a recruiting band played the men of one of the service battalions of the Manchester Regiment through the streets there were many loud and hearty cheers. "Bravo, our boys!" and a real "Hip, hip, hurrah!" greeted them right in the very centre of the city. How different from the almost reverent respectfulness which greets a battalion of the same wonderful Army as it marches through London's streets. Yet, with it all, I do not believe Manchester or Lancashire has any warmer feeling for the boys than London town. The metropolis is merely more restrained in its ebullitions of approval and regard.

Sides at Full Strength.

In spite of the drizzle there was a continuous stream from the city towards the ground, and when the gates opened at half-past twelve the early birds were ready to capture the best positions. By half-past two the compact ground of the Manchester United Club, one of the best arenas in the country from a playing point of view, looked well full, and there were evident indications of something in the nature of a record crowd. Still the constant stream kept the men at the turnstiles very active, and gradually the vast assembly became denser and the thin places filled until the terraces were packed with tier upon tier of eager football enthusiasts.

It was early announced that both Sheffield and Chelsea would have their full teams in the field, but Thomson, the Chelsea centre forward, it was stated, would play with a bandaged elbow. Lieutenant V. J. Woodward, although he made the journey from London in case of anything untoward happening, was not included in the side. All through the forenoon the one topic of conversation wherever little groups of footballers were gathered was whether the Cup would go to London again, it will be remembered that the 'Spurs won it for the South in 1901, after its stay of nineteen years in the North and Midlands. Since then the only occasions on which southern clubs have reached the final stage were in the following year, when Sheffield United defeated Southampton after a drawn game at the Crystal Palace, and in 1909, when Bristol City were beaten by Manchester United.

It is something of a coincidence that Sheffield United, who were conquered by the 'Spurs, and who vanquished Southampton, should again be the club opposed to the hopes of the South.

By three o'clock it was estimated that there were nearly 60,000 spectators on the ground, and the steady stream seemed hardly interrupted. The absence of favours was most marked, there were no parti-coloured umbrellas to denote the sympathies of their owners, and no fanatics had dressed themselves up in the royal blue and white of Chelsea or the red, white and black of the United. There was no parading of the touch line by any mascots or small boys on bicycles, and no mountebank acrobat attempted awe-inspiring feats over the backs of chairs, or threw handsprings on the turf.

Lord Derby, when he arrived, received a very hearty welcome, which the band, having just concluded a selection, mistook as an appreciation of their efforts. As minutes drew on towards the time for the teams to come out all were agog with excitement, and despite the heavy, damp atmosphere there was unquestionably a real touch of Cup-tie electricity in the crowd. They had come to see the national trophy won and lost and as they were not particularly favourable to either team they were prepared to be impartial judges.

Chelsea had reached the final stage by beating Swindon, Woolwich Arsenal, Manchester City, Newcastle United and Everton in the preliminary stages, while Sheffield's road had been via Blackpool, Liverpool, Bradford, Oldham and Bolton Wanderers. In this respect it must be admitted that Chelsea had vanquished the more formidable Cup-fighting sides. The teams were as follows:—

Right. **CHELSEA.** Left.

Molyneux

Bettridge Harrow

Taylor Logan Walker

Ford Halse Thomson Croal Neil

O

Evans Masterman Kitchen Fazackerley Simmons

Utley Brelsford Sturgess

English Cook

Gough

Left. **SHEFFIELD UNITED.** Right.

Chelsea were the first to take the field. They were cordially cheered, but the roar which saluted them was as nothing compared with that which greeted the United a moment or so later. The start took place three minutes before the advertised time, and both teams began with great dash, although the play was a bit scrambling at the start. Ford was fouled by Utley in the first minute of the game, and had to be led from the field and attended to on the touchline. Sheffield initiated a fast combined movement from the right wing, and the ball came across to Simmons, leaving the Sheffield left-winger in an excellent position, but Taylor cleared cleverly. Ford was soon back, and play continued rather scrambling and slightly in favour of Sheffield, Kitchen getting in a fast shot, which went just too wide.

Ford's Bad Luck.

Ford dashed away on Chelsea's right wing, and just as he looked like getting in a characteristic centre he stumbled, and the ball went behind.

Just after this the Chelsea goal was placed in jeopardy by Evans, who centred right across the goal mouth. Bettridge headed out, but Brelsford, fastening on the ball, shot just wide with a hard, low drive. A moment later Simmons put in an oblique shot across the Chelsea goal, but none of his colleagues were in a position to correct the aim and deflect the ball towards the goal. Sheffield were undoubtedly having the balance of the play, and seemed cooler in their methods than Chelsea, whose men were certainly not at this early stage displaying their best form. The game veered round in their favour, however, and, forcing a corner on the left wing, they kept play near the Sheffield goal for some moments until a weak shot by Croal relieved the pressure. Although pretty fast, the play was rather uneventful, and there were few interesting incidents in the first quarter of an hour. Then a miskick by Bettridge let the Sheffield forwards through, and Fazackerley drove in a terrific shot, which Molyneux saved magnificently.

The light improved considerably, and with it the play reached a decidedly higher standard, but always with Sheffield slightly the better side. Logan was doing some great stopping work during this critical time, and was always in the picture as the Sheffield inside men bore down on the Londoners' goal. Once he sent his left wing away in a nice movement, but Croal gave MacNeil a weak pass, and Sturgess broke up the attack. Sturgess a little later on fouled Croal rather badly, and the referee indulged in some finger wagging at his expense in awarding a free kick.

A Wonderful Escape.

Then Chelsea's goal had a miraculous escape, Evans placing a free kick so accurately that the ball fell among a group of Sheffield forwards, and how it was scrambled out of the danger zone few who took part in the mix-up could have had any clear conception. Now and again the Chelsea forwards got away smartly, but Cook and English were very sure in their tackling, and the movements were seldom very dangerous. A fine shot by Simmons was fisted out of the Chelsea goal by Molyneux, who was certainly having much more to do than Gough, who did not have to stop a shot in the first half-hour.

Contrary to expectations, the Sheffield forwards were maintaining their early dash, and in addition were playing better combined football than the Chelsea vanguard, who could not break through the sound defence of the United half-backs and backs. A shot from Kitchen struck Harrow and went just wide of the post, and from this corner the Chelsea goal had another narrow escape, as, after the ball had bobbed about on the heads of two or three players, Masterman, with almost an open goal, shot wide from a range of four yards. Towards half-time the Chelsea forwards improved, and after Gough had saved from Croal, Utley had to concede a corner to stop a combined dash of the Londoners.

This came to nothing, and then, after thirty-five minutes' play, Simmons scored from a cross by Evans. It was a fast rising shot with which Molyneux had no chance whatever. This was not an undeserved success, for up to this point the Blades were undoubtedly the better team. Then we saw a few flashes of the real Chelsea.

Some wonderfully clever criss-cross passing between McNeil and Croal left Ford with the chance of a lifetime, but he topped his shot and the ball rolled weakly over the line. After this play was very dull, and, with the United apparently confining their efforts to defence, Chelsea had more of the game. Several free kicks were awarded them, but none led up to dangerous movements until Ford got away and gave Halse a beautiful opening. Gough saved the shot, and half-time came with Sheffield leading by one goal to none.

The pall of fog, mist and smoke settled down heavier than ever during the interval, and it was impossible to distinguish the faces of the spectators on the other side of the ground. It was difficult to follow the play when the game was restarted at 4.25. Sheffield at once attacked and Masterman nearly broke through, but he was bowled over by Bettridge a few yards from goal. Now and again the Chelsea forwards got away nicely, but, kicking a little too hard, they were not given many opportunities against two such safe men as Cook and English, whose tackling and volleying were admirable throughout the match. It must, however, be said that their efforts were splendidly backed up by a resolute and determined line of half backs, who gave the opposing forwards very little rope.

Chelsea's Futile Efforts.

Sheffield United, with a goal in hand, played rather too much on the defensive, however, and one missed the fine sweeping movements which characterised their play in the first half. Chelsea made desperate efforts to break through, but were spasmodic and scrambling in their methods and lacked the necessary finish to bring their work to a successful issue.

It became darker and darker as time wore on until the endeavour to distinguish players on the far side of the field was mere guesswork. The conditions also seemed to affect the play, which became more and more of the kick and rush order, and, save the fine work of the backs on both sides, rarely rose beyond the level of mediocrity.

Play settled down in the Chelsea half, and remained there, but Molyneux had not nearly so much to do in defending his charge as in the first half. He saved smartly once from a free kick well placed by Simmons, but for the most part Harrow was quite capable of dealing with the desultory attack and random kicking of the Sheffield forwards. It wanted a goal from Chelsea to enliven a very dull and certainly uneventful game, as it almost seemed as if Sheffield considered the result a foregone conclusion, while Chelsea were too excited to show their best form.

Molyneux was beaten once by Kitchen, but the latter was off-side, and the goal was disallowed. A little later on the Chelsea custodian made a very fine save indeed from a daisy-cutter by Evans, which steered its way through a crowd of red and blue players, and thus must have practically unsighted him. Then, for a brief spell, Chelsea, helped by a couple of free kicks, kept the game in the Sheffield half, but there was no flash of inspiration, no outstanding player to pull the line together, and one sat and wondered whether the genius of Woodward was not just what was missing.

A Sheffield Collision.

In clearing from a free kick close in the Sheffield goal, Cook and English, the Sheffield backs, came into collision, and the game had to be stopped for a few minutes while they were attended to. An exhibition of temper by Harrow nearly brought about the downfall of the Chelsea goal, for Simmons went right on and Molyneux only just managed to deflect his shot round the post. From the resulting corner the Chelsea goalkeeper made another good save, bouncing the ball well out of his goal before he could clear from the opposing forces.

In these closing stages Sheffield showed some return to their early dash, and although it was difficult and at times almost impossible to follow the game, the play certainly became faster and more interesting than at any time since the interval.

Yet another corner fell to the United, but it came to nothing, and from still another Masterman hit the bar and Fazackerley headed in from the rebound, making victory safe for Sheffield. In the last moments of the game Kitchen ran clean through the Chelsea defence and scored a third goal for the United. The crowd at this point, with only a minute or so to go, broke through the barriers, but were got off again, and the whistle sounded with Sheffield United the winners by three goals to none.

Their victory was well deserved, for all through they had been much the better side. But the play will not entitle the last match of the 1915 season to rank as a classic among English Cup finals. Just on the finish Molyneux, who had played a great game for his side, saved finely again from a high dropping shot from Masterman.

There was a rare rush to the grand stand at the conclusion of the game to see Lord Derby present the cup and medals. In a few well-chosen words he congratulated Utley, and was not missing in words of sympathy for the losers. Later, in responding to a vote of thanks, Lord Derby said they had had their fun that afternoon; they had now their duty to do, and he knew they would do it.

P. J. MOSS.

LEAGUE RESULTS AND POSITIONS TO DATE.

THE LEAGUE.—Division I.

Blackburn (h)	4	Middlesbrough	0
Bradford (h)	3	Manchester C.	1
Notts Co. (h) ...	1	Newcastle ..	0
Sheffield W. (h)	0	Burnley	0
Sunderland (h)..	5	Tottenham H.	0
W. B. Albion (h)	3	Bradford City	0
Liverpool	2	Oldham (h)	0

	P.	W.	L.	D.	Goals F.	Goals A.	Pts.
Everton	37	19	11	7	74	45	45
Oldham A. ...	38	17	10	11	71	57	45
Blackburn R..	38	18	13	7	83	61	43
Burnley	38	16	15	7	61	47	43
Sheffield Wed.	38	15	10	13	61	54	43
Manchester C.	38	15	10	13	49	39	43
Sunderland	38	18	15	5	81	72	41
Sheffield U. .	37	14	10	13	48	51	41
W. Brom. A..	38	15	13	10	49	43	40
Bradford C.	37	13	10	14	55	46	40
Bradford	37	16	14	7	66	67	39
Middlesbro' ..	38	13	13	12	62	74	38
Aston Villa ..	36	13	21	11	62	68	37
Liverpool ...	38	14	15	9	65	75	37
Bolton W. ...	37	11	18	8	68	83	30
Newcastle U..	37	10	17	10	43	48	30
Notts C.	37	8	16	13	39	57	29
Chelsea	36	8	16	12	49	61	28
Manchester U.	37	8	17	12	45	62	28
Tottenham H.	38	8	18	12	57	90	28

THE LEAGUE.—Division II.

Arsenal (h)	7	Notts Forest	0
Birmingham (h)	1	Bristol City ...	1
Clapton O. (h)	2	Leicester Fosse	0
Derby Co. (h) ..	2	Preston N. E...	0
Blackpool	1	Fulham (h)	0
Grimsby (h)	0	Huddersfield ...	0
Hull City (h)	2	Glossop	0
Stockport (h) ..	2	Wolverhampton	2
Bury	3	Lincoln (h)	2
Barnsley	2	Leeds City (h)	0

	P.	W.	L.	D.	Goals F.	Goals A.	Pts.
Derby C.	38	23	8	7	71	33	53
Preston N.E.	38	20	8	10	61	42	50
Barnsley	38	22	13	3	51	51	47
Wolverh'pt'n..	38	19	12	7	77	52	45
Arsenal	38	19	14	5	69	41	43
Birmingham	38	17	12	9	62	39	43
Huddersfield	38	17	13	8	61	42	42
Hull City	37	18	14	5	61	53	41
Clapton O.	38	16	13	9	50	48	41
Blackpool ....,	38	17	16	5	58	57	39
Bury	38	15	15	8	61	56	38
Bristol City ..	38	15	16	7	62	56	37
Fulham	38	15	16	7	63	47	37
Stockport Co..	38	15	16	7	54	60	37
Leeds City ..	38	14	20	4	65	64	32
Lincoln City	38	11	18	9	46	65	31
Grimsby T. ..	37	11	17	9	47	72	31
Notts F.	38	10	19	9	43	77	29
Leicester F. ..	38	10	24	4	47	88	24
Glossop	38	6	26	6	31	87	18

SOUTHERN LEAGUE.

Plymouth (h)	3	Gillingham	2
Cardiff	5	N'hampton (h)	2
S'hampton (h)	3	Exeter	0
Reading (h)	4	Luton	0
Bristol Rvrs. (h)	1	Swindon	0
Q.P.Rangers(h)..	3	Crystal Palace .	2
West Ham (h).	1	Norwich	1
Watford	2	Brighton (h) ...	1
Southend	4	Millwall (h)	1

	P.	W.	L.	D.	Goals F.	Goals A.	Pts.
Watford	38	22	8	8	68	46	52
Reading ...	38	21	10	7	68	43	49
Cardiff City	38	22	12	4	72	39	48
West Ham ..	38	18	11	9	58	47	45
Southampton	38	19	14	5	78	74	43
Millwall	37	16	11	10	50	47	42
Swindon	38	15	12	11	75	59	41
Portsmouth	37	16	12	9	54	42	41
Northampton.	37	15	11	11	51	51	41
Q.P. Rangers.	38	13	13	12	55	56	38
Exeter City	38	15	15	8	50	41	38
Brighton	37	15	15	7	45	47	37
Norwich City	37	11	13	13	53	56	35
Crystal P.	37	13	16	8	47	60	34
Luton T. ...	38	13	17	8	61	73	34
Bristol R.	38	14	21	3	53	75	31
Plymouth A..	37	8	15	14	50	58	30
Croydon C. ..	38	9	20	9	47	63	27
Southend U.	37	9	20	8	41	63	26
Gillingham ..	38	6	24	8	43	83	20

'SPURS DOOMED.

Tottenham in Last Place—Everton Champions.

DERBY'S FINE FINISH.

Everton are champions of the English League for the first time in their history, and Tottenham have the doleful distinction of finishing absolutely last in the competition. Which club will bear them company at the bottom of the table is not yet certain, but it will probably be Manchester United.

Manchester City's defeat at the hands of Aston Villa during the week put them out of the running for the honour which at one time appeared well within their grasp. A certain measure of sympathy is due to the City, inasmuch as they made a big sacrifice in the cause of discipline by dropping Howard and Taylor and employing two men, George Wynn and Peter Fairclough, one of whom had never previously participated in this class of football, and the other a stranger in First League football this season.

This left Everton and Oldham Athletic to fight for the premiership, and, as the first named were not engaged yesterday, interest centred in the match between Oldham Athletic and Liverpool. Although playing before their own crowd, Oldham could not produce their best form. Their defence was beaten twice, without their being able to retaliate. By this victory Liverpool practically presented their neighbours of Everton with the championship, as they have a match in hand of Oldham and possess the superior goal average.

Almost as interesting as the struggle for the headship was the battle between Notts County, Tottenham Hotspur, Manchester United, Chelsea and Bolton Wanderers to escape being awarded the "wooden spoon." Purposely the word "relegation" is not used, for reasons which readers of the *Sunday Pictorial* will readily appreciate.

As the 'Spurs had lost to Sunderland 6-0 at home they did not make the journey North in very hopeful spirit and, coming in for a decisive thrashing by five goals to none, dropped to the bottom of the table. Notts County, at home, defeated Newcastle United, after a very hard match, by the only goal scored.

There was a full card in the Second Division. Derby County and Preston North End, the only teams concerned in the championship of the division, met on the ground of the former, who had a lead of one point. Consequently they had only to draw to win outright. As Derby had won at Deepdale by 3-1 last December, they started strong favourites for yesterday's contest, and justified expectations by a 2-0 victory. Two of the London clubs, Arsenal and Clapton Orient, wound up with victories, but Fulham failed against Blackpool.

The Southern League championship was determined a week ago, as was the question of "going down," so that little beyond local interest attached to yesterday's games in the competition. The tables of results and positions published on this page will tell all there is to know.

RESULTS AT A GLANCE.

MIDLAND LEAGUE.—Mexborough (h) 1, Chesterfield 1; Castleford (h) 1, Bradford R. 0; Rotherham Co. (h) 3, Leeds City R. 2; Doncaster Rov. (h) 4, Grimsby Town 1.

SCOTTISH LEAGUE.—Dumbarton (h) 0, Falkirk 1; Ayr (h) 3, Clyde 1; Kilmarnock (h) 2, Greenock Morton 2; Motherwell (h) 1, Celtic 1; St. Mirren 1, Partick (h) 0; Rangers 4, Queen's Park 0.

SOUTHERN LEAGUE.—Division II.—Swansea town (h) 1, Stoke 0; Stalybridge Celtic (h) 4, Ebbw Vale 0.

SOUTH-EASTERN LEAGUE.—Luton R. (h) 4, Reading R. 1; Croydon R. (h) 2, Portsmouth R. 0; Bristol City R. (h) 3, Chelsea R. 0; Boscombe (h) 3, Queen's Park Rangers R. 2; Arsenal R. 3, Swindon R. (h) 1; Tottenham Hotspur R. 1, Gillingham R. (h) 0.

LONDON LEAGUE.—Grays Athletic 5, Finchley (h) 1; Page Green Old Boys (h) 3, Catford Southend 1.

LONDON JUNIOR CUP—Final.—Crusaders 1, Alston Rangers 0 (at Wimbledon).

TOTTENHAM CHARITY CUP—Final.—Tottenham Argyle 1, Mildmay Radical 0 (at Tottenham).

SCHOOLS' INTERNATIONAL.—Wales 1, England ? (at Cardiff).

MID-WEEK FOOTBALL.

Monday.—League—Div. I.: Everton v. Chelsea.

Wednesday.—League—Div. I.: Newcastle United Aston Villa, Bradford v. Bradford City, Notts County Chelsea.

TO-MORROW'S BOXING.

The final of the light-weight trials to find an opponent for Champion Fred Welsh in a belt match is to take place at the National Sporting Club tomorrow night, when Jerry Delaney and Willie Farrell meet in a twenty rounds contest. Delaney has beaten Farrell in less than two rounds at Birmingham about two years ago, but the story goes that the actor-boxer was ill-conditioned then, and avers the shoe will be on the other foot this time.

Jack Greenstock is to take Patsy Cokeley's place against Kid Harris in a twenty rounds contest at the Ring on the morrow. Harris is a favourite over there, and, apart from height and reach, he would have many advantages over Greenstock. In the afternoon at this popular rendezvous Jack Goldswain is to take on Eddie Elton—a match worth the seeing.

The last night of the season at the New Cross Baths will bring out the best match of the year there. Fred Jones, the wonderful little bantam from Rushden, who has had a signally successful career since coming to London, is to oppose Bill Beynon, the ex-amateur champion, in a twenty rounds contest.

SPORT IN BRIEF.

At the Ring last night Dai Roberts knocked out Waldemar Holberg in the seventh round.

Hitch, the famous Surrey bowler, who joined the Sportsman's Battalion together with Hayes and Sandham, has been invalided out of the Army.

Inman and Newman have been matched to play a game of billiards of 18,000 up for £50 a side, Newman receiving 2,000 start, at Leicester-square, commencing May 10.

A cricket bat, specially selected by Tom Hayward, was sold at the recent Red Cross sale at Christie's to two schoolboys, Masters Leonard and Claude Duveen, for 70 guineas.

A report has reached London that Young Ahearne knocked out Gunboat Smith in a round over in the States early in the week, but no confirmation of it has been cabled over from that country.

After a fine game Inman yesterday beat Gray by 459 in the billiards match of 18,000 up. Inman led by over 1,000 on Wednesday, and, in spite of some good breaks, the Australian could not catch the English champion.

Followers of the ring will be sorry to hear that the father of those well-known boxers, Arthur, Harry and Charley Duncan passed away on Thursday. The funeral is to take place at Finchley Cemetery, at two o'clock next Thursday.

'TO-MORROW—THE MILLENNIUM?' BY BRITTEN AUSTIN

SUNDAY·PICTORIAL

SALE VASTLY IN EXCESS OF ANY OTHER PICTURE PAPER IN THE WORLD

No. 702 — Registered at the G.P.O. as a Newspaper — SUNDAY, AUGUST 26, 1928 — Twopence

LEAGUE FOOTBALL STARTS—CHELSEA WIN

Numbers carried on the team's backs helped the identification of Chelsea players, here seen attacking the Swansea Town goal, in the football match at Stamford Bridge yesterday. Chelsea won by 4 goals to 0 after outplaying their opponents for most of the match. Other football pictures are on page 32.

FRENCH STEAMER SUNK IN COLLISION WITH GERMAN SHIP IN CHANNEL

The crew of the French steamer Daphne, which sank after being in collision with the German four-masted barque Passat off Dungeness yesterday, travelling on the Hythe and New Romney miniature railway after being rescued by the Passat and landed at Dungeness. The Passat suffered considerable damage.

MYSTERY OF ZOO TRAGEDY

Said Ali, an Indian elephant driver, found dead in an apartment at the London Zoo with serious injuries about the head and body. Another mahout, Sanniri, known as Sandy Wee, dropped from a window and was rushed to hospital with injuries. Both men were known by sight to thousands of visitors to the Zoo. Ali, who was about forty, was regarded as an exceptionally skilful trainer of elephants.

READY FOR EAST TO WEST ATLANTIC VENTURE

Mr. Charles Levine, who is believed to be contemplating an east-to-west Atlantic flight, leaving his machine on arrival at Croydon last night from Amsterdam. He was met by Miss Mabel Boll, who hopes to accompany him on the trip. See pages 16 and 17.

EVERTON SAY FAREWELL TO THE FIRST DIVISION

Shipman (left), Leicester's opening batsman, displayed fine form against the Australians at Leicester yesterday. M. J. C. Allom, the Surrey bowler, who captured three Worcester wickets for 11 runs at the Oval.

Burnley Also Share Relegation—Goal Average Saves Sheffield United

CHELSEA BEATEN BUT GAIN PROMOTION

On a day when both football and cricket were rivals for public favour, football's engaging problems were finally settled for the season. Five clubs in the First Division were vitally concerned in the finish. One of them, Sheffield United, crowded on four goals in the second half against Manchester United to make themselves safe, but it was only goal average that kept them from relegation.

Everton beat Sunderland by 4 goals to 1, but they finish a point behind any other side in the competition. It is the first time since the foundation of the League that they have been out of the First Division.

Although Chelsea were beaten at Bury they regain the senior division as Oldham were beaten at Barnsley. Hull City were relegated to the Third Division by a fractional difference in goal average compared with Bristol City. Notts County's fate has been known for some time.

The Australians' attack was feeble to begin with at Leicester, but there was a change later, when Grimmett took three wickets with four balls.

Millington (left), Chelsea's goalkeeper, whose work for his club this season has been largely responsible for the success they have gained. T. White, Everton's utility man, has played a large part in his club's effort to avoid relegation.

GRIMMETT'S WONDERFUL BOWLING SPELL

Three Wickets Taken with Four Balls

By P. J. MOSS

LEICESTER, Saturday.

Australians left out Woodfull, a'Beckett, Oldfield and Hornibrook from the side that beat Worcester, and Victor Richardson captained the Tourists.

Thus in the first two matches I have seen all fifteen Tourists in the field, as they lost the toss to-day.

It was a dull, cold morning, with rain threatening when the game started. Shipman and Berry were Leicester's first pair, and on a good, easy, paced wicket they gave the County a good start.

Wall, the fast bowler, and Hurwood, who had not played at Worcester, opened the bowling.

Hurwood, a medium-spin bowler, opened the attack, and although neither batsman took the slightest risk, runs came steadily, and before fifty was hoisted Richardson had tried Fairfax and Grimmett for a time.

There were few incidents, but Berry, who started the slower of the pair, played some fine shots when he settled down. A late cut to the rails off Grimmett, and a square cut off Fairfax to boundary, brought the first real applause of the match.

After half an hour's play a slight drizzle fell, and both bowlers and batsmen made use of sawdust.

The impressions formed at Worcester that the Australian bowling is not very formidable seemed borne out by the happenings of this morning, for the attack never looked deadly. Although it is early yet to say they are not up to standard of previous teams I fancy that will prove to be the case.

The drizzle, after an hour and a quarter, developed into rain, and players were driven to shelter at 1.15, Berry then having 34 to his credit and Shipman 25.

The score had just passed the century when Berry was caught by Ponsford off Grimmett.

Following the dismissal of Berry, Grimmett experienced a remarkable run of success, taking three wickets in four balls.

Leicester.—First Innings.

Shipman, c Wall, b Grimmett	63	A. T. Sharpe, st Walker, b Grimmett	5
Berry, c Ponsford, b Grimmett	50	Astill, c McCabe, b Wall	7
Armstrong, st Walker, b Grimmett	3	Geary, not out	3
Bradshaw, lbw, b Grimmett	0	J. A. De Lisle, not out	1
Riley, c and b Grimmett	0	Extras	5
		Total (7 wkts.)	137

All out 148.

WORCESTER COLLAPSE

Worcester were dismissed by Surrey at the Oval for 40 runs, the innings lasting less than two hours. Morning rain had left the wicket wet on top. Allom and Stroud were responsible for the collapse. Score:-

Worcester.—First Innings

Wright, Ducat, b Peach	0	Root, c Peach, b Stroud	14
Fox (J.), run out	0	Brooke, c Brooks, b Stroud	3
Nichol, c Brooks, b Allom	0	Perks, run out	0
Gibbons, c Fender, b Stroud	6	Styler, lbw, b Allom	2
Fox (V.), by Allom	0	Jackson, not out	0
C. F. Walters, b Stroud	13	Extras	2
		Total	40

Bowling: Allom 3 for 11, Stroud 4 for 17.

Surrey.—First Innings.

Hobbs, c Brooke, b Perks, 66; Sandham, not out 54; extras 2; total (1 wkt.) 122.

GLAMORGAN DO WELL

M. J. Turnbull and Hills were associated in a useful partnership against Warwickshire at Birmingham Score:—

Glamorgan.—First Innings

Bates, c Mayer, b Paine	20	Rhys, b Mayer	0
Dyson, b Sanders	16	Davies (D.), b Sanders	8
M. J. Turnbull, lbw, b Mayer	54	Every, not out	13
Bell, c Smith, b Paine	8	Davies (E.), not out	10
Hills, b Mayer	36	Extras	14
		(Total (7 wkts)	179

OXFORD U. v. KENT—At Oxford

Kent.—First Innings.

Hardinge, not out, 9; Ashdown, c Melville b Wellings, 2; Woolley, not out, 3; extras, 2; total (1 wkt.), 16.

WINNERS AT SANDOWN

2.0.—BURNING BUSH (8-1, Speck), 1; Monarchy (100-7), 2; Ballymurphy (10-1), 3. 13 ran. (Woodland.) Tote: Win, 23s. 6d.; places 7s., 8s., 7s. 6d.

2.30.—BORJOM (100-30, Speck), 1; Always Blue (6-1), 2; Magic Bird (7-1), 3. 11 ran. (Butchers.) Tote: Win, 7s. 3d.; places, 3s. 3d., 5s., 5s. 3d.

3.0.—GATE BOOK (9-2, T. Morgan), 1; Donegal (5-4), 2; Slieve Grien (100-6), 3; nine ran (F. Barrett). Tote, win 11s. 3d.; places 4s. 3d., 3s. 9d., 7s.

3.30.—MONTPELIER (2-1, Stott), 1; Paradeisos (8-1), 2; Irish Lord (100-30), 3. 10 ran. (Thrale.) Tote: Win 7s. 6d.; places, 3s., 6s. 3d., 3s. 9d.

4.5.—THE BROWN TALISMAN (8-1, Everett), 1; Roi de Saba (8-1), 2; Residue (13-8), 3. 11 ran. (Blair.) Tote: Win 15s. 3d., places 4s., 4s. 9d., 3s. 6d.

4.35.—DESERT CHIEF (7-1, Capt. Davy), 1; Cross Gate (2-1), 2; Victor Noir (100-7), 3. 10 ran. (Private.) Tote: Win 20s. 9d.; places, 5s. 6d., 3s. 6d., 7s. 3d.

THE UNFORTUNATES

Everton and Burnley Go Down to Second Division

Everton and Burnley will be relegated from the First Division.

Up to yesterday six clubs were in the danger zone, and though all finished on the winning side, Everton are still left in the bottom position. A superior goal average keeps Sheffield United up at the expense of Burnley.

Yesterday Burnley ran up six goals against Derby County, who replied but twice, but this result failed to save them, as Sheffield United won 5—1 at Manchester after being level at the interval.

Everton, too, did well to beat Sunderland 4—1, but even with this win they have failed to total more than 35 points, which is one fewer than the total obtained by Sheffield United and Burnley.

Grimsby, who have made a gallant struggle to get clear, finally got out of danger by claiming the only goal at Huddersfield.

Newcastle saved themselves by beating West Ham 1—0, and Middlesbrough got clear as a result of a 3—1 win over Bolton Wanderers.

HOW THEY FINISHED

The following is a complete list of this season's winners of honours and the sides who are relegated:—

DIVISION I

Champions: Sheffield Wednesday
Relegated: Everton and Burnley

DIVISION II

Champions: Blackpool.
Runners-up: Chelsea.
Relegated: Hull City and Notts C[illegible]

DIVISION III (S)

Champions: Plymouth Argyle.
To apply for re-election: Merthyr [illegible] Gillingham.

DIVISION III (N)

Champions: Port Vale.
To apply for re-election: [illegible] Halifax.

BLACKPOOL CHAMPIONS

Barnsley, in Beating Oldham, Do Chelsea a Good Turn

Blackpool, who knew their fate concerning promotion some time ago, just scraped home with the championship of the Second Division by getting the solitary point necessary as the result of a goalless draw with the Forest at Nottingham. This was Dexter's benefit match, and the Forest goalkeeper celebrated it by keeping his goal intact.

Chelsea have to thank Barnsley for beating Oldham by the odd goal of three, which enabled them to gain promotion. Chelsea were not able to help themselves in this respect since they were beaten at Bury by the only goal of the game. Chelsea may thus count themselves a trifle lucky.

Bradford City put up a good performance in beating Charlton Athletic at the Valley by 3 goals to 1. They needed the victory badly to escape relegation and they won on their merits.

Although Hull City won their home game against Wolverhampton by 2 goals to 0, they have to accompany Notts County into the Third Division. They tie on points with Bristol City, who shared points with Preston, but Bristol City have the better goal average.

WIDNES WIN THE CUP

St. Helens Mastered in Rugby Trophy Match at Wembley

There was something of a surprise in the Rugby League Cup Final match at Wembley yesterday, when Widnes beat St. Helens by two goals and two tries to a try.

Widnes played brilliantly in the first half, while their opponents were sluggish, and in the second half the winners put up such a magnificent defence that they foiled St. Helens' attempts to break through.

Play had been in progress for about five minutes when Ellaby, the most dangerous man in the St. Helens's attack, put in a magnificent swerving run and crosskick. Radcliffe tried to gather the ball but it bounced awkwardly, and Houghton rushed up to touch down a try that Lewis failed to convert.

Widnes returned to the attack, and Radcliffe was nearly through when Crooks obstructed. For this the referee awarded a penalty try that Hoey converted.

The lead, slender though it was, was deservedly held by Widnes, for while they were not so polished as St. Helens, they tackled magnificently, and their forwards brought off some thrilling rushes.

Widnes forwards were magnificent, and in addition to fine open work they scrummaged splendidly. Five minutes before the interval Radcliffe passed to Dennett, who scored a try after a fine run which Hoey failed to convert.

A minute before the interval a penalty was given against Lewis for not playing the ball, and Radcliffe kicked a goal. Thus at half-time Widnes led by two goals and two tries (10 points) to one try (3 points)

In the second half St. Helens showed up rather better, but Widnes played a strong game and never relaxed their efforts. Ellaby did his best to pull the Saints together, but he was not well supported.

St. Helens then began to make some definite headway, and they maintained strong pressure on the Widnes line, only to find themselves met by a brilliant defence.

The second half was fought with intense earnestness by both sides, but Widnes held grimly to their lead and eventually won by 10 points to 3.

YORKSHIRE AT LORD'S

A strong M.C.C. side which welcomed Yorkshire to Lord's did not fare very well against the Northerners' bowling, N. Haig and Hearne proving early victims. Rain also held up the game for brief periods. Score:—

M.C.C.—First Innings

N. Haig, c Robinson, b Macaulay	2	Hendren, no.	40
Lee, not out	57	Extras	15
Hearne, lbw, b Robinson	9	Total (2 wkts)	123

NORTHANTS' POOR START

In good weather, at Manchester, on an easy-paced wicket, Northampton lost wickets cheaply against Macdonald and Sibbles. Bellamy and Thomas came to the rescue of their side with useful contributions. Score:-

Northants.—First Innings

Woolley, lbw, b Tyldesley (R.)	14	Bellamy, not out	33
Bakewell, run out	0	Liddell, b Tyldesley (R.)	10
Timms (J.), c Tyldesley (E.), b Macdonald		Cox, run out	18
V. W. C. Jupp, c Tyldesley (E.), b Sibbles		Thomas, b Hopwood	27
Matthews, lbw, b Tyldesley (R.)	4	Partridge, not out	0
		Extras	2
		Total	122

NOTTS v. SUSSEX.—At Trent Bridge

Notts.—First Innings.

Whysall, not out	90	Payton, not out	6
Walker, b Wensley	10	Extras	3
Staples (A.), run out	7		
A. W. Carr, c Parks (H.), b Langridge	45	Total (3 wkts,	166

VITAL FIGURES IN THE FINAL FOOTBALL LEAGUE TABLES

DIVISION I

	P.	W.	Pts.
Sheffield Wed.	42	26	60
Derby Co.	42	21	50
Man. City	42	19	47
Aston Villa	42	21	47
Leeds United	42	20	46
Blackburn R.	42	19	45
Sunderland	42	18	43
Leicester City	42	17	43
Huddersfield	42	17	43
West Ham	42	19	43
Liverpool	42	16	41
Birmingham	42	16	41
Portsmouth	42	15	40
Bolton W.	42	15	39
Arsenal	42	14	39
Middlesbrough	42	16	38
Manchester Utd.	42	15	38
Grimsby	42	15	37
Newcastle Utd.	42	15	37
Sheffield Utd.	42	15	36
Burnley	42	14	36
Everton	42	11	35

DIVISION II

	P.	W.	Pts.
Blackpool	42	27	58
Chelsea	42	22	55
Oldham Ath.	42	21	53
Bradford	42	19	50
Bury	42	22	49
West Bromwich	42	21	47
Southampton	42	17	45
Cardiff City	42	18	44
Nottingham F.	42	13	41
Wolverhampton	42	16	41
Stoke City	42	16	40
Millwall	42	12	39
Charlton Ath.	42	14	39
Tottenham H.	42	15	39
Swansea	42	14	37
Preston N.E.	42	13	37
Barnsley	42	14	36
Bradford City	42	12	36
Reading	42	12	35
Bristol City	42	13	35
Hull City	42	14	35
Notts County	42	9	33

DIVISION III (N.)

	P.	W.	Pts.
Port Vale	42	30	67
Stockport	42	28	63
Chesterfield	42	22	50
Darlington	42	21	50
Lincoln City	42	17	48
South Shields	42	18	46
York City	42	15	46
Hartlepools Utd.	42	17	45
Southport	42	15	43
Rochdale	42	18	43
Crewe Alex.	42	17	42
Tranmere R.	42	16	41
New Brighton	42	16	40
Carlisle United	42	16	39
Doncaster Rovers	42	15	39
Accrington S.	42	14	37
Wrexham	42	13	34
Nelson	42	13	33
Wigan Borough	42	13	33
Rotherham Utd.	42	11	30
Halifax	42	10	28
Barrow	42	11	27

DIVISION III (S.)

	P.	W.	Pts.
Plymouth Argyle.	42	30	68
Brentford	42	28	61
Q.P.R.	42	21	51
Northampton	42	21	50
Brighton and H.	42	21	50
Fulham	42	18	47
Coventry City	42	19	47
Norwich City	42	18	46
Crystal Palace	42	17	46
Bournemouth	42	15	43
Southend Utd.	42	15	43
Clapton Orient	42	14	41
Luton	42	14	40
Watford	42	15	38
Swindon	42	13	38
Exeter City	42	12	35
Newport Co.	41	12	34
Walsall	42	13	34
Torquay Utd.	42	10	31
Bristol Rovers	42	11	30
Gillingham	42	11	30
Merthyr	41	5	19

FOOTBALL RESULTS

How League Sides Fared in Their Final Games

RUGBY LEAGUE CUP.—Final—Wid[illegible] Helens 3 (at Wembley).

DIVISION [I]

Sheffield Wed.	5	Manchester City	
Birmingham	3	Leicester	
Middlesbrough	3	Bolton	
Manchester United	1	Sheffield United	
Portsmouth	0	Leeds	
Burnley	6	Derby	
Everton	4	Sunderland	
Blackburn	1	Liverpool	
Huddersfield	0	Grimsby	
Newcastle	1	West Ham	
Arsenal	2	Aston Villa	

DIVISION II

Bradford	6	Millwall	
Preston	2	Bristol City	
Nottingham F.	0	Blackpool	
West Bromwich	5	Southampton	
Hull	2	Wolverhampton	
Bury	1	Chelsea	
Charlton	1	Bradford City	
Barnsley	2	Oldham	
Stoke	1	Spurs	

DIVISION III (N.)

Stockport	2	New Brighton	
Crewe	0	Port Vale	
Rochdale	4	York	
Rotherham	0	Hartlepools	
Barrow	0	Southport	
South Shields	2	Accrington	
Wrexham	5	Nelson	
Carlisle	5	Wigan	

DIVISION III (S.)

Coventry	1	Swindon	
Walsall	1	Norwich	
Gillingham	2	Luton	
Plymouth	2	Watford	
Bristol Rovers	4	Brentford	1
Northampton	5	Southend	1
Crystal Palace	1	Bournemouth	1
Clapton Orient	4	Brighton	1
Torquay	2	Exeter	1
Fulham	0	Queen's Park Rangers	2

BELFAST CUP.—Bangor 2, Linfield 3; Cliftonville 2, Portadown 0; Derry 0, Belfast Celtic 0; Distillery 6, Coleraine 3; Glenavon 4, Newry 1; Glentoran 1, Ards 1; Larne 2, Ballymena 1.

CENTRAL LEAGUE.—Blackpool 1, Huddersfield 3; Bolton 2, Everton 0; Leeds 5, Stoke 0; Oldham 3, Sheffield Utd. 3; Wolverhampton 2, Aston Villa 2.

MIDLAND LEAGUE.—Chesterfield 4, Worksop 2; Doncaster 0, Frickley 1; Grimsby 7, Wath 2; Loughborough 1, Hull 1; Lincoln 1, Wombwell 0; Scunthorpe 2, Newark 0; Staveley 4, Nottingham F. 4; Boston 5, Mansfield 0.

SOUTHERN LEAGUE.—Peterborough 0, Southampton 0; Bath 4, Plymouth 1; Bristol C. 1, Barry 3; Ebbw Vale 2, Bristol R. 3; Lovells 7, Swindon 0; Newport 3, Merthyr 1.

LONDON COMBINATION.—Brighton 6, Orient 1; Luton 1, West Ham 1; Millwall 5, Coventry 1; Q.P.R. [illegible], Chelsea 1; Southend 2, Portsmouth 4.

STOCKTON RETURNS

2.0.—RHYOLITE (5-2, G. Richards) and GALA PRINCE (7-1, Forsyth), dead-heat 1; Golden Gauntlet (3-1), 3. Also ran: Catanian (11-4), Desormais, Indian Eagle (100-8), Prefect, Belle Mount, Oh Crikey, and Carpathia (20-1). (Rhyolite by F. Hartigan, Gala Prince by G. Sadler.)

2.30.—EHEU FUGACES (8-1, Adley), 1; Tuffan (5-2), 2; Hindustan (6-1), 3. Also ran: Radio, Glen Gowan (5-1), Golden Glow (11-2), Happy Gazelle (10-1), Grey Hill, Heronslea and Argos Lad (33-1). (Leach, sen.)

3.0.—GOOD MINT (10-1, Simpson), 1; Pickle (100-6), 2; Sept (100-6), 3; also ran: Pauli (evens), Doura, Gloucester Hussar (4-1), and Sir Picton (100-6). (Barling).

3.30.—GOOSANDER (5-4, P. Beasley), 1; Young Ben (8-1), 2; Leg Puller (20-1), 3. Also ran: Queen of Love f (2-1), Mastersinger (5-1), Byronia, Blea Tarn and Lava (20-1). (Leach, jun.)

4.0.—DISARMAMENT (5-2, Caldwell), 1; Sans Doute (5-2), 2; Atherton (7-4), 3. Also ran: Estelle f (10-1), Fullolite (100-7), Tivoli Boy, Semi Royal, Scatterum, Lady of the Snows, Fanciful (33-1). (Elsey.)

4.30.—POMMAME (4-1, H. Wragg), 1; Maugre (10-1), 2; Joan Haste (20-1), 3. Also ran: Abitibi (3-1), Secret Paper (5-1), Pomerellen (6-1), Polo (13-2), Salamis, Uppercourt, High Brambles, Knotweed, Tinkers Well, Wink, Dawpool (20-1). (Elsey.)

JOAN FRY'S VICTORY

Miss Joan Fry defeated Mrs. W. D. List in the final of the women's singles in the British hard court lawn tennis championship at Bournemouth by 6—1, 2—6, 6—2. In the final of the men's singles H. G. N. Lee beat E. C. Peters by 6—3, 2—6, 6—4, 6—4.

BOURN WINS GOLF TITLE

In the final of the English amateur close golf championship at Burnham, Somerset, yesterday, T. A. Bourn (Sunningdale) beat C. E. Hardman (Manchester) by 3 and 2. Bourn, who was one of the original nominees for the Walker Cup team, is a former champion of France.

INTER-'VARSITY GOLF TITLE

Glasgow won the Scottish Universities golf championship at Gleneagles yesterday. They beat Edinburgh University by six matches to four, for an aggregate of three wins to two by Edinburgh University.

82,905 SEE SOCCER GIANTS DEADLOCK

WEST HAM'S TRANSFER DEAL

At a fee which Mr. Paynter, their manager, states is one of the biggest they have ever paid, West Ham last night secured the transfer of Lawrence Conwell, the Portadown inside forward.

Conwell went to Portadown from Aberdeen. He played for the Irish League at Blackpool a fortnight ago.

Another transfer yesterday was that of Rhodes, the Sheffield Wednesday right half, to Wolverhampton.

Too Much Punch for Pompey

BEES GATE CRASH A HOME RECORD

Portsmouth 1, Brentford 3

Brentford's busy bees gave Portsmouth a rare stinging at Fratton Park.

It was the first time since the old Southern League days that they had visited Portsmouth, and they gave 24,000 spectators an exhibition of delightful football.

The game opened sensationally and before Portsmouth realised what was happening, Brentford were two goals in the lead. And Pompey have not conceded a point at home this season.

Fletcher shot and hit the post. He smartly captured the rebound, however, and placed it over to Hopkins, who beat Gilfillan with a flashing effort.

L. Hopkins.

Worse followed for Pompey, Salmond blundered over a through pass down the centre and Holliday snapped up the chance to score Brentford's second goal.

Salmond began to keep a closer watch on the Brentford centre forward and Holliday was not given much scope.

But the right wing, Hopkins, made some flashing runs along the line which were an outstanding feature of the game and he rarely wasted a ball. Once, when Portsmouth forced three corners in succession, the Brentford defence looked like breaking down, but Mathieson finally cleared with a brilliant save.

Later he had to push a hard drive from Symon over the bar, and from Rutherford's flag kick Weddle headed in.

The trouble with Portsmouth was that they were not able to press home their attacks in the centre.

Rutherford and Worrall were willing wingers, but both Easson and Bagley missed chances.

Even during the brief spells when the home side were definitely on top the work of the inside forwards lacked finish.

Midway through the second half, Hopkins showed his opportunism by cutting in to slip a centre by Fletcher over Gilfillan's head into the net, and Portsmouth retired well beaten.

HAMMERS HIT HARD

Extra Punch in Attack Gives Them Points Against Swansea

West Ham 4, Swansea 0

A most resolute defence and the ability of their forwards to make the most of their chances were the chief factors which enabled West Ham to gain the victory.

Swansea actually gave a far better display than the score would suggest. The half backs were consistently good in both defence and attack, while their forwards, combining speed with skill, showed capital form in all respects with the exception of finishing.

The visitors made an unfortunate start, Milne turning the ball into his own net within the first ten minutes when endeavouring to clear a centre from Ruffell. Then it was touch and go until Marshall netted No. 2.

Swansea pressed persistently for long spells in a keenly fought second half packed with incident. While their forwards again spoiled fine efforts by finishing weakly, there were occasions when West Ham were decidedly fortunate in keeping their goal intact, and Conway who showed splendid form in goal, was severely tested by the whole of the visitors' forwards. Goulden completed the scoring.

NORWICH COME BACK

Norwich City 4, Port Vale 2

The point gained by Norwich at Southampton a week ago evidently acted as a tonic, for they played a very aggressive game against Port Vale, and fully deserved their victory. The match was impressive also on the score of fine goalkeeping.

Norwich scored through Vinall and Warnes before Caldwell reduced the deficit. Port Vale threatened with clever approach work, but the Norwich defence stood sound.

The second half was hard fought, Rhodes scoring the equaliser before Warnes restored Norwich's lead.

Rousing exchanges followed, and Vinall headed a brilliant goal from Warnes's centre.

CHELSEA AND ARSENAL IN REAL DERBY

Forwards So Clever—Defences So Keen

LAW THE STAR

By P. J. MOSS

Chelsea 1, Arsenal 1

IT was a battle of giants at Stamford Bridge—giants in the truest Soccer sense.

The passing of both sides was so good that hardly a ball was wasted. The tackling was so quick and keen that, well as the forwards played, openings were few and far between.

In this battle of giants—watched by 82,905 people, a record crowd for a League match in London and the second biggest League crowd ever—the greatest giant of them all was Tommy Law.

Time and again this veteran came out of a ruck of players with the ball at his toes, and most of the centres met his head, so clever was his positioning. He has never played better in his long and brilliant career.

Yet tragically it was Law's head that led up to Arsenal's equalising goal. He tried to head the ball to Jackson, but instead put it behind, and from the corner kick Crayston equalised after Jackson had fisted out Bastin's well-placed flag kick.

HONOURS FOR CRAIG

Comparisons are odious, but I thought that Craig, as a centre half, was more effective in stopping Drake than his vis-a-vis, Roberts, in controlling Bambrick. Good as Roberts's heading was, Bambrick frequently beat him for the ball, and often slipped him. Drake had to work out to the wings for the most part to get past Craig.

In forward play of the highest class—better than any I have seen this season—Gibson's was perhaps the most artistic. He had Crayston, the best wing half on the field, against him, but worked the ball so cleverly that he was always making openings.

So well did the four backs play that it was very rarely that any one got a clear run through. I liked O'Hare, the new Chelsea right back, and Hapgood and Neall were their usual selves.

So in this grand game we saw super—as well as keen—football. I thought Chelsea were a trifle the cleverer, but there was precious little in it. I should like to see such football every week at Highbury, Chelsea and anywhere else.

BARRACLOUGH'S MISS

Both goals had narrow escapes in the first half, but generally speaking the defences were on top. After the interval Chelsea set up many hot attacks, Barraclough coming the nearest to getting a goal, and also missing a sitting chance.

The second half was eight minutes old when Mitchell put in a long drive at the Arsenal goal. Wilson shaped to take it, but in some miraculous way Bambrick got a touch to the ball and, from close in, turned it into the net. How he got into the position is still a mystery to me.

Then the Arsenal attacked in desperation, and for a time their shots flew all round the Chelsea goal.

Jackson once tipped the ball over the bar from Drake's head, and Bastin skimmed the bar with a fast one. Scrambling play round the Pensioners' goal at last brought its reward, Law making his one lapse.

Then in the closing minutes Argue had two gilt-edged chances of putting Chelsea in front, but missed them both.

The last incident was a regular pile-driver from Drake, which Jackson saved on his knees.

Spectacular flying save by Scott, of Burnley, from a shot by Spurs.

Spurs' 5 Might Have Been 8

HIGHEST SCORES	
Plymouth	7
Partick	7
HIGHEST AGGREGATE	
Plymouth 7, Barnsley 1	8

DON'T BE DOWN-HEARTED, FULHAM!

Beaten at Manchester, but Side Is a Good One

By BILLY MEREDITH

Manchester United 1, Fulham 0

I was more pleased with Manchester United's attack than I have been on any previous occasion this season at Old Trafford. Not only did they show a better understanding of each other but they also overcame their old fault of ballooning the ball.

Rowley, at inside left, set them a fine example in ball control, and some of his passing runs in partnership with Chester were delightful.

They made rings round Fulham's big defence at times, and when Rowley got the only goal of the game fourteen minutes before half-time we saw the prettiest move of the whole match. Rowley worked over to the right wing, then turned the ball to the centre for Bamford to take it in his stride.

ROWLEY SCORES

Bamford responded by turning the ball back to Rowley, who beat Tootill all the way with a slanting shot which passed inside the left-hand post.

No one thought the scoring would stop at this, and it should not have done so. Unfortunately, the United's wing men did not finish well. Even so, Keeping, the best back on the field, saved a goal by heading over the bar when Chester lured Tootill out of goal.

Fulham need not be downhearted by their string of defeats. They have the makings of a very good side, but need more punch in the inside forward positions.

Perry, their tall centre forward, had little chance of beating Vose because too many passes meant for him were over-kicked. Hammond found the tackling too quick for him to do his usual spadework as he wished.

Tootill's goalkeeping was one of the best features of a match

ELECTRIFYING RIGHT WING TRIO

By TED HUFTON (England and W. Ham).

Tottenham H. 5, Burnley 1.

If you can imagine a match in which one side has most of the attributes of greatness and the other is too inexperienced to survive against almost classic football, you have a fair impression of yesterday's match between Spurs and Burnley.

The result tells you which was the great side and which the inexperienced.

The afternoon's play confirmed my previously-expressed opinion that the Spurs' real level is Division I, and that given an adequate centre half—Jones does not fill the bill—they will get there at the end of this season.

What I liked most about the Spurs' play was the perfect understanding between Duncan and McCormick, the right wing forwards, and Howe, the half back behind them. To some extent Duncan was the leader of the whole side; he was certainly the mainspring of this trio, varying the play from the old-fashioned triangular movement to the more modern open methods.

Another conspicuous Spur was Fullwood, the left back. His clean first-time kicking delighted me, and I think he is going to hold his position for a long time to come.

THREE GOALS DISALLOWED

Burnley were outplayed, out-paced and outmanœuvred. The methods of their opponents caused them to endeavour to do things too hastily. So their attempts at holding up the Spurs misfired, and the wonder of it was that they were level at the interval.

As a matter of fact the Spurs got the ball in the net eight times—but only five counted. This goes to show that the score does not do the Spurs justice.

The Burnley men I liked best were Hindmarsh (right half) and Kilcar (inside left). With their team suffering so much by comparison, they were 100 per centers. Kilcar was always looking for a chance to reduce arrears.

I should have included Scott, the goalkeeper, in the list of the impressive men of Burnley, but he deserves a paragraph all to himself. Some of his saves were magnificent, while he could not have prevented any of the goals

McCormick gave the Spurs the lead in six minutes, and Smith scored the goal which enabled Burnley to cross over level. In the second half Morrison, Howe, Hall (G. W.), and Evans brought the Spurs' score to 5.

Evans's goal was a delight. It followed a long bout of passing between the scorer and Duncan which electrified the crowd and left Burnley standing.

ORIENT STUMBLE ON BEST TEAM

After an Accident and a Draw with Crystal Palace

By TOMMY CLAY (England and Spurs)

Palace 2, Orient 2

For fifty minutes the Orient had only ten men and a passenger at Selhurst Park, and yet even without the services of Taylor, their regular left back, they did enough to merit taking away both points. It ended all square, so perhaps no one has cause to grumble.

After seeing the Orient's reorganised team I should strongly advise Mr. Proudfoot, their manager, to give it another trial providing, of course, Taylor is not fit to come back and that there is another right winger good enough to step into the first team.

After Taylor's accident Miles (right winger) went to outside left, McAleer (outside left) moved to the inside position while Pateman crossed over to inside right, which position was vacated by Smith, who dropped into left half as if he was born for the place to allow Heinemann to drop to left back.

The changes proved to be for the good. Especially as Affleck at centre half did two men's work beside shutting out Dawes, the Palace centre forward, who showed he could be very dangerous by getting the first goal of the match.

Actually the Palace did enough good work before Taylor's injury to have obtained a good lead, but once Dawes was quietened the effectiveness of the attack gradually disappeared. It must be said, though, that Manders did a lot of scheming and Waldron much hard work in the inside forward positions.

There was nothing particularly exciting about the Palace defence, although W. S. Smith at left half took my eye as a promising player.

Too often did the Palace defence allow themselves to become a trifle rattled by the dodges of McAleer, who virtually made the first equalising goal obtained by Crawford, a man who can get them if given the right passes.

When the Palace again obtained the lead in the second half the Orient appeared a trifle rattled, but their opponents never seemed to realise it. Eventually Smith, the Orient's emergency left half, made a perfect tackle, a dribble and a goal, and put his side in a happy frame of mind.

So much so, in fact, that had the Orient's attack made the ball do the work and the right wing given Crawford more assistance, they might have snatched a win.

Scramble in the Chelsea goalmouth during "derby" game with Arsenal

CHARLTON'S SHOCK

Newcastle Faulty in Finishing and The Pay the Penalty

Newcastle 1, Charlton 2

Only once before this season have Newcastle lowered their colours at home. In the circumstances Charlton can be very proud of their success.

Charlton provided a shock by scoring twice in six minutes through Welsh and Allen, but Newcastle rallied and created many exciting situations in the Charlton goalmouth.

Welsh, a splendid forcing half, often came into the picture during the Charlton attacks, in which the Newcastle defence did not carry conviction.

Newcastle's wing halves, Imrie and Weaver, prompted their attack with great effect, and it was after the latter had had a great shot saved by Bartram that Harris reduced the lead.

Newcastle carried on the attack in the second half, but they were not a sound finishing force, some very good openings being missed by Cairns, the centre forward.

While Charlton chiefly concentrated on defence there was always a danger in their breakaways, in which the most effective player was Hobbis.

Against this player the Newcastle defence had some very lively times, but in the end Charlton ran out worthy winners

SAINTS CAUGHT IN TRAP

The offside trap and Ashton were Southampton's enemies-in-chief at Nottingham. Ashton, the Forest 'keeper, was even more brilliant than the man in the Saints' goal—and the Forest saw plenty of Light!

Neil and Gurry troubled Ashton a lot, but the Saints just couldn't emulate the scoring shots of Gardiner and Stubbs for Forest.

But they fought every inch of the way, and McIlwaine was the stumbling block of many Nottingham attacks. The Forest won by 2—0.

PAYNE FOR CHELSEA, DIXIE DEAN MOVES, TOO

WALES SHOULD MAKE SHORT SHRIFT OF "NEW" IRISH XV

By FORAGER

WALES meet Ireland at Swansea for the forty-eighth time this afternoon. Of the previous matches, Wales have won twenty-seven, Ireland eighteen and two have been drawn.

This is the last international to be played at Swansea. Future matches will be at Cardiff.

West Wales Rugby fans are upset by this decision of the Welsh R.U., and bands of young men threaten a protest march through the streets of the town.

International results have been so unexpected this season that one hesitates to state definitely that Wales will win.

Nevertheless, barring accident, I do not see how Wales can help winning to-day. The team is practically unchanged from the two previous matches, whereas the Irish selectors have made so many changes as almost to incur the charge of being panic-stricken.

There are ten alterations from the side beaten by England, and six from that which went down to Scotland.

Wales, too, have made one surprising change. Arthur Bassett drops out, and to fill his place on the wing Idwal Rees is moved from the centre, where Claude Davey returns.

For Wales and Welshmen there is one sad connection with this afternoon's match. Claude Davey has let it be understood that it will be his last international. It was, I understand, only at the urgent request of the Welsh selectors that he played against England.

ENGLAND OUT TO LAY HOODOO

By REFLECTOR

ENGLAND have yet to win an amateur international match on Scottish soil, and I doubt their ability to break the "hoodoo" at Hampden Park to-day.

Various reasons have been given for Bernard Joy's omission, and I feel we should be told whether the reason is official or personal. It will make a big difference to England.

I do not wish to disparage the merits of L. N. Hockaday, who now gets Joy's former position. The only doubt in my mind is whether he is sufficiently matured for such a big ordeal.

I question Scotland's wisdom in calling up W. Whitehead at inside left. The Kingstonian player is past his zenith.

At the last minute R. Gordon (Queen's Park) is reported unfit. His place at right back in the Scottish side will be taken by J. Clyne (Queen's Park).

It is mainly on the strength of their defence that I expect Scotland to win. This is composed entirely of Queen's Park players, which assures a perfect understanding, allied to the advantage of playing on their own ground.

Rugby Star for Soccer

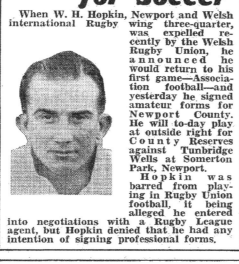

When W. H. Hopkin, Newport and Welsh international Rugby wing three-quarter, was expelled recently by the Welsh Rugby Union, he announced he would return to his first game—Association football—and yesterday he signed amateur forms for Newport County. He will to-day play at outside right for County Reserves against Tunbridge Wells at Somerton Park, Newport.

Hopkin was barred from playing in Rugby Union football, it being alleged he entered into negotiations with a Rugby League agent, but Hopkin denied that he had any intention of signing professional forms.

By JOHN THOMPSON

LUTON TOWN'S "ten goal" Joe Payne will play for Chelsea to-day. His wife is delighted.

"Dixie" Dean, Everton and England leader, will wear a Notts County shirt.

Another new face in the Chelsea side will be Smith full back from Swindon Town.

That's not all in a day of transfers.

Dunkley, Northampton Town's outside right, has gone to Manchester City, in exchange for Tilson (centre forward), McCullough (right half) and Rodger (outside left).

Then Bristol City got busy. Signed Frank Gallacher, Barnsley inside right, and followed up by taking Thorley, Cheltenham outside left. Thorley used to be with Sunderland and Hull City.

Pretty auburn-haired Mrs. Payne, bride of a fortnight, told me last night:—

"I'm not a bit sorry about leaving Luton.

"If I'd been given a choice of saying where Joe should go I should immediately have said Chelsea. I'm just delighted."

Chelsea's fee for Payne is estimated at about £5,000—only half what he could have commanded last season. Since then the player has been in ill-health, but is now back to his old form.

Last season he scored fifty-five goals, and with Joe Harston headed the list of League scorers. This season he has played in twenty-four games and scored nineteen goals.

His ten goals against Bristol Rovers still stands as a record.

Mr. Knighton, Chelsea manager, said last night: "Payne will certainly be in the Chelsea side to-morrow against Bolton, but I cannot say where he will play."

Dean, who leads Notts County to-day, set up an English record in 1927-28 when he scored sixty goals. On September 2, 1936, he scored his 353rd goal, beating Steve Bloomer's record.

Northampton's three newcomers all play against Exeter.

Payne (above) and Tilson.

BOB JACK IS LEAVING ARGYLE

THIS is Mr. Robert Jack's last season as secretary-manager of Plymouth Argyle. He is to resign at the end of the present campaign.

His latest "deal" for Plymouth was the transfer of Harry Lane from Southend. This was the outcome of negotiations with his son, Mr. David Jack, manager of Southend.

Lane will play at inside left for Argyle to-day.

"I am confident the club that I have loved and worked for for so many years will safely emerge from the danger of relegation. If I felt otherwise, the thought of parting would not have entered my mind," Mr. Jack said yesterday.

Mr. Jack added: "I shall remain in football for many years to come."

Mr. Jack's association with Plymouth Argyle as secretary-manager is one of the longest ever known in professional football.

After a spell with Preston and Glossop, he went to Plymouth in 1903.

Within two years he became secretary-manager and after acting for a time as manager of Southend United returned to Plymouth in 1910.

LENIN'S RING, NATIONAL DOG, SHOULD WIN TO-NIGHT

By THE HURDLER

AS the Grand National is the first of the classics at the White City, we can expect a number of open hurdle races within the next few weeks. Four almost certain starters for the National are competing at the White City this evening.

Connor's Company is the popular choice, but I prefer Lenin's Ring—a hurdler that should be able to show his best form on a large track.

To-day's selections:—

White City.—8.0, Bryn Rising; 8.18, Hanging Lie; 8.36 (H), Congleton Row; 8.54, Peerless Odds; 9.12, Cheerful Sandals; 9.30 (H), Lenin's Ring; 9.48, Stevenon Abbot; 10.6; Melksham Nutcracker.
Place Selections.—Faithful Umslopogaas, Jorrock's Hunt, Admiral Sparks, Half Semitic, Forest Don, Connor's Company, Chance Meeting, Pitcher Full.
Stamford Bridge.—6.30, Racing Vonnie; 6.45, Ryan; 7.0, Dusty Mick; 7.15 (H), Half Irish; 7.30, Kyle Luck; 7.45, Gay Robinetta; 8.0, Blue Danroil; 8.15, Jubilee Record.
Place Selections.—Carioca, Nap's Best, Dreaming Ry-

land, Socialist Leader, Raw Recruit II, Dogberry Genobrel, Sudbury Seagull, Wish Now.
Clapton.—8.0, Charlot; 8.18, Herring Bone; 8.36, Plum Tree II; 8.54, Seldom Society; 9.12, Neidin's Elmstead; 9.30, Bundle; 9.48, Bob Gath; 10.6, Red Guide.
Place Selections.—Defiant Lady, Generous Guide, Escaped the Guards, Wangler II, Kemp, Duna Cutlet, Coast Guide, City Editor.
Catford.—8.15, Cheerful Nobleman; 8.31, Joliambler; 8.47, Fever Chill; 9.3 (H), Stanbridge Slick; 9.19, Crindles Lass; 9.36, Busy Day II; 9.53, Tall Joint; 10.11, Shoveller.
Place Selections.—Krakajax, Totnes Hero, Bachelor's Share, Forged Javelin, Seaside Banker, Ravenglass, Great Roundup, Welli B.
Double.—Lenin's Ring (nap) and Steventon Abbot, at White City.

OTHER SELECTIONS

Wandsworth.—8.15, Brown Bear; 8.32, Goulane Swift; 8.49 (H), Markham's Might; 9.6, Noble Bounder; 9.23, Typed Letter; 9.40, Chic Chic; 9.57, Spur of the Moment; 10.14, Thanet Wanderer.
Charlton.—Afternoon—3.0, Reeve's Boy; 3.15, Red Pete; 3.30, Selworthy; 3.45 (H), Chartist; 4.0, Bayview Farm; 4.15, Just Pounce; 4.30, Jumping Boy; 4.45, Love Letter.
Walthamstow.—8.0, Ruddle Star; 8.18, King's Highway; 8.36, Stock Pot; 8.54, Hi-De-Hi; 9.12 (H), Blackilon Roboy; 9.30, Bended Lion; 9.48, Cannon Hill Prince; 10.6, Jerry's Joke.
Place Selections.—Kippet, Keep Left, Walking Home, Breffni Hills, Fairview Genesta, Jack's Hope, Crownville Hero, Clones Man.
Hackney Wick.—Afternoon—3.30, High Colour; 3.45, Convoy; 4.0 (H), Broadwater; 4.15, Batania; 4.30, Warwick Cub; 4.45 (H), Maxdale; 5.0, Newmarket Jockey; 5.15, Coldharbour Lass.
Place Selections.—Deasie, Warwick Peter, Gaelic Reputation, Deloney, Flying Machine, Fairlike Trip, Fashion's Joker, Borderero.

YESTERDAY'S RESULTS

Park Royal.—Afternoon—3.15, Burnsall (T.3) (3-1, T. 7s. 3d.); 3.33, Noble Nature (T.1) (evens F., T. 4s.); 3.51, Emperial (T.1) (7-4 F., T. 5s. 6d.); 4.9, Steady Con (T.4) (7-2, T. 10s. 3d.); 4.27, Hot Poker (T.3) (2-1 F., T. 3s.) and Morning Music (T.6) (3-1, T. 4s. 3d.) dead-heat; 4.45, Winker (T.2) (7-2, T. 5s.) and Geisha (T.6) (9-4 F., T. 3s. 9d.) dead-heat; 5.3, Kaffir Bangle (T.1) (11-8 F., T. 5s. 3d.); 5.21, Venetian Gondolier (T.2) (2-1 F., T. 4s. 6d.).
Wembley.—8.0, Ringside Luck (T.4) (3-1, T. 9s.); 8.15

land, Bid for Fortune (T.1) (3-1, T. 8s. 3d.); 8.32, Sleive Braddan (T.3) (9-2, T. 16s. 3d.); 8.46, Maher's Return (T.6) (3-1, T. 10s. 3d.); 9.5, Nanki's Future (T.6) (3-1, T. 12s.); 9.21, Sheehan (T.6) (9-4, T. 7s.); 9.38, Broomhill Bird (T.5) (9-4 F. 6s. 6d.); 9.55, Vanderveide (T.5) (7-1, T. 19s. 9d.).
Wimbledon.—8.0, Irish Caprice (T.2) (7-1, T. 21s. 3d.); 8.15, Point Steak (T.6) (7-4 F., T. 5s. 6d.); 8.30 (H), Melbourne Laddie (T.5) (evens F., T. 4s.); 8.45, Loppinger Harmony (T.2) (4-1, T. 11s. 3d.); 9.0, Junior Classic (T.1) (1-5 F., T. 2s. 3d.); 9.15, Tipperary Champion (T.4) (8-1, T. 18s. 6d.); 9.30 (H), Cambridge Dandy (T.1) (evens F., T. 4s. 6d.); 9.45, Caislean Luac Maig (T.1) (20-1, T. 43s. 3d.).
Tote Double.—71s. 6d. (13 tickets). **Second Tote Double.**—£33 (1 ticket).
Harringay.—8.0, Little Tom II (T.2) (4-1, T. 12s.); 8.17, Woodlands Bay (T.6) (9-2, T. 12s. 9d.); 8.34, Gipsy Rendezvous (T.6) (10-1, T. 19s. 6d.); 8.51, Kit Cutlet (T.1) 11-2, T. 14s. 9d.); 9.8, Robert Ashley (T.5) (6-4 F, T. 5s.); 9.25, Poetic Bluff (T.5) (5-2, T. 6s. 8d.); 9.42, Grampian Range (T.5) (9-4 F, T. 7s.); 9.59, Marquis Congleton (T.4) (7-2, T. 9s. 9d.).
Hendon.—8.15, Lonesome Laura (T.3) (2-1 F, T. 6s. 3d.); 8.30, Gin Flip (T.5) (3-1 J.F., T. 9s. 6d.); 8.45 (H), Coorado Kid (T.3) (11-8 F, T. 4s. 3d.); 9.0, Good Fault (T.4) (4-1, T. 15s. 3d.); 9.15, Batavian Nurse (T.2) (5-2 F, T. 8s. 6d.); 9.30 (H), Pastime (T.1) (7-2, T. 9s. 9d.); 9.45, Magic (T.5) (10-1, T. 30s. 6d.); 10.0, Sturdy and Staunch (T.3) (9-2, T. 11s.).

ENGLAND 'B' CAP FOR PLAYER WHO WAS 'TOO SLOW'

"Daily Mirror" Reporter

THE England selectors have apparently decided that Arsenal are certain to beat Luton in the Sixth Round of the F.A. Cup next Saturday!

They have picked two Luton players, inside right Jack Taylor and outside left Bert Mitchell, for the England B team to meet Holland in Amsterdam on March 26—three days before the Cup semi-finals.

No, they hadn't forgotten about the semi-finals. That is proved by the fact that Bolton's Jack Ball is named as deputy for Phil Gunter, the Portsmouth right back —if Portsmouth are still in the Cup.

If Luton beat Arsenal they will naturally seek the release of Taylor and Mitchell for the semi-final. So the selectors might at least have named two more alternatives from their "shadow" team.

His Reward

Choice of Taylor, a Stockton lad and Luton's leading goal-scorer, is the final reward for a player who last season had to endure the barracking of some Luton supporters.

"They thought he was too slow," manager Dally Duncan told me earlier this season, "but I was determined to keep him in the team because he has a fine football brain, courage and a good shot."

The team illustrates the selectors' new policy of restricting their choice of "B" team men to players who have not yet received a full England cap.

Tommy Harmer, brilliant ball player in his first League season, was omitted from Spurs' team last Saturday. But he now becomes an England challenger to Eddie Baily, who returned to the Tottenham team in his place.

Goalkeeper Charlie Ashcroft is another player who has taken less than a season to impress the selectors.

Piquant point about the full backs is that Gunter gets a chance to strengthen his claims to Alf Ramsey's place in the England senior team—and Spurs' Charlie Withers a chance to become clubmate Ramsey's international partner!

Other strong challengers for full England caps are Jack Wheeler, Bolton's right half, and Charlie Vaughan, Charlton centre forward.

THE TEAM

Ashcroft (Liverpool); Gunter (Portsmouth) or Ball (Bolton), Withers (Spurs); Wheeler (Bolton), Greenwood, capt. (Brentford), Boyd (Birmingham); Berry (Man. Utd.), Taylor (Luton), Vaughan (Charlton), Harmer (Spurs), Mitchell (Luton). Reserves: Paisley (Liverpool), Hines (Leicester).

Arm-in-arm together during today's fifth round Cup replay at Villa Park were Harris of Chelsea (right) and Kirk of Leeds.

No mistake this time —Chelsea romp home in 2nd replay

By BOB FERRIER

CHELSEA at their sparkling best swamped Leeds 5—1 in their F.A. Cup Fifth Round second replay at Villa Park yesterday.

Maintaining the peak they so often reach—and then infuriatingly lose—Chelsea swept aside the Leeds opposition, and into the sixth round.

For Bobby Smith, chunky Chelsea centre forward, it was a triumph—he scored a hat-trick in his side's five goals.

Leeds never got off their heels. The defence was too often hesitant, the forwards downright inaccurate, but Chelsea can go forward with a deal of faith in themselves on this show.

They had played sixteen minutes. Don Mills fouled Bentley twenty-five yards out. Dickson chopped up a lob, over the defence's line. Dunn, Leeds' right back, headed it back to his goalkeeper. But before Searson could get his hands to it, the blue wraith from Chelsea, Roy Bentley, materialised from nowhere to score with a perfectly controlled head flick! Chelsea, without striking any breathless form, were ahead.

Some boisterous roaming from Roy Kirk, Leeds' centre, put United back in the game with a bang, and they got a glorious equaliser on the half-hour.

Don Mills, angled from about eighteen yards, hit a first-time cross-smash at terrific pace. The ball was bulging the netting before Robertson got his hands up.

And just ten minutes later, when we were already thinking of extra time, so close was the whole thing, Bobby Smith, Chelsea's centre forward, made a twisting twenty-yard run. Resisting four challenges, he held on with complete control, and squeezed his shot in at Searson's near post.

Smith Makes It Three

Armstrong, D'Arcy and Bobby Smith combined well on the Chelsea right wing before Johnny Smith wasted the effort by shooting over the bar.

After fifty-five minutes Chelsea went further ahead, Gray intercepted a pass by Bentley, and the left winger put over a perfect centre for Bobby Smith to head it home.

Two minutes later Bobby Smith, the Chelsea centre forward, completed his hat-trick, when he picked up a loose ball, raced past Charles and scored with a grand shot.

After Chelsea's fourth goal, Charles went centre forward, Kirk dropping back to centre half for Leeds, who had lost their earlier poise. When Leeds did attack, Charles and Mills both wasted chances by weak shooting.

To add to Leeds' woes, Mills was taken off with an injured leg, and immediately Chelsea added a fifth goal, when Gray shot through from a corner after seventy-four minutes.

Chelsea now meet Sheffield United at Bramall-lane in the Sixth Round.

TELEGRAM II MAY BE HER FIFTH CHAMPION

By NEWSBOY

TWO great hurdlers, National Spirit and Hatton's Grace, whose records need no explaining, will attempt to give their younger rivals a lesson in the Champion Hurdle Challenge Cup at Cheltenham today.

There comes a time, however, when racehorses deteriorate, and I feel certain National Spirit has reached that state.

Hatton's Grace may be a different proposition, but the going is not in his favour. One thing certain, however, is that he will not fail through lack of vocal encouragement from his Irish supporters. Even so, I feel forced to overlook him this year and concentrate on the younger challengers.

Three of the runners, Sir Ken, Telegram II and Hunza, are unbeaten over hurdles, but I cannot imagine Hunza being good enough for such a race.

Four to Watch

The other pair come well into the reckoning, however, and I do not intend to overlook the prospects of Wye Fly, Average, Fellah II or Noholme. Wye Fly is a stable companion of Hatton's Grace and will be ridden by Freddy Winter. He has put up good performances in Ireland when carrying big weights in handicaps.

Fellah II comes from France, and is another difficult to assess. He is well enough fancied and it is in his favour that he has been schooled over English hurdles and will be ridden by an English jockey.

Stamina Doubt

The dry ground will favour none more than Noholme, but the fast gallop which is set in this race may sap his reserve. He will probably be right with the leaders at the last hurdle, with insufficient speed left to carry him up the final stiff hill.

Average has a great chance and the fast going will suit this delicately-framed horse. He has always been a favourite of mine, and if all had gone well might have been my choice. I still expect a good show from him, but the fact that he has been off a racecourse for so long makes me wary.

The favourite, Sir Ken, has done everything required of him, but whether he can rise to this great occasion has still to be proved. He cannot be labelled the best of jumpers, and that is important. To lose just a little ground at each hurdle proves disastrous.

Telegram II has won his only three hurdle races. I am convinced he needs the present going to show his best form, and he has the right temperament.

From what I have seen, Telegram II does only what is required and keeps pulling out that little bit extra when necessary.

A better jumper than Telegram II could not be wished for, and I visualise Dave Dick having him with the leaders at the last hurdle and then staying on to give Miss Dorothy Paget her fifth champion hurdle victory.

For the places I choose Average and Sir Ken.

HE NETS THREE

Scottish F.A. beat the Army, 3—1 at Newcastle yesterday, McMillen, of Airdrie, scoring a hat-trick. Parry (Derby County) scored for the Army.

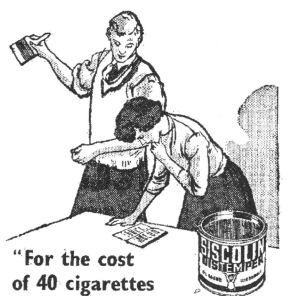

Chelsea sign new manager

'DYNAMITE' DRAKE TO BOOST THEM

By Bob Ferrier

TED DRAKE
"Long contract."

CHELSEA'S new manager is Ted Drake, "Mr. Dynamite" of pre-war Soccer, and probably the hardest-punching, toughest and most courageous centre forward Arsenal and England ever had.

He will succeed Billy Birrell, whose contract ends this month.

Joe Mears, Chelsea chairman, said last night that Reading have agreed to release Drake to take up the appointment when Mr. Birrell's contract expires, and although details of the new Drake contract have not been finally settled, it will be for a "period of some years."

This may well prove to be the best thing Chelsea have done in their long and tangled history.

Drake, with five England caps in his day, was second to none in courage.

His appointment, almost on the eve of an Arsenal Cup Final, recalls the Arsenal-Sheffield United final of 1936, when Drake played with a badly injured knee swathed in a towel-sized bandage.

Against all instructions he took a shot with his injured leg—and falling in agony, he scored the only goal of the match.

With Third Division Reading he has proved himself a first-class manager. With almost no expenditure on players, Drake took the team to second place in 1948-49.

Last season they were third; this season they are fighting for second place.

These efforts have made Drake one of the highest paid managers in football, and in 1949 he was said to have turned down a £2,000 a year offer from Leicester.

He is not quite forty, was a gasworks apprentice in Southampton before signing for the local club, from which he moved to Arsenal in 1934.

The following year he cracked seven goals past Aston Villa at Birmingham to set up a First Division scoring record which still stands.

After RAF service during the war, his playing career was ended by an injury, oddly enough, on the Reading ground in 1945.

Chelsea for years have persisted in spurning the best of their opportunities. With a huge stadium within minutes of the heart of London, with a huge and generally loyal support, they have never quite made the most of it.

Now they have found a young dynamic manager. Let the board of directors, the players and the fans back Drake to the hilt, and we can see a new Chelsea.

Drake goes to Chelsea with the chance of a lifetime. Let Chelsea, and Drake, make the most of it.

That disputed goal makes Spurs No. 2

By GEORGE HARLEY

THE Spurs' two Leslies, Bennett and Medley, scored a couple of goals worth £110 last night. The 2—0 victory at Chelsea made Spurs runners-up for the League championship, thanks to a better goal average than Arsenal, and that meant £440 talent money instead of £330.

But the goal which really gave them the £10 apiece extra was that celebrated double corner-kick effort against Huddersfield on April 2—the goal that wasn't according to the laws of the game.

And only a few hours before Spurs' win at Chelsea yesterday, Huddersfield had taken the dispute to the F.A. Appeals Committee after the Football League had declined to take action on their protest.

Huddersfield accept their relegation as inevitable, but want a F.A. ruling on principle.

It's a pity there should be any question about Spurs finishing runners-up on merit, for they completed their programme playing the rhythmic push-and-run football which has made them such an attractive team.

Medley, in particular, delighted the 46,000 crowd as he harassed the Chelsea defence with intelligent roaming backed by dazzling ball control.

Outside left on the programme, he made the first goal from outside right and scored the second from centre forward.

The first was a gem. Bennett, with his back to the goal, cleverly headed the ball into the net, after a clever Medley move and centre to the far post.

Biggest thrill was a glorious drive by Bentley which Ditchburn tipped against a post. Many thought the ball had hit the iron support at the back of the net, but Bentley confirmed that it struck the post.

THREE SHARE GOLF LEAD

MAX FAULKNER, Open champion, Harry Bradshaw (Portmarnock) and Sid Scott (Carlisle) shared the lead in the Dunlop 2,000 guineas golf tournament at Sunningdale yesterday with second-round aggregates of 141 a single stroke ahead.

Jack Butterworth, 31, of Worcester, beat reigning champion Geoffrey Roberts (Southport and Ainsdale) by three and one in the third round of the English Amateur championship at Burnham and Berrow, Somerset.

Scots win 6-0

Scotland beat America 6—0 in the first official Soccer international between the countries at Hampden Park, Glasgow, last night before a crowd of 107,765. Reilly scored three.

RESULTS

INTERNATIONAL.—Scotland 6 (Reilly 3, McMillan 2, O'Connell o.g.), U.S. 0, at Hampden.
LEAGUE.—Division I: Chelsea 0, Spurs 2 (Bennett, Medley). Division II: Brentford 1 (Morrad), Doncaster 0. Division III (S.): Aldershot 3 (Cushlow o.g., Laird, Durkin), Crystal Palace 0; Millwall 2 (Saward, Morgan), Northampton 1 (Ramscar); Norwich 3 (Ashman 2, Summers), Plymouth 0; Swindon 1 (Bain), Shrewsbury 2 (Jackson, McCulloch). Division III (N.): Accrington 5 (Watkinson 2, Darcy 2, Hindle o.g.), Bradford 1 (Wright); Grimsby 2 (Johnston, Maddison), Chesterfield 0; Hartlepools Utd. 0, Tranmere Rovers 1; Wrexham 0, Stockport 0.
Olympic Trial.—Olympic XI 0, England "B" XI 3 (Stubbs, Hamer, French). At Highbury.
Other Matches—Blackpool 0, Hamburg 2; Crewe 1, Derby 3.
Rugby League Featherstone 18, Batley 5.
Southern League.—Merthyr 4, Dartford 1.

TODAY'S MATCHES

Division I.—Fulham v. Derby (6.15).
Division III (S.).—L. Orient v. Bristol C. (6.15); Bristol R. v. Exeter (6.30); Colchester v. Brighton (6.30); P. Vale v. Millwall (6.15).
Division III (N.).—Scunthorpe v. Barrow (6.30).
Other Match.—Grimsby v. Lincoln (6.30).

Battle with the Silver Fury ends in success

By BERNARD VENABLES
'Daily Mirror' Angling Correspondent

HERE in Devon now, the primroses are under the hedges and anemones shine in the spinneys; the cuckoo sings and swallows sweep the river's surface again. The white owl that flew before us down the road as we returned from the river, went with its kill through the barn's open loft window. There are young in its nest again.

These things are part of the fervour of April everywhere. Not in Devon alone, but in much of the West and North, spring brings as well the salmon, the great silver fish still strong in its sea vigour. In the River Torridge's brassy tinted pools it leaps before the eager eyes of the angler.

When I started to cast my bait in the Hut Pool the easy flexing of the long spinning rod was an old pleasure, but one freshly found again, as it always is in each spring's new salmon season. It seemed that a salmon must wait under every foot of that creaming water.

And, indeed, at about the fifth cast there came that sudden heavy tug that to the dreaming mind of the angler is an ecstasy. But that would have been, perhaps, too early a success. The fish soon kicked off.

Half-way down the pool the water slid quietly over submerged rock ridges that came out from the further bank. Here, if anywhere, a salmon should lie.

Salmon Was on

I threw my bait, a translucent orange plug, so that the pull of the current should work it along the lie, out towards the centre of the pool.

Wriggling and diving as plugs do, it had worked no more than two feet when it stopped, suddenly deadly resistant. A moment's endless pause, and the rod-top plunged. A salmon was on.

Now it was across the pool, rolling just in the surface, now it rushed up the pool towards me, I winding furiously to keep a tight line. If it would stay thus in the pool all would be well. Down stream I could not follow it for the trees on the bank. But it turned and rushed down, The line hissed and grew less on the reel. The drum began to scorch under my controlling thumb. The salmon was becoming distant between the tree-lined banks. I must stop it or lose it.

I stopped it. The rod bowed and laboured, the tensile power of split cane against the silver fury of the salmon. I drew the fish up again, ten yards, twenty yards, then it was away again.

But the peak of its fight was past, its runs were shorter, soon it was fighting in the pool again. It thrashed on the surface, striving for the snags in the bank.

Then, at last, the noose of the tailer snapped round its tail, it was on the bank, it was mine.

It was silver, deep bluish on its back, lilac on its flanks, wonderfully beautiful. fifteen-and-a-half pounds of splendid symmetry.

Lost His Rod

THE doctor loved his fishing. It was the joy of his leisure hours, in season, to fish for the salmon and sea trout on this Devon river. For a modest sum the rights of a stretch had been his for a number of seasons, and would, he supposed, continue to be.

But then the colonel came, a wealthier man. He offered a higher rent and took from the doctor his fishing, his beloved fishing.

One day the colonel was fishing the water; down the opposite bank came the doctor. The sight was painful to the doctor. He shook his fist at the colonel and swore. The colonel swore back. The air became thick.

A cow in the field behind the colonel, in the way of her kind, was curious. She walked up quietly to see what was to happen. The colonel in his rage did not see her.

At the battle's height the doctor said: "Well, anyway, the cow's eaten your ruddy rod." and stumped off.

And so she had.

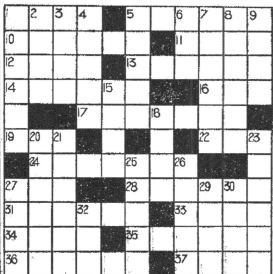
YESTERDAY'S CRICKET SCORES

M.C.C. v. YORKS.: At Lord's. M.C.C. 318 (Willatt 87, Jakeman 48, Eager 46, Bailey not 27. Close 5 for 64; Padgett 2 for 66, Leadbeater 2 for 62). Yorks 54 for 2.

CAMBRIDGE UN. v. LEICESTER. At Cambridge. Cambridge 317 (May 42, Sheppard 148, Tordoff 52; Walsh 4 for 95, Lester 3 for 47). Leicester 51 for 0.

CHELSEA, CHAMPIONS!

JUBILEE CURE FOR THE BLUES

★ "This is the happiest moment of my life," says Chelsea manager Ted Drake as he acknowledges the call of the fans with stalwarts Harris, Bentley, Parsons and the other lads around him.

AFTER fifty inglorious years as Football's laughing boys, Chelsea are Champions of the Football League, writes JACK PEART.

Their 3—0 defeat of relegated Sheffield Wednesday assured them of their first major Soccer honour in the Golden Jubilee Year of the club.

No wonder manager Ted Drake bubbled over with pride and joy when I spoke to him after the game.

Loyalty

"This is the happiest day of my life," he said. "We have had a wonderful response from every member of the staff—and our loyal supporters have been behind us all the way.

"I've had my share of football honours," added Manager Drake. "That is what makes me so happy for some of the older players.

Men like former skipper Johnny Harris, Roy Bentley and Ken Armstrong must have seen their chance of winning anything big slipping away.

"Now we have started, it's up to the youngsters to keep us at the top. Maybe we can win the Cup next year."

Maybe Ted was thinking of the record of the reserves teams—top of Football Combination (Div. I), top of Metropolitan League, top of S.E. Counties League, second in London Mid-Week League.

There's no doubt that Ted Drake, nicknamed "The Lionheart" when he was Arsenal and England's centre forward, has injected Chelsea with his own never-say-die spirit.

A model penalty

Yesterday's match that crowned Ted Drake's triumph in his third year as manager, was, however, hardly worthy of the occasion.

For the record, outside right Eric Parsons scored a goal in each half and right back Peter Sillett showed how a penalty should be taken.

Wednesday played without goalkeeper McIntosh for most of the second half, conceded a penalty that should never have been given, and substitute 'keeper, left back Curtis, gave away a gift goal.

Tension

BUT no more of this game in which Football struggled against the overpowering atmosphere of grim excitement and nervous tension.

These detached yet delirious Chelsea fans—over 1,000,000 of them watched the home games—this season—wouldn't leave until manager Drake and his boys took their curtain calls in front of the stand.

Well, they have waited a long time. I imagine there will be scenes like a theatre opening night when they attend a civic reception at the Fulham Town Hall later this year.

As a postscript, I'm going to risk a prophecy. I believe that amateur inside forward Seamus O'Connell will be persuaded to sign as a professional for Chelsea before next season.

Fate

IN this hour of triumph for Ted Drake, I can't help thinking of another London manager whom the Football Fates have shunned.

I refer to Arthur Rowe, of Spurs, forced by illness to follow his once-great team's struggle against relegation from a sick bed.

Yesterday's 0—2 defeat at Leicester was a body blow.

Arthur, whom I regard as one of the finest tacticians in the game, raised Spurs to the heights.

Such brilliance could not last, but few would have dared to forecast that Spurs could slump so badly.

Everybody in football knows what Arthur Rowe is going through. He has our sincere wishes for a speedy and complete recovery.

HE'S WORTH A MEDAL

● If young J. M. McAllister, of the John Fisher School, Surrey, had not been honest, he would be the proud owner of a medal today.

● He finished third in the junior 110yds. hurdles at the London Athletic Club's Schools Challenge Cups meeting at the White City, then told the referee he had run out of his lane.

● McAllister had to be disqualified but the "Sunday Pictorial" is happy to award him a medal to mark his fine sporting gesture.

PIRIE WINS

Gordon Pirie was only two seconds outside his own British record when winning the A.A.A. Southern Counties 6 miles title in a championship best time of 28m. 21.4s. at White City, London.

WHO GOES DOWN?

FIRST DIVISION managers at the start of each season usually remind players that if they can get thirty-five points quickly then they are safe from relegation.

It isn't so this season:

Who's going down with Sheffield Wednesday to the Second Division — Bolton, Blackpool, Huddersfield, Sheffield United, Cardiff Spurs or Leicester?

Look at the table. Anything can happen.

Now study the remaining fixtures of the clubs involved:

BOLTON: April 27, Huddersfield (home); April 30, Burnley (home); May 4, Leicester (away).

BLACKPOOL: April 25, Newcastle (away); April 30, Sheffield U. (home).

HUDDERSFIELD: April 27, Bolton (away); April 30, Leicester (home); May 2, Cardiff (home).

SHEFFIELD U.: April 30 Blackpool (away); May 2, Portsmouth (home).

CARDIFF: April 27, Newcastle (away); April 30, Wolves (home); May 2, Huddersfield (away).

SPURS: April 27, West Bromwich (away); April 30, Newcastle (home); May 5, Charlton (away).

LEICESTER: April 30, Huddersfield (away); May 4, Bolton (home).

Spurs went down in the 1927-28 season with 38 points!

Championship-chasing Portsmouth discovered how tough can be clubs who face relegation.

At Cardiff they scored in four minutes, through Harris and the enterprise of Dale, Henderson and Harris alone was worth success.

It didn't come. Cardiff equalised, despite the work of Dickinson, Reid and Pickett. And goalkeeper Uprichard complained of double vision after one clash with the fiery Welsh attack.

Spurs fail

Despite the hard work of Marchi at half back and Baily and Gavin in attack, Spurs just couldn't get going at Leicester.

The two Dereks of Leicester, Hines and Hogg, got the two goals and the latter gave Alf Ramsey one of his hardest games ever.

For the first time for several months Leicester played more like a First Division team and Hines and Arthur Rowley were always ready to take advantage of Hogg's speed and centres.

Credit for Reynolds in the Spurs goal that he was able to hold some of the shots of sharp-shooters Rowley and Hines.

Luton's high hopes

THE fight to get up to the First Division is as complex as which club will go down to Division II.

Leeds, Luton, Stoke, Rotherham, Birmingham, Blackburn and West Ham are the sides involved—but it looks as if the last-named two are the outsiders.

Take a peep at the final matches, which are:

LEEDS: April 30, Fulham (away).

LUTON: April 27 Bristol R. (home); April 30, Doncaster (away).

STOKE: April 25, Port Vale (away); April 30, Plymouth (away).

ROTHERHAM: April 25, Swansea (home); April 30, Port Vale (away); May 2, Liverpool (home).

BIRMINGHAM: April 25, Hull (away); April 30, Liverpool (away); May 4, Doncaster (away).

BLACKBURN: April 30, Bury (home).

WEST HAM: April 26, Liverpool (home); April 30, Lincoln (home); May 2, Nottm. F. (away).

Note the fact that Leeds, Stoke and Birmingham have five away games to fulfill between them. So Luton and Rotherham must be regarded as favourites.

New look

Pic reporter **BOB EDWARDS** was at the Luton-Port Vale clash, which Luton won 4—2.

Bob Edwards says manager Dally Duncan blames the hard ground and "the run of the ball" for Luton dropping twelve points in their previous eleven matches.

The confidence of the side had suffered. That's why he made startling changes to meet Port Vale.

Wing halves Jim Pemberton and Charlie Watkins made a new left wing, and Bob Morton reverted to wing half with MacEwan at centre forward.

In a Cup-tie atmosphere, Gordon Turner (10 minutes) and Roy Davies (32) put Luton in a comfortable position. But brilliant goals by Done (55) and Griffiths (70) had them panicky.

West Ham were never in the hunt at Bury and lost 4—1. Allison was at sea against Bury's two centre-forward plan. Dick's goal came when all was lost. He charged down a clearance to score.

SPORT PICTORIAL RESULTS, SCORERS AND TABLES

(Half-time scores in brackets)

DIVISION I

Arsenal .. (2)..2 **Man. Utd.** (2)..3
Lishman 2 — Blanchflower 2, Goring (o.g.) 42,754

Burnley .. (0)..0 **Sund'land** (1)..1
Fleming 19,227

Cardiff . (0)..1 **P'rtsmouth** (1)..1
Williams — Harris 25,000

Chelsea .. (1)..3 **Shef. Wed.** (0)..0
Parsons 2, Sillett (pen) 51,421

Everton .. (1)..2 **Charlton** .. (1)..2
Parker, Wainwright — O'Linn, Leary 27,869

Leicester .. (1)..2 **Spurs** .... (0)..0
Hines, Hogg 23,908

Man. City (1)..1 **Blackpool** . (1)..6
Fagan — Brown, Mortensen 2, Perry 3 44,339

Newcastle (0)..0 **Bolton** .... (0)..0
48,028

Preston .. (0)..0 **A. Villa** .. (1)..3
Thompson 2, Walton (o.g.) 15,160

Shef. Utd. (1)..1 **Wolves** .. (1)..2
Ringstead — Wilshaw, Hancocks 25,000

W. Brom. . (1)..2 **Hudd'sfield** (0)..1
Allen 2 — Glazzard 21,000

	P.	Home W.	D.	L.	Goals F.	A.	Away W.	D.	L.	Goals F.	A.	Pts
Chelsea ..	41	11	5	5	43	29	9	7	4	37	28	52
Wolves ..	41	13	5	3	58	30	6	5	9	29	37	48
Man. City	41	11	5	5	45	36	7	5	8	31	31	46
Sund'land	41	7	11	2	36	27	7	7	7	25	27	46
Portsm'th	39	12	4	3	40	18	5	7	8	28	36	45
Man. Utd.	40	11	4	5	42	29	8	2	10	39	43	44
Arsenal ..	41	12	3	6	44	25	5	6	9	24	36	43
Everton ..	40	9	6	5	32	23	7	4	9	30	41	42
A. Villa	39	10	3	7	36	31	8	3	8	31	40	42
Burnley ..	41	11	3	7	29	19	5	6	9	21	29	41
Newcastle	39	11	4	4	49	26	5	4	11	35	48	40
W. Brom.	40	11	5	4	43	31	5	3	12	32	58	40
Charlton ..	39	8	5	5	41	27	7	4	10	33	41	39
Preston ..	41	8	5	8	47	33	7	3	10	32	31	38
Bolton	39	10	6	3	44	28	2	7	11	17	36	37
Blackpool	40	8	6	6	32	24	6	3	11	26	37	37
Huddersf'd	39	8	4	7	23	22	4	9	7	35	44	37
Sheff. U. ..	40	9	3	8	36	32	6	4	10	27	51	37
Cardiff	39	8	4	8	38	36	4	7	8	21	33	35
Spurs	39	8	4	8	40	34	5	4	10	26	36	34
Leicester .	40	8	6	6	39	32	3	5	12	30	51	33
Sheff. W.	41	6	7	7	37	38	1	3	17	21	62	24

FOOTBALL COMBINATION—Div. 1.—Spurs 2, Norwich 1; West Ham 1, Portsmouth 1.

FOOTBALL COMBINATION—Div. 2.—Bristol R. 2, Southampton 0; C. Palace 1, Aldershot 0; Fulham 2, Swindon 0; Q.P.R. 4, Northampton 2; Southend 2, Watford 2; Swansea 4, Plymouth 1.

SOUTHERN LEAGUE.—Bath 1, Kidderminster 1; Chelmsford 5, Merthyr 3; Dartford 1, Kettering 2; Exeter 0, Headington 2; Gloucester 0, Yeovil 1; Guildford 5, Llanelly 1; Hastings 4, Cheltenham 0; Tonbridge 1, Hereford 4; Weymouth 5, Gravesend 1; Worcester 3, Barry 4.

IRISH CUP—FINAL.—Dundela 3, Glenavon 0 (at Windsor Pk.)

DIVISION II

Birm'gham (0)..1 **Notts C.** . (0)..1
Brown — Wills 28,018

Bury .... (1)..4 **West Ham** (0)..1
Robinson, Kelly, Fletcher, Pearson — Dick 9,746

Hull ...... (1)..1 **Doncaster** (1)..1
Bulles — Jeffrey 14,000

Ipswich (1)..1 **Swansea** . (1)..1
Brown — Charles 19,000

Leeds .. (1)..2 **Blackburn** (0)..0
Brooke 2 39,400

Lincoln .. (0)..3 **Derby** (0)..0
Munro, Finch, Garvie 9,380

Luton .... (2)..4 **Port Vale** . (0)..2
Turner 2, Davies, MacEwan — Done, Griffiths 16,700

Middlesbro (0)..1 **Liverpool** . (1)..2
McPherson — Rowley, Liddell 16,000

Notts F. .. (1)..2 **Fulham** .. (0)..0
Small, McLaren 9,871

Rotherham (1)..2 **Plymouth** . (0)..0
Farmer, Grainger 18,000

Stoke .... (1)..2 **Bristol R.** (0)..0
Oscroft, Finney 18,139

	P.	Home W.	D.	L.	Goals F.	A.	Away W.	D.	L.	Goals F.	A.	Pts
Leeds	41	14	4	3	43	19	8	3	9	24	33	51
Luton	40	17	2	1	53	18	4	6	10	30	35	50
Stoke	40	12	5	4	38	17	8	5	6	30	27	50
Rotherham	39	15	1	3	51	21	8	3	9	35	41	50
Birm'ham	39	14	4	3	56	22	6	5	7	26	22	49
Blackburn	41	14	3	3	72	30	8	2	11	41	48	49
West Ham	39	12	4	3	46	24	6	5	9	27	41	45
Notts Co.	40	13	2	4	44	26	7	3	11	28	44	45
Bristol R.	40	15	3	2	50	21	4	3	13	23	45	44
Swansea .	40	14	3	3	55	28	2	6	12	28	53	41
Midd'sbro'	40	13	0	7	47	30	5	4	11	23	49	40
Bury	40	10	5	6	44	35	5	4	10	31	35	39
Liverpool	39	11	6	3	53	35	4	3	12	33	53	39
Fulham ..	40	10	5	5	45	26	4	5	11	30	50	38
Nottm. F.	40	8	3	9	28	28	8	3	9	27	30	38
Doncaster	40	10	5	4	34	26	4	2	15	23	61	35
Hull	40	7	5	8	30	32	5	5	10	14	31	34
Lincoln ..	39	8	5	6	38	33	4	4	12	28	44	33
Port Vale	39	9	6	4	30	20	1	5	14	16	50	31
Plymouth	41	9	4	7	27	26	2	3	16	28	56	29
Ipswich	40	10	3	8	37	28	1	2	16	18	61	27
Derby ...	41	5	6	9	36	34	1	3	17	14	48	21

KENT LEAGUE.—Ashford 3, Tunbridge Wells 1; Betteshanger 2, Sittingbourne 3; Dover 0, Folkestone 0; Margate 4, Bexleyheath 1; Snowdon 2, Deal 1.

NORFOLK AND SUFFOLK LEAGUE.—Beccles 6, Fakenham 2; E. Coachworks 3, Sheringham 2; Gothic 0, Thetford 5; N. Walsham 4, C.N.S.O.B.U. 2; Wymondham 1, Norwich C.E.Y.M.S. 3; Holt 0, Bungay 1.

ATHENIAN LEAGUE.—Enfield 1, Finchley 1; Hayes 2, Barnet 3; Redhill 4, Hendon 4; Southall 4, Wealdstone 0.

DIVISION III (South)

Brentford (1)..3 **Watford** . (1)..2
Dudley, Towers 2 (1 pen) — Cook, Brown 9,400

Brighton .. (1)..1 **B'nemouth** (0)..1
Leadbetter — Newsham (pen) 10,392

Bristol C. (0)..0 **Newport** .. (0)..0
27,499

Coventry .. (0)..0 **North'pton** (0)..0
11,610

Gillingham (0)..1 **Southend** (0)..1
Marks (pen) — Baron 9,820

L. Orient . (0)..1 **Aldershot** . (1)..5
Lee — Gaynor, J., 2, Cheney, Flint, Menzies 8,207

Millwall . (0)..1 **Swindon** .. (0)..0
Shepherd 6,271

Reading . (1)..1 **Norwich** . (0)..1
Uphill — Chung 7,324

Shrew'bury (0)..2 **Colchester** (0)..0
Price, McCue, 6,735

South'pton (0)..2 **C. Palace** (1)..2
Day 2 — Andrews, Belcher 8,788

Torquay .. (1)..3 **Q.P.R.** .... (0)..2
Dobbie, Collins, Rutter (o.g.) — Longbottom, Cameron 6,000

Walsall .. (1)..1 **Exeter** (0)..0
Richards 10,953

	P.	Home W.	D.	L.	Goals F.	A.	Away W.	D.	L.	Goals F.	A.	Pts
Bristol C.	44	17	4	2	62	22	11	6	4	36	24	66
South'pton	44	16	6	1	49	19	7	5	9	21	27	57
L. Orient	43	16	2	5	48	20	8	6	6	34	24	56
Gill'gham	43	12	8	3	41	28	8	4	8	32	34	52
Millwall ..	43	14	5	3	42	23	5	5	11	24	41	48
Brighton	42	12	4	5	40	24	6	5	10	27	33	45
Watford ..	43	9	8	3	38	23	7	5	11	26	36	45
Coventry	41	14	5	2	44	21	3	5	12	16	27	44
Norwich	43	13	3	5	38	21	5	5	12	20	35	44
Torquay .	42	10	6	5	46	37	6	5	10	30	39	43
N'hampton	44	12	4	5	45	26	6	3	14	26	54	43
Aldershot	43	11	5	5	40	21	4	7	11	28	43	42
Brentford	42	10	5	6	41	34	5	7	9	35	42	42
Q.P.R. ..	43	13	5	3	44	23	2	7	13	22	45	42
B'rnem'th	43	7	7	7	32	28	5	10	7	25	33	41
Reading .	42	7	10	6	32	26	6	4	9	31	39	40
Southend	41	11	5	5	44	26	3	6	11	28	45	39
Newport .	43	8	7	6	30	26	3	8	11	28	43	37
Shrewsb'ry	41	12	4	4	38	23	2	4	15	19	51	36
C. Palace	43	8	10	2	28	21	2	5	16	20	56	35
Exeter	42	8	7	6	26	26	2	6	13	14	39	33
Swindon	42	8	7	5	25	19	1	7	14	16	38	32
Walsall ..	42	8	6	7	44	31	1	6	14	24	48	30
Colchester	43	7	5	9	28	33	2	7	13	19	49	30

EASTERN COUNTIES LEAGUE.—Gorleston 2, West Ham "A" 1; Lowestoft 1, Stowmarket 3; Norwich "A" 2, Spurs "A" 2; Yarmouth 5, Crittall 0; Cambridge Utd. 3, Harwich 0; Eynesbury 0, Arsenal "A" 0.

DIVISION III (North)

Accrington (0)..3 **Darlington** (0)..0
Wright, Stewart, Devlin 7,000

Barnsley (3)..3 **Carlisle** (0)..1
Mitton (o.g.), Chappell 2 — Atkinson 13,510

Barrow .. (1)..2 **Stockport** (0)..0
Collins, Gordon 4,222

Bradf'rd C. (0)..0 **Chester** (0)..0
6,795

Halifax (0)..0 **Bradford** (0)..0
6,700

Mansfield (0)..0 **Gateshead** (0)..1
Ingham 4,336

Oldham .. (1)..4 **Grimsby** (0)..0
McShane, Walker, Scrine, Travis 4,555

Scunth'rpe (0)..3 **Crewe** . (0)..1
Gregory, McGill, Brown — Samuels 5,306

Southport (0)..0 **Tranmere** (0)..0
2,230

Work'gton (0)..0 **Hartlepools** (1)..1
McGuigan 5,161

Wrexham . (0)..0 **Chesterf'ld** (1)..2
Stiffle, Smith 4,558

York . (1)..2 **Rochdale** . (0)..0
Fenton 2 9,948

	P.	Home W.	D.	L.	Goals F.	A.	Away W.	D.	L.	Goals F.	A.	Pts
Barnsley ..	41	16	2	2	45	15	11	2	8	32	26	58
Accrington	43	18	2	3	65	32	5	9	6	24	28	57
York ...	42	13	5	4	42	23	10	5	5	43	32	56
Hartlepools	43	16	2	3	38	17	9	2	11	25	28	54
Scunth'pe	42	14	5	3	44	17	8	4	8	32	32	53
Chesterf'd	43	14	1	5	42	30	7	5	11	27	37	48
Gateshead	43	10	7	4	35	23	8	5	9	25	42	48
Work'gton	43	10	7	5	38	23	7	6	8	26	28	47
Stockport	44	13	3	6	48	23	5	8	10	34	43	47
Oldham	43	14	5	3	46	20	4	5	12	23	41	46
Rochdale ..	42	12	6	3	33	17	4	7	10	29	41	45
Mansfield	44	14	4	5	40	28	4	4	13	22	38	44
Southport	41	9	8	4	26	17	5	6	9	17	25	42
Halifax ..	43	9	9	5	41	27	5	3	12	18	36	40
Darlington	44	9	6	6	37	26	4	7	12	21	45	39
Bradford ..	43	10	7	4	28	19	4	3	15	26	48	38
Barrow ..	42	12	4	6	38	29	4	1	15	26	50	37
Carlisle ..	43	11	1	8	46	33	3	5	15	25	50	34
Tranmere	43	8	5	8	35	29	4	5	13	17	38	34
Wrexham	43	8	6	8	35	35	3	5	13	22	40	33
Chester ..	44	10	3	9	23	23	2	6	14	19	48	33
Bradf'd C.	42	8	5	8	28	22	3	5	13	13	27	32
Grimsby ..	43	9	4	8	25	27	3	4	15	19	41	32
Crewe	44	7	9	5	42	33	2	4	17	23	56	31

ISTHMIAN LEAGUE.—Oxford C. 2, Dulwich H. 1; Romford 1, Bromley 0; Walthamstow Av. 7, Barking 1; Wimbledon 1, Kingstonian 2; Wycombe W. 2, Clapton 1.

BOYS' INTERNATIONAL.—England 6, Wales 0 (at Wembley).

SCOTTISH CUP—FINAL

Celtic ... (1)..1 **Clyde** ... (0)..1
Walsh — Robertson 106,234

(At Hampden Park)

(Replay Wednesday (6.30) at Hampden Park)

SCOTTISH LEAGUE—Div. "A"

Aberdeen .. (3)..3 **Raith** .... (1)..2

Falkirk ... (1)..2 **E. Fife** .... (1)..2

	P.	Home W.	D.	L.	Goals F.	A.	Away W.	D.	L.	Goals F.	A.	Pts
Aberdeen	30	14	0	1	41	9	10	1	4	32	17	49
Celtic	29	10	4	1	42	16	8	4	2	31	21	44
Rangers ..	29	12	2	0	38	8	6	1	8	27	25	39
Hearts	29	10	2	2	40	22	6	5	4	34	20	39
Hibernian	29	8	2	5	28	23	7	2	5	35	29	34
St. Mirren	30	8	3	4	31	23	4	5	6	24	31	32
Clyde	30	6	7	2	33	20	5	2	8	26	30	31
Dundee ..	29	9	2	4	32	21	4	1	9	14	25	29
Partick ..	30	5	5	5	24	29	6	2	7	25	32	29
East Fife	29	6	1	8	32	35	3	5	6	19	26	24
Kilm'nock	29	4	3	7	16	23	5	3	7	28	34	24
Falkirk ..	29	6	5	3	26	21	2	2	11	14	31	23
Motherwell	29	5	2	8	23	31	4	2	8	19	29	22
Qn. of S.	29	6	2	6	21	29	2	4	9	16	27	22
Raith R.	29	8	1	5	32	22	1	2	12	15	34	21
Stirling A.	29	2	1	12	15	40	0	1	13	13	63	6

SCOTTISH LEAGUE—Div. "B"

Airdrie .. (2)..4 **Queen's P.** (1)..2

Arbroath (1)..1 **Albion** .... (0)..0

Ayr U. .... (1)..1 **Dunf'mline** (1)..1

Brechin C. (1)..2 **T. Lanark** (1)..1

Cowd'nb'th (2)..3 **Dundee U.** (0)..1

Hamilton . (1)..1 **Sten'muir** (0)..1

St. J'stone (0)..2 **Forfar** .... (0)..0

AMATEUR INTERNATIONAL

England .. (3)..3 **Wales** ... (0)..1

(At Bournemouth)

RUGBY UNION.—Bedford 16pts., Bath 5; Devonport Serv. 6, Gloucester 10; Northampton 39, Old Alleynians 3.

RUGBY LEAGUE.—Championship Semi-final— Oldham 25 pts, Leeds 6.

RUGBY LEAGUE.—Barrow 44 pts, Widnes 13; Blackpool Boro 15, Swinton 10; Bramley 10, Batley 14; Featherstone R. 43, Hull 16; Huddersfield 42, Doncaster 14; Keighley 5, Halifax 23; Leigh 16, Workington Town 15; Salford 7, Rochdale H. 10; Wakefield T. 25, Hunslet 7; Whitehaven 22, Liverpool C. 12.

A.F.A. INVITATION CUP—First Round.—St. Albans C. 2, Histon 1.

SURREY COMBINATION CUP.—Woking 2, Guildford City 3.

A.F.A. SENIOR CUP—Final Round.—Alexandra Park 4, Polytechnic 1 (at Wealdstone).

HIGHEST SCORE: 6—Blackpool.
HIGHEST AGGREGATE: 7—Man. City 1, Blackpool 6.
Total number of goals scored in League and Cup matches: 148

PICTORIAL

GREAVES AND THE GOALIES

THERE was woe at Stamford Bridge yesterday, where Chelsea notched a hollow 5—1 win against Birmingham City.

Only four minutes after the kick-off Birmingham's 'keeper, Gil Merrick, and Chelsea inside left Jimmy Greaves, collided.

Merrick crashed heavily to the turf.

Players and officials crowded round, and looked glum as Merrick rolled in pain. He had to be carried off on a stretcher.

Greaves, injured, left the field for ten minutes.

Merrick had a gashed chin, and was later found to have concussion. Five stitches were put in his chin, and then—

HE SAW THE MATCH FROM THE STAND.

Saw, too, how his substitute in goal, left half Dick Neal, also had a collision with seventeen-year-old wonder boy Greaves.

Neal and Greaves both escaped unhurt.

Then outside right Gordon Astall went in goal.

DOWN GOES BRUM GOALIE NUMBER 1

● CASUALTY! A second after this tackle by Chelsea inside left Greaves yesterday, Birmingham goalie Merrick was out of the match. Below, Merrick (right) and Greaves (left) are surrounded by worried players and officials.

Merrick suffered concussion — had five stitches in his jaw.

DOWN GOES BRUM GOALIE NUMBER 2

● AGAIN! Same forward, substitute 'keeper. Greaves collides — above — with left half Neal, who took Merrick's place. This time there were no serious injuries..

HELP YOUR NEWSAGENT

ORDER YOUR PIC

Printed and Published by SUNDAY PICTORIAL NEWSPAPERS (1920). Ltd., at Geraldine House, Fetter-lane, London E.C.4 Tel. Holborn 4321, and at Mark-lane, Manchester 4.—Sunday September 1. 1957.

Blasted by Greaves lightning

BANG GOES THE SPURS DREAM

By ROSS HALL

GREAVES' lightning shattered Spurs' League championship hopes yesterday with one of the most sensational goals that young Jimmy, Chelsea and England inside right, has scored.

It came after twenty-seven minutes of desperate Spurs endeavour.

A clearance goes chest high to Greaves, who is closely marked by two Spurs men. With an amazing twist of his body he takes it with him to the left and his two rivals go the right.

Greaves beats a third defender; moves away from a fourth and blazes in a glorious drive from twenty yards.

Attack Splutters Out

It was a great goal worthy of beating the sparkling Spurs.

But in defeat they were magnificent. Although victory meant so much to them there was never any sign of assault and battery replacing skill.

Unfortunately it was their shuffled attack that spluttered out without the guiding genius of left half Dave Mackay, who was injured, behind them.

Welsh outside right Terry Medwin couldn't find the confidence that he musters up for his country, centre forward Bobby Smith was shaky and Cliff Jones, in the makeshift position of inside left, covered a tremendous amount of ground without achieving much.

Inside right John White was their most effective forward—but he won't remember this game with pride.

As for Chelsea, their defence was superbly marshalled by skipper and left back Peter Sillett, while seventeen-year-old 'keeper Peter Bonetti was as cool and safe as a veteran.

Hammers led, led and led

Man. Utd. 5, West Ham 3

THREE times West Ham took the lead and three times they lost it.

They had a grand half back in Andy Smillie, the best of a teen-age trio who did not put a foot wrong until late in the game.

Dave Dunmore gave West Ham the lead after five minutes. His fierce twenty - five - yard drive went in off the post.

Alec Dawson headed an equaliser. But a penalty by Noel Cantwell put West Ham in front again. Then Bobby Charlton equalised once more.

Right winger Tony Scott scored West Ham's third, but Charlton Dawson and Albert Quixall scored for Manchester United in the second half.

Well done!

● Spurs' captain Danny Blanchflower (left) goes across to congratulate Chelsea 'keeper Peter Bonetti, 17, and say "Well done, son!" after yesterday's game at White Hart-lane.

DOOMED LUTON HAD NO SPIRIT

Luton 1, Blackburn 1

LUTON'S doom was sealed in this match, but there were only just over 14,000 mourners. Those who stayed away were lucky—they missed a deadly dull match in which Cup Finalists Blackburn were merely careful to keep out of trouble.

In the circumstances, Second Division bound Luton should have won by a street. But they had no spark of life and looked resigned to the dogs.

Irish international outside right Billy Bingham, appearing for the first time on the left wing, scored after three minutes, but afterwards he was seldom brought into the game.

Blackburn stirred themselves, just once in the second half, and Peter Dobing strode past a bemused Luton defence to hammer in the equaliser.

WATFORD GOING UP?

Chester 0, Watford 1

SIX points from three holiday games — and that means Watford look like hot-footing it out of the Fourth Division. Right winger Mike Benning slammed the all-important goal just before half-time at Chester and they're now in fourth spot.

Northampton, who had no game yesterday, are still in with a promotion chance—but it looks like Watford, with Walsall, Notts County and Torquay.

ICE HOCKEY

BRITISH LEAGUE.— Wembley Lions 7 (Saunders 3, Beach 2, Shepherd, Robertson, Murray), Brighton Tigers 6 (Macdonald 2, St. John, Hamilton, Turple, McNeil).

Reading down at the Dell

Southampton 1, Reading 0

READING, who beat promotion - chasing Southampton on Good Friday, were never in the hunt before the biggest League crowd at the Dell this season.

Reserve inside left Brian Clifton put the Saints ahead with a glorious header after fifteen minutes.

The Reading defence reeled under constant second half pressure, and their rare attacks were blunted by a dour Southampton rearguard, in which skipper Cliff Huxford was outstanding.

GREAT WIN BY BRITISH CYCLE ACE

TOMMY SIMPSON, the Doncaster cyclist, scored the best-ever road race win by a British cyclist when he beat a host of Continental stars in France yesterday.

He won a 100-mile race which ended at L'Orient, Brittany, in 4h. 4m.

In the final sprint, he beat Tour de France winner Jacques Anquetil.

Two more Tour de France winners, Louison Bobet and Charly Gaul, were equal ninth.

Pass your driving test

Learn the theory the armchair way. Don't miss this important feature starting in the May issue of *Scooter & Three Wheeler*, the magazine for all scooterists.

You won't want to miss the many other features including :—

■ Retreading scooter tyres
■ Preparing your machine for touring at home and abroad
■ Exploring Central Spain
■ Road Tests—
   Quickly S moped
   Triumph Tigress 175 c.c.
■ Around the clubs
■ Mainly for women
■ New Accessories and equipment etc.

In case of difficulty send 1/3d. p.p. to Department SM8, Link House, Store Street, London, W.C.1.

SCOOTER & THREE WHEELER 1/-

OUT NOW 1/-

ALL NEWSAGENTS AND BOOKSTALLS

RESULTS, SCORERS AND TABLES

FIRST DIVISION

Birmingham 1 W.B.A. 7
Gordon Allen 3 (1 pen.),
  Jackson,
H.T: 1-3. Kevan 3 28,685

Blackpool 0 Everton 0
25,697

Bolton 3 Man. C. 1
Stevens, Barlow 35,592
Holden, Birch H.T: 1—2.

Fulham 0 Arsenal 0
Key, Jones, H.T: 1—0. 31,058
O'Connell

Leicester 2 Burnley 0
Wills, Cheese- Meredith
brough H.T: 2-0. 24,429

Luton 1 Blackburn 1
Bingham Dobing
H.T: 1—0. 14,107

Man. U. 5 West Ham 3
Dawson 2, Dunmore, Cant-
Charlton 2, well (pen.),
Quixall Scott
  H.T: 2-3. 34,676

Preston 2 Leeds 1
Sneddon Gibson
H.T: 0—0. 15,789

Sheffield W. 2 Newcastle 1
Fantham, H.T: 1—0. 33,332
Froggatt

Tottenham 0 Chelsea 1
H.T: 0—1. 37,205 Greaves

Wolves 3 Nottm. F. 1
Murray 2,
McDonald (o.g.) Younger

	P	W	D	L	F	A	Pts
Wolves	39	23	5	11	100	63	51
Spurs	40	19	11	10	79	54	49
Burnley	38	22	5	11	81	59	49
Sheff. Wed.	40	19	10	11	77	54	48
W.B.A.	40	19	10	11	80	54	48
Newcastle	40	18	8	14	74	74	44
Bolton	40	18	8	14	55	50	44
Man. Utd.	40	18	7	15	95	75	43
Preston	39	15	12	12	75	72	42
Fulham	40	16	8	16	71	79	41
Blackpool	40	15	9	16	57	66	39
West Ham	40	16	6	18	73	87	37
Chelsea	40	14	9	17	75	84	37
Leicester	40	12	13	15	64	73	37
Arsenal	40	14	9	17	63	77	37
Everton	40	12	11	17	72	73	35
Blackburn	39	15	5	19	57	66	35
Nottm. F.	40	12	9	19	47	73	33
Birmingham	38	11	9	18	57	76	31
Leeds	38	10	10	18	60	87	30
Luton	40	8	12	20	42	70	28

ATHENIAN LEAGUE.—Carshalton Athletic 2, Redhill 4; Grays Athletic 2 Finchley 2; Hornchurch and Upminster 1, Enfield 2; Leyton 2, Haves 1; Southall 0, Sutton United 2.

SECOND DIVISION

A. Villa 2 Stoke 1
Lynn (pen.), Bowyer
Thomson H.T: 0—0. 25,000

Brighton 3 Lincoln 3
Thorne, Buick Chapman,
(o.g.) McNeill Hawksworth 2
H.T: 0—3. 15,000

Bristol C. 5 Ipswich 2
Atyeo 3, R. Curtis
Williams, H.T: 2—1. 10,890
Rogers, 2

Charlton 5 Scunthorpe 2
Summers Bakes,
Lawrie 3, Donnelly
Leary H.T: 4—0. 10,497

Derby 1 Hull 3
Darwin King, Sewell,
H.T: 0—1. 11,107 Shiner

Huddersfield 1 Bristol R. 1
H.T: 0-1. 13,820 Hooper

Liverpool 3 Rotherham 0
Hunt, Hickson 2 H.T: 1-0. 26,776
  Sheffield U. 2
Middlesbro' 1 Simpson, Pace
Clough H.T: 0-0.
H.T: 0—0. 18,453

Portsmouth 1 Sunderland 2
Newman Taylor,
H.T: 1-1. 16,151 Lawther

Swansea 0 L. Orient 0
Dodson H.T: 0—0. 10,000

	P	W	D	L	F	A	Pts
Aston Villa	40	24	9	7	86	40	57
Cardiff	39	23	10	6	87	58	56
Middlesbro'	39	19	8	12	88	59	46
Huddersfield	40	18	9	13	69	50	45
Liverpool	39	18	9	12	84	65	45
Sheff. Utd.	39	17	11	11	64	50	45
Rotherham	38	17	11	11	54	58	45
Charlton	40	18	13	11	84	82	45
Ipswich	40	19	6	15	73	65	44
Bristol R.	40	17	10	13	68	76	44
Leyton Orient	40	14	13	13	71	58	41
Lincoln	40	15	7	18	72	74	37
Swansea	39	14	9	17	76	84	37
Scunthorpe	40	13	10	17	55	67	36
Sunderland	40	13	11	17	51	61	35
Brighton	40	11	13	17	72	80	35
Stoke	40	13	7	20	62	80	33
Portsmouth	40	10	11	19	57	70	31
Derby	40	11	9	21	55	79	31
Plymouth	39	12	6	21	62	87	30
Bristol C.	40	12	5	23	57	96	29
Hull	39	10	9	20	46	75	29

METROPOLITAN LEAGUE.—Bedford Town 3, Haywards Heath 1; Canterbury City 1, Arsenal 2; Crawley 2, Chelsea 1, Dunstable 2; Eastbourne 0, Luton Town 2; Hastings 2, Tonbridge 0, Guildford 2; Windsor and Eton 0, Newbury 1; West Ham 0, Headington 5.

THIRD DIVISION

Accrington 0 Newport 0
  2,054

Bournemouth 1 Chesterfield 0
Coxon (pen.) Bain 9,008
H.T: 1—0.

Bradford C. 0 Q.P.R. 1
Webb, Reid 2 Andrews
 (1 pen.) H.T: 2—0.

Mansfield 0 Brentford 1
Curtis Parsons
H.T: 0—1. 7,536

Norwich 0 Halifax 1
Allcock 2 H.T: 0—0.
Brennan 32,942

Port Vale 1 Bury 0
Portwood 3 H.T: 2—0.
Poole (H.) 7,875

Shrewsbury 2 Barnsley 2
Starkey, Ireland Brooks, Oliver
H.T: 3—2. 8,460

Southampton 1 Reading 0
Clifton H.T: 1—0. 35,042

Southend 1 Colchester 0
Corthine H.T: 1—0.
  12,533

Swindon 1 Tranmere 0
Gauld K. Williams
H.T: 0—1. 10,524

Wrexham 2 York 1
Griffiths Powell
Evans (B.), H.T: 1—1. 4,842
Harbertson

	P	W	D	L	F	A	Pts
Southampton	43	24	9	10	99	71	57
Norwich	43	22	10	11	75	51	54
Bury	43	21	8	14	62	45	50
Coventry	42	20	9	13	74	57	49
Shrewsbury	42	17	13	12	93	73	47
Brentford	43	19	9	15	71	59	47
Grimsby	42	16	14	12	80	69	46
Q.P.R.	43	17	11	15	71	53	45
Colchester	44	17	11	16	77	70	45
Bournemouth	43	18	13	14	70	66	45
Port Vale	43	18	7	18	70	71	43
Halifax	41	17	9	15	65	68	43
Southend	43	17	8	18	67	68	42
Bradford C.	43	15	12	16	66	65	42
Newport	43	16	6	20	78	77	42
Swindon	43	17	8	18	64	71	42
Barnsley	43	13	16	14	60	65	42
Reading	43	16	8	19	81	76	40
Chesterfield	43	16	7	20	63	80	39
York	43	15	9	19	55	69	39
Tranmere	42	12	13	18	68	76	37
Mansfield	43	15	6	23	74	105	34
Wrexham	43	13	7	23	66	113	33
Accrington	44	11	5	28	56	113	27

SOUTHERN LEAGUE: Premier Div.—Cambridge City 1, Chelmsford 2; Gravesend 2, Poole 0; Headington 3, Wellington 0; Nuneaton 8 0; Tonbridge 1; Kettering 0, Cheltenham 1; Bath 2, Yeovil 1; Barry 2, Weymouth 1; Hastings 1, Bedford 0.

FOURTH DIVISION

Barrow 2 Workington 1
Reid, Bannan McGarry 6,783
H.T: 1—0.

Chester 0 Watford 1
H.T: 0—1. 5,962 Benning

Crewe 2 Oldham 1
Llewellyn 2 Bourne, Birch
H.T: 0—1. 6,629

Exeter 1 Crystal Palace 2
Wilkinson Gavin 2
H.T: 0—1. 8,000

Gateshead 1 Darlington 3
Amstrong Baxter 2, Carr
H.T: 0—1. 1,933

Gillingham 1 Doncaster 1
Brown, Walker
Pulley (pen.) H.T: 1—0. 6,960

Hartlepools 1 Carlisle 2
Clark Bevan, Robson
H.T: 0—0. 3,800

Notts Co. 2 Walsall 1
Hateley, Roby Hodkisson
 (pen.) 22,788 H.T: 1—1.

Rochdale 2 Aldershot 0
Cairns, Barnes H.T: 0—0. 4,300
Torquay 2 Millwall 1
Bond, Mills Broadfoot
H.T: 2—4. 9,317

	P	W	D	L	F	A	Pts
Walsall	41	26	7	8	93	51	59
Notts County	42	24	6	12	96	62	54
Torquay Utd.	42	24	6	12	77	54	54
Watford	42	22	7	13	84	61	51
Millwall	44	21	17	10	77	59	51
Northampton	41	20	7	14	79	57	47
Crystal Palace	43	18	11	14	80	67	47
Bradford	42	17	13	12	66	61	47
Rochdale	43	18	10	15	64	55	46
Exeter	43	17	11	15	74	66	45
Gillingham	44	18	9	14	66	64	45
Aldershot	43	18	7	18	76	71	43
Crewe	43	17	8	18	77	86	42
Chester	44	14	11	19	56	68	39
Doncaster	43	15	8	18	63	69	38
Barrow	42	15	8	19	63	82	38
Carlisle	42	14	10	18	45	61	38
Gateshead	42	9	11	21	43	86	29
Southport	43	9	11	23	42	86	29
Hartlepools	44	10	7	27	58	105	27
Oldham	43	7	12	24	58	103	26

SCOTTISH LEAGUE: Div. 1.—Rangers 0, Motherwell 3; Airdrie 2, Celtic 2.

CENTRAL LEAGUE:—W.B.A. 8, Sheff. Utd. 1; Stoke 4, Chesterfield 0; Newcastle 1, Sheff Wed. 1; Man City 3, Bolton 3; Burnley 4, Preston 0; Barnsley 2, Derby 4; Everton 1, Huddersfield 1.

MOTOR CYCLING

INTERNATIONAL (Cesenatico, North Italy).—500 c.c.: 1, J. Surtees (Britain), M V Agusta—av. 81.05 m.p.h.; 125 c.c.: 1, C. G. Hocking (Britain)—av. 69.73 m.p.h.

SPEEDWAY

WIMBLEDON.—British Match Race Title (1st leg): R. Moore (Wimbledon) bt P. Craven (Belle Vue, holder) 2—1. Metropolitan Cup: P. Craven 14 pts. Bt R. How. 14 pts. in run off; 3, R. Moore, 13 pts.

● GEORGE EASTHAM back in action—for Arsenal reserves.

EASTHAM THE SCOUT DOES HIS GOOD TURN

GEORGE EASTHAM, the latest in a long line of glittering Gunners, squelched through the mud of a South London park yesterday to watch Sunday Soccer.

I shared a plastic mac with Arsenal's new £47,500 inside forward star on a rain-soaked scouting mission—finding talent for Surrey amateur side Redhill.

There were no T V cameras, no flash-bulbs. Only one small boy recognised Soccer's man of the moment.

And that was the way unassuming Eastham wanted it.

Twenty-four hours earlier he had kicked a ball in earnest for the first time in five months, when he made his debut as an Arsenal player in a reserve game against Leicester at Highbury.

It turned out to be one of the most glamorous matches the Football Combination has ever produced, with 9,600 fans turning up to see him.

Eastham, who ended his Soccer strike when he signed for Arsenal on Friday, got the film star treatment.

The game over, he slipped quietly away to my home to discuss his form and his future.

He slipped a cup of tea, rubbed the stiffness out of his legs and said:

"Thank goodness that's all over. The first one is always the toughest after a long lay-off."

He hadn't tried to bring

FOOTBALL FOCUS
By Ken Jones

the house down at Highbury.

He made no special efforts to justify that club-record price tag.

"But I enjoyed myself," he told me.

"If Arsenal are willing, I would like to play in the friendly against Ramsgate this week.

"It's the only way to get match fit again . . . play as much as possible."

As we watched flashes from Arsenal's game on T V, Eastham cracked: "It doesn't look as though I am playing."

That was Eastham on the day he came back to Soccer from the wilderness.

Yesterday we kept an appointment with Redhill official, Syd Hawkins for that scouting mission . . . because Redhill are the club who have helped Eastham keep fit.

And he intends to help them.

Get Out the Cheque Book

WITH Eastham finally off their hands, Newcastle went to Everton and were thumped five nil.

No wonder manager Charlie Mitten and every director bar the one who went with the team to

Everton, were out looking for new men !

But they are finding it tough to get rid of money when you want talent in return.

The Unhappy Return . . .

POOR Jimmy Bloomfield ! He waits for a month to get away from Arsenal.

Then he walks straight into a Soccer storm that goes by the name of Spurs.

Two hours before the kick-off at White Hart-lane on Saturday, Jimmy signed the form that made him a £28,000 Birmingham inside forward.

Fifteen minutes after the start he was lining up for a kick-off for the FOURTH time.

Not that he flopped. In fact, for half an hour, he played as well as I have ever seen him.

I think he knows he faces a big job in welding

this Birmingham side together.

For that is why they have bought him.

But it will never be tougher than on Saturday. In those first fifteen minutes, Spurs rocked the Blues back on their heels, ripped them wide open.

John White started a ruthless goal rampage when he thundered in a Bobby Smith pass.

Dyson made it 2—0 from a great Les Allen pass. And Cliff Jones swayed past 'keeper Alan Withers for No. 3.

Then Spurs soft pedalled until the last fifteen minutes, when Dyson, Smith (penalty) and Jones rushed in three more.

They're Fit for Wembley

AFTER the game, Cliff Jones reported no ill-effects on the knee he injured in Milan. . . .

He's fully fit to line up for Wales in the international against England at Wembley on Wednesday.

And good news for England !

Bryan Douglas, who missed Blackburn's game on Saturday, yesterday reported fit for the international, too.

Cantwell says 'Yes'

NOEL CANTWELL, West Ham's Eire international left back, will fly to Manchester today and sign for United in time to play in tonight's friendly against Bayern (Munich) at Old Trafford.

Cantwell, who wanted the week-end to talk over the move with his singer-fiancee, Margaret Ross, tele-phoned his decision to United manager Matt Busby last night.

Greaves makes Law look so ordinary
100 UP—BUT A GEM GOT AWAY!

By BEN WRIGHT, Chelsea 6, Manchester City 3

JIMMY GREAVES made Denis Law, Britain's costliest inside forward, look ordinary, though the blond Scot never stopped trying to be much more than that.

But the brilliance of Greaves was only one gem in a diamond-bright cluster that made this such a memorable game.

Law hit an upright after twenty seconds. New-boy Gerry Baker had a fine header smack the same spot ten minutes later.

If those, and two shots from George Hannah that hit the bar in the forty-sixth and sixty-fourth minutes had gone in, this might have been a different story.

As it was, Chelsea were 5—1 up in thirty-eight minutes.

Jimmy Greaves fairly raced to the hat-trick that gave him his 100th League goal and a tremendous ovation. And each goal was better than the last.

Greaves slipped two tackles before shooting in from an acute angle after three minutes.

Magic Moment

He took a return pass from Bobby Tambling for his second after nineteen minutes.

He started and finished the move that brought the third.

But the one that got away provided the game's most magic moment.

It was a flashing twenty-yard volley in the second half that Bert Trautmann miraculously tipped over the bar.

Tambling and Peter Brabrook were magnificent on the wings. Bobby Evans never failed to get his red head to the dangerous cross.

Peter Bonetti was as uncannily catlike as ever.

Tambling (20m.), Law (30), Tindall (38 and 55), Betts (penalty 39) and Baker (49) got the other goals.

Brown inspires Luton to a great win

Luton 6, Middlesbro 1

LUTON inside left Allan Brown turned in a superb performance.

Brown, recalled after a spell in the reserves, bewildered the Middlesbrough defence.

In a sensational ten minutes he laid on two goals and grabbed one himself.

Luton, inspired by Brown, were always on top, and this performance makes their lowly position in the Second Division look ridiculous.

SCORERS.— Luton: Spencer, Tracey, Brown (2), Turner 2 (2 pens.).
Middlesbrough: Waldock.

A tragedy for 'keeper Rhodes

By RON BEAGLEY

West Ham 2, Nottingham Forest 4

TRIUMPH for Forest goalkeeper Peter Grummitt, and tragedy for opposite number, Brian Rhodes.

Grummitt, 18, played a blinder and kept West Ham at bay with some superb saves in the last fifteen minutes.

Rhodes brought off many fantastic saves in the first forty minutes, then made two blunders which put Forest back in the game.

The Forest youngster was playing in only his second League match, but he proved he is ready for the big time—after a nightmare start.

I think Grummitt will take his chance and help Forest to get away from the foot of the table.

This win, Forest's first away victory of the season, was gained by fighting spirit and good football.

Rhodes, on the other hand, has now to prove himself again in a team that deserves a kick for playing too casual.

He started the season badly, but he has played some great games in West Ham's recent run of victories.

The next few weeks will be vital for him.

Scorers—Forest: Vowden (21 and 61 mins.), Gray (44), Le Flem (47). West Ham: Palmer (own goal 20 mins.), Dunmore (34).

'TOSH' MAKES FLYING START

Aston Villa 2, Fulham 1

WHILE Fulham manager Frank Osborne was watching Manchester United's Albert Scanlon, his own left winger, "Tosh" Chamberlain, had a flying start against Aston Villa.

A Chamberlain corner in the fiftieth second was headed in by Graham Leggat.

But Fulham faded, and lost 2—1 through goals by Jimmy Mac-Ewan and Ron Wylie.

MATTHEWS NEARLY FOOLED ARSENAL

By HOWARD BOOTH

Blackpool 1, Arsenal 1

ARSENAL nearly fell for Stanley Matthews's old lullaby trick.

The score was 1—1, Ray Charnley having equalised the Arsenal goal scored by David Herd.

Then Matthews, who hadn't been much in the game, decided to take a hand.

That's part of the fun in watching him these days, waiting to see when he turns on the magic.

Matthews became an inside left-cum-deep centre forward.

Although there were no more goals to show for it, Jack Kelsey was forced to prove himself a goalkeeper of world class.

Vic Groves and Co., too,

had to pull out all the stops to brake a Blackpool front line that was suddenly transformed.

Neither side deserved both points. But Arsenal played enough football to make one realise the kind of force they could be—with Tommy Docherty, Mel Charles and George Eastham !

A FREE 'TONIC' FROM FRANK

Charlton 1, Liverpool 3

CHARLTON goalkeeper Frank Reed will want to forget this—his second first-team game.

He took his eyes off the ball for a fraction of a second—and Liverpool were a goal up in the eighth minute as Sammy Lawrie's back-pass spun out of his

hands into the net. The "free" goal was a tonic to Liverpool and they dominated the game for the next hour.

But it was only after Lawrie equalised in the 73rd minute that they snatched the goals they deserved, through Roger Hunt and Johnny Wheeler.

FIXTURES

LEAGUE CUP—Third Round
Blackburn v. Rochdale (7.30)........
Portsmouth v. Man. City (7.0)........
OTHER MATCHES (7.30).—Manchester Utd. v. Bayern (Munich);
Peterborough v. Managers XI;
Tranmere v. Clyde.

SUMMER POOLS

Strong boys for draws

From BILL FLEMING
Melbourne, Tuesday

SUMMER Pools are here again, and I kick off the season with this advice for the treble chance — follow the strong men.

This season promises to be the best ever in Australia, for the standard of play has been lifted by a huge "invasion" of good players from overseas.

Most have been snapped up by the top clubs in New South Wales and Victoria, and it is in these States that competition will be strongest.

I expect them to prove it this week-end by providing eight draws.

Welcome

Already this season we have had some indication that these "strong men" will be good bets for the treble chance.

And that's a welcome sign, for most promoters are keeping to their normal winter eight-match pool instead of making their usual switch to the "summer seven."

The northern section of New South Wales started with four draws out of five games, and the First Division record three out of six and two out of six.

In Victoria's First Division (North), every club has drawn at least once. In the State League, only Lion have yet to chalk up an X.

Selections:

TWELVE HOMES.—Awaba, Apia, Prague, Dnipro, Polonia, Fiorentina, Moreland, Malta, S. Coast, Sutherland, Latrobe, Medina. Next best: University (Q).

TEN AWAYS.—Merewether, Budapest (NSW) Polonia (NSW), Sydney A., Hellenic (Q), George C., Slavia, Alexander, Austria (V), Tricolore. Next best: Brighton.

THREE DRAWS.—Melbourne v. Croatia, Wilhelmina v. Juventus, Canterbury v. Hellenic. Next best: Moonee P.

TREBLE CHANCE.—Melbourne, Wilhelmina, Canterbury, Moonee P., Oakleigh, Yallourn, Wallsend, Melita. Next best: Croatia (SA).

TEST TEAM 'FIGHTERS' TO FOLLOW

By EXTRA COVER

BASE your first cricket treble-chance entry of the season on batsmen fighting for a place in England's team for the first Test against the West Indies.

The big match is only a fortnight away and the selectors are looking for new faces.

Some of the men they have in mind are:

Phil Sharpe (Yorks), Colin Milburn (Northants), John Edrich (Surrey), Graham Atkinson (Somerset).

This quartet will obviously be all out to clinch a Test place in the remaining few matches. And so will these England "old boys": Peter Richardson (Kent), Mickey Stewart (Surrey), Brian Close (Yorks). Selections:

LITTLEWOODS.—Nos. 6, 12, 18, 36, 37, 38, 42, 43, 51. VERNONS.—Nos. 4, 15, 19, 35, 48, 31, 45, 49, 54. COPE'S.—Nos. 6, 16, 20, 31, 37, 40, 43, 52, 53. SOCCER.—Nos. 5, 26, 27, 30, 36, 37, 41, 51. ZETTERS.—Nos. 3, 7, 13, 19, 25, 28, 31, 38, 48.

CHELSEA'S 7—UP!

First Division, here we come. . . . Chelsea's skipper Bobby Tambling bursts through to score the first of his four goals.

By KEN JONES
Chelsea 7, Portsmouth 0

ON a night of football fantasy that could only happen at Stamford Bridge, Chelsea swept back into the First Division last night.

They began needing two precious points to pip Sunderland to a promotion place on goal-average.

But high drama became a promotion picnic as Chelsea, seven goals to the good and roared on by a 54,558 crowd, coasted out time with a tidal-wave of fans waiting to pour on to the pitch.

Swarmed

With four minutes still to go, the pitch was suddenly a seething mass of people, as the fans, believing the game was all over, swarmed over the dog-track fence.

Ipswich referee Reg Aldous was powerless. The players were powerless. And a loudspeaker plea was lost in the wave of sound.

Eventually they got the crowd back as far as the dog-track. But no farther.

And when it was all over, the fans came again—a chanting, almost frightening flood that enveloped the Chelsea players as they struggled to the dressing-rooms.

Skipper Bobby Tambling, a four-goal hero after months of despair, was carried farther and farther away from the tunnel.

Fans invade pitch

Afterwards there were tears of joy in the eyes of the team when they came out to spill champagne over the crowd.

THE WHOLE SCENE WAS SHEER FANTASY.

And fantasy it had been as Chelsea, on a night when one goal would have been enough, steam-rollered their way to the Second Division's biggest win of the season.

Stoke City and Stan Matthews, already assured of a First Division place, were in the crowd as Chelsea tore into Pompey's veteran defence.

And it was Derek Kevan, written-off as a £48,000 flop a few weeks ago, who hammered home the first vital goal.

Header

Suddenly hitting the peak of his old power, Kevan sent a 30-yarder skimming out to Tambling and then met the winger's return cross with a thudding header, to put Chelsea in front in the second minute.

Frank Upton, passed fit to assume his role as the centre forward and No. 1 harasser in Chelsea's attack, made the second for Tambling in the fourteenth minute.

On the half-hour, Tambling tore into a panicky defence to snatch the third.

The champagne corks were already beginning to pop, when the Chelsea skipper clinched a "hat-trick" two minutes after half-time.

Chelsea were now on to a runaway win. In the sixtieth minute, Frank Blunstone got the fifth—the best of the match—after a slick one-two with Tambling on the edge of the area.

Five minutes later Tambling was brought down in the penalty-area by left half Alan Brown.

Brown went off for the rest of the match with a hand injury—and Terry Venables cracked home the spot kick, to make it six.

Another dazzling inter-passing movement gave Tambling his fourth and Chelsea their seventh ten minutes from the end.

Manager Tommy Docherty, shouting between cupped hands, told the jubilant crowd in front of the directors' box: "Now

Manager Tom Docherty . . . champagne celebration.

we'll give you a team that you'll be proud of for many years to come."

Tambling, at 21 the youngest captain of a promotion-winning team, said: "We were a bit down-hearted when we lost to Stoke, but the boss picked us up again. When we saw he still had faith in us, we knew we could do it."

SAFETY MATCH IS A WASHOUT

By HARRY MILLER: Walsall 0, Charlton 0

(Abandoned at half-time)

REFEREE Gordon Roper abandoned this Second Division relegation decider last night after torrential rain had flooded the Fellows Park pitch at half-time.

The match that was so vital to both sides was finally brought to a halt after referee Roper had allowed the interval to run for thirty minutes on the hope of an improvement.

Then he sent Walsall's biggest crowd of the season home by saying: "Conditions are quite impossible."

It was announced afterwards that the game will be replayed on Friday at 7.15 p.m.

Charlton must win it to remain in the Second Division—and send Walsall down. A draw is all Walsall need for survival.

A crowd of 18,820—Walsall's biggest of the season—had turned out for the match.

RESULTS AND SCORERS

FIRST DIVISION

Ipswich 1	A. Villa 1	
Moran	Thomson	
H T: 1—0	17,222	

SECOND DIVISION

Chelsea 7	Portsmouth 0	
Kevan,	H T: 3—0	
Tambling 4,		54,558
Blunstone,		
Venables (pen)		
Middlesbrough . 6	Norwich 2	
Metcalf (o.g.),	Burton,	
Gibson, Kaye,	Sutton	
Peacock 2,	H T: 3—0	
Orritt		7,413
Walsall 0	Charlton 0	
18,820		

Abandoned at half-time owing to heavy rain. Match will now be played on Friday (kick-off 7.15).

Top Positions

	P	W	D	L	F	A	Pt
Stoke	41	20	13	8	73	48	53
Chelsea ...	42	24	4	14	81	42	52
Sunderland	42	20	12	10	84	55	52

Bottom Positions

Walsall ...	41	11	9	21	52	87	31
Luton	42	11	7	24	61	84	29
Charlton ...	41	12	5	24	60	93	29

THIRD DIVISION

Halifax 3	Millwall 0	
Tait, Roscoe	H T: 1—0	
Worthington		1,243

F.A. YOUTH CUP — Semi-Final Replay : West Ham 4, Wolverhampton 2.

FOOTBALL COMBINATION.— Southampton 1, Orient 1; Q.P.R. 1, Coventry 3; Brentford 2, Fulham 2.

TOUR MATCH (Gdansk, Poland).— FC Lechia 0, Plymouth 3.

MIDDLESEX SENIOR CUP FINAL (Finchley).— Enfield 0, Wealdstone 2.

ISTHMIAN LEAGUE.— Barking 2, Oxford City 0; Leytonstone 2, Maidstone 0; Tooting and M. 2, Wimbledon 2.

ATHENIAN LEAGUE.— Barnet 3, Southall 0; Hayes 1, Hornchurch 3.

TODAY'S FOOTBALL

EUROPEAN CUP FINAL (Wembley, 3.0).—Benfica v. Milan.

SECOND DIVISION.—Southampton v. Stoke, 7.30.

THIRD DIVISION. — Barnsley v. Crystal Palace, 7.15; Q P R v. Coventry, 7.30.

FOURTH DIVISION.—Chester v. Chesterfield, 7.15; Crewe v. Exeter, 7.30.

SCOTTISH LEAGUE.—First Division: Clyde v. Rangers, 7.30.

AMATEUR INTERNATIONAL TOURNAMENT. — Final: Scotland v. West Germany (Sunderland, 7).

Over-the-top Benfica bid for hat-trick

BENFICA, the new masters of European club Soccer, may lose their crown at half-empty Wembley Stadium this afternoon, writes Ken Jones.

A crowd of only 50,000 is expected to watch Benfica defend the European Cup against Milan.

A Wembley official told me last night: "At roughly a pound a head, plus TV fees, it will still be a big money match."

I feel that Benfica will falter on a three-in-a-row Cup triumph because, like Spurs, they have to rebuild and reblend a side that is almost over the hill.

In attack the Portuguese club still have inside forward Eusebio, a deadly finisher, and dangerous wingers in Santan Augusto and Simoes.

But I expect Milan, and the graceful play of inside forwards Dino Sani and Rivera to supply the unforgettable moments this afternoon.

PLAYBOY!

DENTIST

"I'd take that Leicester scarf off if I were you — he's a Manchester United supporter!"

ORDERED OFF

Alan O'Neill, Plymouth Argyle inside left, was sent off last night in a friendly against FC Lechia in Gdansk, Poland.

0-0 Chelsea grab League Cup

By KEN JONES

Leicester 0, Chelsea 0
(Chelsea win 3-2 on aggregate)

A TRIUMPH THAT CAME LIKE THE DAWNING OF A BRIGHT NEW DAY

CHELSEA captured the Football League Cup last night.

It was not the big one . . . the one that really mattered to them.

But to a Chelsea side shorn for weeks of the class and confidence that has promised so much this season, it was a triumph that came like the dawning of a bright new day.

The League championship remains the greatest prize of all . . . still to be fought for, still to be won.

And Chelsea needed last night's result to re-establish the discipline and rhythm that has made them a top team.

They had a vital goal lead from the first leg at Stamford Bridge two weeks ago, on which to base and fashion their tactics.

And in Terry Venables, back in the side after being dropped against Birmingham on Saturday, they had a player who rediscovered the sharpness and accuracy of earlier days.

By winning the Cup last night, Chelsea took not only a trophy but also a passport to Europe back to Stamford Bridge.

They are certain of Continental combat next season as Inter-Cities Fairs Cup representatives.

With that 3—2 lead from the first leg, it had to be defensive for Chelsea last night.

And defensive it was, with lucky mascot wing half John Boyle, yet to be on a losing Chelsea side, coming in at inside right in place of George Graham.

Dropped Back

Boyle dropped back to subdue Leicester inside left Davie Gibson, the one man who might have had enough ideas and skill to break down Chelsea's defensive formation.

But Boyle won the battle and Gibson was forced to play square passes and try lofted but unproductive centres into the goalmouth

Chelsea's only moments of trouble came when goalkeeper Peter Bonetti had to push over a dropping ball in the first half

Then, again, when he hurled himself to clutch the only real menacing shot Leicester produced all night.

Space

With Venables finding space and using it so well, it was difficult to accept Chelsea were only hanging on to their slim lead.

They might have scored three goals. But first Venables fired a good chance over the top. Then Leicester centre half John Sjoberg cleared off the line after goalkeeper Gordon Banks dropped the ball.

And finally Banks showed why he is playing for England at Wembley on Saturday with a splendid save from Bobby Tambling

There was one more moment of anguish for Chelsea when centre half John Mortimore handled desperately close to the penalty area, with fifteen minutes to go

But that was the end of Chelsea's troubles and, they hope, the beginning of a proud run in to take the First Division title.

SMITH, NEWTON IN UNDER-23 SIDE

Tom Smith (Liverpool) and Henry Newton (Nottingham Forest) are England's new wing halves in the Under-23 international against Czechoslovakia at Leeds tomorrow.

Smith replaces injured Leeds left half Norman Hunter and Newton comes in for Chelsea's John Hollins (ankle injury).

Here it is . . . the Cup! Chelsea's Terry Venables (centre) and goalkeeper Peter Bonetti proudly show off the Football League Cup to their fans at Leicester.

Fire—it was hotter than the tennis

FIRE destroyed a tent at the Cumberland Tennis Tournament, Hampstead, yesterday—and it caused more excitement than the play.

Nell Truman looked very shaky in beating Celia French 4—6, 6—3, 6—4.

Joyce Williams, another British top ten player had plenty of luck in her 6—8, 6—3, 8—6 victory over Rosemary Deloford.

CURRY GIVES MANSFIELD A 4-GOAL 'LIFT'

By PETER INGALL

Mansfield 6, Southend 1

BILL CURRY, Mansfield's £10,000 centre forward, sent his team racing towards the Second Division with four brilliant goals.

Their win put them in second place in the Third Division two points behind Carlisle.

Mansfield were leading through a thirty-fifth-minute penalty by left half Peter Morris when Curry started his goalrush a minute after the interval.

Right winger Bobby Gilfillan pulled a goal back for Southend and Mansfield left winger Geoff Anderson made it 3—1.

Then Curry struck with three more goals in fifteen minutes.

Manikintime

GREYHOUND RESULTS

PARK ROYAL.—1.30: Orchard Pride 4-1, Garryawn Prince 7-2 (5-3, 101/6). 2.46: Devil in Red 7-2, Half Mast 7-2 (4-6, 31/-) (Hiver Swanky ran for Arizona Man). 3.3: Kans 7-1, Captain Pike evens f (2-1, 50/3). 3.20: King Pressure 2-1 f, Borris-in-Ossary Prince 5-1 (5-2, 28/3). 3.38: Adamstown Chief 11-8, Southland Boy Blue 5-1 (1-5, 20/9). 3.56: Chittering Cheapjack 6-1, Fairlands Sayderite 20-1 (1-2, 129/6). 4.13: Moreen King evens f, Keen Snub 9-2 (6-3, 17/3). 4.30: Come On Sandy 4-5 f, Cherished Forever 7-1 (1-2, 18/6).

HARRINGAY. — 7.45: Impacts Girl 3-1, Hi There Poldy 9-4 (5-6, 19/9). (Good Deal ran for Queen of the Clan). 8.21: Cloudesley Fair 5-4 f, Pride of Broadway 13-2 (2-5, 30/9). 8.35: Longacre Wasp 7-1, Master Scholar evens f (4-2, 42/3). 8.36: More Hope 5-1, Foot Wrap 5-1 (1-3, 91/3). 8.54: Big Scheme 7-2 jf of 3, Cloudesley Folly 7-2 jf (6-3, 36/-). 9.12: Metallic 11-4, South Gate 9-4 f (5-3, 58/5). 9.31: Bolan Pass 7-2, Hi Parachute 6-1 (3-1, 50/6). 9.50: Newport Prince 10-11 f, Gogiri 6-1 (1-3, 25/6).
QUINELA: £24/16/3.
DUELLA: £10/9/3.

HENDON.—7.45: Life Indeed 15-8 f, Georgina 3-1 (5-4, 17/-). 8.3: Agapantha 7-1, Barnawee 9-4 (2-1, 50/8). 8.21: Dromorin Lass 6-1, Alvaston Viscount 2-1 f (1-2, 47/-). 8.39: Hanslope Pathan 9-1, Hackney Turnery 20-1 (4-3, 151/9).

8.57: Lawous Girl 5-2, Burning Bright 13-8 f (2-4, 22/-). 9.16: Flying Deuces 6-4 f, Kilrickle 7-2 (1-3, 18/6). 9.34: Midnight Crosspatch 9-2, Shady Twilight 3-1 (5-1, 39/6). 9.52: Tully Eagle 7-2 jf, Mallagh an Ois 8-1 (2-6, 131/6).
QUINELLAS: £385/14/6: £376/5/-.
WEMBLEY.—7.45: Filed Steel 11-2, Gloria Dawn 8-1 (2-5, 82/-). 8.0: Paddlewheel King 10-1, Matton 11-8 f (3-1, 96/6). 8.18: Berkeley Bouquet 7-1, Fair Orlana 15-8 (5-6, 63/9). (Buzzy Wingse ran for Stirling Panter.: Fleur Petite ran for Mitzanne.). 8.34: Hi Swagman (ran for Kilquane Mixer) 10-11 f Baytown Nap 7-1 (1-3, 15/6) (NR Caeueauel). 8.50: Giant Maple 4-1, Knockrour Betsy 9-2 (3-5, 88/3). 9.6: Cloudland 4-1, Irish Jungle 9-2 (3-2, 55/6). 9.22: Ring of Fire 5-1 and Cam's Pride 5-1 dd-htd. (1-5, 36/-). 9.38: Greenane Flame 5-1, Gorey Gold 4-1 (5-2, 72/6).
QUINELLA: £1,379/3/-.
WANDSWORTH. — 7.45: Kings Counsellor 5-1, Glory Paddy 2-1 f (3-2, 102/-). 8.0: Tinkers Parson, 3-1; Coolkill Trotter, 5-2 jf (5-6, 27/3). 8.17: Sly Jack, 7-2; Kifaru, 6-1 (5-8, 77/6). 8.35: Bevans Lad, 10-1; Halfpenny King, 3-1 (1-2, 95/3). 8.53: Ballyroyal Prince, 8-1; Ringside, 9-2 (4-2, 137/6). 9.12: Kelly's Brindle, 3-1; Conna Jester, 8-11 f (5-6, 14/6). 9.29: Gurrane Jet, 4-1; Boeing Prince, 4-1 (2-5, 57/3). 9.46: Automation, 5-4 f; Hillside Buck, 100-8 (5-3, 34/6).

BRAWL AS CHELSEA WIN..

United spurt to lead—then they dither

From FRANK McGHEE

Helsinki, Wednesday

Helsinki 2, Man. Utd. 3

IT took Manchester United just thirty seconds to prove how easy it should be for the professionals to beat the amateurs here tonight.

That was how long they spent strolling to a nonchalant lead in their European Cup preliminary round first leg tie through centre-forward David Herd.

Hard Work

But for the rest of the ninety minutes, United made hard work of what should have been an easy job.

It was fifteen minutes before they scored the second goal through John Connelly.

Then a thirty-fourth minute shock for United—inside left Kai Pahlman scored with a swerving free kick.

Within two minutes United went further ahead when Denis Law scored, but Helsinki still had a shock left and closed the gap to only one with a shot from Markku Peltoniemi.

Scusi! That's Italian for "Excuse me"—and it's Chelsea skipper Terry Venables politely stepping over Roma's spreadeagled Leonardi during the flare-up that resulted in Eddie McCreadie being sent off.

McCreadie sent off, but 3-goal Venables slams the Italians

By KEN JONES   **Chelsea 4, Roma 1**

EDDIE McCREADIE, Scotland's left back, was sent off at Stamford Bridge last night as Europe became a battleground for Chelsea.

Raiding along the left wing after 30 minutes McCreadie turned to retaliate. He threw a punch that poleaxed Roma's inside right Leonardi and ended this Fairs Cup clash—his first game in European competition—back in the dressing room.

It was the beginning of a savage night punctuated by the ugly tackles and bad refereeing that now seem part and parcel of Continental combat.

Chelsea, forced to fight on with ten men and at one point with nine after skipper Terry Venables was carried off in the 43rd minute, rode out the trouble to win a game in a style that matched anything they had done before.

It was a night that demanded courage and heroes. And Chelsea had them.

Venables hit a brilliant hat trick, governed the game with midfield decision and defensive deployment and emerged as a player of great stature.

Little left winger Joe Fascione worked himself dizzy as a deputy defender, and the football of left half Ron Harris, outside right Barry Bridges and inside right George Graham contained quality and courage.

It was a team effort on a night when Chelsea met a side who came determined not to lose, satisfied to survive for the second leg in Rome on October 6.

Brutally Kicked

With a defence that rarely had less than six players between Chelsea and their target, Roma rode out a fiery beginning.

But what had gone before was nothing to what came after Dutch referee Schalks had ordered McCreadie to the dressing-room.

Within a minute, Venables had been body-checked as he was going through and Fascione brutally kicked by Roma inside left Benitez.

Then the ball was pushed square and Venables's shot raked through a nine-man Italian "wall" to put Chelsea in front.

In the thirty-third minute Chelsea paid the penalty for forgetting that left winger Barison has a "banana" shot as deadly as any in Europe.

A free kick given against Harris on the edge of the area gave Barison his chance and goalkeeper Peter Bonetti was left helpless as the ball swerved past him.

Deceived

In the 40th minute Chelsea went back in front, when Venables deceived the Italians from a free kick. He walked at—and then ran around—their defensive "wall" to turn a Harris pass in.

Three minutes later, he was carried off, after being hacked down by Barison, who was booked when it seemed obvious he should go off.

Venables came back to start the second half and immediately volleyed in a George Graham cross.

In the 67th minute Graham ran in, unmarked, for the fourth.

New Posh hand Cup ko to Newcastle

QUITE a day for **Peterborough**! Their chairman, 70-year-old Tommy Peake, was voted out of office—and a few hours later the Third Division side sensationally knocked **Newcastle** out of the Football League Cup.

Peake, the centre of a bitter boardroom battle, was deposed as Posh chairman after a unanimous vote of no confidence in him at a special meeting attended by seven of the club's nine directors yesterday.

The vice-chairman Vic Grange succeeds Peake as chairman.

But the boardroom squabbles certainly did not affect the Posh players, who pulled off the shock of last night's second round League Cup games with a 4—3 win at St. James's Park.

It was a great night for the League Cup. The fans

flocked in, and there was a new record gate for the competition with 40,168 at the Hawthorns to see the Midlands clash between **West Brom** and **Walsall**.

First Division leaders West Brom got home 3—1 after two late goals had wrecked their plucky Third Division neighbours.

And Colchester had their biggest crowd for four years with 7,777 turning up for the match against **Middlesbrough**. Unfortunately, Colchester lost 4—2.

Martin Chivers, the Young England forward who scored four in **Southampton**'s 9—3 thrashing of Wolves on Saturday, hit a hat-trick in Saint's 3—0 win over Rotherham.

CHELSEA HELD TO REPLAY

By KEN JONES: Chelsea 2, Milan 1

Teams level 3—3 on aggregate.

CHELSEA must travel to Italy for a third crack at A C Milan, probably on Wednesday, March 2.

The two teams ended this Inter-Cities Fairs Cup third round tie at Stamford Bridge last night all square on aggregate at 3—3.

Then Chelsea lost the toss that decided the replay venue.

Nearly 60,000 fans packed Stamford Bridge for last night's brave and brilliant battle.

Terry Venables set a pattern of neat composure for Chelsea—first with two accurate build-up passes, and then a fine and speedy run by young Peter Osgood nearly opened up the Milan defence.

But it was the Italians who threatened first, and Chelsea were nearly two down on aggregate when centre forward Angelillo broke from a deep position to hit a fierce shot against the foot of a post.

A long shot from Venables was pulled down by Milan goalkeeper Balzarini.

At the other end roaming right winger Sormani was nearly through on a Rivera pass.

Urgent

When it seemed as if Chelsea's urgent early pressure was going to be repelled without reward, they got a brilliant tenth-minute goal.

Bobby Tambling's corner kick cleared the tall Milan defenders and George Graham scored with a fierce header.

Nine minutes later

They play again in Milan after Fairs' Cup clash ends all-square at 3-3

Chelsea went two up and into an aggregate lead when Osgood scored a great goal.

Taking a difficult pass from Graham, the young Chelsea forward pulled the ball on to his left foot on the edge of the area and then exploded a tremendous left-foot shot past Balzarini.

Switch

Milan now switched their marking.

They sent West German international full back Karl Schnellinger to mark Osgood and were forced to release players from the back in a bid to get into the game again.

A bad tackle by left half John Boyle sparked off a note of trouble in midfield.

Then Rivera, who had been strangely quiet, made space for himself on the right and nearly pulled a goal back with a centre that ran just wide of the far post with Chelsea's defence beaten.

Venables was working prodigiously in midfield and from one centre Graham went just wide with a header.

Balzarini saved from Tambling when a goal looked likely and then another Boyle foul seemed to rob Chelsea of some of their composure.

Their marking became slack and a minute before half-time Sormani was free to pull down a Rivera pass and shoot viciously past Bonetti.

Superb

Inspired by a superb performance from Schnellinger, the Italians seemed to stroll into command of the game in the second half.

Their passing was accurate, and Rivera, now at the furthermost point of their attack, was a constant threat.

Chelsea lost John Hollins for a spell after he had been hurt in a tackle—and while he was off the field inside right Lodetti was pulled down by McCreadie.

It looked a certain penalty, but play went on.

Rivera missed from close in and left half Madde wasted another chance when he shot into the side-netting with Rivera unmarked on his left. Then centre forward Angelillo shot over.

With time running out, Chelsea turned on pressure and Barry Bridges, Graham and Tambling all went close in a hectic last five minutes.

Yipee! Peter Osgood turns in triumph after scoring Chelsea's second goal from the edge of the penalty area at Stamford Bridge last night.

HAMMERS NAILED BY McEVOY HAT-TRICK

By HOWARD BOOTH: Blackburn 4, W. Ham 1

A FIRST-HALF hat-trick by Blackburn goal-grabber Andy McEvoy shattered West Ham's cup hopes in last night's fourth-round replay at Ewood Park.

Playing at centre forward, the former inside striker cracked home goals in the fourteenth, forty-first and forty-third minutes.

John Byrom—who hit a hat-trick in last Saturday's tie—got the other first-half goal in the thirty-third minute.

Hammers seemed well in the game when Geoff Hurst, the country's leading scorer, wiped out McEvoy's opening goal within a minute.

But Byrom deftly put Blackburn back in front after outside left Harrison had placed a fast cross to his feet.

Then McEvoy completed his hat-trick.

In the forty-first minute he picked up a long clearance by full back Billy Wilson which West Ham skipper Bobby Moore had mis-headed and scored from thirty yards.

Two minutes later another glorious long ball from Harrison found McEvoy once more the eager finisher.

BOLTON HAVE TALKS WITH £60,000 BELL

Bolton last night led the chase for 19-year-old Colin Bell, Bury inside forward and skipper who is on the transfer list at £60,000.

Bell was interviewed by Bolton, but with the talented youngster preferring a move into the First Division, Arsenal and Spurs cannot be ruled out. Both have watched him this season.

Blackpool's board met yesterday to discuss England inside froward Alan Ball's request for a new contract. The player will get their answer today.

Quiz word

ACROSS

1. Son of Enoch and grandfather of Noah (10).
8. See "3."
9. Afrikaans is "South African ——" (5).
10. Citizen of Copenhagen, perhaps (4).
11. The first socialist premier of France (4).
12. Kind of pigeon so named from the hood-like appearance of the feathers of its head (3).
14. Vessel with a narrow neck (6).
15. Dog like a large greyhound (6).
18. "—— Glory" is the "Stars and Stripes" (3).
20. Statesman whose death resulted from a riding fall in Hyde Park (4).
21. "Pineapple ——" is a ballet (4).
23. Judicial examination (5).
24. Such fishing, for example, is done near the coast (7).
25. Composer of "The Rite of Spring" (10).

DOWN

1. Picture or statue of the Virgin Mary (7).
2. What word is missing from the brackets? ANIMAL (HOSE) PAST (RAID) WEARY (— — -) (4).
3 and 8. Film star who has been called the most beautiful woman in the world (6, 7).
4. In legend, Selene the moon-goddess was the mother of fifty daughters by him (8).
5. "Adolph —— Wilhelm Wohlbruck," born in Vienna, became a film star (5).
6. Name of certain suites of music by Elgar (4, 2, 5).
7. Name for a cock, like "Reynard" for a fox (11).
13. Well-known ballet in which the title-role is not a star part (8).
16. The science of animal life (7).
17. Constellation containing the stars Castor and Pollux (6).
19. Just float along (5).
22. Insert what is missing from the brackets: PRESERVE (CANCAN) CAT (TOM-TOM) EXISTS (— — — -) (4).

Yesterday's Solution

ACROSS.—1, Galop; 5, Pause; 9, Overact; 10, Lever; 12, Hutch; 14, Even; 16, Mere; 17, Sir; 18, General; 20, Widen; 21, Strange; 23, Bit; 25, Neon; 26, Four; 27, Adage; 29, Norma; 30, Clarion; 31, Ether; 32, Pleat.

DOWN.—1, Gales; 2, Lover; 3, Oven; 4, Per; 5, Pah; 6, Acumen; 7, Utter; 8, Ethel; 11, Evicted; 13, Cranium; 15, Ledge; 18, Gin; 19, Nee; 20, Wangle; 21, Snake; 22, Roach; 23, Borne; 24, Tract; 26, Fool; 28, Ear; 29, Nip.

CHELSEA WIN—ON TOSS !

Sensational finish to Fairs Cup play-off

From KEN JONES   Milan, Wednesday

Milan 1, Chelsea 1 (after extra time)

CHELSEA won their Fairs Cup play-off in the giant San Siro stadium here tonight—on the toss of a coin !

The match ended sensationally, going into extra time after Milan had equalised in the 90th minute.

There were no more goals, and the German referee H. Baumgartner had to spin a coin to decide which team went into the fourth round.

Bobby Tambling went close after a fine pass by Peter Osgood, as Chelsea kept their promise to "come out and fight."

Milan, too, produced skilful attacking play even though they were without their three top international stars, Rivera, Schnellinger and Amarildo.

Then in the twelfth minute Chelsea went ahead.

The goal was brilliantly designed by George Graham and skilfully finished by right winger Barry Bridges.

Graham held the ball on the edge of the area, and then swapped passes with Bridges to send the winger in to score.

The Italians came back immediately. Inside right Madde swept through on the left touchline, centred over Bonetti's head and left back Eddie McCreadie had to clear wildly for a corner.

Brave

Left winger Fortunato met the kick bravely with a near-post header that sent the ball into the crowd.

The Italians, missing the skill of Rivera in attack, were now producing little more than a series of centres slung into the Chelsea penalty area.

A fierce shot from Madde had Bonetti leaping, but Chelsea, playing the more attractive and intelligent football, were on top.

But then John Boyle conceded a free kick on the edge of Chelsea's penalty area—and it very nearly brought the Italians a goal.

Smart gamesmanship opened up Chelsea's defensive "wall" and Sormani found a gap to hit a tremendous shot that disappeared into the crowd with Bonetti still leaping to save.

A bad foul by Sormani on Osgood sent the young Chelsea forward rolling in agony on the floor and the incident brought some tension into the game.

There was an angry flare-up in the corner when the German referee Baumgerter first gave a free kick to Chelsea and then changed his decision to a throw-in for the Italians.

Chelsea did well to keep their heads and refuse to be drawn into trouble.

Chelsea were back on defence for most of the second half and had anxious moments when a shot from Lodetti seemed to be handled in the area, and when inside left Angelillo shot dangerously close.

There was a sensational finish. Milan equalised in the last minute with Fortunato scoring from a corner on the right.

Chelsea protested vigorously that there had been a goalmouth infringement but the referee let the goal stand and the game went into extra time.

Left winger Peter Cooper (second, right) bursts through to head the first Leeds goal at Elland-road last night.

Hungarians get a four-goal hiding

By DEREK WALLIS   Leeds 4, Ujpest Dozsa 1

LEEDS UNITED, 4—0 up at half-time, crushed the Hungarians in their first leg quarter final tie in the Fairs' Cup at Elland-road.

Leeds, who had scored only six goals in six Fairs Cup matches so far, swarmed into attack on a swamp of a pitch.

Norman Hunter, Peter Lorimer, Terry Cooper and Mike O'Grady all went close in the first three minutes.

The barrage eased a little, but only momentarily, and after seven minutes Leeds inevitably took the lead with a header by left winger Cooper.

Play was then held up for ten minutes by a dog that sprinted over the pitch before finally being trapped.

More than a dozen policemen joined in the hunt, and German referee Schaulenburg clearly despaired of ever catching it and sent for a net.

Header

Seven minutes from half time Leeds increased their lead with another header—this time by left back Willie Bell.

Leeds clinched the match — and possibly the tie — when they went 4—0 ahead with two goals in the last two minutes of the first half.

Jim Storrie got the first —another header — and Billy Bremner completed the first-half rout.

Dunai scored for Ujpest after 75 minutes.

SPANIARDS KO HEARTS

Real Zaragoza 1, Hearts 0

HEARTS went out of the Fairs Cup after a fighting display in Spain last night—and Real now meet Dunfermline in the quarter-finals.

This third-round play-off was settled by a goal from Marcellino ten minutes from time. Hearts got the ball in the Spanish net five minutes before half-time, but the referee had whistled for a foul by Wallace on goalkeeper Rodri.

WILTS TRIUMPH —AT LAST !

Wiltshire are through to meet Cheshire in the County Hockey Championship—after four and a half hours' play against Middlesex.

They won their semi-final second replay 2—1 at Camberley yesterday, the winning goal coming three minutes from the end of extra time.

Now Clay fights in Montreal..

IF THEY'LL LET HIM OUT OF THE COUNTRY !

CASSIUS CLAY'S world heavyweight title defence against Ernie Terrell has been moved from Chicago to Montreal, Canada. It will still take place on March 29.

The fight has been approved by the Montreal Boxing Commission, and it was switched to Canada after the Illinois State Athletic Commission yesterday barred the bout in Chicago.

One snag, however, in staging the fight in Montreal, is that Clay will have to get permission to leave the United States until his military future is cleared up.

'OP' FOR TOURIST

West Indies fast bowler Lester King, one of the nine players already chosen to tour England this summer, has entered hospital for a cartilage operation on his right knee.

ATHLETICS

INDOOR MEETING (Leningrad). —5,000 metres: A. Kakarov (Russia) 13m. 49.8s. (world indoor record).

Quiz-word

ACROSS

1. Giant whose tongue sheltered a whole army from the rain (10).
8. Great river of South America (7).
9. Brazilian Negro dance, originally (5).
10. What word is missing from the brackets ?
   PRIMATE LIGHT BLOW (RIME); CAPTURE, FELINE ANIMAL (PURE); SOUTHERN. BITTER (---) (4).
11. Indian ox with a large fatty hump near the shoulders (4).
12. Drink introduced into England in the seventeenth century (3).
14. Saint said to have made a pilgrimage to Rome with 11,000 maidens (6).
15. Cut up fine (6).
18. "--- constrictor" (3).
20. "Wendy" theatrical producer and film director, etc. (4).
21. What word is indicated on either side of the brackets ? EXTRA (---) SWEEPING (4).
23. One kind of terrier (5).
24. Largest ocean of the world (7).
25. Familiarly, the opera from which comes: "Flight of the Bumble Bee" (4, 6).

DOWN

1. "—— Finn," novel by Trollope (7).
2. Mid-day (4).
3. Wading-bird with a long, curved, elastic bill (6).
4. "Holy man" who for years was the real power behind the Russian throne (8).
5. Ant (5).
6. One of the ancient English kingdoms (11).
7. Famous novel dealing with Russia and France at the time of Napoleon Bonaparte (3, 3, 5).
13. "Christian" was the ringleader of the rebellious crew of H.M.S. Bounty (8).
16. Thin material (7).
17. Shortness of sight (6).
19. First sign of the zodiac (5).
22. Sir Walter Scott was one (4).

Yesterday's Solution

ACROSS.—1, Tuber; 5, Brews; 9, Amateur; 10, Sorij; 12, Dirge; 14, Trot; 16, Noun; 17, Yen; 18, Demerit; 20, Salad; 21, Defamed; 23, Dig; 25, Odin; 26, Penn; 27, Serif; 29, Forgo; 30, Station; 31, Satyr; 32, Elate.

DOWN.—1, Tasty; 2, Baron; 3, Emit; 4, Rag; 5, Bed; 6, Ruined; 7, Pool; 28, Far; 29, Fie. Error; 8, Spent; 11, Precede; 13, Mad; 20, Sanity; 21, Doses; 22 First; 23, Derna; 24, Gnome; 26.

10 mins left..Osgood's there!

Peter Osgood (right), unmarked by the Munich defence, flashes home the header that put Chelsea into the Fairs Cup semi-finals.

Pictures by Mirror Sport
Cameraman Monte Fresco

Chelsea 1, Munich (1860) 0
(Chelsea win 3-2 on aggregate)

CHELSEA rescued themselves from the agony of another match in an ever-lengthening Cup campaign.

And they did it with time snapping at their heels at Stamford Bridge last night.

A John Hollins throw-in from the right . . .

A ballet of headers in the German goalmouth . . .

Suddenly, there was Peter Osgood free, unmarked, gratefully accepting the chance to send home a header and his club on to the semi-finals of the Fairs Cup.

Back To Bed

Away went Osgood, leaping into the night, finally engulfed by his colleagues, who happily accorded him the honour of hero in a match in which he might not have played.

Chosen at the last minute, after five days of tonsillitis, Osgood secured a European semi-final for Chelsea with just ten minutes left and with a play-off a ghastly possibility.

Osgood was ordered straight to bed after the match.

He said: "I knew this before the game. Before today, I had been in bed since last Thursday.

"I had no idea when I left home this morning that I had a chance of playing. I felt great when Mr. Docherty told me I was in."

Mastery of Munich means Chelsea can go on to F A Cup combat against Third Division Hull City in tomorrow night's replay happy that the first hurdle in a week of great effort has been safely cleared.

But how much last night's game took out of them will not be known until they tangle with the Tigers of Hull in the election night battle.

Certainly, Chelsea were forced to run as hard as they have ever had to run before, against a Munich side that matched all their effort and enterprise.

Until Osgood's goal it seemed that every shot would end safely in the hands of the giant Yugoslav goalkeeper, Radenkovic.

Artiste and actor, the Munich 'keeper treated Chelsea's fiery finishing almost with indifference—almost as though this was a pre-season practice.

He made fine first-half saves from Osgood, Barry Bridges and George Graham.

Best Save

And with Chelsea turning on the heat in a fiercely-fought second half, he made the save of the match at Bobby Tambling's feet.

Early on, there was trouble for Chelsea as

LAST-MINUTE CHOICE ENDS CHELSEA AGONY

KEN JONES says:
They had to run their hardest to beat Munich

Munich's clever movement and intelligent, incisive running opened up gaps.

Right winger Heiss twice shot wastefully wide and centre forward Konietzka might have scored instead of bringing a brilliant save out of Peter Bonetti.

Marvin Hinton, for once adopting an orthodox centre half role, found trouble with it, and must have longed for the security of the position he normally holds at the rear of the defence.

Unchanged

But this was a night when Chelsea had to attack, and the effort had to be 100 per cent.

They got it, but despite the planning of Terry Venables, and swift running from the other forwards it looked as though the right result was going to be beyond him.

Now Chelsea take an unchanged side to Hull, confident they can surmount this second hurdle in a week that could have been a crisis.

● Chelsea meet Barcelona in the Fairs Cup semi-final. The first leg will be at Stamford Bridge on April 20, with the return in Barcelona on April 27.

BEST WILL MISS TONIGHT'S REPLAY

Irish international outside right George Best (knee injury) will miss Manchester United's F A Cup sixth-round replay against Preston—and possibly the first leg of the European Cup semi-final against Partisan in Belgrade on April 13

Now Chelsea will win Cup

"I think Chelsea will now win the Fairs Cup. I am sure they can beat Barcelona in the semi-finals."

—Max Merkel, Munich coach.

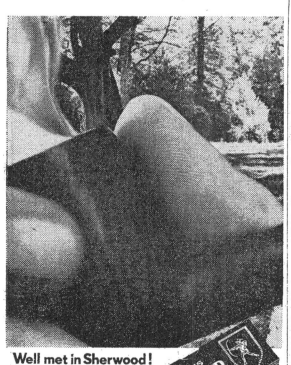

Well met in Sherwood!

Venables gashed by goalkeeper

By HARRY MILLER

CHELSEA inside left Terry Venables had two six-inch gashes down his right thigh, after a last-minute clash with Munich goalkeeper Peter Radenkovic.

Venables said: "The goalkeeper jumped on me."

But Radenkovic, one of Munich's stars in that magnificent Cup Winners' Cup final with West Ham at Wembley last May, told me: "The referee had already blown his whistle, but No. 10 wanted to win time. I came from the goal to get the ball. I was sorry for what happened. I apologised to Venables."

Left back Eddie McCreadie — dropped yesterday from Scotland's "possibles" for Saturday's international against England —also had a legacy from last night's Cup-tie. There was a criss-cross of cuts on his left thigh.

But both Venables and McCreadie will be fit for tomorrow's F A Cup replay at Hull.

FOOTNOTE: Many Hull City fans are expected to start queueing for the tie late tonight with blankets and vacuum flasks. The match is not all-ticket and Hull are preparing for a siege of 70,000 fans. Official capacity is 39,500.

'SUB' STEALS HATELEY'S

Now fighting Fulham crash to Blackpool

Blackpool 4, Fulham 2: By HOWARD BOOTH

SPURS, Chelsea, Fulham. All London teams come alike to Blackpool these days.

In completing this hat-trick at Bloomfield Road last night, Blackpool put themselves into the fifth round of the League Cup — another step towards what could be their first serious assault on Europe.

For make no mistake, this incredible revival that has brought four wins and 16 goals in ten days, has given them the confidence to take on any side in England.

Fulham, it must be said, did not surrender without protest.

Indeed it was Fulham who scored first after 20 minutes, through slim winger Terry Parmenter.

But within a minute, Ian Moir equalised, and three minutes later a Ray Charnley header left Fulham trailing.

Pounced

Before half-time Blackpool were three-up as Jimmy Robson crashed in a headed pass from the hardworking Charnley.

Allan Clarke, best of Fulham's forwards, spoiled a fine night's work when, fifteen minutes from time, he rammed the ball across his own goal-mouth where Charnley pounced to score.

Fulham, still battling bravely got a second goal near the end through Fred Callaghan.

Chelsea's £100,000 centre forward Tony Hateley (No. 9) turns away almost unnoticed as his new team-mates salute substitute Tommy Baldwin's first goal.   Pictures by Monte Fresco.

PETER WILSON

'Amonti' won't be a pushover

Bodell must be at his best tonight

WITH Billy Walker very much in the headlines again and Henry Cooper nearing the end of his career, Jack Bodell's fight at Liverpool tonight against the Italian, Sante Amonti, assumes more than usual interest.

For clearly Bodell and Walker are likely to be called on to meet in an eliminator for the British title which by next month will have been Cooper's property for a record-breaking period of nearly eight years.

Amonti, 28, has lost only seven of his sixty-four bouts.

Tough

But the five men who beat him inside the distance include ex-world champion Floyd Patterson, European heavyweight champion Karl Mildenberger, and Piero Tomasoni, who regained the Italian heavyweight title from Amonti with a nine-round knock-out a year ago.

He may be a little past his best and he has had only one fight this year, outpointing the little regarded American, Leroy Green.

Amonti outpointed Brian London over four years ago and has three opponents in common with Bodell — America's Freddie Mack and two Italians, Giuseppe Migliari and Tomasoni.

Mack beat Amonti in three rounds in 1961 and Bodell in five in 1964. But the big Midlander avenged that defeat by outpointing Mack just over a year ago.

Both men beat Migliari, Amonti stopping him in ten rounds last year and Bodell outpointing the Italian over ten rounds just over six months ago.

Tomasoni took only three rounds to defeat Bodell in June against the nine round k.o. of Amonti.

Although Amonti may well be ring rusty, Bodell will have to be at his best to win.

JACK SOLOMONS has submitted a purse offer for Howard Winstone's British and European featherweight title defence against fellow Welshman, Lennie "The Lion" Williams.

Aberfan

Solomons plans to put it on at Grosvenor House, London—NOT as a World Sporting Club promotion for private clubs cannot stage championship bouts—but to charge luxury prices for a really "posh" evening in the 1,250-seater Great Room.

If he gets the fight Solomons will arrange for live television in some ten Welsh cinemas.

And all the profits will go to the Aberfan Disaster Fund — which, alone, should ensure the most distinguished attendance at Grosvenor House.

£100,000 TONY HURTS BACK

AFTER his first match for Chelsea, £100,000 Tony Hateley said: "I am slightly stiff from a kick in the back, I feel sure I shall be O.K. for Saturday.

"I couldn't have had a harder test, having to meet Mike England. I usually score against him, but he was ready to mark me and I had to try to pull him away. It worked, because Tommy Baldwin got the goals."

Manager Tommy Docherty said: "Tony came through well."

GLORY...

Dropped—then Baldwin hits two and puts Chelsea top

Chelsea 3, Spurs 0

CHELSEA paid Aston Villa £100,000 for the headwork of Tony Hateley yesterday—and then discovered they dropped a match-winner to make way for him!

Former Arsenal forward Tommy Baldwin, left out to let in Hateley, returned to the side as substitute for a second half of urgent action and two goals that shattered Spurs

By KEN JONES

Baldwin's part in a match that he was detailed to miss until he came on for the injured Peter Houseman, is in keeping with the character—and occasionally the calamities —of Chelsea.

But they will have no complaint. Hateley's power won them a penalty and that along with Baldwin's two goals takes them to the top of the First Division.

Hateley, signed early yesterday, will have few more difficult tasks than the one he faced last night—the barrier of Welsh giant Mike England, Spurs' £95,000 centre half.

Mid-air

Their duel was inevitably a mid-air one fought with power and with England answering the challenge that a sudden transfer deal had thrust at him.

With the luxury of Hateley's height to aim at, it was perhaps predictable that Chelsea's passes should be played to the point at which the big centre forward hoped to connect.

But it wasn't until their attacks flowed in more traditional well-supported style that Chelsea achieved mastery of a match in which they might easily have been beaten.

For long periods a cool and confident Spurs side built their attacks intelligently.

They created chances

which, if they had been taken, would not have made this such a storybook start for Hateley and a wonder finish for Baldwin.

A courageous save by goalkeeper Pat Jennings cost Spurs a doubtful penalty in the 62nd minute.

Hateley, hurtling through in the box, was pulled down by the 'keeper, and Bobby Tambling scored from the spot.

Baldwin entered the scene ten minutes later, curiously unmarked on the far post and heading in a long cross from Charlie Cooke.

Chelsea's victory was complete and Baldwin's delight obvious when he finished off a goalmouth scramble ten minutes from time.

EDDIE WINS

Eddie Avoth, the Cardiff light-heavyweight, stopped Bermondsey's Johnny Ould in the fourth round of an eight-round bout at the National Sporting Club last night. The referee stepped in when Ould's right eye was almost completely closed.

PREMIER MIDWEEK FLOODLIGHT LEAGUE.—Hounslow Tn. 1, Walton & Hersham 3.

Baldwin leaps in triumph after his second goal.

Hat-trick boost for Leeds

LEFT winger Albert Johanneson scored a hat-trick for Leeds as they swept into the third round of the Inter-Cities Fairs Cup against DWS of Amsterdam last night.

Leeds' 5—1 victory in this second leg means they win the tie on an 8—2 aggregate.

There was trouble in Dunfermline's 4—2 first-leg triumph over Dynamo Zagreb. The Yugoslavs cut up rough in the closing minutes and full back Braun was sent off.

Trouble too, in Madrid, where Penarol of Uruguay became world club champions by beating Real Madrid 2—0 (aggregate 4—0). Police had to clear the pitch of angry Spanish fans after the South Americans had scored from a penalty.

THE 'BEST' GOAL FOILS BRIGHTON

Brighton 1, Northampton 1: By NIGEL CLARKE

BRIGHTON failed by five minutes to reach the quarter-finals of the League Cup.

Their bid to join the small band of Third Division survivors ended when Billy Best put Northampton level in the eighty-fifth minute—to earn a replay next Tuesday.

That goal saved Best's face. Earlier he had missed three golden chances.

Brighton never stopped

running, but lacked skill and science before their biggest crowd of the season —17,238.

Their attempts at goal were rationed to long-range efforts that rarely troubled ex-Spurs keeper Bill Brown.

Their goal, in the 60th minute, came from the only chance they created inside the penalty area.

After two shots had been charged down, Jimmy Collins took a rebound from Kit Napier to fire wide of Brown.

WEST HAM'S SHAKE-UP ENDS HOME HOODOO

West Ham 3, Nottm Forest 1: By HARRY MILLER

WEST HAM last night began to live on level terms with every other team in the League. They won a home First Division match for the first time this season.

They did it after manager Ron Greenwood's shock shake-up that sent Johnny Byrne to the sidelines and relegated John Sissons to substitute.

The new-look team's response was a display from Bobby Moore and his men that had Forest flattened from the moment Hammers scored in the fifteenth minute.

It was a victory fashioned from non-stop drive and determination.

Greenwood shrewdly sent Martin Peters out in a No. 11 shirt—and he played a vital part in Hammers' first two goals.

In the fifteenth minute he crossed from the left. Peter Bennett, who took over the number nine spot from Byrne, headed towards the far post, and Geoff Hurst dived to score.

Flash

Eleven minutes later Peters flashed the ball low into the goalmouth and Hurst was there again to shoot past Peter Grummitt. West Ham got their third in the 74th minute.

Forest centre half Bobby McKinlay failed to clear a Peter Brabrook centre and Eddie Bovington cracked the ball home.

Forest, unlucky when Jack Birkett cleared an Alan Hinton shot off the line, and when Johnny Barnwell had a goal disallowed, scored three minutes from time.

Hinton centred and Ian Storey-Moore was there to turn the ball wide of Jim Standen.

ALDERSHOT FIFTH

Aldershot kept up their promotion bid with a three-minute goal by 20-year-old right winger Ron Walton against Lincoln. They moved into fifth place, but missed many more chances against the bottom team in the Fourth Division.

Results, scorers

FAIRS CUP
2nd Rnd., 1st Leg
Dunfermline ... 4   Dynamo Zagreb 2
  Delaney,   Gucmirtal,
  Edwards (pen)   Zambata
  Ferguson 2   H-T: 1—1
                      10,000
Plovdiv Bulgaria: Spartak Plovdiv 1, Benfica 1. Prague: Sparta Prague 2, Bologna. Italy 2
2nd Rnd., 2nd Leg
Leeds 5   DWS Amst'dam 1
  Johanneson 3,   Geurtsen
  Giles,   H-T: 3—0
  Madeley   27,096
  (Leeds won 8—2 on aggregate.)
Pitesti, Rumania: Dynamo Pitesti 5. Toulouse, France 1   Dynamo won 5-4 on aggregate.

LEAGUE CUP
Fourth Round
Blackpool 4   Fulham 2
  Moir,   Parmenter,
  Charnley 2,   Callaghan
  Robson   H-T: 3—1
                      15,349
Brighton 1   Northampton .. 1
  Collins   Best   17,238
  H-T: 0—0
Carlisle 4   Blackburn 0
  Wilson 3,   H-T: 1—0
  McVitie   14,054
Grimsby 2   Birmingham ... 4
  Tees,   Bridges 2,
  Cockerill (pen)   Fenton,
  H-T: 2—1   Vowden
                      11,298
Sheff. Utd. ... 2   Walsall 1
  Woodward 2   Taylor
  H-T: 1—1   13,910

FIRST DIVISION
Chelsea 3   Tottenham ... 0
  Tambling   H-T: 0—0
  (pen.),   54,191
  Baldwin 2
West Ham ... 3   Nottm For. ... 1
  Hurst 2,   I. Moore
  Bovington   H-T: 2—0
                      23,000

Top Positions
	P	W	D	L	F	A	Ps
Chelsea	13	7	5	1	28	13	19
Stoke	13	8	2	3	21	11	18
Burnley	12	6	5	1	24	13	17
Tottenham	13	8	1	4	24	20	17
Leicester	13	6	4	2	32	21	16
Everton	13	6	4	3	21	18	16

FOURTH DIVISION
Aldershot 1   Lincoln 0
  Walton   H-T: 1—0
                      5,036
WORLD CLUB CHAMPIONSHIP.—Second leg (Madrid): Real Madrid J. Penarol, Montevideo 2 (Rocha, pen., Spencer). H T: 0—2. Att.: 80,000. Penarol won 4—0 on aggregate.
INTERNATIONAL (Copenhagen) Denmark 3, Israel 1.
EUROPEAN CUP.— Preliminary round, play-off (Budapest): ASK Vorwaerts, East Germany 1, Gornik Zabrze, Poland 3.
EUROPEAN AMATEUR CUP.— Second leg (Hendon): England 2 (D'Arcy, Eason), Austria 0. H T: 0—0. Att.: 3,000. Austria won 3—2 on aggregate.
SOUTHERN LEAGUE CUP.— Trowbridge 2, Guildford 3; Kettering 2, Cambridge 1; Romford 6, Sittingbourne 1; Kings Lynn 4, Nuneaton 3 (after extra-time.)
SOUTHERN LEAGUE.—Div. 1 Dover 2, Crawley 1.
OTHER MATCHES.—Oxford Univ 1, Arsenal 0; Oldham 9 (Collins 6, McIlroy, Bebbington, Towers), FC Thun 2 (Benko, Gasser). H T: 4—0. Att.: 5,577.
FA YOUTH CUP.— First round proper: Leicester 2, Derby 0.
LONDON MIDWEEK LEAGUE.— Colchester 0, Millwall 5; L. Orient 1, Luton 0.

YESTERDAY'S SPORTS SUMMARY

GREYHOUNDS

WEST HAM.—7.45: Crimson's Express 10-1, Kilcaskin Sport 6-1 (4-5, 137/-). 8.0: Wise Clo 7-2, Torreador 9-4 f (1-2, 29/9). 8.15: Garry Enterprize 6-1, Crazy Court Paving 6-1 (6-2, 48/6) (N R: Lady Linwood). 8.33: Hi Dean 11-4, Never Seen 5-2 f (1-3, 20/3) (N R: Perry Castle). 8.50: Claymill Wonder evens f. Her Bambi 100-8 (5-6, 29/6). 9.7: Mr. Ireland 4-1, Steady Rain 11-10 f (6-2, 27/9). 9.24: Luska Major 7-4, Flameless 5-4 f (6-1, 12/-). 9.40: Lovely Rover 3-1, Miley's Lane 4-1 (4-2, 36/-). Couplets: £12/15/3 (paid on first leg), £37/18/-. £26/8/9.

WIMBLEDON.—7.45: Rip Cord 2-1, The Pilgrim 7-2 (4-5, 30/6). 8.0: Easter Countess 11-8 f. North County 3-1 (1-4, 14/3). 8.15: Red Mahogany 100-30, Master Cook 5-2 f (4-1, 36/6). 8.30: Space

Bird 13-8 f. Munster Queen 6-1 (3-1, 28/3). 8.45: Tarvin Sane 11-4, Tornado Clo Clo 7-1 (5-1, 51/6). 9.0: Glen Presto 5-1, Skin Again 5-2 (1-6, 44/3). 9.18: Precious Miss 9-4 f. Ballyloo Lark 7-2 (4-1, 23/-). 9.30: Murkish Blue 3-1 jf of 2, Corville Trip 3-1 jf (3-4, 33/6).
Plums: £14/7/3. £35/10/- £21/9/3.

RUGBY UNION

TOUR MATCH.—Oxford Univ 9 pts., Australians 11.

COUNTY CHAMPIONSHIP.— Bucks 19, Herts 8; Kent 14, Sussex 3; Hampshire 8, E. Counties 6; Middlesex 3, Surrey 3; N. Midlands 14, Staffs 3.
OTHER MATCHES.—Cambridge Univ. 17, Cambridge Univ. LX Club 6; Ebbw Vale 11, Cardiff 0; Newport 22, Pontypool 6; Bristol 24, St. Luke's Coll. 3.

BOXING

NATIONAL SPORTING CLUB (London).—8 Rnds Light-heavy: Eddie Avoth (Cardiff) bt Johnny Ould (Bermondsey) stpd 4th. 6 Rnds. Welter: Fess Parker (Battersea) outpd Bunny Stirling (St. Pancras) 6 Rnds. Light: Billy Attfield (East Ham) bt Bernard Fenn (West Ham) stpd 5th.

JONES QUITS LEAGUE

Berwyn Jones, 26, former British international sprinter who joined Wakefield Trinity in 1964 for a £6,000 signing-on fee, has quit Rugby League for personal reasons.

HOW THEY WON THEIR BATTLES

CHELSEA		SPURS	
Huddersfield	2—1	Millw'l 0—0	1—0
Bri'ton 1—1	4—0	Portsmouth	3—1
Sheff. Utd.	2—0	Bristol C.	2—0
Sheff. W.	1—0	B'ham 0—0	6—0
Leeds	1—0	Nottm. F.	2—1

SUNDAY MIRROR CUP SPECIALS

WALLACE LANDS CELTIC DOUBLE

CELTIC cruise on to another Scottish honour. Two goals by Willie Wallace won them the Scottish Cup against Aberdeen. They have won the Glasgow Cup and the League Cup, and are in the European Cup final. (Celtic's Jinx Mission—See Page 37.)

IT'S A COCKNEY FINAL!

LAST-GASP LEEDS GOAL DISALLOWED

Leeds 0, Chelsea 1 at Villa Park

ONE direct hit by Tony "The Head" Hateley, £100,000 air ace in Tommy Docherty's Stamford Bridge squadron, was sufficient to smash Chelsea's Cup semi-final hoodoo.

From a Villa Park clash that erupted in the last minute like a volcano, they go on to Wembley for the first time.

By KEN MONTGOMERY

But while lauding Chelsea, lament with unlucky young Leeds.

Chelsea, for whom seven out of eight previous semi-finals had been their heartache hurdle, tasted all the sweetness of luck this time.

Their luckiest break was reserved till the final furious minute of a battle that was never a classic but ever a cliff-hanger.

Blitzed the goal

Leeds, with skipper Billy Bremner drafted into the attack, blitzed Peter Bonetti's goal for the final half hour.

By a series of weird and often wonderful escapes, the Stamford Bridge defensive wall remained intact.

Then, with referee Ken Burns looking at his watch, Hateley pulled Norman Hunter down from behind, way out on the left.

Johnny Giles quickly pushed the free kick across the face of the penalty box to 21-year-old Peter Lorimer, who came on 18 minutes earlier as substitute for Rod Belfitt.

Lorimer's fierce first-time drive flew past Bonetti to send Yorkshire fans in a 62,378 crowd delirious with delight.

Referee said 'No'

But the referee refused to allow what I—and almost everyone else—thought a perfect equaliser—and a goal which would have meant the perfect ending.

Instead he ordered Leeds to retake the kick and, that done, it was all over. Chelsea, finalists only once before, 52 years ago at Old Trafford, were Wembley bound.

Immediately the whistle went, Leeds boss Don Revie leaped from the trainer's bench and strode defiantly across the pitch to ask Mr. Burns why the score had been disallowed. The referee, behind a heavy police escort, did not reply.

Later, from the comparative quiet of his dressing room, Mr. Burns explained that he had not blown for the first free kick to be taken because the Chelsea players were not ten yards from the ball.

In face of such a tragic finale, the young men of Leeds emerged as sportsmen supreme, offering their conquerors immediate congratulations and hiding their own bitter disappointment.

Leeds, lacking the vital link of centre half Jackie Charlton, never dominated up front.

Juggling wizards

Chelsea, on the other hand, had grafters from goal to outside left.

Charlie Cooke, spoken to after 19 minutes for a lunging kick at Willie Bell, was the ball-juggling wizard Leeds could not contain.

Significantly, it was from a Cooke run that Hateley headed his glory goal.

Danger seemed remote as a harmless ball bobbed around the centre line on Chelsea's left wing. But Cooke struck like a viper, wriggling magnificently between Bremner and Paul Reaney and setting off hell for leather for the corner.

He steadied, saw Hateley and put over a perfect cross. The squadron leader just couldn't miss and Chelsea had struck at the most crucial moment, the 44th minute.

Leeds were far from beaten. Bremner switched himself to lead the attack and all Chelsea's assurance seemed to ebb. It became a case of the Londoners clinging defiantly, desperately, to what they held.

JUBILATION!—Chelsea's scoring hero, Tony Hateley is buried beneath his exuberant team-mates.

● **Harlequins beat Richmond 14—11 in a fabulous Middlesex Sevens Final before 55,000 at Twickenham, writes GARY NEWBON.**

● **After tailing 11—3 to unfancied Richmond, the superb 'Quins produced a fantastic last-gasp finish to give the club their first win in this Rugby Union competition since 1935.**

● **Man of the competition was 'Quins' captain, Hiller. His lethal right boot and intelligent running planned victory in each round. He scored 40 of their 61 points.**

● **But it looked as if brilliant South African Bedford would come between Harlequins and the title. Four times he pulled off last-ditch tackles when 'Quins looked through.**

● HARLEQUINS.—Tries: Lloyd (2), Rutter. Pen. goal: Hiller. Conv.: Hiller. RICHMOND.—Tries: Stoneman, Cormack, Bedford. Conv.: Moffatt.

● FIFTH ROUND: Northampton 16, Lon. Welsh 5; Rosslyn Pk. 8, Streatham and Croydon 11; Lon. Scottish 10, Harlequins 15; Blackheath 15, Headingley 16; Moseley 13, Cambridge 0; Richmond 13, Wasps 5; St. Luke's Coll. 14, Saracens 8; Lon. Irish 8, Loughborough Coll. 23.

● SIXTH ROUND: Northampton 11, Streatham and Croydon 10; Harlequins 16, Headingley 13 (after extra time); Moseley 11, Richmond 13; St. Luke's Coll. 13, Loughborough 14.

● SEMI-FINALS: Harlequins 16, Northampton 8; Richmond 16, Loughborough 5.

LAZARUS BID FAILS

Bristol R. 2, Q P R 1: By BRUCE PERRY

RANGERS, fielding five reserves, just failed to save a point against promotion hopefuls Bristol Rovers.

They went down to only their fourth League defeat of the season, beaten by two goals from Bristol leader Alfie Biggs.

Slightly outplayed in the first half, Rangers came into their own after the interval when Mark Lazarus set about confusing a suspect Bristol defence by constantly switching wings.

It was one such switch which led to Rangers' goal in the 60th minute. Moving out to the left Lazarus slipped through a shrewd pass for Mike Leach to score from close range.

Leach had earlier been unlucky with a splendid drive which bounced clear off the Bristol upright. But it was Alan Wilkes who had the best chance of equalising.

He seemed certain to score from only five yards out—until Ray Mabbutt nipped in and took the ball off his toe.

Biggs was the home hero. He was mobbed at the end and had to seek police aid to fight his way off the pitch.

His first goal in the twenty-fifth minute came after he had been put through by Harold Jarman.

Peter Springett got a hand to the ball as it sped to the back of the net, and referee Jim Finney brushed aside Rangers' claims that Biggs was offside.

His second goal came a minute after half-time after a shot from Wayne Jones had bounced off Springett's leg.

Oxford Utd. 0, Watford 0

ACE Watford marksman Terry Garbett tarnished his reputation with two astonishing misses against Oxford.

But Garbett wasn't the only Watford forward out of touch. Left winger Brian Owen also boobed badly when he scooped wide from six yards ten minutes before time.

Oxford although sure of avoiding relegation and with little at stake, were tougher than expected.

They never matched Watford's midfield skill but fought hard enough to win.

Typical of their misses was Jones' well-wide shot while the Hornets' defence was in utter confusion.

'Keeper Brian Sherratt never faltered in dealing with Scullion's steady flow of centres as Watford pressed.

GREGSON'S SUPERB 65

MALCOLM GREGSON, 23-year-old golfer from Dyrham Park, Herts, was £1,000 richer today after cracking the course record with a 65 at Hunstanton, Norfolk.

It helped him win the 72-hole Schweppes championship and his first major tournament victory.

His final round clipped a stroke off the course record, set the previous day by Irishman Hugh Boyle.

Boyle finished second on 278 to collect £750. Third was Dave Thomas (281), who got a £500 cheque.

In an incredible run of ten holes during his final round, Boyle needed only one putt on nine of them.

275—**Gregson** (74, 69, 67, 65).
278—**Boyle** (70, 66, 73, 69).
281—**Thomas** (70, 68, 71, 72).
284—**Barnes** (69, 74, 68, 73), **Hitchcock** (70, 71, 69, 74).
285—**Muscroft** (74, 70, 72, 69), **Hood** (70, 73, 67, 75), **Lynch** (71, 72, 72, 70), **Will** (73, 67, 71, 74), **Jones** (68, 69, 74, 74).
286—**Skerritt** (72, 71, 71, 72), **Weetman** (72, 71, 70, 73).

Arsenal ease up after four goals

Burnley 1, Arsenal 4

ARSENAL won with such arrogant ease that twenty minutes from the end hundreds of disgusted Burnley fans drifted away to watch the cricket next door, writes JIM BEECROFT.

Everything went wrong for Burnley, who had a nightmare game.

Arsenal were a cool, compact outfit, who played crisp football until they eased up midway through the second half.

They took command early and Addison and Graham scored in the first half-hour.

Burnley, knocked off their stride by the robust methods of taller and heavier opponents threatened a serious rally only once.

That was near the interval when full back Smith scored an excellent goal.

Three minutes later Arsenal's superiority was re-established by winger Armstrong, who cracked a brilliant shot in off the post.

With wing-half McLintock and inside forward Sammels creating chances with devastating regularity, it did not matter very much when Addison went off early in the second half to be replaced by Court.

It was no surprise when winger Simpson scored Arsenal's fourth goal in 56 minutes with a flying header that left 'keeper Thomson floundering.

Fulham 2, Blackpool 2

IT used to be Johnny Haynes's role to haul Fulham clear of relegation. Now it falls on the slender shoulders of Allan Clarke.

Two opportunist goals by him in this end-of-the-season frolic saved them from humiliating defeat by doomed Blackpool.

Clarke pounced on anything loose in Blackpool's penalty area. But on either side of him Fulham never reached the heights they have shown on occasions.

Prompted by Green, McPhee, and Armfield, Blackpool produced a calculated—if spasmodic—brand of football that was too often wasted by Skirton, Charnley, and Oates.

Clarke opened the scoring in the thirty-second minute when he lobbed a ball with the flight of a spin-bowler's delivery into the net at the acutest of angles.

The lively, if erratic, Oates equalised. But Clarke appeared to seal the issue with a goal in the seventy-fifth minute. It was a gem of opportunism made by Haynes.

But Blackpool were not finished and a bad mistake by the retreating Fulham defence let in Charnley for the equaliser.

SWIM SHOCK.—Fourteen-year-old Alex Jackson, from the Isle of Man, beat Britain's No. 1 girl swimmer Pauline Sillett at the British trials at Crystal Palace. She also set a British junior record of 62.7s. for the 110yds. freestyle.

GREYHOUNDS 1, 2

Dead Heats.—New Cross (2nd): Dunkeld Playboy (T3) 5-1 and Dunkeld Praise (T4) 9-2, F 2-3 19/6, F 2-4 23/3.

* Winning favourite † Joint favourite ● Triple favourite § Quadruple favourite

Catford	Clapton	Hackney	New Cross	Romford	S. Bridge	Walth'stow	White City
Mini Rose 100-8 M's Talent evs F 6-2 67/6	H'bury Lass 2-1 C'kill Shaggy 5-1 *F 2-1 19/-	Frank Friend 6-4 St. Wharf 5-1 *F 6-2 25/6	Karen 8-1 Leeky Boy 4-1 F 2-3 81/3	Foll. It Away 9-2 Crozier M. 4-1 F 5-6 72/9	T. T. Star 8-11 Bally Lad 3-1 *F 1-5 16/-	Busy W'ker 3-1 B' Neale T V 7-1 F 2-1 48/9	P'k Abbey 9-4 Paddock F'n 100-8 †F 6-2 60/-
Stewardess 11-4 Mon. Champ 4-6 F 6-1 17/9	J's Queen 2-1 Ard. Chariot 7-4 F 4-1 13/9	Val's Star 5-1 Win. W'der 2-1 F 2-1 48/-	Front Ave. 4-1 Dd Ht 2nd See Above	St. Mustbe 3-1 Aw. Sabana 9-2 †F 1-4 43/9	Mitchel M'd evs Gl's Paddy 100-7 *F 3-6 31/-	H'uva Good 3-1 Secret Aff. 5-1 F 3-5 47/6	E. Y. Dog 11-2 G. Brindled 6-4 F 2-1 38/-
Dusty Trail 2-7 Mexico 10-1 *F 1-2 9/6	Glen Strm. 13-8 Hi Halo 4-1 *F 2-4 13/3	Rath. Streak 4-1 Sup. Teddy 7-1 F 4-6 54/3	Shameless 3-1 The Fear 10-1 F 6-2 94/-	St. Return 7-4 Mon. Cheers 3-1 *F 2-3 23/6	R. Snowman evs Big Scheme 5-2 *F 3-5 15/6	Can Trap 7-4 Jist 6-1 *F 1-2 28/-	All Here 4-1 Lea Valley F. 7-2 F 4-5 44/3
Stylish Lad 3-1 Tric Trac 2-5 F 2-1 14/9	L'more Dandy 9-4 Hollymount 5-4 F 1-3 15/-	W'pk Jackal 4-1 Mr. Topaz II 6-1 †F 6-5 100/6	Waltrop 5-4 Champ. Pr. 6-1 *F 1-2 22/6	Gl. Symbol 7-1 Trop. Flash 7-1 F 2-3 104/-	S's Chief 4-1 Peep O'lite 8-11 F 6-4 24/-	Tinvane K. 8-1 Ch. Court 11-8 F 3-4 58/9	Rayden 7-2 Rickersland 5-1 *F 3-2 38/9
C'kill W'der 9-2 Sp. the Case 7-2 F 6-1 45/6	Larry Charm 8-11 Daisy Knock 100-8 *F 2-3 23/6	Modulus 13-8 Tr. a Mink 5-1 *F 2-3 35/6	Cl. to Fame 9-2 Gl. Maigue 7-4 F 4-1 34/-	J'ty Abbot 3-1 Appian K. 10-1 †F 1-3 53/-	Nessies M. 20-1 In Exchange 5-4 F 2-5 119/3	Ch. Overall 8-1 Brightside 6-1 F 4-5 132/3	N. Ruliene 2-1 Rayhill J. 5-1 *F 4-2 39/6
Cons Duke 7-4 N. Errand 100-30 *F 4-5 15/-	S. of Wonder 3-1 Tall Str. 2-1 F 3-4 27/3	No race.	Mus. Tansy 7-4 Bally Duck 6-1 *F 2-1 30/9	B's Convict 2-1 Cons Orbit 7-4 F 1-6 17/6	Cave V.S. 13-8 Here's the K. 6-4 F 3-5 14/6	Cosy Ave 7-1 Estalis. F. 7-4 F 5-3 75/6	Cricket F. 3-1 Calisto 7-4 F 4-1 28/9
D'ble Rock 2-1 G. Present 4-1 F 6-3 26/-	Misery Me 8-13 Vista Sherry 9-2 *F 3-6 9/3	Cullen Era 5-1 Tsai Cham. 3-1 F 1-6 73/3	Tuners Spec. 4-1 Straight R. 3-1 F 5-1 67/9	Hello N'bour 3- Prin. Pine 4-1 †F 3-2 24/-	Albany Pride 9-2 Killeen B. 33-1 F 5-4 91/9	B'neale Kim. 8-13 M's Cheatha 6-1 *F 2-4 14/9	Parker Hill 7-2 Innsbruck 7-4 F 5-6 20/-
Roamin B'ty 2-1 And. Romulus 5-1 *F 2-5 20/-	Dalcais Fm. 9-4 L'more Guest 7-2 F 6-2 17/3	Mr. Cash 11-4 A's Venture 5-1 ●F 1-6 23/-	Ring. Chief 3-1 D'kld Prince 4-1 † F 3-4 28/9	Seans Canal 5-1 Aud. Hill 3-1 F 3-2 66/6	F'land An. 11-4 Kn. Mick 4-1 F 5-4 40/-	B'neale Luck 3-1 M'days Fug 15-8 F 2-5 27/9	Cinder Rock 2-1 Kilure 6-1 *F 6-3 34/6

Brighton	Crayford	Reading	Rochester	Slough	Southend	Ramsgate	Oxford
T's Privet 7-4 Kit. Salt 5-1 *F 4-1 37/9	C. Playboy 5-1 Low Flying 5-2 F 4-6 49/9	Bash. Lady 5-1 Joden's T. 8-1 F 5-4 138/-	F. L. Tom 4-1 Welcome D. evs. F 3-2 17/3	B. Bender 2-1 Bal. Girl 11-4 *F 3-2 19/6	D. of Foxes 2-1 Cowboy F. K. 7-2 †F 6-3 25/3	St. Flyer 5-1 Bl. Laces 4-1 F 3-2 88/3	B'ham Olive 9-4 L. Sixty Six 3-1 F 2-5 69/6
The Pilg'm 100-30 Woodlock 7-2 F 4-2 50/-	Moate Pr. 5-1 T. S. Hare 3-1 F 3-2 69/3	Red Wing 5-2 Sandy Acre 9-4 F 2-5 26/6	Fairy Wand. 5-1 W. Pirate 10-1 F 5-3 128/3	C. V. Pook 4-1 M. Victor 11-8 F 2-1 29/9	Bal. Tess Evs. Sw. Wind 8-1 *F 2-3 37/9	Cito Cito 3-1 Can. Away 7-2 F 5-1 36/-	Jet Stream 3-1 Fir. Pace 5-1 †F 3-2 93/3
My Prospect 3-1 Lucerna 100-30 F 4-5 25/9	D. Brandy 3-1 Miss Linda 5-2 F 3-1 36/6	Dunloy 4-1 Rose Para 9-4 F 6-3 33/6	Solo 9-4 C. Spinner 6-1 *F 3-2 49/9	Velvet L'n 7-4 Social Sec. 6-4 F 2-3 12/3	Kit's Alice 7-2 B. Grandee 7-2 F 5-6 37/3	St. Swift 6-1 St. Docile 7-4 F 4-1 84/3	Ken. Pilot 4-1 Book Jigs 3-1 F 5-1 97/9
N's Grove 9-2 Peachey's K. 3-1 F 2-6 44/3	Rosies J. 10-1 Marbelle J. 5-1 F 6-4 311/-	T. Tanner 3-1 Lovely F. 7-2 †F 6-2 26/-	Bell Top 6-4 Cracker 6-1 *F 6-5 36/6	A's Printer 11-8 Pop Tune 2-1 *F 2-6 15/6	T's Plastic 2-1 Right R'd 7-2 *F 3-1 23/-	Star Char. 5-1 Two to T. 5-1 F 5-1 83/-	Jade Lady 7-4 Our Chris 5-1 *F 5-1 51/6
L. Dashwood 11-8 Patch Dusty 4-1 *F 2-1 16/6	Coqueed 100-8 And. Remus 9-4 F 3-1 92/3	S. Windsor 3-1 Conna Pr. 10-1 ●F 1-6 71/3	H. Printer 5-2 Waxwork 7-4 F 4-2 21/3	Fear Burn 11-4 Sp. Guest 9-4 F 5-2 24/-	Kel's Halo 8-1 Fob. Star 7-1 F 5-4 150/-	C. Renown 7-2 S. Robin Par. 4-1 F 6-4 70/9	Sunny Hue 4-1 K. Karen 11-4 F 5-2 85/6
Hurst Rag 5-2 Hey Bruce 6-1 F 1-5 55/3	Br. Watch 6-1 St. Champ 5-2 F 6-3 37/6	Find Out 7-1 Renaldo 10-1 F 2-6 129/6	Martian 2-1 G. Nuisance 9-2 *F 2-4 24/3	R. T. Ruby 10-1 Un. Keith 11-4 F 6-5 88/9	T. Gr. Fox 13-8 Cl. Goldie 7-2 *F 4-6 18/6	G. Safari 3-1 St. Charlie 5-1 F 6-2 61/6	H. Fungus 6-1 Gen. Jumbo 5-1 F 2-4 90/9
Valley Cat 3-1 Gor. Abbot 5-1 F 2-1 48/6	Knoc. Fly 100-8 C. Second 7-1 F 4-5 91/9	Callela 5-1 T's Thumb 2-1 F 3-6 41/-	F. Printer 5-1 W. Icicle 7-4 F 6-4 78/-	Joan's Fawn 5- En. Breeze 3-1 F 5-1 67/3	Busy Bob 11-4 Bal. Pine 5-1 F 3-1 47/3	Cl. Fancy 6-4 Ball. Rod 4-1 *F 1-2 26/6	J's Post 5-2 Sum. Rock 7-1 F 1-3 127/-
Burn. Sands. 8-1 Cr. Acorn 3-1 F 4-6 89/9	Des. Track 8-1 F. Cougar 6-4 F 3-1 49/-	H't Break 7-1 Farloe Gig 7-4 F 1-5 59/-	P. Triumph 5-2 W. Tartan 4-1 *F 4-1 60/3	Roseville N. 2- Remir Sally 6-4 F 2-5 21/3	P's Patch 15-8 Better Kn. 5-1 *F 3-5 38/9	Ball. Rufus 6-1 Tree Top H. 2-1 F 5-1 41/3	B. Breaker 4-1 Pr. Demon 7-4 F 3-6 85/-

NON-RUNNERS.—Brighton: Enaffa. Hackney: Galbally Present. New Cross: Mandy's Brother, Kylerue Bobbie. Stamford Bridge: Glenshane Judy. Crayford: John Henry. Rochester: Know Knowing. Oxford: Muswell Tiger, Good Banker, Forest Kim, Hidden Willow. Slough: Mill Addo, Husky Haven.

TOMORROW'S BEST BETS.—Harringay: 7.45, Ballyloo Hind; 8.47, Double Rock; 9.9, Jerpoint Button; 9.31, Jerry's Memory; 10.15, Silver Churn. WEMBLEY: 7.45, Nimrod; 8.35, Applecart; 8.51, Proud Heron; 9.23, Baby Mine; 9.39, Any Hare.

CHELSEA (Blue shirts, blue shorts)

SKETCHES BY SALLON

1. PETER BONETTI   2. ALLAN HARRIS   3. EDDIE McCREADIE   4. JOHN HOLLINS   5. MARVIN HINTON   6. RON HARRIS (Captain)   7. CHARLIE COOKE   8. BOBBY TAMBLING   9. TOMMY BALDWIN   10. TONY HATELEY   11. JOHN BOYLE

TOTTENHAM HOTSPUR (White shirts, white shorts)

1. PAT JENNINGS   2. JOE KINNEAR   3. CYRIL KNOWLES   4. ALAN MULLERY   5. MIKE ENGLAND   6. DAVE MACKAY (Captain)   7. JIMMY ROBERTSON   8. JIMMY GREAVES   9. ALAN GILZEAN   10. TERRY VENABLES   11. FRANK SAUL

S !

followed Spurs the disappoint-their only Final

h of the Cockney
d up the first of
n 1915

LLER

the teams step up to the

giants of Tottenham
istory has been so

years before Chelsea
ned by Sheffield United.
beaten the Yorkshire-
in the Final at Crystal

Spurs took the Cup
ing Wolves 1—0 at
Bridge of all places.

namic Dave

ns need reminding of
ips super Spurs took to
in 1961 and 1962, when
Leicester 2—0, then
—1

Mackay, that dynamic
sted Scot, was there on
sion. He'll be back today
or his hat-trick.

Final history is against
then the history of
clashes between these
ondon clubs at least
on a level footing.
on the first meeting—a
und tie in 1910—by the
Forty-seven years later
Spurs slammed Chelsea
—0 in the fourth round.
But in two ties since
hen. the tide has turned
Chelsea's way They beat
Spurs 2—0 in the 1964
hird round after a 1—1
draw And in the fifth
ound the following year
Chelsea won 1—0.

At 4.45 this afternoon,
he score in the record
ooks—one way or the other
-will need revising.

JOE IS SUBSTITUTE

Chelsea yesterday named
ull back Joe Kirkup as
heir substitute. Spurs
anager Bill Nicholson will
ecide on his twelfth man
day

SINGING IN THE RAIN . . . A Gene Kelly-style act by Chelsea manager Tommy Docherty at Wembley yesterday. He hopes to go into a victory song-and-dance routine with his team this afternoon, and won't be satisfied to see that scoreboard stay at 0—0. Picture MONTE FRESCO.

TAMBLING IS MAN SPURS MUST TAME

CHELSEA'S strategy is built around tight marking and the deployment of centre half Marvin Hinton as a "free" defender at the back of their defence, writes Ken Jones.

Hinton's role is that of a "sweeper," moving quickly to cover at each point of attack.

Chelsea are rarely interested in competing in midfield. preferring to fall away on their own penalty area where they form a tight front to attacks.

Bobby Tambling, Tommy Baldwin and Tony Hateley form a three-pronged attacking squad. but they are often supported by runs from full backs Allan Harris and Eddie McCreadie, who break along the touchlines.

Tambling is dangerous across the whole width of the field and watch for the runs that take him from the left to an inside right position.

His strength on the ball and his ability to shoot from impossible angles makes him the biggest threat to Spurs.

Hateley's headwork is equally lethal and Chelsea will attempt to play the ball up to him in the air hoping he can flick on for Baldwin and Tambling.

If a spark of genius can win this final it may well come from Scottish international forward Charlie Cooke.

Cooke a phenomenal dribbler has the skill and balance to worm his way out of tight situations. and with non-stop John Hollins and John Boyle makes up Chelsea's motor unit in midfield.

If Chelsea stick skipper Ron Harris to match the menace of Jimmy Greaves, then his tackles will be fierce and his marking skin tight.

ENGLAND CAN BE MASTER OF THE AIR

IT is no coincidence that Spurs' more resolute attitude has brought them an unbeaten run stretching to twenty-three games.

But although their defence now gives little away. this new found determination has not changed their approach to the game.

They will be more ambitious than Chelsea and build their attacks from deep in their own half

They will probably use Alan Mullery to subdue the dangerous Tambling. Look for his strength in the tackle and the effort he puts into his game.

In Mike England, Spurs have the complete answer to Hateley's menace in the air

The tall England is probably better in the air than any other player in the world.

Spurs play the ball up to the feet of skilful for-wards Jimmy Greaves and Alan Gilzean—watch how they break back towards their own goal to receive passes that begin dangerous moves.

They work well together and Gilzean will roam wide hoping to flick passes into the path of the quicksilver Greaves.

On the right side of the field, Spurs attack in orthodox fashion with winger Jimmy Robertson a swift and determined runner

On the other wing Frank Saul often operates inside. opening things up for attacks by Cyril Knowles and Dave Mackay

Mackay's spirit is legendary and his skill in the highest bracket.

Terry Venables supports him in midfield. and see how he becomes the support for players when they have possession.

NO LUCK AT ALL FOR CHELSEA ★ TAMBLING GOAL CAME TOO LATE

SPURS 2
Robertson, Saul
CHELSEA 1
Tambling

SPURS NEVER

● Spurs manager BILL NICHOLSON said: "Chelsea played as we expected. Ours was a great team effort, but I think special mention must go to youngsters Joe Kinnear, Frank Saul and Jimmy Robertson."

● Beaten boss TOMMY DOCHERTY said: 'My lads gave me everything. Nobody will beat you if you are meant to win it. Spurs obviously were. We are good enough to come back next year."

● Chelsea's RON HARRIS, at twenty-two Wembley's younger-ever skipper, said: 'It was a rebound from an Alan Mullery shot off my calf which gave Jimmy Robertson his vital opening goal. But I don't blame myself."

● FRANK SAUL added: "I struck the ball blindly, but who can complain—it was the winner."

● JIMMY ROBERTSON, Spurs first scorer, said: "This was my first Cup goal but I promised it to the boys."

You were brilliant babes says skipper Dave Mackay

By KEN MONTGOMERY

DAVE MACKAY, warhorse of White Hart Lane, gave the credit to Tottenham's young ones for winning him his third medal at 31 after yesterdays 2—1 victory at Wembley.

And the Spurs sensation was the youngest and smallest, 20-year-old Southern Irishman Joe Kinnear, only 5ft. 7in., but a giant in Spurs' well deserved win.

Little Joe was left out of Eire's home international with Czechoslovakia today, in Dublin by selectors who felt two games in 24 hours were too much.

KINNEAR said: "I'd have loved to pick up my second cap so soon after a first Wembley medal but the selectors were right, It took a lot of strain off."

Skipper Mackay added: "I've played here about ten times and the pitch has never worried me. I felt great this afternoon.

"I think this is the nicest of all three triumphs, including internationals, for we had so many youngsters at Wembley for the first time and they all played magnificently."

TERRY VENABLES, sold by Chelsea to Spurs, injured his back early in the match but played on without telling anyone.

He said: "It was all right as long as I didn't stand still—so I simply kept on moving."

BOBBY TAMBLING, Chelsea's record goal-scorer who scored a late goal, said: "I didn't realise it was so late and genuinely felt we had a chance of taking them to extra time.

"But on the whole I think Spurs just fractionally deserved it."

One Spurs supporter who didn't see the game was **MRS. GRACE NICHOLSON**, wife of the Spurs manager. Her husband asked her to stay away as she is a jinx on the White Hart Lane men.

She said: "I'm so glad Bill got his Wembley hat-trick. I didn't even watch the game on T V, I was too busy preparing for the celebrations."

BRILLIANT

JIMMY GREAVES said: "It's a great feeling to finish in a team winning a major trophy after my big disappointment of being left out of the World Cup.

"I am especially delighted for Jimmy Robertson and Frank Saul, their goals were brilliant."

CLIFF JONES (12th man): "I thought I had a blinder from the bench

"I certainly felt as though I had worked for a tough ninety minutes. It's not quite the same as playing, but I am really pleased for the players."

The eager goal-hungry leap by Robertson is foiled this time by the safe, clutching hands of Chelsea 'keeper, Peter Bonetti

CAMPBELL DASHES OUR WALKER CUP HOPES

By ALF GOVER

THE Campbells are coming was not a popular tune to whistle at Sandwich, where Britain's amateur golfers staged a great fight-back in the Walker Cup.

It was America's Big Bill Campbell who held us in check.

Just when Britain seemed to have an outside chance of pulling back their 1—8 overnight deficit, in stepped the big, slow swinging Campbell.

In a key singles match he beat our No. 1, Ronnie Shade, 3 and 2.

Soon it was all over—and America had retained the Cup.

It was a disappointing moment in view of our three-out-of-four victories in the morning foursomes.

FIGHTING BACK

Joe Carr, Britain's captain, had been super-optimistic earlier in the day. He said: "I told you last night we were not done yet. This is Baltimore in reverse."

He was referring to two years ago when America snatched away Britain's winning lead to get a draw.

But yesterday Carr's team had to win seven matches—America only two—to make sure of retaining the cup.

And fight back we did. Oosterhuis was two up on Dixon at the turn. Bonallack was four up on Gray at the 14th and Saddler all square with Fleckman at the 9th.

Campbell, veteran of six Walker Cup matches, was first off in the afternoon singles against Shade.

He set the pace for his side. He won the first hole in par figures, then went two down as Shade won three holes in a row.

Campbell bounced back. He took the 451-yard fifth in three. Halved the short sixth.

The seventh, 493 long windswept yards, saw Campbell hit a great 3-iron second shot to within one foot of the stick, for what must have been a hard three for opponent Shade to swallow.

All square. Campbell finished the first nine with two perfect threes to be out in 32.

A win in four to Shade's five at the tenth put him three up. He dropped the 12th, restored his lead at the 13th, then took the 14th to be dormy four up

Campbell's example spread over the course. It inspired Cerrudo to go one up at the 13th on Foster, and Dixon two up at the 13th on Pirie.

Joe Carr's optimism had not been justified.

LEFT BY PARTNER

Campbell had also stolen the limelight in the morning foursomes.

He stopped Britain reversing Friday's match-play results when we were very nearly whitewashed by eight matches to one.

Campbell, partnering Lewis against the all-Scots combination of Saddler and Pirie, had turned one down.

The Americans took the 380yd. tenth with a drive, pitch and one putt. They arrived at the 15th still all square.

Campbell had been left by his partner fifteen feet from the stick. Saddler, with a teeny putt, was only inches from the hole for a win if Campbell missed.

No touch of nerves for Campbell. A bold putt hit the back of the hole and rattled the cup.

Saddler and Pirie hit back by winning the short 16th. A win at the 17th and they would be home and dry.

SUPERB PITCH

Here they were four feet from the hole. Campbell twelve feet away. Again he did his disappearing act with the ball.

Saddler missed to get his four, and off they went to the 18th all square.

Campbell did it again. Saddler, playing the second shot to the green first, left his partner twelve feet short.

Campbell played a superb pitch from eighty yards to within six inches of the hole. Pirie missed the hole by a mile.

Singles: Shade lost to Campbell 3 and 2; Bonallack beat Murphy 4 and 2; Saddler beat Gray 3 and 2; Pirie lost to Dickson 4 and 3; Craddock beat Lewis 5 and 4.

Foursomes (British names first): Craddock and Bonallack beat Murphy and Cerrudo by 2 holes; Saddler and Pirie lost to Campbell and Lewis, 1 hole; Shade and Oosterhuis beat Gray and Tutwiler, 3 and 1; Foster and Millensted beat Allen and Fleckman 2 and 1.

CARDIFF BEATEN. — Northern Transvaal defeated Cardiff by 25 pts. to 5, after leading 12—5 at half-time in Pretoria. This was Cardiff's final match of their short Rugby tour of South Africa.

● Eighteen-year-old Allan Martin, the Welsh secondary schools Rugby international second row forward, continues his unrivalled reign as the discus and weight kingpin in Welsh junior athletics.

● Currently the Welsh junior title holder in both events, he easily retained both Glamorgan junior men's county titles at Bargoed in the Glamorgan AAA's county championships.

● He took the discus with a throw of 138ft. 2½in., and the weight with 48ft. 9½in.—both distances well below his personal best—in wintry conditions.

● Two county titles in successive weeks were claimed by 14-year-old high jumper June Hirst from Neath Grammar School.

● After her triumph last week in the intermediate women's high jump, she took on all-comers in the senior women's grade and soared to victory, clearing 4ft. 10½in. — five inches ahead of her nearest rival.

● Michelle Smith, aged 12, of Barry, rated by Welsh AAA officials as possibly their brightest sprint prospect for many years, came through strongly in the final of the women's short sprint, which she took in 12.3 seconds.

● The junior men's half-mile brought the toughest struggle of the day. Seventeen-year-old Wynford Leyshon, of Neath grammar school, shook off the persistent challenge of Birchgrove Harriers' Keith Jones only in the last few strides.

● Leyshon's time of 2 minutes 0.5 seconds, was way outside of his personal best of 1m. 57.4s.

● No tennis at Sofia yesterday where rain prevented any play in the doubles. Britain are leading Bulgaria 2—0 in their second round Davis Cup match.

INDIANS NOW HIT BY SNOW

MCC pace twins John Snow and John Price tore through India's top batsmen at Lord's yesterday. The tourists crashed to 5-4 in just over half an hour, Snow snatching three wickets for two runs in 23 balls.

Opener Engineer and Saxena went in the same over to Snow.

Then anchor man Sardesai scooped a gully catch off Snow with the score at five, and Price ousted Borde soon after.

Then came the fight-back, led by skipper Pataudi. With Hamumant, he put on 75 before he lost his partner for 38.

Tony Buss's cutters produced a few scars in Leicester's pre-lunch batting. They slithered to 38-4 under the Buss blitz, the Sussex man taking all four wickets for 11 runs in forty-nine balls.

Hauled

Leicester were hauled out of the crisis by the patient Booth who stayed until the last ball before tea when the score was 121-7.

Booth smoothed his way to 42 in 195 minutes.

Somerset, having elected to bat on a soft Worcester pitch, crashed before Flavell and Coldwell and were all out by lunch for 80.

The pair bowled unchanged and Flavell took six wickets for 32 runs and Coldwell four for 45

Virgin was the first to go, beaten through the air by Coldwell's sixth delivery. Then Flavell, in twelve overs, took the next six for 22.

Clayton, last man out, was top scorer. Alley was the only other batsman to reach double figures.

Worcester, in their turn, found themselves struggling against Rumsey and Alley. Three fent for 28, but Graveney and D'Oliveira settled in.

Dodging in and out between heavy showers, Kent batted sedately against Northampton. They lost Wilson at 2?, but Luckhurst and Leary pulled them round.

It was not until Mushtaq came into the attack that they found scoring easier. The Pakistani conceded 37 runs in ten overs.

Middlesex opener Russell hit a century against Oxford University. He took two and a half hours over his first fifty, and seventy minutes later reached three figures with his fifteenth boundary.

Glamorgan had a long wait at Pontypridd and when they got started they soon lost Alan Jones against Gloucester.

MCC v. INDIANS
At Lord's

INDIANS—First Innings

Sardesai, c Denness, b Snow	3
Engineer, c Denness, b Snow	2
Saxena, b Snow ..	0
Borde, lbw. b Price	0
Pataudi, b Price	70
Hanumant, b Price	38
Surti, c Murray, b Price	8
Mohol, b Pocock	1
Prasanna, b Snow	0
Guha, not out	2
Bedi, not out	0
9 wkts (extras 3)	...127

CLOSE: 133 all out. MCC 1 for 0.

OXFORD UNIV. v. MIDDLESEX
At Oxford

MIDDLESEX—First Innings

Russell, c Walsh b Smith	153
Harris, lbw, b Gamble ..	2
Parfitt, c Khan, b Smith	32
Radley, run out	30
Manasseh, lbw, b Easter	19
Ling, b Gamble	2
Titmus, not out	45
Bick, lbw, b Ridley (G.)	7
Latchman, c Ridley (G.), b Smith ...	4
Sturt, not out	4
8 wkts (extras [illegible])	304

WORCESTER v. SOMERSET
At Worcester

SOMERSET—First Innings

Virgin, b Coldwell	
Willetts, b Flavell	
Kitchen, c Booth, b Flavell	
Burgess, lbw, b Flavell	
Alley, lbw, b Flavell ..	
Atkinson (C.), b Flavell	
Palmer, c Booth, b Coldwell ..	
Robinson, b Flavell	
Clayton, c Richardson, b Coldwell	
Langford, b Coldwell	
Rumsey, not out ..	
Total (extras 3)	

Flavell 6-32, Coldwell 4-45.

WORCESTER—First Innings

Headley, lbw, b Rumsey ...	11
Fearnley, c Clayton, b Rumsey	8
Ormrod, lbw, b Palmer	4
Graveney, c and b Langford	45
D'Oliviera, c Rumsey, b Langford	32
Richardson, not out	3
Slade, not out	0
5 wkts (extras 6)	1[illegible]

LEICESTER v. SUSSEX
At Leicester

LEICESTER—First Innings

Hallam, c Cooper, b Buss (A.)	2
Booth, c Grieg, b Lewis	42
Norman, c Buss (M.), b Buss (A.)	3
Inman, lbw, b Buss (A.)	0
Marner, lbw, b Buss (A.)	16
Constant, b Bates	24
Birkenshaw, b Lewis	26
Tolchard, c Graves, b Lewis	4
Lock, c Oakman, b Lewis	2
Spencer, c Suttle, b Lewis	0
Cotton, not out	11
Total (extras 8)	138

Lewis 5-66, Buss (A). 4—36.

SUSSEX—First Innings

Oakman, not out .	
Buss (M.), not out	
0 wkt.	

LATER: 19 for 0 wkt.

KENT v. NORTHANTS
At Gravesend

KENT—First Innings

Wilson, b Kettle . ..	
Luckhurst, not out	
Leary, not out	3[illegible]
1 wkt. (extras 1)	88

GLAMORGAN v. GLOUCESTER
At Pontypridd

GLAMORGAN—First Innings

Jones (A.), c Mortimore b Smith	11
Davis, not out	12
Slade, c Nicholls, b Brown (A.)	1
Walker (P.), not out	16
2 wkts	40

Later: 53 for 2 wkts.

● Because of rain no play was possible in the Derby v. Surrey, Lancashire v. Warwick and Yorkshire v. Notts matches.

TWO CUP-WINNING SNAP SHOTS ★ FIRST ROBERTSON THEN SAUL

HAD IT SO GOOD

Magnificent Mullery keeps fighting until he drops

By SAM LEITCH

SPURS must have been staggered at the ease with which they won the 1967 Cup final.

Only when Chelsea scored a too-late goal in the eighty-fifth minute did the famous Wembley occasion capture its traditional passion and drama.

Trojan-hearted Spurs skipper Dave Mackay never had it so composed in 1961 and 1962, when Tottenham last triumphed.

Chelsea disappointed their fans although their magnificent sporting spirit commended them to Wembley's 100,000 audience.

I admired the way manager Tommy Docherty rushed on to Wembley to congratulate Mackay even before Dave's Spurs boss Bill Nicholson.

TREMENDOUS BOOST

Spurs had the luck and two magnificent snap-shot goals at vital moments.

They received a tremendous boost when Scottish right-winger Jimmy Robertson hit an opportunist's goal one minute from half-time.

Then Frank Saul, a reserve for the 1961 and 1962 finals, and the only man in this Tottenham team who is not an international, slashed home a startling second goal in the sixty-seventh minute.

One of the finest sights of a Final which was so one-sided for long stretches, was Alan Mullery, running around at the finish in his bare feet, holding the Cup high and proudly.

Mullery had a marvellous match. So had the Spurs 20-year-old Dubliner, Joe Kinnear at right back, reading the game so adroitly, looking so craftily for the vital open spaces.

It was only when Chelsea, more desperate than cohesive, forced an eighty-fifth-minute goal that the match exploded.

ROVING BOYLE

John Boyle, forever roving in his usual midfield capacity, slung over a high and dangerous ball. Three Chelsea men rose for it, £100,000 centre forward Tony Hateley, Tommy Baldwin, and top scorer Bobby Tambling.

Spurs' Irish international 'keeper Pat Jennings made his one error, missed the ball with his huge pawing gloves, and Tambling glanced it over the line.

Perhaps if Chelsea's goal had come five minutes earlier we might have had the draw I expected.

But let us not take one iota of credit away from Tottenham for the convincing manner in which they won the richest FA Cup of all time.

Kinnear has never played so well, with so much time to spare.

Left back Cyril Knowles, quieter than I have seen him, found life easy against this wingless Chelsea outfit.

What powerful confidence stemmed from the Spurs half-back line! Mullery drove himself on and on.

When Bolton housing officer Ken Dagnall, blew his full time whistle, Mullery collapsed on the Wembley grass in exhaustion.

Mullery turned the game Spurs' way in that last minute of the first half.

Frank Saul slipped him a short ball and the former Fulham right half surged on goal.

It was the first time this defence-packing Chelsea team had bared their goal. Mullery pounded on and released a fierce blast at goalkeeper Peter Bonetti.

The ball never reached Chelsea's England keeper because it rebounded hard from his skipper Ron Harris. Robertson's reaction was fast and deadly. His left foot drive to the corner of the net looked a goal all the way.

The Spurs' right winger had his arm raised in goal-expectancy the minute the ball roared from his boot.

Chelsea protested that their former skipper Terry Venables, was offside. But I did not think so, nor did I see any sign of a linesman's flag being raised.

This was the perfect time for Tottenham to score. A little lucky perhaps because although their football had been super and more entertaining, they lacked real penetration.

GREASY SURFACE

But immediately the second half kicked off there was no doubting Spurs superiority.

A rainstorm half an hour before the teams were presented to the Duke of Kent had made Wembley's grass greasy on top and even the surefooted Jimmy Greaves could not dance so daintily.

Right from the first kick Alan Gilzean was beating Chelsea sweeper centre half Marvin Hinton in the air.

But the tight and competent way Ron Harris marked Greaves gave the Spurs' goal-thief little chance to exploit Gilzean's headed-down flicks.

A Saul half-volley in the tenth minute felled Alan Harris. It looked a dangerous shot.

Then a Robertson left footer in the thirteenth minute was magnificently pushed over the bar by the somersaulting Bonetti.

Charlie Cooke's dazzling dribbles took the eye. But the Chelsea finishing was confined to the headwork of Hateley and he could make little impression on Mike England.

Twice Cooke released that dynamic Chelsea right half John Hollins in the fifteenth and forty-first minutes with beautifully-timed crossfield passes to the right corner flag.

Just before Robertson got the goal which turned all Tottenham's flair into a deciding lead, Chelsea might have scored.

Mackay slashed thin air in a tough attempt to halt Cooke and Charlie floated down on goal, that deceptive body swerve confusing the Tottenham men.

CONFIDENT JENNINGS

Knowles and Venables were passed. Then Cooke fired right on target but the Jennings composure and handling was a model of class goalkeeping.

Tottenham turned on all their power in the second half. Chelsea sagged and Hateley found it increasingly difficult to make any headway against England.

Bonetti's save from Mullery in the 49th minute was a sign that he was going to have much more work.

A panicky miskick by Alan Harris as early as the 50th minute from an England header at a Spurs corner kick gave Saul the perfect opportunity to shoot home the second goal.

Greaves went in with his only decisive danger spot of the match and Harris, his constant shadow, fell back.

Suddenly Greaves shuffled those expensive feet and unleashed a snap shot which Bonetti just got over the bar.

It was marvellous for skipper Mackay to start the move which led to Tottenham's second goal in the 67th minute.

AERIAL BLAST

From one of his famous long throw-ins, the nippy little Robertson touched on the ball to Saul.

The red-haired Canvey Islander, scorer of Tottenham's important second goal in the semi-final against Nottingham Forest, spun round to poke an unstoppable right footer past Bonetti.

It was the hammer blow which sank Chelsea. Spurs slowed down the game with insolent ease.

At last Hateley got in one of his famous headers in the 84th minute—a glorious twisting aerial blast from a Baldwin cross.

The header was so fast it even beat the clockwork reactions of Jennings but it was off target.

But Chelsea surged in with a desperate late rally and their goal came in the 85th minute.

It was noticeable that several Spurs players—Venables, Mullery, Saul and Gilzean—were tiring.

Spurs got more of the luck which chased them throughout the match when Mullery brought down Baldwin just outside the goal area, but no free kick was given.

Another Baldwin header—and it was all over for an easier victory than any Tottenham player had expected.

HOW THEY GOT TO WEMBLEY

SPURS
Rd. 3: Millwall, 0—0. A
  Replay: 1—0, H.
  (Gilzean.)
Rd. 4: Portsmouth, 3—1. H.
  (Gilzean 2, Greaves.)
Rd. 5: Bristol City, 2—0. H.
  (Greaves 2.)
Rd. 6: Birmingham, 0—0. A.
  Replay: 6—0, H.
  (Venables 2, Greaves 2, Gilzean, Saul.)
Semi-final: Nottm. For., 2—1.
  Hillsborough.
  (Greaves, Saul.)

CHELSEA
Rd. 3: Huddersfield, 2—1. A.
  (Houseman, Tambling.)
Rd. 4: Brighton, 1—1. A.
  (Tambling.)
  Replay: 4—0, H.
  (Tambling 2, Hateley, Young.)
Rd. 5: Sheffield Utd., 2—0. H.
  (Tambling, Hateley.)
Rd. 6: Sheffield Wed., 1—0. H.
  (Baldwin.)
Semi-final: Leeds, 1—0. Villa Pk.
  (Hateley.)

Me and my shadow! That could be the theme song of Jimmy Greaves (right) after the way Chelsea skipper tailed him throughout the match.

COMEBACK FOR MOORE

By TUDOR JAMES

GRAHAM MOORE, Northampton's Welsh international inside forward, whose fortunes nose-dived when he left Cardiff City, wants to return home.

After being signed by Chelsea for £35,000 six years ago, Moore played during the London club's relegation and promotion seasons, then joined Manchester United before signing for Northampton who have now also been relegated.

Moore has asked for a transfer, saying he wants to join a First or Second Division club.

Still only 27 years of age, Moore may get his wish, for a Cardiff official said: "Moore helped to get us into the First Division. He might repeat the act. We made an offer some time ago but were priced out."

It was a sad Cup Final day for Moore yesterday, who must have been thinking what might have been had he stayed with Chelsea.

Bolton Bid

CARDIFF CITY'S dynamic centre-half Don Murray has alerted Bolton Wanderers' scouts, who have sent "bid now" messages to Burnden Park.

Bolton may make the plunge before Murray gains full Scottish honours, when the price would soar.

Scouts from Liverpool and Birmingham saw Newport's last game to check on a quartet of teenage players.

The talent spotters are assessing inside-left Jeff Thomas, right-back Lyn Collins, outside-right Ken Wookey, and inside-right David Pugh.

County manager Trevor Morris has started his campaign to save the club by signing full back Joe Wilson from Wolves.

Swansea manager Billy Lucas, appalled at Swan's relegation record of conceding eighty-nine goals, is hotting up his search for defenders.

His top targets are Swindon centre-half Mel Nurse, and Newport full back David Williams.

Promising

IN a bold bid to win back the crowds Glamorgan CCC may play Rugby's golden boy Keith Jarrett against the Indians, at Cardiff, on Wednesday.

An aggressive right-hand batsman, and medium pace bowler, Jarrett has been showing great promise in practice.

Said an official: "If the lad does half as much in his county cricket debut as he did against England, in his first Rugby International, he'll be a marvel."

Jarrett's chances of making an early County game soared when he took seven wickets for seven runs for Glamorgan's second team against Swansea University.

With players like Jeff Jones and Tony Cordle nagged by injuries, Glamorgan may urge Ossie Wheatley to carry on—at least until he gets his thousand wickets. He needs just seven more.

TOMMY PULLMAN, Mountain Ash skipper, is attracting the attention of Cardiff selectors.

Pullman scored 73 points last season to become runner-up in the points stakes.

Twenty-three tries for a scrum-half is a fine record in these days of close marking.

Look out for hot competition for the hooking berth in the Cardiff team next season.

Abertillery's Brian Wilkins joins the queue, which includes capable Peter Thomas and Gary Davies for the spot vacated by Bill Thomas.

Regular top class Rugby will ensure an international place for Newport's ace lock forward John Jeffrey.

That is why John is being urged to appeal to Cardiff Training College to allow him to put club before school.

Right Man

WELSH RUGBY UNION are ready to toss a timebomb at British Rugby chiefs when they meet in London next month.

Wales have never sent a manager on an overseas tour, and for the job of manager of the British Lions' South African tour next year, Wales feel they have the right man.

They will nominate Llanelli secretary Handel Rogers, who will command grudging respect from the three other nations.

One more snub could set up a wave of resentment which might sweep Wales out of British tours, and make them go it alone.

SPORT MIRROR 7

WATFORD WIN OUR GIANTKILLER CUP

Watford might have lost their first-ever F A Cup semi-final to Chelsea 5—1, but the Second Division strugglers will be pleased to learn that their magnificent performance in this season's competition has won them the Sunday Mirror Giantkiller Cup. Details about when and where the presentation is to be made will be announced later.

CHELSEA SAY

Leeds Utd 0

Manchester Utd . . 0

By FRANK McGHEE

IN the end it only proved something Chelsea should already know — whether it is Leeds or Manchester they meet in the F A Cup Final they will be up against a defence to respect and forwards to fear.

It was so close a contest, so fierce a battle that no clear favourite could emerge.

Manchester had the better of the first half. Leeds came back with pressure few others could have resisted in the second.

You couldn't even separate them on the scores of either individual stars or chances created. Each had their equal quota of both.

To match the Leeds defensive marshal, Norman Hunter, Manchester had David Sadler reading every moment of danger as adequately.

The midfield was shared equally between Bremner and Giles for Leeds, Crerand Charlton and Sartori for United.

It looked like following the one-sided route almost everyone expected for just the first sixty seconds.

That was when Manchester centre half Ian Ure found himself caught halfway between deciding whether to chest or head a clearance.

He missed it completely and Jones, through on his own, had a crisp right-foot thump saved by Stepney for a corner.

Leeds didn't get another chance as good in the whole first half.

They were managing to snuff out the main dangers, with right back Paul Reaney policing George Best and Paul Madeley shadowing Bobby Charlton.

It produced a situation recalling Manchester's great days—for every key man tightly marked another couple blossomed elsewhere.

Manchester at this stage were winning the midfield, normally Bremner and Giles's territory, so competently they were able to dictate the flow of play.

The traditional depth of the Leeds defence prevented them from penetrating too deeply.

But the pressure kept Leeds at such an anxious full stretch that they were unable to introduce many attacking ideas.

There were only brief spasms of alarm for Leeds in the second half, however.

Notably when Best spun on a ball from the right in the 67th minute and struck so powerfully that 'keeper Gary Sprake had to react with instant reflex to tip it over the bar.

Almost all the rest was one-way traffic as Leeds pushed forward intelligently and kept United penned and pinned in their own half.

George Best blamed himself for having to face the might of Leeds United a second time.

"We should have won the match in the first half. I should have won the match. I had two chances, the first was a half chance and I could see Gary Sprake was going to save the second."

The replay will be at Villa Park on Monday, March 23.

ARSENAL MAY BID HIGH FOR QUEEN

One ball that Gerry Queen didn't get. This time John McGrath outjumped him to head away and clear Southampton's lines.

He jumps on shaky Saints

Crystal Palace 2, Southampton 0: By ROY PESKETT

ARSENAL are poised to make a £100,000 bid for Gerry Queen, the Scottish centre forward whose goals are easing Crystal Palace out of the First Division relegation area.

For the fourth successive home game Arsenal sent chief scout George Male to check on him.

The Gunners have only until midnight tomorrow to decide whether they need Queen this season.

Male's report will show that Queen is an even greater player than when Palace manager Bert Head bought him from Kilmarnock last year.

His incredible leaps in the Saints penalty area not only materially helped Palace to two points, but made him look a better player than Southampton's Welsh international Ron Davies.

Manager Head refused to say anything about a possible move other than: "What can Arsenal offer more than Crystal Palace?"

Southampton could have considered themselves lucky if they had stopped Palace in this match.

Hammering away against a strong, icy wind, Palace carried on from where they had left off against the League Cup-holders, Manchester City.

In the twenty-fifth minute, from a Hoadley free-kick, David Payne gave a great display of juggling with the ball before lifting it over Southampton's shaky defence for Roger Hoy to drive home.

GREAT

The only danger to the Palace defence looked like coming from the determined efforts of Jimmy Gabriel on the half-hour. A great pass from Gabriel gave Jenkins a chance, but Blyth intercepted

There was a spontaneous penalty appeal from the Palace players when Fisher appeared to pull back Queen in the box.

Referee Kevin Howley was right up to the mark, though, and said no.

The game hung on that one goal until the eighty-sixth minute when Queen sent Taylor through to fire against goalkeeper Martin. The ball ran free to Cliff Jackson who blasted it into the net.

ENGLAND PAYS HEAVY PENALTY

Everton 3

Spurs 2

MIKE England can rarely have had a match like this, writes EDGAR TURNER.

The Spurs skipper conceded two of three penalties awarded and was given 90 minutes of trouble and frustration by skilful Joe Royle.

Everton's 75th - minute winner—they're three points clear in the championship race—came from Royle who figured in all their goals and both penalties.

England was spoken to for a foul on Royle before being penalised it seemed harshly, in the 40th minute.

England and Royle fell together, but referee Dan Lyden was right on the spot.

There was little doubt about the second penalty in the fifty-sixth minute, even though England protested again. He barged Royle in the back after a long throw-in by Brown.

This time, Ball, who had scored from the first spot kick, was foiled by Jennings. Though a linesman vigorously waved, play was allowed to continue.

There were thirty-two fouls, seventeen against Everton, who scored against Spurs at Goodison for the first time in four years.

Whittle, scorer of the only goal at White Hart Lane last week, put Everton ahead (30 minutes). Gilzean and Bond penalty, were scorers for Spurs, who also had Pearce booked.

Portsmouth 0

Millwall 1

MILLWALL broke their sequence of twenty-six away matches without a win after being mainly on the defensive in this drawn-out battle.

Their "break" came in the final minutes. Derek Possee was brought down, and Weller's free-kick was nodded home by Bolland.

But Portsmouth only have themselves to blame. They left him unmarked.

Instead of sinking to their eighth home defeat of the season, they should have made sure of victory long before Millwall scored.

They lacked the striking power of little left winger Nick Jennings, who is nursing a thigh injury.

And although Mike Trebilcock, the former Everton Cup finalist, made a powerful substitute, he did not have the same finish.

He went nearest with an early twenty-yard drive which whistled over the top, but later he was ably covered by the agile Bryan King in Millwall's goal.

Millwall's five-man defensive wall, with Burnett acting as sweeper, was able to smother the Portsmouth attack by sheer weight and power.

Only Ray Hiron looked a possible gap finder in the centre.

Once he tested King with a low level effort and, midway through the second-half, another shot shaved over the bar.

Charlton 1

Aston Villa 0

CHARLTON'S first League win after a twelve-match-four-point run should have been more convincing, writes PETER KINLAN.

While their approach work is promising, their failure to penetrate for the pay-off in goals still persists.

The sturdy Villa defence had snuffed out a series of dangerous moves. Then towards the end of the first half Harry Gregory's goal-mouth prompt gave Peacock a chance.

The winger was lucky. His first shot rebounded off defender Keith Bradley's body and he was also to clinch the second.

After the interval Villa nearly snatched an equaliser as their relegation-haunted companions' composure was ruffled by a searing reprisal.

Charlton survived uneasily when goalmouth shots from Welsh international Barry Hole and Turnbull struck defenders, and burly George Curtis hammered a shot inches off target.

But after this panic, Charlton regained their poise and earlier control, although they still could not find a finishing punch.

Industrious Ray Treacy, foiled by Villa goalkeeper John Dunn, earned most credit in the Charlton attack.

Enfield 1

Skelmersdale . 0

ENFIELD, those ace trophy hunters, are through to their third F A Amateur Cup Final in six years. They did it the hard, nail-biting way.

Brave Skelmersdale, to their eternal credit, gave the London club some anxious moments.

But with a 75th minute smash and grab goal from centre forward Peter Feeley, Enfield cashed in on a Skelmersdale midfield boob.

There were no fancy thrills about Enfield's play, with straight-for-the-line attacks which smashed through.

However, Skem refused to be knocked off their sure, swift and, on occasions, skilful game.

St Albans . . . 1

Dagenham . . . 1

What was bubbling into a breezy battle for a first ever Wembley place with a Dagenham goal after 14 minutes—through a John Still header—equalised by a 4th minute injury-time effort by John Butterfield—fizzled flat.

Within minutes of the final whistle at Millwall both managers were seeking postponements of midweek games.

But Dagenham will play at Redhill tomorrow night. St. Albans are due to meet Hertford on Tuesday.

Dagenham's dynamos shredded the St. Albans defence in the first fiery forty minutes. But St. Albans lost their ragged look when they tightened up

NEW STRIKER BELL ROCKS THE CROCKS

Halifax 1, Reading 1

READING are probably wishing that Alan Ball's request to have this game postponed had found favour with the Football League.

At least it would have spared them the embarrassment of being held to a draw by a team including two half-fit men and a reserve winger.

Former Hartlepool inside forward Terry Bell showed up well in his debut and paid back part of the £6,000 Reading paid for him when he crashed home a cross from left winger Bobby Williams after 44 minutes.

Reading, jittery defence and all, looked to have the points parcelled up. But Halifax finally got the goal they deserved, when Dave Shawcross thumped home a corner by McCarthy two minutes from time.

Blackburn 2

Oxford 0

OXFORD'S stubborn defence, one of the best in the Second Division, fell to second-half goals by Darling and Goodwin.

They made a lively start and for a brief spell looked as though they might gain control. This promise had faded badly by the interval

In the first half Oxford missed two easy chances of snatching the lead. A Colin Clarke shot was brilliantly saved at close range by Barton.

Oxford had no raider to compare with Darling and they couldn't produce a defender to match full back Charter.

WALES GET TRIPLE-CROWN BLUES

Ireland 14 pts, Wales 0: By TUDOR JAMES

THIS was not just a win for Ireland. Champions Wales were almost annihilated in a staggering second-half collapse.

They had piled on the early pressure, yet the game changed hands when Irish hero Barry McGann dropped a stunning 57th minute goal. Wales never recovered.

So Wales slithered badly off course on the final lap of their Triple Crown chase. It is eighteen years since Wales won the Crown in Ireland and the hoodoo persists.

The fiery Irish never looked the underdogs; nor Wales the champions.

Fly-half McGann played his best game for Ireland; the power and speed of wing forward Fergus Slattery made a great impact, and Ken Goodall was an eager ally in the destruction of Wales.

Another Irish hero, Tom Kiernan, who has broken all British Rugby records with his 47th cap, wept openly as he was chaired off the field after his greatest—and perhaps his last—game for Ireland.

There were occasional flashes of brilliance from Mike Gibson, while Duggan made his mark with an epic try. He ran over fifty yards to touch down.

The Welsh play was sometimes as patchy as an old quilt. For once, famous half backs Gareth Edwards and Barry John made incredible mistakes, with John dropping the ball constantly.

There was a lamentable lack of skill among the backs. Too often they were like prisoners on parole—afraid to run.

Wales slid from brilliance to mediocrity to suffer their biggest defeat by Ireland since 1925.

Wales won the lines-outs with Delme Thomas dominating, while Jeff Young won the hooking duel.

With these advantages it was amazing to see Wales slip to ignominious defeat.

Once again Wales suffered because they had no recognised kicker. There was a complete mix-up over the goal kicking.

Skipper Edwards relieved John Williams after one attempt and they were seen to be arguing during the match.

IRELAND. — Tries: Duggan, Goodall. Drop: McGann. Conv.: Kiernan. Pen.: Kiernan.

Staffordshire 11 pts, Gloucestershire 9

SALUTE Staffordshire—county Rugby's new boys who become county champions after this thriller final at Burton-on-Trent, writes GARY NEWBON.

Staffs, the under-dogs, only entered the county championship in 1964.

At the end of their greatest hour Staffs skipper and England lock-forward Mike Davis was carried shoulder-high to the dressing-room.

Waiting for him there alongside a crate of champagne was a cork-wrencher given to Davis by an optimistic fan before the match.

Davis told me: "We were very confident of justifying the champagne."

They certainly were! Determined Staffs, with scrum-half Jan Webster in sparkling form, rushed to an early lead before issuing Glos with a "catch us if you can" challenge.

Staffs, whose choice of second-half weapons was a superb tackling performance, will now play a Rest of England XV later this season.

Saddest man this weekend is Glos scrum-half John Morris, the county's prolific points-scorer who must have left his kicking boots at home in Lydney.

Morris, who has scored two-thirds of his side's points this season, missed four penalty-goal attempts and two conversion attempts.

CUP TICKETS.—Chelsea's allocation of 16,000 F A Cup Final tickets will be distributed by the programme voucher system that they have operated all season. Six thousand season ticket holders will automatically get a ticket.

BACHER SKIPPERS SPRINGBOKS TOUR

The South African cricket touring party for England this summer is one of the strongest sent. There are 148 Test appearances between them and only two of the fourteen didn't play in the victorious series against Australia. They are opener Arthur Short (22) and fast bowler Gary Watson. Ali Bacher leads the team. Other players are: Eddie Barlow, Barry Richards, Graeme Pollock, Lee Irvine, Denis Lindsay, Tiger Lance, Mike Procter, Peter Pollock, Pat Trimborn, John Traicos and Grahame Chevalier.

THEY WERE SO WORRIED

BUT HERO HOUSEMAN PUTS THEM THROUGH TO WEMBLEY

Chelsea 5, Watford 1: By KEN MONTGOMERY

INEVITABLY, and eventually irresistibly, Chelsea's team of all talents swept through the sands of White Hart-lane and into their third FA Cup Final.

Poor Watford, 50-1 outsiders of the Cup's last quartet, were left like twelve battered bodies—riddled by a football firing squad.

Yet Chelsea, now unbeaten in their last eleven outings, gave their supporters bouts of first half heart failure with probably their worst forty-five minute performance of the season.

Even manager Dave Sexton confessed: "I was worried until we got our second goal."

That was understandable. For, with half the match gone, Ken Furphy's gold-shirted Watford warriors were still level—and giving their First Division rivals as good as they got.

The Cup shock of this or any other season looked on.

But dreams of a 20th century David slaughtering a Soccer Goliath were wrecked by Chelsea's superb second-half goal blitz.

Sexton's super-side went into their tea break looking like a side who needed their batteries recharged.

They re-emerged as the cultured aristocrats with the in-built killer instinct that could take the FA Cup to Stamford Bridge at long last.

Watford had no complaints. Furphy himself walked straight into the Chelsea dressing-room at the end to say: "Well done—now go on and win the Cup. You can do it."

Furphy did not forget his own shattered players, who had made such a remarkable fight of it.

"We really stretched them until well into the second half. We've done tremendously well, even getting this far," he said.

Watford looked set up for complete annihilation when they went one down after only 154 seconds.

But with Stewart Scullion giving Eddie McCreadie a rare old wing roasting, Watford forced a shock equaliser, and might even have gone in front before referee Gordon Hill turned the teams round.

Chelsea just couldn't get into top gear, and while there was still an obvious class difference, Watford's tremendous effort more than made up for their lack of skill.

OSGOOD BOOED

It was a totally unhappy half for Chelsea, the hottest semi-final favourites for years, and Peter Osgood was booed constantly after crash-tackling centre half Walter Lees.

Lees, who handcuffed Chelsea's man-of-menace throughout the opening half, recovered after treatment.

But, like the rest of his enthusiastic team-mates, he was overwhelmed when Chelsea put on the second-half style.

Chelsea's opening goal came from a left-wing Alan Hudson corner, headed on by John Dempsey for full back David Webb to scoop the ball home.

Watford equalised after eleven minutes with that busy little blonde, Terry Garbett, taking a Scullion pass forty yards out and sprinting unchallenged for another twenty before sending his shot skimming over the sand dunes and over Peter Bonetti's outstretched arms.

The second half slaughter chart read like this:

Fifty-seven minutes: Osgood silenced his barrackers with a beautifully-headed goal from man-of-the-match Peter Houseman's superbly chipped left-wing centre.

Seventy-three minutes: Houseman raced on to Ian Hutchinson's through-ball to stab home Chelsea's third.

Seventy-five minutes: Hudson put Osgood through, he helped the ball on to Hutchinson, and the shot flew high behind Walker to make it four.

Seventy-nine minutes: Houseman completed the nap-hand with Hudson's assistance to round off his memorable match and take Chelsea's goal tally to an impressive twenty-one in six ties this season.

Osgood flashed home a sixth in the final seconds, but referee Hill refused to allow it, because Osgood's shouting had distracted Watford's already demoralised defence.

But whether Chelsea, who have written London's greatest sporting story for years, meet Manchester United or Leeds at Wembley on April 11, they will have to get cracking earlier than they did here.

■ Chelsea striker Tommy Baldwin, who asked for a transfer on Friday, could get a beat-the-deadline move to Newcastle.

Five helpless Watford men might have guessed. David Webb, who opened Chelsea's scoring in the sixth round tie against Q P R, does it again. It's Wembley ahoy.

Ref raps Moore

West Ham 0, Ipswich 0

AFTER ninety minutes of niggling fouls, pushes in the back, and wild kicking, Ipswich gained a precious point in their fight against relegation.

They just about earned it, if only because neither side deserved to win.

It was a sad, sad match. Even Geoff Hurst and Bobby Moore were spoken to by referee Roger Kirkpatrick as the ill-feeling bubbled over.

Hurst was ticked off for disputing a throw-in and Moore for mimicking the referee.

The England skipper was annoyed when a foul was given against him and imitated Mr. Kirkpatrick's roly-poly run.

But Moore had a great match. He was everywhere, pushing out accurate ground passes and through-balls which his forwards never used.

Only Hurst showed punch in front of goal for the Hammers. It looked as though he had clinched the match eight minutes from time. But David Best made an india-rubber save

Hero Best, injured in the fourth minute after falling on his right shoulder, spent the rest of the match lurching along his goal-line, his arm hanging limply.

Twice he fell on the shoulder, and had to be treated.

Ipswich, with Peter Morris and Ian Collard combining well in midfield, had their chances and missed them.

A goalless draw looked on the cards from the early minutes. If anyone had scored, it would probably have been the frisky Mr. Kirkpatrick.

Colchester 1
Brentford 1

BRENTFORD plundered the first half honours and looked worth far more than their one-goal interval lead.

But United did enough second half work to win.

And Ken Jones blasted home a fifty-eighth-minute corner from Brian Hall.

Skipper Bobby Ross gave his side their thirty-seventh minute lead just when Brentford looked worth a hatful.

They ran riot among the Colchester forwards, winning most of the loose balls and coming out of tackles in possession.

New leader Roger Cross, the £10,000 buy from West Ham, was always lively and had a hand in Ross's goal.

Barnet 8
Mossley 1

GOALKEEPER Wyn Dicken's bravery was about the only thing the Cheshire League side had to offer in this FA Challenge Trophy quarter-final.

Ricky George slipped two first-half goals past Dicken—one direct from a corner—before ex-Manchester City player Dave Roberts got one back with a fiftieth-minute penalty.

Mossley pressed hard for five minutes after that—and were then hit for six more. Les Eason scored a hat-trick, Colin Powell got two and Billy Meadows scored the other.

It was a triumph for Barnet captain Gerry Ward. The ex-Arsenal man plans to retire at the end of this season . . . and hopes to lead Barnet to victory at Wembley in his last match.

Hillingdon 0
Chelmsford . . . 0

THESE two Southern League sides will have to replay tomorrow to decide who goes into the FA Challenge Trophy semi-final.

Neither side had a forward clever or penetrating enough to settle the game.

Hillingdon's most dangerous moment came two minutes before the break when defenders Dickie Moore hit a post

John Cozens, Hillingdon's top scorer, may miss the replay because of a leg injury.

Tommy Knox, the ex-Chelsea player signed from St. Mirren, had a good home debut

QPR 0
Bolton 4

RANGERS' promotion hopes were gunned down by a Bolton line brilliantly led by former England and Liverpool star Roger Hunt.

He scored two goals and set up the others as he overshadowed the considerable talent of Rodney Marsh.

It was Rangers biggest home defeat of the season.

Hunt scored in the 12th minute and had one ruled offside before he headed in No. 2 in the second half. It was all Bolton after that, with Roy Greaves and John Byrom getting the others.

Rangers' full back Ian Gillard was carried off minutes from the end with a leg injury and Alan Harris substituted.

ARSENAL PAIR STRIKE AGAIN

Arsenal 2, Liverpool 1: By GEORGE CRANFIELD

ARSENAL'S Fairs Cup heroes Jon Sammels and John Radford, fresh from their triumph in Rumania last week, gave Highbury an encore.

The men who boosted Gunners to a 2—0 first leg win against Dinamo Bacau were on target again. And if anything they found Liverpool even easier opponents.

Arsenal were never in danger of dropping a point, not even when Liverpool skipper Yeats scrambled a goal from Bobby Graham's corner seven minutes from time.

Solid in defence with the return of Simpson and free moving in attack, where George Graham shone, Arsenal coasted home after going in front.

Goalkeeper Wilson picked up his easiest win bonus of the season. He never had a serious shot to save and only once had to put himself out.

That was when he daringly dived at the feet of clean-through Bobby Graham in the twenty-ninth minute.

Five minutes earlier George Graham took on and beat Hughes and Lawler to give a perfect cross which Sammels roared to meet and head in.

Arsenal should have been at least three up at half-time.

MAGNIFICENT

George headed against the bar in the third minute, after another good move by George Graham, and busy goalkeeper Clemence made a magnificent save from George a minute before the break.

Frank McLintock sent Charlie George racing through, but the goalkeeper came out to narrow the angle and then dived superbly to his right to deflect the shot for a corner.

It was George again, sending a header against the bar in the fifty-sixth minute, who set up Arsenal for their second.

Radford seized on the rebound and with a saucy overhead kick lobbed the ball over Clemence just inside the far post.

Marinello, whom Arsenal said in their programme would not be at his best until next season, decided to show some of his class.

The £100,000 winger from Hibernian started the move which led to Arsenal's second goal went off on his own straight down the middle.

He raced on, drew Clemence off his line, and whipped the ball high into the net.

It had him dancing with joy until he found he had been given offside.

It was a near thing and certainly pleased the fans who had been waiting for such a show from the new man.

FAIRBROTHER KEEPS ORIENT TOP

Bury 0
Orient 1

CRAFTY Orient let Bury do all the early running and then pulled out the important goal in the seventy-fifth minute to keep them at the top of the Third Division.

Bury could say they were unlucky, for they had a Hince "goal" disallowed, two other shots were headed off the line and they lost winger Grundy after fifteen minutes with a hip injury.

But Orient were much the better team. They back-pedalled for much of the game but never lost control.

When they were sure Bury had no more steam, they moved assuredly into top gear and went for the win.

It was from a Brabrook cross that Barry Fairbrother hit a 25-yard rising shot to score the all-important goal.

For Bury, Kerr had the probing skill and Jones the dash and enthusiasm, but they received little support

Bury had no one to compare with Orient's midfield generals, Plume and Dyson.

On the two occasions Jones and Kerr went close, 'keeper Goddard made great saves.

Slips cost Luton dear

Luton 2, Mansfield 2

LUTON are placing far too much reliance on the probing qualities of Malcolm MacDonald, their chief match winner this season.

He had a good, but unlucky first half in which he could have had a hat-trick.

This was the margin by which Luton should have led at half-time. Instead, they were limited to a deflected goal from right back John Ryan.

The second half began with a burst of three goals in six minutes.

First Roberts levelled, then Harrison restored Luton's lead, only for Partridge to make it 2—2. The Luton defence must take the blame for both Mansfield goals.

After their second goal Mansfield withdrew into a defensive shell which Luton were unable to penetrate.

Fulham 2, Rochdale 0

VIC HALOM, Fulham's expensive buy from Orient, stepped out of a long stint in the reserves to snap two first-half goals and victory. But for the brilliance of Rochdale's keeper Harker, he could have hit a hat-trick.

Fulham ran riot and only Harker prevented them shooting into an unassailable lead at half-time.

Wingers Les Barrett and Jimmy Conway and strikers Steve Earle and Halom carved openings galore from menacing passes by Barry Lloyd, who improves every outing.

Earle should have had an early goal when the Rochdale 'keeper dived at his feet and pulled him to the turf. But the referee refused a penalty.

After the break the old Fulham failing was apparent again. Their early sparkle and punch vanished and they struggled against Rochdale's very ordinary defence.

Doncaster 1, Gillingham 0

AN early penalty award gave Doncaster victory. And Gillingham are now almost certain to pay for it with relegation.

Gillingham centre half David Galvin brought down Rovers winger Archie Irvine in the box. And centre forward Steve Briggs had no trouble beating 'keeper Simpson from the spot.

At times Gillingham played good football and did most of the early pressing. Right-half Ray Bailey was only inches off target with a glancing header

In the second half a back-pass was intercepted by Brian Yeo who rounded Rovers' 'keeper John Ogston and squared the ball back across the face of the goal.

But none of his team-mates were in position to take the simple chance. Gillingham came back toward the end but despite the efforts of Andy Smillie, their best forward. Doncaster held on.

This was only the sixth occasion extra time has had to be played since the Final was switched from Stamford Bridge to Wembley in 1923. Leeds have been involved in two of them, the other in 1965 when they

lost to Liverpool 2—1. The others were in 1938, when Preston beat Huddersfield 1—0, 1946 with Charlton going down to Derby 4—1, 1947; Charlton beat Burnley 1—0, 1968; Everton crashing to W B A 1—0.

LEEDS KEEP A PROMISE

That vital twenty-first minute when Chelsea fell behind to a sloppy goal. Charlton (7th left) was the scorer after a goal-line catastrophe by Harris and McCreadie.

NEWPORT TAMED BY TIGERS

Leicester 13 pts. Newport 3

NEWPORT made a flattering start and led by a penalty goal at half-time, but they could not keep up a cracking pace.

A Leicester win seemed far away in the first-half, for rarely have they gained less of the ball this season.

They were outplayed in the line-out, thanks to Gareth Jones and Len Martin.

Alan Evans was a controlling force at scrum half for the Welshmen, kicking shrewdly to help his forwards and checking some big Leicester rallies in which Matthews, Rowell and Andrews were prominent.

Short kicks by Raybould and Cornwall gave the Tigers plenty of trouble, but Robin

Money came through a tough match with colours flying.

One exciting bout of handling ended with Skirving crossing the home line but the referee ruled that the ball was not grounded correctly.

With half-time three minutes away, Anthony landed a penalty goal for Newport from twenty-six yards, but it did not do full justice to the Welsh grip on the game.

Even the Leicester crowd did not count on their side bouncing back in such decisive action as they did less than a minute after the interval.

The try by Rowell was entirely due to the forwards, who wheeled on the Newport line for the big second-row

forward to gain the touchdown.

Barker lifted the Tigers in front with a first-class conversion from a wide angle.

From then on the contest developed along dour lines with breathtaking tackles by both sides.

Garry Sutton, the Newport prop, made a big impact on the game fith his intelligent work in the loose, and the Newport back row tried all they knew to penetrate the Leicester barrier.

A penalty goal by Barker was followed by a splendid interception tha gave Harrison a ry in injury time, converted by Barker.

LEICESTER. — Tries : Rowell, Harrison; convs: Barker (2); pen.; Barker.

NEWPORT.—Pen: Anthony.

Pontypool . 10 pts
Rugby . 8

RICHIE PUGH snatched this game out of the fire for Pontypool with a try in the last two minutes of injury time.

With scores level, the former Welsh youth international took the conversion attempt himself and the ball bounced over from an upright.

Scrum-half Gwyn Williams went off with a bruised rib after 35 minutes and Pugh had to switch from centre to full back

It was Pontypool's skipper Terry Cobner whom Rugby had mainly to blame for their defeat.

He rallied his depleted pack in fine style and did the work of two men in the loose. And Cobner paved the way for Pugh's try by following up a punt into Rugby's 25 and then shaking off a defender to leave a clear path to the line.

PONTYPOOL.—Tries: T. Cobner, R. Pugh, Convs: Pugh (2).

RUGBY. — Try: G. Melville. Pens.: S. Martin. Convs.: S. Martin.

Coventry in Gwyther bid

By TUDOR JAMES

TEARAWAY David Gwyther, Swansea's 21-year-old goal-bomber, is a top target of Coventry City.

Their scouts saw David score the two golden goals at Newport which made promotion certain for Swansea and have written rave reports.

With 23 goals, powerfully - built Gwyther helped to sweep Swans through a great spell of ten away games without defeat

David is piling up a substantial bonus for himself. Five thousand pounds is being awarded Swansea players on a points system, and the goal-hungry centre forward hasn't missed a match.

It's the kind of service which has impressed Coventry, who believe he is ready for First Division Soccer.

SELECTION PROBLEMS

THE ironclad midfield club partnership between £110,000 Terry Hennessey and Alan Durban, of Derby, can provide the Welsh padlock to hold world champions England, at Cardiff, on Saturday.

Manager Dave Bowen can play the pair with Leeds' 19-year-old Terry Yorath in a devastating middle trio.

Major selection problems for Bowen will be to decide whether he plays John Toshack (Cardiff) or Dick Krzywicki (Huddersfield) with Ron Davies (Southampton) and Wyn Davies (Newcastle) up front.

Another surprise choice could be Charlton's strongman Graham Moore.

A FLY HALF windfall is on the way for the talent-crammed Cardiff Rugby club.

Lining up for the key role, in the hard training sessions planned for the summer will be British Lion star Barry John, Secondary School's cap Ian Lewis, who is captain of the successful Cardiff Training College side, and Gabe Servini, of Aberdare.

Another star in the queue, to play with the great Gareth Edwards, is skilful Barry born Vaughan Williams.

Edwards and Wiliams played together for the famous Millfield school, winning Wales secondary schools honours against Yorkshire and France.

Lucky Cardiff also have versatile Gary Samual waiting in the wings.

SOUTH AFRICA CO-OPERATES

IT'S the big break through in world Rugby.

This week England send out invitations to the three coloured Rugby Unions in South Africa to attend their centenary celebrations this year.

Most significant is that the white South Africans have concurred, and even provided the addresses of the coloured Unions.

WELSH wonder boy John Williams, of Maesteg, will be quitting the track to return to the Rugby scene.

Captain of the strong Cardiff Training College atheltic team, linking John will compete in this year's Commonwealth Games before leaving the track

Convinced that athletics and Rugby don't mix, the Bridgend flyer turned away from Rugby when he was ignored for the trials this year.

Now he has made a welcome about-turn and said: "Rugby is in my blood, and I want to get back."

NEATH LOSE TWO STARS

DOUBLE blow for Neath Rugby club will be the loss of their flying winger Hywel Williams and flank forward Alan Thomas.

Sprinter Hywel is finding the journey from Cardigan for training and matches too irksome and he intends playing for the seaside club. Former Wales and Newport star Thomas is taking a job in London.

Better news is that Owen Jones, the Amman Valley utility player, will join Neath next season.

Boyo James, Bridgend's popular tough prop forward, is joining valley club. Penycray.

Farthing too much for Tredegar

Taunton 12 pts., Tredegar 9

A GAME peppered with penalty kicks and dropped goal attempts ended with Taunton's sixth victory in a row.

Main interest for home supporters centred on Taunton's place kicker Roger Farthing, who reached a season's total of 200 points with the third of his four penalties.

The sides were evenly matched. Tredegar three times equalising Taunton's scores before Farthing's boot again edged his side in front.

Barry Burridge, Taunton's powerful young second row

forward, was the outstanding player on the field.

Tredegar's best try-scoring opportunity came when scrum half Terry Francis made a fine break but he held on to the ball too long and the chance was lost.

TAUNTON.—Pens.: Farthing (4). **TREDEGAR.** Drop: Davies; pens.: Thomas (2).

Penarth 14 pts., Weston 14

PENARTH'S last home match of the current campaign sprang to life after half an hour.

Bryn Davies, Ken Davies, and Mike Edwards, who went off midway through the second half with a

broken collarbone, drove into the rucks with determination.

Penarth's left wing, Alan Barham, playing only his second game, scored two first-half tries, following good approach work by his forwards.

Debut-making centre Bob Fry opened his account with a second-half try, showing good initiative in supporting Barham following a breakdown in the Weston handling.

PENARTH.—Tries: A. Barham (2). R. Fry. Conv.: Woodham. Pen.: Woodham.

WESTON.—Tries: P. Anderson, C. Brown, R. Hazzard. Conv.: Hazzard. Pen.: Hazzard.

EDDIE GRAY, the Leeds left winger, was voted man-of-the-match by the Football Writers. He got a decisive 72 votes, with second man Peter Bonetti (Chelsea) receiving 24. Billy Bremner was third with four votes.

For referee Eric Jennings (Stourbridge) it will be his second Cup Final replay. In 1967 he was in charge of the Enfield-Skelmersdale F A Amateur Cup Final at Wembley which ended goalless. Enfield won at Maine-road 3—0.

BUT CHELSEA HOLD ON

GREAT WEMBLEY GAME ENDS EVEN, FIRST FINAL DRAW SINCE 1912

Chelsea 2, Leeds 2 (after extra time) By FRANK McGHEE

LEEDS won everything at Wembley except the F A Cup. For the first time ever at this stadium the Final will have to be replayed—at Old Trafford on April 29.

The last time it was needed was in 1912, when Barnsley and West Bromwich Albion drew 0—0 at Crystal Palace and Barnsley won 1—0 at the second attempt.

Only consolation for Leeds is that they can never surely play so well again without winning.

They can never go through again with so much domination and so little luck.

Almost throughout the match they were on top and in control, hitting the woodwork three times and rendering Chelsea virtually unrecognisable from the side which has played so excitingly this season.

Chelsea were there mainly to survive somehow, and it was virtually a miracle that they made it.

WEBB WAS MESMERISED

For the first fifteen minutes it was Leeds who controlled the most important part of the field—helped by the unaccountable failure of Chelsea to even attempt close marking on Bremner and Giles.

It gave Leeds freedom from the midfield to spray the ball to all corners of the field.

It was especially dangerous when Gray, the young Scottish left winger, was loping forward and mesmerising full back Webb.

There was nothing frantic about Leeds in this spell.

They were keeping their promise to entertain and play adventurously.

The sort of pressure Leeds were mounting might have given them a goal in the 16th minute when a great tackle by right back Madeley on Cooke launched him in a run up the right.

He fed Lorimer with a neat through ball and Chelsea 'keeper Bonetti had to go up in a back-wrenching arc to tip over a tremendous shot for a corner.

Within a minute Madeley was in action in his own penalty area, just beating outside right Baldwin to a cross from the left in the first worthwhile Chelsea attack—which was promptly followed by another.

Baldwin flighting a ball forward to the strangely lethargic Cooke who pushed it further for inside left Hutchinson to snap a header wide.

But this was no lengthy Chelsea revival. It ended in the twenty-first minute with a Leeds goal as sloppy as the rest of their play had been attractive.

Jack Charlton, up for a corner curled carefully in from the right by Gray, made contact in the air with Bonetti impaled by the cluster of men around him the ball almost trickled over the line with two Chelsea defenders well placed to block it.

Chelsea should have scored in the thirty-ninth minute when Osgood angled a tremendous right-foot drive after Hollins had crossed and Hutchinson helped the ball forward.

The shot went past 'keeper Sprake, but Charlton, after getting the ball tangled between his legs almost on the line, managed to turn with it dangerously and scrape it away.

Two minutes later Chelsea were level—and again the goal was a freakish affair.

Inside right Houseman was fully twenty-five yards out when he let fly more in hope than expectation.

Sprake seemed to have the shot comfortably covered, but although he gathered it into his arms it still slipped through for the equaliser.

Leeds had one brief spell of alarm early in the second half when Chelsea, by sheer strength, managed to force themselves out of the morass of attacks threatening to swamp them.

ONE SPELL OF ALARM

Sprake had to come out bravely to smother a shot from Hutchinson and was still stranded when it broke clear for Osgood to drive for goal and Hunter to thunder up from nowhere to clear on the line.

From that point I have seldom seen a side dominate a game as completely as Leeds did without any luck at all.

Again Chelsea had to pull every man back in an attempt to cope. An extract from my notes tells me how they scrambled through.

Fifty-five minutes: Giles reaches Lorimer on right with firm pass headed forward for Jones to hit perfectly—with Bonetti making a marvellous diving save as Bremner rushed in hunting a rebound.

Fifty-seven minutes: A cross from the right and again Bonetti was perfectly placed to make the save from a Jones header look easy.

Sixty-two minutes: Gray tormented and left behind Webb for the umpteenth time, but couldn't score.

Sixty-four minutes: Cooper makes a run past three men, keeping the ball close to the byline with impeccable control, but McCreadie crushed Jones' lunge for the cross with a great tackle and appeals for a penalty firmly rejected.

Seventy minutes: Chelsea centre forward Osgood back in defence like the rest got his face in the way of a Lorimer blast and Jones was injured going for the rebound.

HAPPIER RESULTS

To make the Leeds frustration all the harder to bear, in the 79th-minute Gray shuffled through on to a Giles through ball then suddenly checked to smash a tremendous shot against the bar.

Five minutes later, Leeds hit the woodwork yet again—but with happier results.

This time Giles crossed from the right. Clarke's diving header came back off the upright and Chelsea centre half Dempsey swivelling in a desperate attempt to clear put the ball to Leeds centre forward Jones who crashed it joyously in.

That joy was only brief. Two minutes later Chelsea were level again.

A free kick taken by Ron Harris on the left was pushed back for Hollins to cross and Hutchinson went up beating Charlton in the air to score with the header of a lifetime.

So it went into extra time with both sides weary, now prone to the sort of mistake Leeds made when a free kick wasn't properly cleared and Chelsea centre half John Dempsey had a right foot thump tipped over by Sprake for a corner.

Then almost unbelievably, Leeds came within inches yet again.

Gray crossed from the byline and Giles cracked it perfectly only for Webb to block on the line.

Aberdeen. . . . 3
Celtic 1

ABERDEEN won the Scottish Cup for the first time in twenty-three years when they beat hot favourites Celtic at Hampden Park.

They just about deserved their victory. Fortune favoured them when they most needed it, but their deep defensive tactics proved the answer to the skill and pace of Celtic.

A hotly-disputed first-half penalty paved the way for Aberdeen.

Brogan handled a harmless-looking Mackay cross in the penalty area and Harper scored from the spot.

Gemmell protested so much about the decision that he was booked.

Celtic's all-out attacking bid to retrieve the situation proved their downfall.

Midway through the second half Forrest broke away and after Williams could only parry his shot Mackay had a simple task to score.

Three minutes from time, Lennox pulled one back for Celtic but Mackay ended any hopes of a comeback when he scored Aberdeen's third a minute later.

It was a great day for Aberdeen, who had a tremendous skipper in 19-year-old Martin Buchan.

It was a sad day for Celtic, who had little luck. They will now be more keen than ever to beat Leeds and reach the European Cup final.

BEVAN WONDER DASH LAUNCHES TIRED CARDIFF ON LATE SPREE

Ebbw Vale 0 pts, Cardiff 16: By TUDOR JAMES

JOHN BEVAN, Cardiff's 19-year-old winger, broke the stalemate after an hour, with a magnificent try, to start a Cardiff spree.

Taking the ball in his stride, the tall, jinking student from Ferndale left a wake of ruin as opponents groped for him, without success.

This 40-yard dazzling try saved the game from a lingering death.

Bevan is obviously of international class, and will come into the reckoning next season.

His college mate from Cardiff College of Education, Robin Williams, the Welsh shadow full-back, converted the try to bring his colossal score for the season to 350 points.

Minutes later Cardiff wing Lyn Jones put in a quicksilver spurt, to make the game safe.

Another penalty goal by Robin Williams, and his conversion of a Lyn Baxter try merely rubbed into the wounds of tired Ebbw Vale.

Showing obvious signs of battle fatigue after a strenuous season, the teams failed to reach the heights.

Two splendid scrum halves Gareth Edwards and Glyn Turner, tried desperately to inject some sparkle into the play.

Turner, who had scored twenty-four tries this season, gave the talented Edwards a hard match, although the Cardiff man many times burst through in his inimitable style, and was three times held up only yards out.

Arthur Lewis, Ebbw Vale's new cap at centre, and a seventeen-try scorer, had an enterprising eager partner in Graham Evans.

They made the experienced Ken Jones and Roy Duggan defend constantly.

Jones sometimes showed his panther-style stride when he took a pass, or snatched a loose ball.

Cardiff reserve Alan Hardwicke, a fourth choice at fly half, showed the club's depth of talent.

Cardiff's front row of Roger Beard, Meirion Davis and Howard Norris were formidable, for the big push won the ball in the scrums.

Still the Vale forwards gave their more illustrious opponents a lesson in loose play, where Peter Eastwood and Peter Moyle gained possession.

The steel town's pack ruthlessly exploited every Cardiff mistake, and made the brilliant Edwards their constant target.

The Welsh scrum half received protection from his back row of John Hickey, John James and Mervyn John, when the floodgates opened with tremendous home forward effort.

CARDIFF.—Tries: Bevan, Lyn Jones, Baxter. Convs.: Williams (2). Pen.: Williams.

London Welsh 29 pts., Wasps 3

LONDON Welsh surged to a crushing victory with the menacing Alan Richards bursting through for two great tries to start a second half rout.

They had an early setback, Mervyn Davies, one of their eight internationals, was off the field for thirty-four minutes with a cut.

Yet still the Welsh kept the play moving their way, although their handling fell below its usual high standard.

They roared in front with tries by Taylor and Phillips. The formidable John Williams converted the second.

Five minutes before half time, Tony Harry gave the Wasps hope by landing a penalty. Later he went on to miss three chances.

With Mervyn Davies back in the second half, the Welsh pounded into the attack. Davies and Phillips added two tries and Williams converted three times and landed a penalty.

Wasps had nothing to offer in attack. Harry's missed penalty chances wrecked their fight to get back into the game.

LONDON WELSH.—Tries: Richards (2), Phillips (2), Taylor, Davies; cons.: Williams (4); pen.: Williams.
WASPS.—Pen.: Harry.

SWAIN BREAKS IN

Aberavon 30 pts, Swansea 9

CONTINUING their end-of-season improvement Aberavon were much too strong for Swansea. It was one way traffic during the second half.

The Wizards made all the running and served up some entertaining Rugby as they gathered in the points.

Ultimately, Aberavon won by three placed goals, two penalty goals, and three tries, against two penalty goals and one try.

Basically this was a good team performance by skipper Billy Mainwaring, and his hard-running Wizards

Every player blended into a purposeful attacking combination.

For exile Malcolm Swain, however, it was yet another good match to make his Easter vacation back home in Wales worthwhile.

This former secondary schools international who is now a PE teacher in the Midlands, had the quick penetrative touch to take the three-quarter line through.

His link-up with fly half Ray Wilkins and veteran centre John Simonson paid dividends.

The hard-running Simonson got a hat-trick of tries as the Swansea defence crumbled before a series of swift assaults.

Swansea skipper Stuart Davies in the second half switched from wing to centre in an attempt to pep up the back play.

Ultimately, it was some good running by Davies that paved the way to Swansea's only try which came late in the game and was scored by No. 8 Roger Hyndman.

Swansea's other points came from two penalty goals kicked by full back Ray Jones.

Aberavon built a commanding 11—3 lead by half-time with tries by Brian Donovan, Robert Fleay and John Simonson, with one conversion by Ray Wilkins.

In the second half Alan Martin kicked a penalty goal and Ray Wilkins also kicked a penalty goal.

The Aberavon tries during this period came from Viv Jenkins and John Simonson (2). Wilkins added the goal points to two of the tries.

ABERAVON.—Tries: Donovan, Fleay, Simonson (3), Jenkins; convs.: Wilkins (3); pens.: Martin, Wilkins.
SWANSEA.—Try: Hyndman; pens.: Jones (2).

JACKLIN TRAILS

BRITISH Open golf champion Tony Jacklin said: "Now I need a pair of 67s" after finishing eight shots behind the second round leaders in the US Masters' at Augusta, Georgia.

Jacklin returned a 36-hole total of 147. Americans Bert Yancey and Gene Littler—on 139—led the 48 qualifiers

The only other British player to survive the cut, made at 150, was Little Aston professional Maurice Bembridge, who scored a 72 to add to his first-round 77 for 149.

Three Britons failed to survive. They were Bernard Gallacher (151), Peter Butler (154) and amateur Michael Bonallack (161).

139—B. Yancey, 69-70; G. Littler, 69-70.
140—B. Lunn, 70-70; B. Casper, 72-68.
142—T. Aaron, 68-74; G. Player (S A), 74-68.
143—T. Kono (Japan), 75-68; D. Hill, 73-70.
144—D. Stockton, 72-72; C. Coody, 70-74; L. Heinsoh, 72-72.
145—G. Knudson (Canada), 73-72; R. Sikes, 70-75; O. Moody, 73-72; C. Coe, 74-71; G. Archer, 73-72.
146—T. Weiskopf, 73-73; D. Lotz, 74-72; B. Greene, 75-71; H. Johnson, 75-71; B. Crampton (Australia), 75-71; C. Rodriguez, 70-76; B. Charles (N. Zealand), 75-71; J. Nicklaus, 71-75; D. Beman, 74-72; B. Devlin (Australia), 72-74; J. Boros, 75-71.
147—F. Beard, 71-76; A. Jacklin (Britain), 73-74; J. Wright, 75-72; D. Sikes, 70-77; K. Still, 74-73.

Bridgend 18 pts
Bristol. . . . 24

BRIDGEND'S hopes of becoming Welsh champions received a rude shock when they went down to a lively Bristol, in a fast free-scoring game.

It was Bridgend's first home defeat since last October and they must now win two of their remaining four games if they are to win the title.

Bridgend sadly lacked a reliable place kicker, whereas Bristol had a fine marksman and match-winner in full back Peter Gunter. He scored twelve points with three conversions and two penalty goals.

It was a tremendously fast game with Bridgend scoring four tries to Bristol's three.

Two powerful packs fought a rare battle in the loose and set pieces.

The home second-row forward Steve Thomas, was a tower of strength in the line-out.

Bridgend held an interval lead of four points after tries by Gordon Collier and Viv Jenkins and a penalty goal by David Griffiths with Bristol pulling back a goal.

Bristol attacked with great speed in the second half, tries coming from Mike Collins on the left wing and Ken Plummer on the right.

Bridgend's second-half points came from tries by Tony Morgan and Max Wiltshire and a penalty goal by Griffiths.

BRIDGEND.—Tries: Collier, Jenkins, Morgan, Wiltshire; pens.: Griffiths (2).
BRISTOL.—Tries: Nichols, Collins, Plummer; convs.: Gunter (3); pens.: Gunter (2); drop. Nicholls.

NOTTS SPOIL LATE RALLY BY JENKINS

Notts 9 pts., Cross Keys 3

NOTTS really had to fight to land their 19th win of the season after a late rally by Cross Keys.

Territorially, Notts were second best to the Welshmen. But Notts won because they turned half chances into tries.

After fly-half Tony Butcher kicked Notts into a second-minute lead with an easy penalty, it was No. 8 Phil Brealey who went over for a corner try after a move by prop John Pearce and flanker Peter Moore.

Notts went further ahead two minutes after the interval, when winger Paul Irons raced forty yards for a spectacular try. Moore again played a key role in the build-up and Irons evaded two tackles before scoring.

Cross Keys hit back as Notts became complacent and fly-half David Hardaker raised the Welshmen's hopes with an angled penalty after sixty-five minutes.

But Notts rallied and time ran out for Cross Keys, who were inspired by full-back Gordon Jenkins and scrum-half Roger Ford.

Notts back-row players Moore and Brealey were industrious performers and winger Chris Hawthorne played well. Cross Keys' best work came from their pack, in which John Troop and John House were outstanding.

NOTTS.—Tries: Brealey, Irons; pen.: A. Butcher.
CROSS KEYS.—Pen.: Hardaker.

Plymouth 18 pts., Newbridge 0: By GARY NEWBON

NEWBRIDGE, without nine of their regular side, arrived with only fourteen men and drafted local policeman Roderick Herbert into the front row.

Their reshuffled team gave unexpected debuts to Derek Jones on the left wing and lock forward Jim Criddle.

Newbridge were also forced to call up youth stars Mel Davies on the right wing and Bernard Knott at flanker. Both played well.

To add to Newbridge's troubles, centre Terry Evans gashed his left hand and after the match went to hospital.

Albion, in the middle of three matches against Welsh opposition, eventually ran in fifteen points in the final seventeen minutes.

To cap an inept display, Albion missed seven penalty attempts and Newbridge five.

Les Ware, the former Plymouth Argyle youth Soccer player turned rugby centre, kicked the only penalty goal of the match in the 47th minute to open the scoring.

Albion full back John Bone missed four penalty attempts, Ware two and lock forward John Williams one in the first half.

Newbridge full-back Brian Anthony missed his side's five attempts in perfect kicking conditions.

PLYMOUTH.—Tries: A. Westlake, Jewell, D. Westlake. Conv.: Bone (three). Pen.: Ware.

DAILY Mirror

6d.   Thursday, April 30, 1970   ✦ ✦ ✦   No. 20,633

WHAT A GAME!

Kennedy 'at fault' over the death of Mary Jo

From DAVID WRIGHT in Boston, Massachusetts

SENATOR Edward Kennedy was probably driving his car negligently before it crashed into a tidal pond on Chappaquiddick Island last July.

And that "appears to have contributed" to the death of his passenger, 28-year-old Washington secretary Mary Jo Kopechne, says a judge's report released last night.

The report — Judge James Boyle's finding from the secret inquest on Mary Jo, held in January—contradicts Senator Kennedy's evidence on several points.

He found that Mr. Kennedy, once a Democratic hope for the Presidential nomination, and Mary Jo did not intend to return to Edgartown on the island of Martha's Vineyard, Cape Cod, Massachusetts, as Kennedy said in evidence.

Their turn on to a lonely sand road after a party was intentional, says the Judge.

Singing

The partygoers—six men and six girls—had been cooking, eating, drinking, singing and dancing, says the report.

Judge Boyle concluded that Senator Kennedy was thoroughly familiar with the road to a ferry landing on Chappaquiddick Island.

He says that Mr. Kennedy's admitted speed of 20 m p h at the time was "negligent and possibly reckless," and that if he knew of the bridge hazard it would constitute criminal conduct.

The judge noted that Kennedy's chauffeur, John Crimmins, had been

SENATOR'S DRIVING 'NEGLIGENT'

among the six men at the party.

"Kennedy had employed Crimmins as chauffeur for nine years and rarely drove himself," he says. "Crimmins drove Kennedy on all other occasions . . . and was available at the time of the fatal trip."

Publication of the inquest report and transcript has been held up by complicated legal manoeuvres.

It includes Senator Kennedy's first account on oath of the accident.

He told the judge: "I remembered t h e vehicle beginning to go off the bridge.

"The next thing I recall is the movement of Mary Jo next to me, struggling, perhaps hitting or kicking me.

"I opened my eyes and realised I was upside down, that water was crashing in on me, that it was pitch black."

In Washington, Senator Kennedy rejected the judge's findings.

He said in a statement that they were not justified.

"At the inquest I truthfully answered all questions asked of me," he said.

THE HERO   *Face masked in pain, Chelsea goalkeeper Peter Bonetti is treated after being hurt in a clash. He recovered to play on . . . limping. And time and again he saved his side.*

Chelsea win Cup thriller

IT'S Chelsea's Cup! They won the trophy for London last night after one of the most dramatic Cup Finals ever.

A glory goal from full-back Dave Webb in extra time gave them a 2—1 victory over Leeds United at Old Trafford, Manchester.

The match went into extra time when the score at the end of ninety minutes was 1—1.

Leeds went ahead in the thirty - fifth minute through their centre forward Mick Jones.

Touts

But Chelsea fought back— and got their reward twelve minutes from the end of normal time when centre forward Peter Osgood equalised.

The match was a washout for ticket touts. Ten minutes before kick-off there were still plenty of tickets left for most parts of the ground.

Touts who had paid inflated prices for tickets were offering them at half their face value.

Among the spectators was Premier Harold Wilson who travelled up from London specially for the match.

Replay Special—Pages 22 and 23.

Chelsea snatch the Cup in extra time

CHELSEA snatched the FA Cup from Leeds' grasp in a bitter battle which went into extra time at Old Trafford, Manchester, last night.

David Webb, who suffered torment in the first game at Wembley, got the winner in the 103rd minute.

There seemed little danger when Jack Charlton played the ball out for a throw-in on Leeds' right flank, but threat gathered as Hutchinson produced one of his longest throws.

The ball hung in the Leeds goalmouth and, when it eluded goalkeeper Harvey, Webb followed up to score in a fashion that has marked much of his play this season.

Leeds began where they left off at Wembley settling down quickly and playing the more assured and competent football.

And they nearly took a goal within two minutes of the start.

Peter Lorimer broke clear of Eddie McCreadie and when he drove his centre low into the Chelsea goalmouth the ball was deflected straight into the hands of Peter Bonetti.

Hurled

It was a sign of things to come as Leeds began to stretch Chelsea with passes hurled forward from midfield.

Leeds had to bring in reserve goalkeeper David Harvey for Gary Sprake who failed a fitness test but their covering was so assured that Harvey was not asked to do more than field back passes from his own players.

Remembering David Webb's humiliating experience at Wembley where he was tortured by Eddie Gray's skills Chelsea rearranged the defensive formation and switched captain Ron Harris to right back and moved Webb across alongside John Dempsey.

But it made little difference to Leeds' attacking threat and Webb was forced to pull Gray down when he broke swiftly through the middle on a brilliant through ball from Billy Bremner.

It was Chelsea who were forced to concede free kicks and they gave away four in quick succession.

They threatened when Ian Hutchinson pulled a shot across goal and then Peter Osgood finished in similar fashion after wheeling clear of Jack Charlton.

Command in midfield belonged to Leeds, and a brilliant move between John Giles and Bremner

By KEN JONES

CHELSEA	2
Osgood (78m.), Webb (103m.)	
LEEDS	1
(Jones (35m.)	
H-T: 0—1.	
(After extra-time.)	

sent Allan Clarke through for a shot which finished in the side netting.

Clarke threatened again on yet another pass pushed through the middle and at this time Webb only just got to him as he was about to shoot.

There was no sign of despair in Leeds' play. They were sharper on the ball, more confident when they had possession and a class above Chelsea when it came to putting their passes together.

Harris was pulled up for a reckless foul on Gray but within a minute Chelsea suffered a severe blow when goalkeeper Bonetti injured his left knee when challenging Mick Jones on a long centre from Paul Madeley.

Treatment

The game was held up for three minutes while Bonetti received treatment and when he continued he was clearly in some trouble.

But it was the sharpness of a Leeds attack built from deep in their own half of the field which led to Chelsea going behind in the thirty-fifth minute.

Clarke skilfully and bravely avoided three tackles in quick succession and then set Jones free with a superb pass through the middle.

Jones went on and as Bonetti attempted to narrow the angle a perfect shot hit with power and accuracy tore past the Chelsea goalkeeper's right shoulder for a brilliant goal.

Some of the tackling

began to get out of hand and referee Eric Jennings did little to cool down the gathering animosity.

Several of his decisions angered players on both sides and Harris was lucky not to receive more than a verbal admonishment after an appalling foul on Gray.

Leeds were content to consolidate their lead and settled for playing the ball towards the corners, forcing Chelsea into errors.

Despair for Peter Bonetti . . . elation for Mick Jones as the Leeds striker scores

Pictures by MONTE FRESCO and ALFRED MARKEY.

It was clear that Jennings was making the major contribution to the violence which crept into the game as it progressed and it was hardly a classical display of refereeing.

Bonetti began the second half with his left knee heavily strapped and Leeds put him under pressure with the certainty of their football and sharp breakaway attacks.

It was an hour before Chelsea really threatened the Leeds goal. But when Baldwin's sharp header was directed down into the goalmouth Harvey made a confident save.

Few matches of such importance can have been so badly handled and eventually booked by referee Jennings when he joined in a skirmish between Bremner and Osgood.

But then came two

threatening raids by Terry Cooper, whose attacking instincts and skill were constantly used as a weapon by Leeds.

Bonetti saved both of Cooper's shots and each of them was good enough to have put the game beyond doubt.

Threatening

But then in the 78th minute Chelsea rescued themselves from a desperate situation.

Cooke burst free attacking Leeds along their left flank and when he aimed the centre behind the line of defenders, Osgood darted in to beat Harvey with a header.

TEAMS. — CHELSEA: Bonetti, Harris, McCreadie, Hollins, Dempsey, Webb, Baldwin, Cooke, Osgood, Hutchinson, Houseman. Sub.: Hinton.
LEEDS: Harvey, Madeley, Cooper, Bremner, Charlton, Hunter, Lorimer, Clarke, Jones, Giles, Gray. Sub.: Bates.
REFEREE: E. Jennings (Stourbridge).

And another British triumph in Europe

COURAGEOUS CITY MAKE IT A DOUBLE FOR ENGLAND

From BOB RUSSELL: Vienna, Wednesday

Manchester City 2, Gornik 1

JOE MERCER'S magnificent Manchester City tonight emulated the super Spurs of the sixties by becoming only the second team to win the European Cup-winners' Cup on foreign soil.

By subduing Gornik, they completed a European double for England, following Arsenal's Fairs Cup success against Anderlecht.

Hitting first and hitting hard with a goal in 13 minutes and then fighting their way through a 24th-minute crisis when Mike Doyle was carried off with damaged ankle tendons, they were every inch champions.

City, with Tony Towers replacing injured Mike Summerbee, took control early on.

Olek, Francis Lee's watchdog, was booked immediately by Austrian referee Paul Schiller after a tackle on the City striker. After five minutes, as if to dispel doubts about his fitness, Oakes burst through and blasted a 30-yard shot just over the top.

City went ahead after 13 minutes. Lee, daring and dangerous, exploded a 22-yard shot that caught Kostka fumbling at the near post. The goal-

keeper could only parry the ball to Neil Young and the elegant striker steered it into the opposite corner.

Four minutes later Mike Doyle crumpled under a crushing tackle by Florenski and lay motionless for two minutes before being taken off and replaced by substitute Ian Bowyer.

After 43 minutes, City struck again. Defender Latocha carelessly tried to round Young and failed. Young headed directly into the penalty area and Kostka committed himself to conceding the inevitable penalty. From the spot, Lee made it 2—0.

A half-time downpour failed to dampen the spirits of City's 4,000 followers and the team responded in a style that made light of the increasingly heavy going.

It was one of City's most resilient and resourceful performances in view of the fact that they were without Summerbee and lost Doyle during the game.

It was essentially a negative second-half judged by City's high standards. Gornik had shown little hope of striking, but in 58 minutes were right back in the game when defender, Stanislaw Oslizlo hooked an eight-yard drive past Joe Corrigan.

IT'S THE FINAL

Two goals that brought hope .. but not glory

OH! What a final of frustration especially for Leeds United.

At Old Trafford last night it was their last chance to win a trophy.

But even though they took the lead Chelsea fought back to take the FA Cup in the 14th minute of extra time.

Mick Jones raised Leeds's hopes when he scored in the 36th minute.

But first Peter Osgood and then David Webb scored , to make it a real final of frustration for poor Leeds.

HOPE for Leeds fans but no GLORY for Leeds

HOPE for Chelsea fans . . PRAISE for Peter Osgood . . but no GLORY for the Chelsea centre-forward. His flying header beat Leeds reserve goalkeeper David Hai

CUP FINAL SPECIAL: Pictures by Mirror

. OF FRUSTRATION

...d centre-forward Mick Jones. He beats Chelsea goalkeeper Peter Bonetti with a ` in the 36th minute . . but it was not enough to give Leeds victory.

in the 78th minute. The goal made the score 1—1 . but it was left to Chelsea left-half David Webb to grab the GLORY with the winner in the 14th minute of extra time.

...eramen Monte Fresco, Alfred Markey and John Walker.

EUROPEAN SOCCER SPECIAL

CHELSEA SHOW THEIR NEW STRENGTH

From KEN JONES: Sofia, Bulgaria, Wednesday

CHELSEA drenched their skills in sweat here tonight and finally established themselves as one of Europe's most powerful teams.

This victory in the second round of the Cup Winners Cup must rank among their most notable. It was achieved against opponents known for

their cunning and strength against a team most would have been happy to avoid. And it was memorable for an abundance of determination and subtle deployment.

Chelsea would not have complained had they

CSKA 0, CHELSEA 1

been able to start equal in the second leg on November 4. Now they are a goal to the good and yet will recall with some annoyance that they could have put the tie beyond the reach of the Bulgars.

Peter Osgood, playing in irresistible style, might have added two goals to the one taken by Tommy Baldwin and Chelsea made enough chances to cause continual anxiety in the Bulgarians' goalmouth.

Chelsea's intentions were as clear as their strategy was familiar—to present a formidable front and to work for the quick productive counter-attack from midfield.

But it was the manner in which this was achieved that makes this performance so worthy of recall.

Osgood and David Webb, a defender of considerable stature tonight, were booked by Swiss referee Scheuer, but these were isolated incidents of technical dispute, rather than examples of flagrant delinquency.

Cleared

Chelsea were at their best in the first half when the Bulgarians were at their most threatening.

CSKA outside left Marashliev broke away in the 18th minute and the ball was cleared only to Penev, but he shot well over the bar.

Hollins had a long, low free-kick blocked by Filipov in the twenty-sixth minute and, soon afterwards, put Osgood through with a high ball into the penalty area. But the Chelsea striker's shot rebounded off the goalkeeper and Peter Houseman missed a chance to score.

Osgood had his name taken in the thirty-third

minute for a foul on Filipov.

The London club went ahead two minutes before half-time when Weller powered down the right wing, cut inside and pushed the ball through to Baldwin, who steered the ball home from five yards.

Former Bulgarian captain Gaganelov came on for Yakimov immediately after half-time and CSKA seemed to have found a new lease of life.

Yet Chelsea had the first scoring chance of the half. Osgood dribbled round Denev in the fifty-ninth minute, but Filipov dived brilliantly to the right to save.

A minute later, Webb had his name taken after bringing down Denev from behind. Then CSKA had a Penev goal disallowed for offside.

In the 83rd minute, Filipov made a good save from an Osgood header from a cross by Houseman, but though it was all Chelsea from then on the Londoners could not increase their lead.

Cardiff's Brian Clark, under pressure from two Nantes defenders, heads towards goal.

Fans fight as Celtic send Irish champions reeling

Waterford 0, Celtic 7

THIS game lasted just twenty seconds —the time it took Willie Wallace to hammer in Celtic's first goal. From then on, little Waterford's only interest was in keeping down the score.

But while Celtic strolled to victory, fierce fighting broke out among rival fans in the 48,000 crowd jammed into

LEE 'DUMMY' CLINCHES IT

Honved 0, Manchester City 1

A BRILLIANTLY - TAKEN free-kick gave Manchester City a great victory over Honved in their Cup-Winners' Cup first-leg tie in Budapest last night.

Striker Francis Lee shaped as if to take the kick thirty yards out in the sixty-fifth minute. But he ran over the ball and Colin Bell slipped it out to Mike Summerbee on the right wing.

Summerbee steered over a perfect cross for Lee to

crash past goalkeeper Bicskel.

City should have no difficulty in reaching the last eight when they meet the Hungarians in the return leg in Manchester in two weeks' time.

On this form, City look capable of becoming the first club to win the trophy twice in succession.

They were robbed of another goal when a powerful Colin Bell drive crashed against a post.

Dublin's Lansdowne-road ground. At one stage, some spectators jumped onto the pitch to escape flying bottles.

But there was no escape for Waterford. Lou Macari netted Celtic's second after ten minutes and Bobby Murdoch added two more before the interval.

In the second half—with fans still lining the pitch—Wallace added two more inside a minute. This was the signal for thousands of Irish fans to start streaming home.

Five minutes from time Macari completed the scoring.

Waterford's hero was goalkeeper Peter Thomas, who stopped Celtic running up a cricket score.

The Irish champions now have another ninety minutes of torture to go through — in the second leg in Glasgow.

FOOTBALL COMBINATION: Bournemouth 0, Arsenal 0. **SOUTHERN LEAGUE CUP:** Hereford 4, Kings Lynn 0.

CRICKET

RAY STARTS OFF WITH A WARNING

From PETER LAKER

Adelaide, Wednesday

RAY ILLINGWORTH got MCC's Australian tour off to a dynamic start here today in a frank and fearless Press interview that surely stamps him as one of cricket's shrewdest politicians.

For forty-five minutes he sat calm and relaxed in manager David Clark's hotel room and told English and Australian newspapermen how, why and by what margin—3-2 —England would regain the Ashes.

If an accolade were required for his performance it came with the admiring comment of an Aussie journalist: "My word that Illingworth is just great. I feel as though

I've known him all my life."

Illingworth said: "I accept that Australia have the advantage of playing on their own wickets but if I go into a series thinking of not winning then I never will win."

There can be no question that Illingworth is hitting where it hurts most in this traditional war of nerves when he continually plugs the frightening hard - wicket pace, bounce and built-in venom of the John Snow-Alan Ward alliance.

The 4-0 hiding Australia took from South Africa's Peter Pollock and Mike

Procter last winter is not a thing spoken of lightly here just now.

The talk tells of the decline at that time of Australia's own speedster, Graham McKenzie, and of the lack of luck and form shown by the batsmen.

So Illingworth chips in with: "I can assure you of one thing. If you think Pollock bowled quick for the Rest of the World in England this summer, let me tell you that my two lads are FOUR yards quicker."

Team practice may or may not get underway tomorrow afternoon, depending on whether the

sixteen - strong MCC party feel up to it following a desperate y-tiring 12,000-mile flight from London.

Token rather than punctilious searches of luggage at Zurich, Tel Aviv, Teheran and Delhi—necessary but tiresome anti-hijack precautions—were bad enough.

But when the aircraft landed at Perth in the early hours of today, a work-to-rule by ground staff delayed them for two hours.

The subsequent scramble to catch the connecting flight from Sydney meant ultimate arrival in Adelaide with all the party's personal luggage left behind—in Sydney!

But, make no mistake, this is going to be a great tour because Ray Illingworth has said so. And the Aussies believe him.

TENNIS

Barrett tells Lloyd: 'Win—or you're out'

By C M JONES

JOHN BARRETT left the Stalybridge Indoor Stadium yesterday fuming—because he'd beaten David Lloyd in the Dewar Cup.

After his 9—7, 6—4 victory Barrett said: "It was embarrassing. I would much rather have lost."

Barrett, as a director of the BP International Tennis Fellowship is virtually Lloyd's manager and coach.

Now he may have to sack Lloyd from the Fellowship as membership is based on merit.

And Lloyd's good performances have been in short supply this season.

Said Barrett: "If he doesn't produce some wins he'll have to go."

Graham quits— crisis looms

By NIGEL CLARKE

DICK GRAHAM
Hurt and upset.

DICK GRAHAM, Colchester manager, admitted last night that he had resigned from the club.

And Graham, who piloted the little Fourth Division club to an FA Cup conquest of Leeds, said: I handed my notice in on Saturday.

I can't withdraw it, either. The reasons for me leaving are too serious for me to want to.

Emergency

After an emergency board meeting, it was unanimously decided to ask Graham to withdraw his notice.

And chairman Bill Graver is even prepared to step down from office to keep Graham at Layer-road.

Peace hopes failed last night when Graver and his vice-chairman, Arthur Neville, waited at the ground for more than two hours to see Graham.

Finally, a letter was delivered at his home requesting a meeting at 10.30 this morning.

I understand that Graham has not had the freedom he has demanded with team selection.

"I can't see any compromise," said Graham. "I'm hurt and upset. All I want is to be treated with respect. There are principles involved that cannot be smoothed out in five minutes."

Said Graver: "Yesterday was the unhappiest day of my life. I was crucified all evening and into the early hours of this morning by angry supporters."

Magnificent Chelsea turn on two-hour thriller

OSSIE MAKES UP FOR LOST TIME!

By HARRY MILLER

CHELSEA 4, BRUGES 0

(er extra time Chelsea win 4—2 on aggregate

PETER OSGOOD pushed aside eight weeks of inactivity with two fine goals, as Chelsea scaled the European heights to reach the semi-finals of the Cup-Winners Cup last night.

It would be unfair to say that one man won this match—and the tie—on an evening of extra-time tension and tremendous football.

But the difference between the Chelsea team that surrendered in Belgium and the one that succeeded so magnificently in this second-leg was spotlighted by Osgood's performance.

He had come back to a match that meant so much to Chelsea, only 48 hours after ending the agony that was his two-months' suspension.

He had come into a Chelsea side desperate for his scoring flair as they set out to pull back from a 2—0 defeat.

And Osgood obliged in a way that 45,558 fans lucky enough to see this marvellous match will never forget.

It was Osgood's goal in the 81st minute that made the aggregate score 2—2 and earned Chelsea extra time.

It was Osgood's goal six minutes from the end of extra time that gave Chelsea the vital breakthrough for a 3—2 lead.

But to go back to the beginning. Chelsea had to get the first goal that would take them halfway up the mountain they were to finally conquer.

Luc Sanders, an excellent goalkeeper, was the main barrier. He made a superb save from an Osgood header before Chelsea scored after 21 minutes.

Tommy Baldwin hooked a John Hollins through ball across the face of goal for Osgood to head the ball down and Peter Houseman to flick it in.

Ron Harris, David Webb, John Hollins, Alan Hudson were all outstanding as Chelsea provided their own non-stop charge of the heavy brigade on a besieged Bruges goal.

Harris raised his arms in anguish after seeing a vicious 35-yarder spin back off the inside of a post just before half-time.

Chelsea started the second half with John Boyle replacing John Dempsey. Centre half Dempsey was suffering from slight concussion and needed two stitches in a head wound following a first-half collision.

Bruges were rarely out of their own half as time ticked away. Centres were poured into their goal-mouth from all angles.

Ironically, Bruges had an outstanding chance to kill off Chelsea in the 65th minute.

In a rare break, Webb missed his clearance, John Phillips was stranded out of his goal but Johnny Thio tamely lifted the ball over the bar.

Then, with 81 minutes gone, Osgood struck that all-important goal that made it 2—2 on aggregate.

Charlie Cooke made the opening and Osgood slammed the ball through a forest of Bruges' legs.

Osgood signalled his delight by leaping the four-foot barrier surrounding the pitch, to be engulfed by excited fans.

Drained Away

Bruges had never won an away leg in six previous European ties. As their energy drained away, you could see the gleam of victory in Chelsea's efforts as they spurted forward.

Two minutes into extra time Baldwin lashed a shot against the underside of the bar. Then, with 114 minutes gone, Osgood struck again.

Hudson made a brilliant run before laying the ball back for Osgood to strike it past the gallant Sanders.

Chelsea's night to remember was not over. Three minutes from the end Hudson and Cooke combined superbly to provide the opening for Baldwin to shoot goal No. 4.

But to both sides, an accolade. They provided outstanding entertainment.

Arsenal angry about being the victims

By KEN JONES

ARSENAL find consolation for the loss of the Fairs Cup in the freedom they now have to manoeuvre at home.

They go forward to their FA Cup semi-final against Stoke on Saturday recognising the strain that was involved in a bid for three titles in one season.

Manager Bertie Mee says: "Although we wanted to win in Cologne —and, in fact, deserved to win—we have to accept that we had taken a lot on.

"Perhaps in May we shall look back on this defeat as one which consolidated our effort in the search for an even greater prize.

"Whatever happened in Germany will not affect what we are setting out to do on Saturday.

"The whole thing was too ridiculous for words. We were never allowed to play by the referee, and the histrionics displayed by the Cologne players should really be of concern to the West German authorities.

"The Germans have a name throughout world football for this sort of thing and they are not doing the game any good. It is not good to see players acting every time they are touched and the Germans should examine the whole business very quickly."

Criticism

Criticism of Rumanian referee Constantin Petres was unanimous and a Cologne official later described him as their best player.

I understand that this was Petres' first experience of European football at this level and Arsenal are understandably angry that they should be chosen as victims of his inadequacies.

Arsenal captain Frank McLintock says: "From the moment he penalised me for a fair tackle in the opening few minutes I knew that we had problems. When he started pulling us up for calling for the ball it became impossible.

"Our whole game was affected and we didn't really settle down to play until the second half. We were the better team and the Germans knew it.

"Their players were laughing when decisions were awarded against us. It will be different in the FA Cup because there will be a common attitude."

Mee adds: "Let's say we have managed to learn something which will stand us in good stead."

Arsenal have no injury problems and will train today and tomorrow before leaving for the semi-final at Hillsborough.

REAL BLAST CARDIFF OUT

From TOM LYONS

Madrid, Wednesday

CARDIFF crashed out of the Cup Winners Cup here tonight in a bad-tempered quarter-final second leg clash with Real Madrid.

Cardiff, who held a 1—0 first leg lead, were beaten 2—0 tonight for an aggregate 2—1 and can now concentrate on their league promotion target.

Velazquez blasted Real into the lead in the forty-eighth minute and four minutes later Felicitas clinched it by flicking the ball over goalkeeper Jim Eadie's head.

Cardiff left back Bell was booked for a foul on right-winger Amancio — and had a couple of beer cans thrown at him.

GOLF

HUGGETT'S DRIVE CAN SWING IT

BATTLING Welshman Brian Huggett will head the seventy-strong British challenge as the £12,000 Italian Open championship begins at the Garlenda golf club here tomorrow.

In fact, Ryder Cup star Huggett is so optimistic about his chances that he is thinking of switching his return flight from Sunday night to Monday morning in order to savour the fruits of victory!

Huggett drove badly in the Algarve Open last week, but still sneaked into third place.

From
BOB RODNEY
Alassio, Wednesday

"It was the wind that wrecked my driving in Portugal," he said. "I'm hitting the ball much better now, and I like this course."

This is a vital event for the leading British players since Order of Merit points are at stake for the first time on the 1971 British-controlled European circuit.

And the top six Order of Merit men in August get automatic selection for the Ryder Cup match against the United States in September.

Yet this Italian Open—the first for eleven years—is lucky to get off the ground, since five days of continuous rain has left the course very soft.

RUGBY UNION

Chances go begging —so England crash

By CHRIS LANDER

England Under-15's 6 pts, Wales Under-15's 8

THE WELSH youngsters cashed in on England's inability to take their chances in the Under-15 international at Twickenham yesterday.

With a swirling gale-force wind behind them in the second half, England had enough opportunities to have finished comfortable winners.

England did some courageous work in defence when the wind was against them in the first half and Wales only led 8—3.

Wales scored two spectacular tries, and John Keene converted one of them.

One try came when full back Paul Simmonds got through from the 25-yard line on his own.

John Harwood and Simmonds moved the ball swiftly for winger Stephen Kohut to score wide out for the second try.

Although Wales were pinned deep inside their twenty-five for most of the second half, England's try did not come until two minutes from time.

Kevin Mason, who had scored a first-half penalty, broke sharply from a line-out and threw a long overhead pass, missing out the centres, for winger Alden Corn to scamper over.

Joe Sass had to land the conversion to earn England a draw—but he miscued.

Alliss quits top golf

By BOB RODNEY

PETER ALLISS yesterday quit tournament golf.

The 40-year-old Ryder Cup star withdrew from the £8,000 Penfold tournament at Bournemouth, saving himself the indignity of having to play in the pre-qualifying rounds.

And he announced that he was no longer interested in selection for representative teams.

Alliss, who missed the Italian Open last month because of ill-health, returned to Britain on Monday after playing in the Spanish and Madrid Open tournaments.

Poor performances in Spain influenced his decision to quit.

For the past few seasons he has struck the ball well from tee to green but has had real trouble on the greens.

Last year he was fifty-ninth in the P G A Order of Merit and won only £920.

In thirty-two rounds he averaged 74.25 strokes against 70.88 in forty-two by Order of Merit leader Neil Coles.

Yesterday, Alliss was in Norfolk on business. In future, he will be fully occupied with business interests, television commentating and his job as senior professional to the new club at Moor Allerton, Leeds.

Graham joins the top boxers

GRAHAM SINES, a self-confessed "lazy trainer," yesterday became Britain's latest heavyweight boxing hope when he signed professional under manager Arthur Boggis, writes Ron Wills.

Sines, 20, stands 6ft. 1in., weighs 13½st. and earns £18 a week as a Post Office worker.

After the signing in London, he admitted: "I have never liked training. I was always looking for excuses to dodge it. I don't suppose I have been more than 75 per cent. fit for any of my eighty-nine amateur bouts. But now I am being paid for it, I am prepared to knuckle down. I know I will have to."

Boggis, who hopes to give Sines his professional debut at London's Royal Albert Hall next month, told me: "This boy has given me a new enthusiasm for boxing.

"In three years I expect him to be getting close to the British title."

CHELSEA STRIDE

No apparent danger as Ron Healey goes up to collect Keith Weller's free-kick

Then the young Manchester City goalkeeper stares in horror as the ball finishes up in the net for the knock-out blow.

TO FINAL

Now comes a clash with Real Madrid

Manchester City 0, Chelsea 1 (Chelsea win 2-0 on aggregate)

CHELSEA'S enviable strength in depth saw them triumphantly through an injury crisis and on to the final of the European Cup-Winners' Cup last night.

They must now beat Real Madrid in Athens on May 19 to emulate Spurs and West Ham, the two other London clubs who have previously won this Cup.

By KEN JONES

Chelsea's success in this second leg semi-final at Maine-road was a tribute to the patience and care with which they have assembled an impressive first team squad.

Manchester City, too, were ravaged by injuries, but it was clear from the opening minutes that they were unable to reach into the same area of accomplishment.

Colin Bell, Glyn Pardoe, Alan Oakes, and Tommy Booth have fallen in recent weeks to leave City short of experience and star quality.

The faces they found to replace them have become steadily more unfamiliar as their manager Joe Mercer has been forced to call on teenagers he would have preferred to hide from such demanding action.

But Chelsea had no such problems. They were without internationals Peter Osgood Eddie McCreadie, and John Hollins. Missing, too, were Tommy Baldwin and Ian Hutchinson.

But the men who came in were almost as well known as those who had been forced to drop out.

A goal ahead from the first game at Stamford Bridge two weeks ago, Chelsea organised themselves to register strength in midfield and power in their counter-attacks.

When they managed to display consistent willingness and aggression it was all too much for the City side which produced only occasional flickers of threatening play.

In midfield John Boyle played with tremendous enthusiasm as a defensive prop for Charlie Cooke and Alan Hudson.

In Trouble

The speed with which Chelsea struck in support of their attackers had City in trouble from the opening minutes, and extravagant play by young Derek Jeffries might have led to early goals when he was twice caught in possession.

There was always the possibility that Chelsea would extend their lead even though City found one brief flourish of form when Francis Lee and Neil Young revealed the skills which have proved influential in the past.

Lee's cleverness once took him between despairing tackles by John Dempsey and Ron Harris, but although he shot well after leaving them in his wake, the ball cleared the crossbar and goalkeeper Phillips.

Two free-kicks gave Chelsea some concern but three minutes before half time they scored a goal which left City short of spirit and inspiration.

Keith Weller curled in a free kick from wide on City's left and close to the corner flag.

It proved tragic for City's young goalkeeper, Ron Healey, who was confused by the flight and could only push the ball against full back David Connor and on into his own goal.

With a two-nil aggregate lead Chelsea were able to play with utmost confidence.

City called off Mike Summerbee, another of their limping internationals and Steve Carter, even more unfamiliar than the rest, came on to play with skilful enthusiasm.

But by then the crowd were streaming from the ground and Chelsea's band of supporters could stand and cheer comfortably over their team's triumph.

EUROPEAN SEMI-FINAL NIGHT

EUROPEAN CUP
Semi-Finals, 2nd Leg

Panathinaikos 3 **Red Star** 0
Antoniades 2, Kamaras. H-T: 1—0. 30,000.
(Agg.: 4—4. Panathinaikos win on rule that away goals count double.)

Ajax .... 3 **Atletico Madrid** 0
Keizer, Suurbier, Neeskens. H-T: 1—0. 67,000
(Aggregate: Ajax win 3—1)
(Final at Wembley on June 2.)

EUROPEAN CUP WINNERS' CUP
Semi-finals, 2nd Leg

Man. City .... 0 **Chelsea** ....
H T: 0-1. Healey (o g). 43,663
(Agg: Chelsea win 2-0)

Real Madrid 2 **P.S.V. Eindhoven** 1
Zoco, Arri. Van Den Dungen
H T: 1—0. 35,000
(Agg: Real Madrid win 2—1)
(Final in Athens on May 19.)

EUROPEAN FAIRS CUP
Semi-Finals, 2nd Leg

Juventus 2 **Cologne** 0
Capello, Anastasi. H T: 1—0. 70,000
(Agg: Juventus win 3—1)

Leeds .... 0 **Liverpool** 0
40,462
(Agg: Leeds win 1—0)
(Two leg Final on May 26 and June 3.)

FIRST DIVISION

Newcastle .... 3 **W B A** 0
Smith, Young, Tudor. H-T: 0—0. 18,310

Tottenham . 1 **Huddersfield** .. 1
Chivers. Cherry. H-T: 0—0. 18,827

Wolves .... 0 **Ipswich** 0
18,827

SECOND DIVISION

Oxford Utd. .. 2 **Luton** ....
Clarke, Cassidy. Busby. H-T: 2-1. 9,531

Watford ...... 1 **Swindon** 2
Wigg. Peplow, Horsfield. H-T: 1—1. 10,793

Hull .... 1 **Carlisle** ..
Butler. Hatton, Webb. H-T: 0—1. 14,363

THIRD DIVISION

Torquay ...... 2 **Halifax** ....
Rudge 2. H T: 1-0. 3,244

Brad. City **Fulham** 3
Hall, Corner. Johnston 2, Lloyd. H T: 1-1. 6,430

Shrewsbury ... 1 **Swansea** 0
Andrews. H-T, 1-0. 4,578

Brighton **Plymouth** 1
Irvine. Allen. H T: 0-0. 8,202

Gillingham .... **Chesterfield** .. 1
Woodley. Archer. H-T: 0—0. 1,887

TOP POSITIONS

	P	W	D	L	F	A	Pts
Fulham ..	45	24	12	9	68	40	60
Preston	44	20	17	7	59	39	57
Halifax ...	44	21	12	11	69	49	54
Chesterfield	45	17	17	11	66	37	51
Bristol R.	45	19	13	13	68	47	51
Aston Villa	44	18	15	11	49	41	51

FOURTH DIVISION

Aldershot ..... 5 **Stockport** 0
Melia, Brown, Howarth 2, Joslyn. H T: 4-0. 3,379

Southend 0 **Exeter** 0
4,471

Crewe .... 1 **Notts Co.** 2
Bowles. Bradd, Masson. H-T: 1—1. 4,222

Lincoln .... 2 **Chester** ......
Freeman, Svarc. H T: 1-0. 3,086

Peterboro' ... 3 **Bournemouth** .. 1
Hall, Robson, Conmy (pen.). MacDougall (pen.). H-T: 1—1. 3,014

SCOTTISH LEAGUE.—Div. II: Brechin 2, Clydebank 0.
FOOTBALL COMBINATION.— Fulham 0, Q P R 2; Leicester 1, Arsenal 0.
SOUTHERN LEAGUE.—Premier Div.: Kings Lynn 0, Hereford 1. **Div 1:** Bexley Utd 1, Rugby 1.
LONDON MIDWEEK LEAGUE CUP.—Millwall 0, Charlton 0; Orient 1, Colchester 1.
F A YOUTH CUP FINAL.— First leg: Arsenal 0, Cardiff 0. Att.: 3,551.

AND LEEDS STROLL INTO THEIR THIRD FAIRS FINAL

By DAVE HORRIDGE: Leeds 0, Liverpool 0

(Leeds win 1—0 on aggregate)

LEEDS successfully reverted to their old policy of dour defence last night to win through to their third Fairs Cup Final.

Relaxing from the frenzy of the League title race, Don Revie's determined professionals smothered Liverpool's eager attack. In fact, there were few moments when either side looked like adding to the goal Billy Bremner scored in the first leg two weeks ago.

But if the match lacked the aggression usual for a semi-final, there was no shortage of entertainment.

The absence of the tension endured by both teams this season encouraged them to indulge in the type of football for which they rarely receive credit.

Intentions

But Revie made his intentions crystal clear when he left off striker Allan Clarke at half-time and brought on defender Paul Reaney. Ten minutes later Mick Jones was replaced by reserve forward Joe Jordan.

Steve Heighway produced some dangerous stuff for Liverpool and twice came near to scoring.

One of his efforts, a left-foot shot on the half-volley, brought the save of the game out of Gary Sprake, who just managed to deflect it over.

But it was Jones who came nearest to scoring with a header in the first half.

It surprised Liverpool goalkeeper Ray Clemence with its pace and precision, but full back Emlyn Hughes cleared as the ball bounced down off the bar.

PUSKAS WILL COME BACK TO WEMBLEY

ATHENS was a city of joy last night after local club Panathinaikos had reached the final of the European Cup by beating favourites Red Star of Belgrade 3—0.

The Yugoslavs, who won the semi-final first leg 4—1, were hotly fancied to win yesterday's return and go through to the final at Wembley.

But the Greeks—managed by former Hungarian ace Ferenc Puskas—scored within a minute through Antoniades.

Antoniades headed the second in the fifty-fifth minute and nine minutes later Kamaras lashed home the third.

In the final on June 2 they meet the Dutch club Ajax, who beat Atletico Madrid 3—1 on aggregate.

Gizzi beaten—McAlinden gets a boost

By RON WILLS

DAN McALINDEN finally lived up to two years of ballyhoo last night—but only just.

The 23-year-old Coventry-based, Irish-born heavyweight outpointed Welsh champion Carl Gizzi at the Cresta Stadium, near Coventry, by the narrowest possible margin of a quarter-of-a-point, or one round.

Referee Roland Dakin scored the fight 49¼pts. to 49, which means McAlinden dropped three rounds and Gizzi four.

But narrow margin or not, the victory hauls McAlinden into third place behind champion Joe Bugner and Jack Bodell in the British heavyweight rankings.

That is reward enough for McAlinden's backers, who have hailed him as a certain future British champion. But on last night's showing, I reckon that is not in the near future.

Within seconds of the finish Gizzi's manager Paddy Byrne issued a £1,000 side-stake for a return match—and the offer was promptly accepted

CURTIS, PAISH HURT AS RAIN HITS CUP TIE

From PETER WILSON

Zagreb, Wednesday

AFTER one of the wettest days I have ever experienced outside a swimming pool, play was abandoned late in the afternoon without a ball being struck in our Davis Cup tie here against Yugoslavia.

The match is due to commence at 1 p.m. tomorrow.

We are, in effect reduced to a two-man team anyway—Gerald Battrick and Stanley Matthews. Peter Curtis who had been expected to play in the doubles aggravated a previous injury when he wrenched the ligaments in his ankle while practising on this very soft, newly laid court.

Today, non-playing captain Headley Baxter told me that standby John Paish was suffering from fibrositis in his back and also a slightly injured ankle.

JENNINGS SLIP IS AGONY FOR SPURS

By HARRY MILLER: Tottenham 1 Huddersfield 1

PAT JENNINGS made the sort of mistake last night that Arsenal will be wishing and willing on him next Monday.

North London rivals Spurs are the team Arsenal look destined to have to beat to take the championship. If Arsenal get the sort of luck Huddersfield had, then the title's theirs.

Tottenham were cruising to victory when goalkeeper Jennings blundered badly just three minutes from time.

He was standing bouncing the ball eight yards from his goal after collecting a Steve Perryman backpass when he unaccountably lost control of an easy situation.

The ball suddenly ran loose and Huddersfield midfield man Trevor Cherry was on it in a flash to shoot into an empty net.

Spurs goal came in the 38th minute — Martin Chivers neatly heading home a free-kick from Alan Mullery.

Williams upsets Arsenal hopes

By WILLIE EVANS

Arsenal 0, Cardiff 0.

ARSENAL face a tough battle to win the FA Youth Cup after being held to a goalless draw in last night's first leg of the final at Highbury.

In a second half which Arsenal dominated with their fast attacking football, centre half Brendon Batson struck the Cardiff bar with a fine header.

But though clever winger Brian Hornsby led numerous thrilling raids, Arsenal were unable to break down a resolute Cardiff defence, in which goalkeeper John Williams played superbly.

SECOND DIVISION

Oxford 2, Luton 1

A BAD miss by leading scorer Malcolm Macdonald twenty minutes from time robbed Luton of a Second Division point.

He blasted a Don Givens pass into the crowd from within the six-yard box.

Derek Clarke scored the first in the fifth minute, racing onto a great pass from Ron Atkinson.

Nigel Cassidy added the second in the twenty-fifth minute before Viv Busby pulled one back for Luton.

Watford 1, Swindon 2

WELSH international Tom Walley faces disciplinary action by Watford after a flare-up.

He hurled his shirt at the trainer's box ten minutes from time after being substituted.

It was an unhappy night for Walley, who was caught out by a perfect John Trollope cross in the seventy-ninth minute when Arthur Horsfield rammed home the Swindon winner.

Swindon took the lead through Steve Peplow after twenty-five minutes. Ron Wigg equalised six minutes later.

FULHAM GO UP—BY GEORGE

Bradford City 2, Fulham 3

GEORGE JOHNSTON headed Fulham back into the Second Division last night with a 76th-minute goal which ended a real thriller of a match.

The two points make sure of promotion for the Londoners, but Bradford City made them go all out and twice fought back to level the scores.

Johnson put Fulham ahead after thirty-two minutes, but John Hall equalised on half-time.

Barry Lloyd restored Fulham's lead in the 58th minute, but three minutes later City equalised again through a spectacular header from Norman Corner.

It was still a ding-dong open battle until Johnston's goal settled the result.

Brighton 1, Plymouth 1

BRIGHTON once again gave an uninspiring display in front of their fans and even a Willie Irvine goal fifteen minutes from time failed to inject life into their play.

John Napier and Norman Gall were Brighton's strong men and deserved a better fate than to see Keith Allen equalise

Gillingham 1, Chesterfield 1

A DISMAL season for relegated Gillingham ended before their lowest league gate of the season, 1,877. But there was one glimmer of hope in the sparkling midfield performance of 19-year-old Graham Knight.

Both goals came in the closing minutes with Derek Woodley putting Gillingham ahead and John Archer equalising with almost the last kick

FOURTH DIVISION

Aldershot 5 Stockport 0

AN AMAZING four-goal burst in the first thirty-one minutes spurred Aldershot to their biggest win of the season.

They went ahead through player-manager Jimmy Melia after two minutes and Dennis Brown forced home a second two minutes later.

Top scorer Jack Howarth made it three in the sixteenth minute and after Henry Bennett had missed a penaly, Roger Joslyn burst through for the fourth.

In a less dramatic second half, Howarth bagged his second four minutes from time.

Southend 0, Exeter 0

SOUTHEND, needing a victory to make certain of avoiding re-election, were kept out by an eight-man Exeter defence.

They were unlucky in the first half when two shots were cleared off the line, but had only themselves to blame after the interval.

Strikers Bill Garner and Terry Johnson both missed clear chances as Exeter held on grimly for a point.

SPORTS SUMMARY

SPEEDWAY

BRITISH LEAGUE.—Poole 39 (Eide 9, Andrews, Fossengen 8) **Reading 39** (Michanek 15, Curtis 9).

WORLD CHAMPIONSHIP.— Qualifying round (Coventry): Lomas (Coventry) Cribb (Exeter) 12; McKinlay (Oxford) 11, Monk (Glasgow) 11

RUGBY UNION

OXFORDSHIRE KNOCK-OUT CUP FINAL.—Oxford 28 Henley 6.

BOXING

CRESTA STADIUM (Nr Coventry) — **10 rnds heavy:** Danny McAlinden (Coventry) outptd Carl Gizzi (Rhyl). **6 rnds light:** Dav Pams (Tottenham) drew with Dave Nelson (Wolverhampton). **8 rnds heavy:** Peter Boddington (Coventry) ko'd Brian Hall (Dartford) 2nd. **6 rnds feather:** Neil McIvor (London) bt Freddie Williams (Nuneaton) stopd 4th.

GREYHOUNDS

WEST HAM.—7.45: Bagpipes 2-1 f (6-5, £1·03). **8.0: Kilcar Song** 4-5 f (5-6, 88p). **8.16: Carnival Pardee** 11-8 jf (6-2, £1·30). **8.33: Ballyfinane Time** 4-1 (6-1, £1·12). **8.50: Princess Mee** 9-4 (4-3 £1·74). **9.7: Wages Day** evens f (5-4, 60p). N R: Mud Bath (T1). **9.24: Hasty Kuda** 10-1 (3-5, £13·16). **9.40: Flashing Blade** 7-4 f (6-4, 78p).

Couplets: £14·33; £22·58; £12·65 (paid on first leg).

WIMBLEDON.—7.45: Sheila's Champ 6-1 (6-1, £2·96). **8.0: Belleen** 25-1 (1-6, £4·03). **8.15: Tallow Fairy** 5-1 (6-5, £1·17) **8.30: Ball O'Yarn** 5-4 f (5-6, 91p). N R: Corral Prince (T4). **8.45: Dacta's Speed** 7-1 (6-3, £4·17). **9.0: Granada Breeze** 9-2 (3-5, £1·99). **9.15: Charville Flash** 7-4 f (5-3, £2·90) **9.30: Idle Thought** 9-4 f (3-4, £1·25).

Plums: £55·96; £14·91, £32·61.

TOP DOG'S BEST

HACKNEY: 2.30, Lucky Boro; 2.45, Sunset Heather; 3.5, Ginger Wolf; 3.22, Mystery Maker; 3.39, Derby Special; 3.58, Flashy Kid; 4.16, Lurleen; 4.35, Black Bazaar.

CATFORD: 8.33, Amigo Freddie; 9.37, Bubbly Pint (nap). CLAPTON: 7.45, Paul's Legacy. WHITE CITY: 7.45, Tiger In Smoke.

DON'T MISS THE TOP TEAM EVERY DAY IN MIRROR SPORT

REAL SHOCK FOR CHELSEA

Last-minute drama as Zoco swoops to force a replay

Chelsea 1, Real Madrid 1 (after extra time)

CHELSEA and Real Madrid battled to a furious 1—1 draw in the European Cup Winners' Cup Final here tonight and will now replay here on Friday.

Chelsea had gone ahead by a fifty-sixth-minute Peter Osgood goal. But Real snatched a last-gasp equaliser to force extra time—and brave Chelsea had to survive tremendous Spanish pressure to gain another chance.

Although Chelsea were under pressure in the opening minutes they were the first to produce a legitimate threat.

Keith Weller nearly broke through following a mix-up between Real goalkeeper Borja and full back Zunecui.

But it was quickly evident that Chelsea were short of form in vital positions and they were embarrassed by the skills and style of the Spaniards.

Unused to sharp inter-passing around their penalty area, they found themselves over-committed to tackles, and Amancio, in particular, took advantage.

When Chelsea did manage to establish some control, they troubled Real with a Charlie Cooke corner kick, but the Spaniards managed to clear under pressure.

Trouble

Faulty positioning by Ron Harris got Chelsea into trouble and goalkeeper Peter Bonetti, coming out to kick clear, could only play the ball against Real's veteran winger Gento.

Fortunately for Chelsea, Gento was unable to control the ball and it ran clear for a throw-in.

Chelsea continued to struggle when trying to put passes together, and Real's tactic of keeping their wingers wide in advanced positions led to concern among the London club's defence.

A fine example of Amancio's skill left David Webb floundering, and a tremendous through pass sent Gento away beyond John Boyle—but, at thirty-nine, Gento no longer had the speed to take advantage.

The one Chelsea player to be aroused by Real's talent was Charlie Cooke. He made two fine

SPASTIC LEAGUE CLUB
PREMIUM BOND
QUALIFYING NUMBERS

01 — 32 — 35	14 — 41 — 59
02 — 14 — 50	15 — 58 — 67
02 — 63 — 68	17 — 21 — 58
03 — 38 — 53	18 — 25 — 44
04 — 23 — 39	19 — 42 — 52
05 — 19 — 35	21 — 22 — 69
06 — 10 — 45	22 — 44 — 61
06 — 62 — 70	24 — 25 — 54
07 — 54 — 67	25 — 48 — 59
08 — 38 — 66	27 — 61 — 65
09 — 38 — 45	29 — 57 — 70
10 — 35 — 54	32 — 35 — 56
11 — 38 — 66	35 — 41 — 44
12 — 47 — 59	38 — 41 — 51
13 — 36 — 48	44 — 59 — 69
	53 — 55 — 65

SPASTIC LEAGUE CLUB, Bristol

KEN JONES
Britain's top Soccer writer reports from Athens, Wednesday

dribbles both of which could have been productive.

The first of them led to a pass to John Hollins, but his shot on the run went high over the crossbar.

The Spaniards were totally uncompromising in defence and Peter Osgood, in particular, suffered from the tackles.

Osgood did well to fight his way on to a free-kick from Alan Hudson, but he was unable to find an angle for a shot.

Another Real burst of slick inter-passing had Chelsea in trouble again, but Grosso was hopelessly off target.

Both Osgood and Hollins seemed to be feeling the effects of injuries which nearly prevented them from playing.

It meant that Chelsea were short of authority in midfield and decision in attack.

But they began the

second half with more determination — and in the fifty-sixth minute they went ahead with a Peter Osgood goal.

Shadow

Cooke played the ball out to Boyle, who crossed. Osgood and his shadow Benito challenged vigorously for the ball.

The Spaniard got there first but only managed to deflect the ball downwards and Osgood, reacting smartly, turned to score with a low, left-foot shot.

In a pile-up in front of Chelsea's goal, he intercepted a Cooke back pass to Bonetti and shot home.

But Real fought back—and grabbed the equaliser in the last minute through right half Zoco.

After Dempsey had miskicked in front of goal, Zoco pounced and drove the ball in from three yards.

Coventry to sell Strong—with a vote of thanks

By PETER INGALL

COVENTRY are prepared to sell three defenders—including Geoff Strong, the former Liverpool and Arsenal star.

The others are Mick Coop and Brian Hill, and Coventry chief Noel Cantwell hopes to collect about £60,000 for the trio.

Strong, signed for £20,000 from Liverpool, solved a Coventry injury crisis at the start of the season, when centre half Roy Barry was ruled out with a broken leg.

But with Barry fit and England youth team skipper Bobby Parker a regular member of the first team squad, Coventry feel that Strong can go.

Cantwell said: "Strong has done the job I bought him to do when we ran into injury trouble and now I feel it is only fair to give him the opportunity to move on with our thanks."

Coop has been listed for some time while Hill has just returned after a period on loan to Bristol City.

SPEEDWAY

BRITISH LEAGUE. — Div. I: Poole 52 Elde 11, Smith 10, Fossengen 9, Belle Vue 26 (Mauger 10, Slosten 8). **Div. II:** Bradford 45 (Schofield 11, Adlington 9), Berwick 33 (Robinson 12, Wyer 11).

RESULTS

HOME INTERNATIONAL
England 0   Wales 0
70,000

(At Wembley)

	P	W	D	L	F	A	Pts
England	2	1	1	0	1	0	3
Wales	2	0	2	0	0	2	2
Ireland	2	0	1	1	1	1	1
Scotland	2	0	1	1	0	1	1

EUROPEAN CUP WINNERS CUP FINAL
Chelsea 1   Real Madrid 1
Osgood   Zoco
H-T: 0—0
(In Athens.)
After extra-time. Score at 90 mins. 1—1. Replay in Athens on Friday.

EUROPEAN NATIONS CUP.—Group Two (Sofia): Bulgaria 3, Hungary 0.

TOUR MATCH (Tel Aviv).— Tel Aviv XI 1 (Spiegal, pen.), Everton 2 (Morrissey, pen., Royle), H-T: 0—0. Att.: 10,000.

KENT LEAGUE—Chatham 1, Faversham 0; Crockenhill 2, Sittingbourne 1; Hastings 1, Bretts Sports 1.

Francis Lee looks dejected as Irish referee Malcolm Wright disallows his goal and points for a free-kick to Wales for offside.
Pictures: MONTE FRESCO

A VENGER COX IS JUST CHAMPION

PETER WILSON
at Bournemouth on the big tennis scene

MARK COX, holder of the Rothmans-sponsored British hard court championships, but ranked second in Great Britain to Roger Taylor, yesterday justified his status as champion.

He also confounded the ranking authorities by reaching the semi-finals at Bournemouth at the expense of fellow left-hander Taylor.

Cox won 8—6, 6—1, 3—6, 6—3, and it seems to me that Taylor—as well as suffering from the effects of a back injury—is suffering from the other "professional disease," an inability to concentrate for any length of time because of too much lawn tennis.

Taylor lost his service to trail 1-3, broke back to 2-3, but foozled a smash when looking straight into the sun, and was beaten by a great pass to fall behind again at 2-4.

Taylor never gave up trying, but when he went for forehand winners they were generally too long.

In the tense and final ninth game Cox also used the drop shot intelligently to enmesh Taylor, who finally had to concede defeat in just under two hours playing time.

Crisp

Certainly, what began as cool play by the Yorkshireman degenerated into a kind of lackadaisical exercise in which he could never get the adrenalin flowing freely or raise his strokes when he needed to, until it was virtually too late.

Cox played as he always plays, striking the ball crisply enough, rarely producing unforgiveable errors, and even more rarely producing memorable shots.

He kept steadily on after he had let two set points get away from him at 4—5 in the first set, and in the fourteenth game Taylor made an unforced error to become a set down.

Alive

Taylor continued to beat himself in the second set, which lasted only seventeen minutes, and in which he won only three points in the three final games.

The Yorkshireman just could not get his touch on the forehand, and when he tried to apply a little

pressure on this wing, he constantly over-drove.

At last Taylor came alive in the third set. For a big man he was doing well on this desperately slippery Centre Court.

But Cox, having been beaten by pass and smash and serve in the third set, went on in his unemotional way in the fourth.

Forty-three - year - old Frank Sedgman, finalist here nineteen years ago, therefore goes forward to meet Britain's Gerald Battrick, twenty years his junior.

Rousing

In the other two men's singles, Zeljko Franulovic, Yugoslavian architect of Britain's first round Davis Cup defeat, beat South African Bob Maud with the loss of only eight games, and the aggressive young Chilean, Jaime Fillol, won a rousing five-setter against France's Pierre Barthes 3—6, 8—6, 6—4, 2—3, 6—2.

Winnie Shaw is Britain's only representative left in the women's singles.

In a match in which her form varied from intelligent aggression to rather pallid lack of inspiration, she defeated Mrs. Ana Maria Pinto Bravo, of Chile, 3—6, 6—3, 6—3.

John and Edwards may miss Meads

THE BRITISH Lions' leading half-back pair of Barry John and Gareth Edwards get an immediate taste of New Zealand rugby power when they face Thames Valley Counties at Pukekohe on Saturday.

It almost certainly means the Lions will not play this precious pair next Wednesday against the powerful King Country side—who are captained by mighty All Black Colin Meads.

YESTERDAY'S RESULTS

BRITISH HARD COURT CHAMPIONSHIPS (Bournemouth)—**Men's singles, 2nd rnd:** F. Sedgman (Aust.) walked over A. Roche (Aust.) scratched. **Quarter - finals :** Z. Franulovic (Yugo) bt R. Maud (S. Africa) 6—4, 6—3, 6—1; M. Cox bt R. Taylor 8—6, 6—1, 3—6, 6—3; J. Fillol (Chile) bt P. Barthes (France) 3—6, 8—6, 6—4, 2—6, 6—2.

Women's singles, 3rd rnd: F. Durr (France) bt B. Hawcroft (Aust.) 6—3, 2—6, 6—0; Mrs. P. Curtis (U.S.) bt Mrs. W. Mowrey

(Aust.) 6—3, 9—8; P. Hogan (U.S.) bt Mrs. D. Dalton (Aust.) 6—4, 6—2; E. Goolagong (Aust.) bt W. Gilchrist (Aust.) 6—4, 6—1; Mrs. M. Court (Aust.) bt H. Gourlay (Aust.) 6—2, 6—3; W. Shaw bt Mrs. J. Pinto-Bravo (Chile) 3—6, 6—3, 6—3.

GOLF
IRISH AMATEUR CHAMPION-SHIP (Ballybunion, County Kerry).—**Semi-finals:** M. O'Brien (New Ross) bt R. Carr (Sutton) 4 and 3; R. Kane (Malahide) bt P. Caul (Malahide) 5 and 4. **Final:** Kane bt O'Brien 3 and 2.

OLE! OLE! CHELSEA!

Chelsea 2, Real Madrid 1

CHELSEA survived gathering anxiety in the final ten minutes here tonight to add the European Cup-Winners' Cup to London's record of glowing achievement this season.

From
KEN JONES
Athens, Friday

Chelsea two up .   scorer Peter Osgood turns in joy as Borja sprawls.

It was finally an ecstatic moment for those other fans who chose to stay on—to sleep rough on the beaches—rather than miss the replay against Real Madrid.

They danced in triumph on the terraces at half-time after Chelsea had powered into a two-goal lead which suggested they had taken total command.

Grimly

But, as in the first match on Wednesday, Chelsea found themselves hanging on grimly to protect a lead which had been reduced to just one goal.

Once again they came close to squandering all they had fought for as the Spaniards reached for

Dempsey, Osgood hit glory goals to clinch the Cup-Winners Cup

the attacking instinct which has enriched their history.

Astonishingly, Real elected at first to allow Chelsea to take the initiative, despite their own vulnerability in defence.

And it was not until the game had been almost won and lost that Real reveaed their true style and surprisingly, some character.

Pushing forward in a desperate effort to save the game, they pulled a goal back through winger Fleitas, and it seemed that Chelsea would commit the error they made on Wed-

Snatched

nesday—of being over-cautious once they were in front.

It was then that goal-keeper Peter Bonetti snatched glory out of the mounting danger.

The darting Amancio almost beat him with a whiplash shot after turning between two Chelsea defenders as though they were not there.

Then came a memorable save as the elegant Zoco soared to meet a centre and drove the ball towards the far corner of Chelsea's goal with his head.

Bonetti arched through the air to his left, clutching the ball in full flight and bringing Chelsea's substitutes to their feet on the touchline in spontaneous applause.

So Chelsea survived to take the cup after what may well be the last replay allowed in this competition. A series of penalties, if scores are level at full-time, will probably be the pattern for the future.

It would have been tragic had Chelsea been forced into a penalty serial to settle the contest tonight.

Obviously better acclimatised than they

were in the first game, they benefited from the shrewd move of bringing in Tommy Baldwin as the spearhead of their attack.

Expected

With John Hollins injured, Chelsea were expected to push John Boyle forward into midfield and to bring Paddy Mulligan in at full back.

But it was Baldwin who was included and Peter Osgood dropped back into midfield to find the space which had been denied him by Benito's belligerent defensive play on Wednesday.

It was some time before Real sorted themselves out, and during that period Chelsea took command.

Charlie Cooke's skills and willingness were vital to them in the opening half-hour, but it was David Webb's persistence and a spectacular volley by John Dempsey which put them ahead.

Webb broke powerfully on a run which led to a centre that had goal-keeper Borja in considerable trouble before he conceded a corner.

When Cooke curled in the kick, Baldwin turned the ball back and Webb forced the Spaniard into

a frenzied clearance. It gave Dempsey the chance to strike a scaring volley which threatened to demolish the goal.

Six minutes later Osgood took a Baldwin pass and beat Borja with a right foot shot to the far corner of the net.

Real looked finished then, but in the second half when their raids became more effective and Fleitas pulled back a goal with a fine shot from just inside the penalty area.

Process

Chelsea were then in process of replacing Osgood with Derek Smethurst, and Osgood departed from the match when Chelsea began to play through their grimmest period.

The veteran Gento came on to add his skill to the Spanish football, but Chelsea were in no mood to make the same mistake as on Wednesday, and Bonetti was more than equal to the challenge when put under pressure.

BATTRICK KEEPS COOL TO SHATTER CHILEAN

PETER WILSON AT THE BIG TENNIS

GERALD BATTRICK, ranked number three in Britain, scored what was probably the most satisfactory win of his career —considering the importance of the tournament—when he reached the final of the Rothmans-subsidised British Hard Court Championships at Bournemouth yesterday.

Battrick beat the man who only last Saturday at Hurlingham defeated him in two straight sets— Jaime Fillol, the Chilean joint number one — by 7—5 1—6 6—3 1—6, 6—3

Battrick played consistently as well as I've ever seen him.

This win ensures Battrick at least £1,000 even if he loses today—it would be £1,700 if he were surprisingly to beat Zeljko Franulovic—and expenses of anything from £250 to £425.

Fillol was not at his best. The evening before

he had played nine sets comprising no fewer than 111 games in the men's doubles and had felt compelled to scratch from the mixed.

The weariness showed in his game.

Nevertheless at the end of both the second and the fourth sets, both of which the Chilean won with the loss of only a single game, the scales seemed to be tipping in his favour.

But Battrick produced far greater solidity than one expects from a player of his volatile temperament. Some of his passing shots in particular, would have been memorable in any company.

Most satisfactory of all was the way the Welshman stood firm in the decisive fifth set. There was a great fight for the

first game with Battrick serving.

There was an even greater one for the second. Twice Fillol played drop shots which died as venomous as rattlesnakes burrowing into the dust.

Terrible

Terrible shots to have to meet at this breath-holding stage of the match, but Fillol failed with a third and his fatigue made him sag into more simple errors.

But he, too, fought back —this was quite the best match of the week—and after they had been playing for over two hours, the score stood at two sets all, two games all, and two points all with Battrick serving at thirty-all in the fifth game.

Battrick broke through

to lead 4—2 when Fillol again started missing easy approach shots and drives and lost the game by netting a simple forehand volley

But even up to the last game, with Battrick serving at 5—3, the result was by no means certain.

He trembled on the brink of victory—and Fillol lassoed him back with a couple of stretching, straining volleys. The Chilean had a point for the break but again put a simple volley out.

Nerves were stretched tighter than racket strings and then on the second match point against him, Fillol rasped the ball down the side-line — to fall out of court — urged on by a shout of triumph from Battrick !

Brave Oosterhuis zips three ahead

By RON WILLS

PETER OOSTERHUIS took an Arnold Palmer-type gamble yesterday to reduce the 6,600-yard Stoke Poges course to 67 shots in the second round of the £5,000 Agfa-Gevaert tournament. And that, with his first round 68, means he goes into today's final two rounds with a three-shot lead in the chase for the £1,000 first prize.

The gamble came when 23-year-old Oosterhuis pushed his drive under trees at the 497-yard fifth He elected to hook a three-iron round the trees in a bid to make the green.

Incredible

Incredibly it came off and he got his birdie four!

Another miracle hole for Oosterhuis was the 507-yard thirteenth He rifled his tee shot 290 yards into the wind, laid a two-iron second six feet from the pin and holed it for an eagle three.

OLYMPIC AIRWAYS

IN a report last Wednesday concerning the delay at Heathrow in the departure of the Chelsea football team for the European Cup Winners Cup final in Athens—due to the possibility that a bomb had been planted in the plane—we stated that the pilot had refused to take off since one of his company's planes blew up in mid-air a year ago

This statement was based on information the accuracy of which at that time our reporter had no reason to doubt.

We are asked by Olympic Airways to state that the accident referred to was not caused in the manner described and that neither last year, nor at any time has any of their planes blown up in mid-air.

LAST NIGHT'S LONDON GREYHOUND RESULTS

CHARLTON. — 7.45: Leaders (5-1 58p) Quinela: £4 99 Duella: 88p.
6.6arm 6-4 jf (2-5, £1-90). 3-1: Airp001 Boy 5-4 f (1-4, 69p). 8-13: Speedy Clipper 12-1 (3-1, £4-51). 8.35: Majestic Ron 5-1 (5-1, £1-77). 8-52: Morden Flash 5-1 (6-3, £5-89). 9.28: Vickris Flash 5-1 (6-3, 1'5-69). 9.45: Amy Farne 11-4 f (3-4, £2-42).
HARDINGAY.—7.45: Quiet Era 5-1 (3-6, £1-80). 4.34: Brighri Glass 5-1 (3-4, £1-53). 8.51: Pune Pencil 8-2 (6-3, £1-95). 9.8: Supreme Fun 1-3 (3-4, £5-22). 9.27: Yellow Sunrise 15-8 f (2-1, 58p). 9.45: The Marshiness 10-11 f

WEMBLEY.—7.45: Fox Hound 4-1 (5-1 £2-87) 8.8: Skilful Lady 3-1 (3-1 £2-67). 3.39: Bon Voyage 9-2 (6-4, £1 89) 8.3: Ballyhea Era 7-2 (1-6, £2-33). 8.15: Proud Lark 11-10 f (2-3, 72p) 9.7: Westmead Rudi 7-2 f (5-4, £1-76) 9.75: Killone Kit 5-1 (5-4, £3-29) 9.38: Prairie Patch 7-2 (1-5, £3 00) Quinella: £95 xj t

WEST HAM.—7.45 Dugs Dasher 10-4 (3-2 £9-37). 8.0: Silver Harm (3-4 £5-5, £5 10). 8.16: Charmageld (74) 2-1 jf and Pigalle Boy CT6 8-1 dd-hL. (1-6, £1-42, 6-4, £1-31) 8.33: Dun Atman Girl 4-1 (3-4,

WIMBLEDON.—7.45: Tito Pete 7-1 (3-6, £5-99) 8.0: African Queen 4-1 (3-2, £1-40) 8.15: Gaultier Chief 10-1 (3-6, C5 87). Non-winner Jingle Book (7-2) 8.30: Call The Tramp 11-8 f (4-2, £1 78) 8.45: Powerful Home 3-1 j f (4-2, £1-51). 9.0: Sandy Desert 2-1 f (6-4, 60p). 9.15: Plus Glory 11-8 f (5-4, 44p) 9.30: Trumps Lad 6-4 f (4-6, 9.5 92) Plums £38-12 Paid on 1st leg: £19-56, £12-16.

8.50: Miss Buzz 5-1 (2-4, £1-77). 9.7: No Gambler 4-1 (5-4, £1.23). 9.24: Wages Day 4-1 (5-6, 1 £2 65) 9.40: Lakeside Lass 2-1 f (5-4, £1 14) Couplets: £2-16 72 pd. on 1st leg: £48 26; £27-19.

NIGHT WINNERS

TAUNTON: Hard

6.30 FRODO (Champion, evens 1), 1: Clear Wave (5-1), 2; Metraned (20-1), 3. 7 ran. Tote 18p 14p 19p; dual forecast 98. 7.0 RICHELEAU (H. M. Ranaugh 5-2 f), 1; Mieux Mount (5-1), 2; Ivy Star (5-1), 3. 7 ran. Tote 34p; 20p, 23p; dual forecast £1-32. 7.30 THUNDERCOPSE (W. Shoemark 14-1), ; Tristram (8-1), 2; Portman (4-1), 3. 14 ran. Tote Winners 3-1 f, Tote £1 11 31p, 34p 22p; dual forecast £1 29. 8.0: BIG GUN II (Starkle 8-1), 1; Maniple (7-2), 2; Bangkok (evens 1), 3. 8 ran. Tote £1 03: 15p, 13p, 12p; dual forecast 88p. Objection to winner overruled.

8.0, DANDY TOM (Forsey 5-2 f), 1; Fort Spirit (5-1), 2; Hewood Lad (11-2), 3. 9 ran. Tote 28p, 19p, 17p, 19p; dual forecast £1 25.

9.0, FARMER (I. Jones, 25-1), 1; Signor Bonemica (11-4), 2. On the Man (10-3) 3, 14 ran. Mascua and Keighero Artist 3-2 1fs. Tote £1 67 38p 18p, 20p Tote Double: £45 25. Treble: £165 45

In the meantime Mrs Margaret Court, playing more from the back of the court than she usually does, nevertheless had no serious difficulty in beating Francoise Durr 6—3, 6—3

Evonne Goolagong, the only girl to have beaten Mrs Court this year—in the Victorian State Championships — meets her again in today's final.

The 19-year-old part-aborigine youngster, beat Mrs Mary Ann Curtis, of the USA 5—7 6 4, 6 -1.

EUROPEAN SOCCER SPECIAL..WITH THE MEN FROM THE MIRROR

LUCKY 13 AS CHELSEA SMASH RECORD!

By KEN JONES: Chelsea 13, Jeunesse 0

(Chelsea win 21-0 on aggregate)

CHELSEA striker Peter Osgood failed by just one goal to grab personal distinction on a record-breaking night at Stamford Bridge.

Osgood needed to score six times against Jeunesse Hartcharage to set a new record for marksmanship in a European competition. He could only manage five, however.

But Chelsea, completely overwhelming the Luxembourg village team passed the 18-goal record aggregate set by Benfica.

Chelsea made a quick-fire start with two goals in the first five minutes—both scored by Peter Osgood.

Osgood turned in his first from Charlie Cooke's low free kick and then drove in another in the fifth minute after goalkeeper Lucien Fusilier had dropped a centre from the right.

Alan Hudson scored a third for Chelsea, striking Cooke's low centre firmly through a crowd of defenders. At that stage it seemed that Chelsea would have their record before half-time.

There was no reason to doubt that prospect when

Chelsea skipper Ron Harris was brought down inside the penalty area by Jeunesse captain Eddy Welscher and John Hollins drove home the spot kick.

But Chelsea had to wait another ten minutes for their next goal.

Injured

It was David Webb who scored with a header from Peter Houseman's corner.

Jeunesse, who had taken time out to repair their injured goalkeeper, hung on until the forty-second minute before Chelsea scored again.

This time it was Harris who netted with a shot

which was wickedly deflected by Osgood.

Chelsea, watched by a near-28,000 crowd kept things going in the second half in search of their record.

Tommy Baldwin got a seventh in the 63rd minute and Osgood made it eight two minutes later.

Baldwin with a back header and then Houseman from an Osgood pass brought Chelsea level with Benfica's record aggregate.

It was Osgood with his fifth goal of the match who put Chelsea ahead in Europe's history with the 11th goal.

Osgood got the 12th—and then Baldwin took the total to 13 in the closing minutes.

Urtain first for Bodell

By PETER WILSON

AS I forecast, the European Boxing Union has nominated Jose Urtain, of Spain, as official challenger for the European heavyweight title acquired this week by Jack Bodell. The contest is to take place by December 15.

Bodell's manager, George Biddles, commented: "We are looking forward to the fight. We don't mind where it is."

No surprise, then, about the second most important heavyweight title in the world — the European—but a bombshell about the world championship.

"Yank" Durham, manager of world champion, Joe Frazier, says the rematch between his man and Muhammad Ali Cassius Clay, scheduled for next March, now probably won't come before late 1972, or even

early 1973.

Durham went on: "All says he wants four or five more fights before he gets back in the ring with Joe, so we're not going to be sitting around doing nothing.

"I'd like Frazier to have a title fight in December—he could fight Joe Bugner, Jose Urtain, of Brazil, Floyd Patterson, or George Chuvalo."

Clearly "Yank" hasn't heard what happened to Bugner last Monday. He doesn't know that Urtain already has a December date with Bodell.

Ken Buchanan's next defence of his world lightweight title may be in Japan. Manager Eddie Thomas has received a £30,000 offer from a Tokio promoter for a fight with Shinnichi Kadota in February or March

Radford double as Arsenal men go sweeping on

By PETER INGALL

ARSENAL moved easily and confidently last night over the first hurdle towards adding the European Cup to the other trophies they have taken to Highbury in the past two seasons.

They did so by brushing aside Norwegian amateurs Stroemsgodset Drammen, on an aggregate score of 7—1 after winning the first leg 3—1 in Norway.

It was Arsenal's first European Cup match at Highbury but the fans must be hoping for better-class opposition in the second round.

It took Arsenal only five minutes to increase their aggregate lead. A clearance from a Norwegian defender struck the referee and the ball eventually went to Eddie Kelly. He put it square past two defenders to the unmarked Ray Kennedy, who gave the goalkeeper no chance.

Then, in the seventeenth minute, Kennedy laid the ball off to John Radford, who was allowed time to bring it under control and let fly with a fierce drive which flashed into the net.

It appeared little more than a practice match for Arsenal. There were times when they overdid the clever stuff, no doubt having some pity for the opposition.

But one man who did capture the hearts of the Highbury crowd was goalkeeper Thun, who

Arsenal		
Stroemsgodset		
Drammen		
(agg. 7-1)		

brought off some fine saves. He produced a brave save from a George Graham effort and then showed his class when keeping out Radford.

His best save came in the thirty-ninth minute when he dived to push a Kelly piledriver round the post.

Unmarked

The Norwegians did little in attack, and Arsenal keeper Bob Wilson's only real work was stopping a header from left winger Pettersen.

Thun had no chance in the 60th minute.

Kennedy tried to bulldoze his way through but the ball glanced off one defender to the unmarked Radford, who scored with a right-foot cross.

Arsenal finished off a competent night's work when George Armstrong scored their fourth goal ten minutes from time.

Injury-hit England send an SOS for Evans

By CHRIS LANDER

Hongkong, Wednesday

GEOFF EVANS, the Coventry and Warwickshire centre, has been asked to fly out as a replacement for England's injury-stricken Rugby team in the Far East.

The tourists were so badly hit by injuries in Japan that the original party of twenty-three has been whittled down to eighteen fit players.

Jim Broderick, Coventry prop, and David Roughley, Liverpool centre, flew home to London today.

Broderick will be transferred from Heathrow to the RAF hospital at Halton for an intensive check on his mystery back injury.

And full back Peter Rossborough, of Coventry, is still in a Tokio hospital recovering from delayed

concussion he suffered during England's bitter struggle to beat All-Japan 6—3 last night.

England hope he will rejoin the tour in Singapore at the weekend.

Meanwhile, manager Bob Weighill and coach John Burgess have extra selection problems because centre Chris Wardlow and hooker Peter Wheeler cannot be considered for selection against Hong Kong.

Wardlow is limping because of an old leg injury and Wheeler has a mild bout of tonsilitis.

This means that Dick Cowman, normally a fly half, will stand in as full back against Hong Kong.

Weighill said: "Tony Richards was the original first choice three-quarter replacement.

"But with so much trouble over the centres we're calling for Evans."

England are upset about criticism of their Rugby in Japan, where they won all three matches.

As they left Tokio, skipper Budge Rogers said: "I reckon the boys can be proud of our achievement here.

"We played three matches in eight days, and had to put up with tremendous humidity and a temperature approaching 90 deg. F. in Osaka. We've had our injuries, too."

SPORT SUMMARY

GOLF

DUNLOP MASTER'S TOURNAMENT (St. Pierre G.C., Chepstow).—First round: 67—A. Jacklin, J. Cook. 68—T. Horton, M. Bembridge, H. Bannerman, 69—G. Player (S. Africa), D. Vaughan, G. Graham (Australia), B. Charles (New Zealand), 70—P. Oosterhuis, B. Hunt, S. Brown, J. Garner, P. Townsend, F. Boobyer, D. McClelland, D. Hayes (S. Africa), B. Huggett, P. Thomson (Australia), P. Leonard. 71—V. Hood, H. Jackson, L. Platts, D. Huish, D. Rees, B. Barnes.

NORTHERN WOMEN'S GOLF CHAMPIONSHIP (Ainmouth.)

Semi-finals: Mrs. M. Pickard (Ainmouth) bt Mrs. M. McCartney (Bolton) 2 and 1; Mrs. V. Stone (Morpeth) bt Mrs. P. Nelson (Ainmouth) 4 and 2. Final: Mrs. Stone bt Mrs. Pickard 2 and 1.

CRICKET

LORD'S. — Gross Arrows 173 (Gale 57; Sprackling 7-56), Amersham 171 (Hughes 41; Latchman 6-61). Gross Arrows won by 2 runs.

RUGBY UNION

Ulster 27pts., Surrey 7; Sussex 19, Army 36; Torquay 15, St. Lukes Coll. 7; Rosslyn Park 10, Loughborough Coll. 30; Old

Alleynians 23, O. Millhillians 0. Glamorgan 14. Canada 14.
Abertillery 15, Cardiff 3.

SOCCER

SCOTTISH LEAGUE.—Div. II: Berwick 3, Albion 1; Clydebank 1, St. Mirren 3; E. Stirling 1, Alloa 2; Hamilton 2, Dumbarton 8; Raith 1, Arbroath 1; Stenhousemuir 3, Queen's Park 0; Stirling 2, Queen of South 0; Stranraer 0, Montrose 3.

TONIGHT'S SOCCER

TEXACO CUP—1st rnd., 2nd leg: Waterford v. Ballymena (4.30).

Mirror Sport

Friday, October 4, 1974
Telephone: (STD code 01)—353 0246

SEXTON GETS THE AXE

Now Chelsea aim to build a glamour side

Stepping in..

Dave Sexton has gone and assistant manager Ron Suart looks grim as he prepares for a caretaker's role in the hot seat at Stamford Bridge yesterday.

BREAKTHROUGH IN TV STRIKE

See story Page Two

Breakthrough in ITV news deadlock when management and striking journalists finally got together for meeting early today.

CHELSEA yesterday sacked manager Dave Sexton—and put into operation phase one of the changes scheduled for Stamford Bridge.

Now there will be a concentrated effort to bring style and appeal to the club, and that could mean a bid to buy back Peter Osgood from Southampton.

Conscious of the need to attract fans to their super stadium, ambitious chairman Brian Mears acknowledges the need for a personality at the Bridge.

Osgood up front again, and the authority and leadership from someone such as Bobby Moore at the back would go a long way to giving Chelsea a Showbiz glitter again.

Young emerging players like Peter Taylor of Crystal Palace could also be transfer targets, and with players to offer now in part exchange, Chelsea are in a position to bargain.

By NIGEL CLARKE

Peace

But first, under the caretaker management of Ron Suart, an effort will be made to make peace with the club's five unsettled players.

Bill Garner, Ian Hutchinson, Tommy Baldwin, Steve Kember, and John Dempsey will all be asked by chairman Mears to see Chelsea through their present problems.

Chelsea will advertise for Sexton's replacement but out of the running will be controversial names like Brian Clough and Malcolm Allison.

Prefer

Mears gave a clue to the kind of man he wants when he said he would prefer someone young who has proved himself, and has a Chelsea background, but not young enough to have played with the present staff.

Alan Dicks, a former player, and now boss at Bristol City, could join the inevitable names that will be linked with the job.

Mears said he told Sexton on Monday that he was out, and adds: "I did not make an immediate announcement because I thought it would be more humane to wait.

"This is a sad day for me, I had the greatest respect for Dave, and I have admired him not only as a man, but for the way he took the news.

"He leaves because we have to look beyond survival in the First Division. The object is to win trophies, and the board felt we had no prospect in the present position."

Pride

"As far as Dave's contract is concerned we shall be honouring our commitments."

That means that Sexton is likely to receive something in the region of £30,000 compensation. He had three years of a five-year agreement to run.

Sexton said: "I've no complaints, but my pride is hurt. Managers always have to walk a tightrope and sometimes you fall off."

Sexton is unlikely to be out of work for long, and will certainly interest Queen's Park Rangers.

Suart, who reluctantly takes over his caretaker duties, said: "Dave is a wonderful man, and a brilliant coach. Everyone had the greatest respect for him."

TWO MORE VICTIMS OF THE PANIC—Page 30.

Stepping out..

A sad moment for Dave Sexton as he prepares to leave Chelsea for the last time after a seven-year reign.   *Pictures: MONTE FRESCO*

SAWARD IN LINE FOR MILLWALL

By KEVIN MOSELEY

PAT SAWARD, the former Brighton boss, could become Millwall's new manager.

Saward, a former Millwall player, took Brighton into the Second Division on slim resources and was dismissed after their relegation. He will be one of those considered to replace Benny Fenton.

After over eight years as manager Fenton resigned yesterday, admitting that "Millwall was a difficult club to run."

The Lions are set to give Fenton, who made numerous shrewd and profitable deals on the transfer market, a golden handshake.

Millwall's poor start to the season—they are fifth from bottom of the Second Division—and last week's resignation of chairman Mickey Purser seemed to have prompted Fenton's decision. "It was a mutual decision and I'm sad to part company with the club," said Fenton last night.

Fenton's most successful transactions involved the buying of strikers Keith Weller, now with Leicester, and Derek Possee, who went to Orient via Crystal Palace. Both of them went for six-figure fees.

Taylor: My head's on the block

BRIGHTON manager Peter Taylor offered to quit last night, if the club felt he was not the right man for the job, writes Kevin Moseley.

Taylor joined Brighton with Brian Clough last November and took over as manager when Clough left. He said: "I am sick at the way things are going. My head is on the block."

THE DAILY MIRROR NEWSPAPERS, Ltd (01-353 0246) at, and for IPC Newspapers Ltd., Holborn Circus, London, EC1P 1DQ. Registered at the Post Office as a newspaper   © The Daily Mirror Newspapers, Ltd., 1974

FRANK McGHEE

THE VOICE OF SPORT

'Paisley had the right answer'

When the pressure starts to tell..

BOB PAISLEY, the Liverpool manager, allowed himself afterwards to admit the unthinkable: "We could still finish up winning nothing."

He doesn't really believe it, of course. Neither do I. But significant signs that the pressure of two Cup Finals at the end of this month is at last getting to the Liverpool team are starting to show.

I have seldom seen them as completely outplayed as they were for most of the first hour at Loftus Road. And a nagging suspicion exists that fear you don't normally associate with Liverpool players was the 'cause

No one was consciously shirking. But an alarming percentage of the 50—50 challenges were being lost, both in a hesitant defence and a meek midfield.

Frankly, I can't help wondering whether a subconscious, perhaps understandable, desire to avoid injury was its cause.

If so, Paisley provided the right remedy

QPR .... Liverpool ....

Bringing on that marvellous ageless veteran Ian Callaghan in place of the still raw and immature David Fairclough after 60 minutes provided an unsubtle reminder to half a dozen of his players that Wembley and Rome team places still have to be earned

And it was probably no coincidence that Paisley's after-match conversation was liberally sprinkled with the names of other contenders.

Pushing

"Steve Heighway is already fit enough to come back into the forward line," he said.

"Phil Thompson is pushing on towards fitness after his cartilage operation. If we get the championship won he could still get in for a League game.

"And John Toshack might put himself into contention for the Rome game."

Paisley might look and sound like everybody's favourite uncle. But there is and has to be a streak of shrewd professional practicality in him

Certainly Callaghan wasted no time in starting to make

his own claim. His alertness, neatness, accuracy and industry immediately restored balance in midfield where the game was being lost

Rangers' Gerry Francis had been particularly responsible for that—re-emphasising what a blow it was for both club and country that injury robbed him of virtually a whole season.

Rangers looked like last season's championship challengers once more as they took a 10th-minute lead through Don Givens in a game that could have been over by halftime.

Peter Eastoe and Givens both hit shots against the two uprights in the same attack.

Francis uncharacteristically, and Givens both missed simple scoring chances

Dave Thomas on the left wing was creating havoc with long twisting intricate runs.

Only the two most senior men, Emlyn Hughes and Kevin Keegan, were operating with anything like normal efficiency and Keegan was suffering from lack of either service or support from the midfield trio of McDermott, Kennedy and Case.

The arrival of Callaghan—

with Case pushed forward into attack—made all the difference. Suddenly Liverpool remembered who they were, what their name means.

Before then Phil Parkes in the Rangers' goal, had made only two saves, one from Keegan, one from Fairclough.

Suddenly he was under siege. Keegan should have had a penalty when Frank McLintock lost his cool control to haul him down. And Case's 69th-minute equaliser might have been the first of several Liverpool goals

Dominating

Ray Kennedy in particular redeemed all his earlier errors to dominate his sector as convincingly as Francis, limping and tired in these later stages, had done in the first half.

Better finishing accuracy from David Johnson once and Terry McDermott twice could have seen Liverpool even further on the road to the title —though come to think of it, that would have been savage injustice for Rangers.

On this form they'll be safe —and deserve to be.

Kevin Keegan collides with Don Masson but helps keep Liverpool on course.

Picture: MONTE FRESCO

EDDIE

WHAT promotion really means to Chelsea will become clear when their creditors meet on July 2.

While the mood won't be exactly euphoric, it will be vastly different to that of a year ago.

Then the same people got together at Stamford Bridge and agreed to a stay of execution only if the most stringent economies were made.

Champagne corks were popping all around at Molineux on Saturday as chairman Brian Mears stood in a corridor and reviewed the most difficult twelve months any club has ever experienced

He had earned the deep-down joy he felt. If there was a tear or two mixed with the bubbly in his glass, it was understandable

Tightrope

Manager Eddie McCreadie and the players were accorded maximum credit as the friendly man everyone in football addresses as Brian said:

"It's been like a tightrope without a net. But I never doubted we would get to the other side.

"I can't believe that any manager in history has even been under the

By HARRY MILLER

| Wolves | 1 |
| Chelsea | |

sort of pressure that Eddie has experienced.

"Those who started this season had to finish it, no matter how badly things had gone. There simply wasn't a penny available to buy players.

"Now we can go to our creditors in July and say we have done everything they wanted us to do and more."

Mears points out that Chelsea's average gate has been well above the break-even 20,000 regarded as the essential base for survival.

And that a drastic drop in the interest rate has made a difference of

SUPER BILLY MOVING ON

By KEVIN MOSELEY: West Ham 2, Derby 2

BILLY JENNINGS came on as a late substitute to snatch a crucial point-saving goal for West Ham a few hours after being put on the transfer list.

Later Jennings, priced at £60,000, said: "My only satisfaction from the goal was that it took me into double figures for the season and it could help me get away.

"I don't hate West Ham. There's no hard feelings. All I want to do is secure my own future.

"I would love to stay in the First Division but

I'm prepared to drop into the Second. I just want to go to a club where I'm wanted."

Derby's controversial winger Leighton James was abused, pelted and nearly belted after an incident which led to Derby's first-half equaliser at 1—1

He went sprawling to win a controversial free-kick—and scored from it himself

"Contrary to public opinion I was fouled," said James. Few would argue after an action replay on television yesterday

THE MONDAY MORNING SOCCER VERDICT

ON A BANKER!

Chelsea kids make the future bright

£150,000 a year to the size of Chelsea's debt.

If Chelsea need to buy to make an impact in the First Division, Mears is hoping they will have earned the go-ahead to spend.

Worthy

The fact that John Richards equalised an earlier Tommy Langley goal to make Wolves worthy champions seemed almost academic on a day of such Chelsea joy.

Wolves, through having to make the match all-ticket in an abortive move to beat the hooligans, reckon that cost

them £10,000 in lost receipts.

It wasn't really team manager McCreadie's concern as he looked forward to the First Division challenge and proudly predicted:

"Give them a couple of years and these players will terrorise the First Division. All they need is time.

"They have done wonders in two years, but the best is yet to come. English football is going to be proud of these kids."

Few will surely disagree this morning, that Wolves as well as Chelsea are back where they belong.

Bubbling over . . Chelsea's youngsters have made it to the First Division, and the celebrations are under way.   *Picture: DICK WILLIAMS*

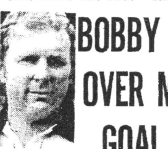

MOORE

BOBBY BUBBLES OVER MITCHELL GOAL BLAST

JOHN MITCHELL'S four-goal spree in Fulham's 6-1 win over Orient guarantees Second Division football at Craven Cottage next season—and Bobby Moore can't thank him enough.

Moore, making his final London appearance before retiring after next week's match at Blackburn, was greeted on the pitch by England manager Don Revie. And a fan ran on to present Moore with a bottle of champagne.

Yet he was apprehensive, and refused Alan Slough's offer to be captain for the day.

"We still had two points to win and that came first," said Moore. "I can't thank John enough for giving me a champagne send-off.

"I want to stay in football, but definitely not as a player."

Mitchell's goals, plus two from Teddy Maybank were capsuled in a magnificent thirty-six minute spell that leaves poor Orient in grave relegation danger.

Finale

CHARLTON manager Andy Nelson was disappointed with their finale at The Valley — a 2-1 win over Oldham — and added: "We're two players short of an excellent side."

An own goal by MILL-WALL'S Jon Moore—his second of the week — gave Nottingham Forest the 1-0 win that could carry them into the First Division.

LUTON'S David Geddis held Bolton — Forest's promotion rivals—with a great equaliser in a 1-1 draw. But manager Harry Haslam said: "We have only borrowed Geddis from Ipswich and he will be going back."

M'M'BLOO

OH WHAT A REFEREE!

BREWERY Rangers staged a breakaway against Sludge Shifters. "Nicker" Steele took the ball to the by-line before turning it back to Studs McShane, just inside the penalty area.

Studs had only one opponent in front of him: Shifters' goalkeeper Tank Thomas. Tank protested furiously, after Studs had put the ball into the net. "Offside!" fumed Tank.

Our referee disallowed the goal and that was a bloomer. MR. McBLOO! Law 11 makes it clear that Studs was not off-side because he was standing behind the ball when it was last played.

Slim Rix is great prospect

Arsenal 1
Middlesbrough 1

GRAHAM RIX, Arsenal's teenage forward, confirmed his growing reputation with an eye-catching performance.

Rix, deputising for the injured Alan Hudson, was unlucky not to be rewarded with two goals as Arsenal left it late to grab a point in their final home game of the season.

He struck the crossbar twice within a minute as Arsenal snapped back an answer to Boro's early burst.

With only a 10st. 3lb. frame, Rix has to rely on skill to combat the fierce demands of the First Division. And he has plenty of that.

The pace caught up with him in the second-half, but manager Terry Neill said: "He can be very satisfied. Coming into the side on the odd occasion can only do him good."

'TERRIBLE' FOR SPURS

SPURS manager Keith Burkinshaw accepted that his team was virtually condemned to the Second Division, but remained as defiant as Manchester City who kept a promise to pursue Liverpool to the finish of the title race.

"Tottenham are a great club and I can say without doubt that, whoever is in charge in the future, the team will soon be back," he said.

Whether Burkinshaw, appointed only last summer to succeed Terry Neill, meant he is more convinced of the club's future than his own remains a question yet to be answered.

"This is a terrible day for us all," he added. "Unfortunately we didn't deserve any better.

"We didn't compete as we might have done. I was expecting much more battle."

If they had played as honestly as Burkinshaw talked, Spurs might at least have gone to the scaffold with dignity and pride.

Tommy Booth, available for transfer a few

months ago, and now the team's outstanding player, scored City's first goal after nineteen minutes.

Spurs heads drooped as Dennis Tueart, Peter Barnes and Asa Hartford scored in a twelve-minute burst before Brian Kidd completed the rout.

By DEREK WALLIS	
Man City	5
Tottenham	0

Peter faces a tough time in Palace push

By TONY STENSON

CRYSTAL PALACE plunge 19-year-old reserve team 'keeper Peter Caswell into first-team duty for their crunch match at Wrexham on Wednesday.

It's a game Palace must win to keep alive their Third Division promotion hopes. A point will give Wrexham a place in the Second Division at Palace's expense.

Caswell steps up for his League debut because first-choice Tony Burns tore a right thigh muscle taking a goal-kick in Saturday's 4—1 win over Lincoln.

"It's an injury that will take him most of the summer to recover from," said manager Terry Venables. "But I have every faith in Peter. He's been doing well in the reserves."

Two penalties from Paul Hinshelwood and further goals from Steve Perrin and Jeff Bourne gave Palace a commanding lead.

Stand-in keeper Nick Chatterton, brilliantly

shielded by his defence, was finally beaten in the closing stages by Alan Harding.

Palace's hopes were kept alive by Oxford, who held Wrexham to a 2—2 draw. Although Oxford were gifted two goals they were well worth their point.

John Shuker, Oxford's long serving defender given a free transfer last week, claimed last night he had had a raw deal.

Shuker, who stopped playing this season to run the reserves said: "It's a bit sickening after all the service I've given them. I thought I was going to be offered a coaching job."

Brentford, who looked re-election candidates in December, beat Scunthorpe 4—, to stretch their points tally to 27 from a possible 34.

Pat Kruse, a £20,000 signing from Torquay, scored the first and set up the fourth for Phillips. In between, Gordon Sweetzer got two

SCOTTISH CUP FINAL

Now Stein faces a big decision

JOCK STEIN completed a great League and Cup double season with his Celtic team's 1-0 victory over Rangers in the Scottish Cup Final at Hampden Park

But today he faces a crunch decision when he gets an official approach to manage the Scottish international team in place of Willie Ormond who has taken over at Hearts.

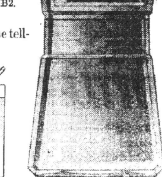
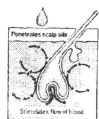
WEEKEND SPORTS SUMMARY

SPEEDWAY

NATIONAL LEAGUE. — Newcastle 53 (T Owen 11, R. Gardiner 10). Scunthorpe 25 (N. Allo 10). Rye House v. Ellesmere Port. Postponed — track waterlogged; Mildenhall 42 (B Coles 11), Canterbury 35 (G. Banks 19); Stoke 41 (E. Mountford 11), Workington 37 (S. Larson 16).

INTER-LEAGUE KNOCKOUT CUP.—Eastbourne 28 (D. Kennett 6, E. Dugard 8), Wolverhampton 49 (J. McMillan, F. Thomsen 12).

CHALLENGE MATCH: Boston 41 (C. Cook 12, S Clarke 10, R. Hollingworth 8), Peterborough 37 (B. Clark, N. Cousens 10, K. Matthews 7).

GULF BRITISH LEAGUE

	P	W	F	A	Pts
White City	8	6	360	162	12
Reading	4	4	174	137	8
Swindon	6	4	252½	214½	8
King's Lynn	6	4	244	223	8
Coventry	9	4	350½	337½	8
Halifax	6	4	332	361	8
Wimbledon	3	3	203	126	7
Belle Vue	4	3	186	174	6
Poole	4	2	214	174	6
Wolverh'pton	6	3	325	243	6
Exeter	3	2	131	103	5
Ipswich	4	2	163	146	5
Sh'field	6	2	218	250	5
Cradley Heath	6	2	234	232	4
Hull	4	2	214	253	4
Birmingham	6	2	271	352	4
Hackney	6	2	186	275	4
Leicester	5	1	173	176	2
Bristol	5	1	91	47	0

WEST GERMAN GRAND PRIX (Hockenheim).—50 cc; 1. A. Nieto (Sp) Bultaco (W Ger Kreidler); 79.4 m.p.h.; 2. E. Lazzarini (Ity. Kreidler) 3. A. Nieto (Sp. Bultaco) 125 cc; 1, P. Bianchi

(Ity. Morbidelli). 88-9 mph; 2, E. Lazzarini (Ity, Morbidelli); 3, A. Mang (W Ger, Morbidelli). 350 cc; 1, T. Katayama (Jap, Yamaha), 105·0 mph; 2, G. Agostini (Ity, Yamaha); 3, O. Chevalier (Fr. Yamaha). 500 cc: B. Sheene (G B, Suzuki) 114·6 mph; 2, P. Hennen (U.S. Suzuki); 3, S. Baker (U.S. Yamaha); 4, S. Parrish (G.B. Suzuki).

MOTOR RACING

SPANISH GRAND PRIX (Madrid. 150 miles). — 1, M. Andretti (U.S. Lotus) 1h. 42m. 52·22s.; 2, C. Reutemann (Arg. Ferrari); 3, J. Scheckter (S.A. Wolf-Ford); 4, J. Mass (W. Ger. McLaren); 5, G. Nilson (Swe. Lotus); 6, H. Stuck (W. Ger. Brabham); 7, J. Laffite (Fr. Matra-Ligier); 8, R. Petersen (Swe. Elf-Tyrrell)

World Drivers' Standings: 1, Scheckter 23pts ; 2, Andretti 20; 3, N. Lauda (Austria, Ferrari). Reutemann 10; 5, J. Hunt (G.B. McLaren) 9.

GOLF

FRENCH OPEN (Le Touquet). —Final Leading Scorers: 287—B. Ballesteros (Sp); 285—D. Stanley (Australia), Bland (S A), A. Garrido (Sp), M. Pinero (Sp); 288—H Baiocchi (S A), M. King (G B); 289—D. Ingram (G B), E. Polland (G B), C. Mason (G B); 290—A. Oosthuizen (S A), G. Garrido (Sp) J. Horton (G B) B Barnes (G B).

BADMINTON

WORLD CHAMPIONSHIP FINALS (Malmoe, Sweden) Women's Singles: L. Koppen (Den) bt G. Giiks (Eng) 12—9, 12—11. Men's Singles: F. Delfs

(Den) bt S. Pri (Den) 15—5, 15—6.

Women's Doubles: E. Togamoo, E. Ueno (Jap) bt J. Van Beusekom M. Ridder (Hol) 15—10, 15—11. Men's Doubles: Tjun Tjun, Wadyudi (Indonesia) bt Christian, Ade Chandra (Indonesia) 15—6, 15—4.

DARTS

DAILY MIRROR JUNIOR CHAMPIONSHIP. — Wiltshire Play-off (Swindon): 1, P. Balcombe (Pewsey); 2, N. Neale (Luckington). Beaten S-finalists: K. McAlpine (Pewsey), P. Cooke (Salisbury).

TONIGHT'S SOCCER

ENGLISH SCHOOLS TROPHY —Finals (First Leg): S. London v Islington (Millwall, 7.0). TESTIMONIAL MATCHES (7.30). — Derby v. Nottingham Forest (Kevin Hector); Ipswich v. Norwich (Colin Viljoen).

HOLLOWAY MUST SHARE TITLE

COVENTRY'S Woodlands School and London's Holloway School drew 3—3 at Highfield Road to share the ESFA Under-16 Individual Championship.

South London meet Islington in the first leg of the English Schools Trophy final at Millwall tonight (7.0).

SPORTS MIRROR for the BEST Cup

COCKNEY

LONDON'S First Division foursome made it a real old Cockney Cuppa in yesterday's third round.

Bookmakers are even linking Arsenal with another double year They are 80-1 (Forest are 22-1) to pull off the League and Cup — as they were last to do in 1971 — after winning handsomely with a nap hand at Sheffield United.

Chelsea sent four past Liverpool, Hammers beat Watford and even Rangers won one — beating little Wealdstone 4—0.

Spurs and Millwall need

Tuesday replays but Fulham, Charlton and Palace all went out. Palace perished at Hartlepool who are more interested in staying in the Fourth Division let alone getting to Wembley.

CHELSEA SUPER KID KOs THE KOP

CHELSEA 4
LIVERPOOL 2

By KEN MONTGOMERY

LIVERPOOL'S mighty Red Army were blasted out of the Cup by a blond bundle of dynamite called Clive Walker.

The 20-year-old winger was the star of a champagne Chelsea show which left the European champions totally punch-drunk.

Walker's two-goal FA Cup dream debut produced only nightmares for Hughes and a Liverpool defence that was torn to tatters.

Don't let the scoreline fool you. Liverpool weren't just beaten—they were blitzed!

And Liverpool boss Bob Paisley had plenty to say about that afterwards.

STORM

Paisley stormed " We gave away all four goals.

The trouble with my players is that they have not learned football's best lesson — you get nothing for yesterday.

" Some of them thought just walking around was enough.

" But don't take anything away from the Chelsea boys. They battled and did their jobs well."

Ken Shellito, Chelsea's delighted young manager, said " I think we threw Liverpool out of their rhythm. And my side cost practically nothing."

The man who started it all was young Walker

His opening goal was out of this world. He took a throw on the left, received Garner's pass in his stride and, from the edge of the box, unleashed a shot which Clemence couldn't even have seen.

Liverpool, parading more than £1 million worth of talent, were just too bad to be true.

Even so, they might still have fancied their chances when Cooke limped off in the 34th minute with a pulled muscle to be replaced by fellow Scot Finnieston.

But in the 49th minute Walker had himself another slice of the action.

STRUCK

From his free kick, Hughes could only head weakly down at Finnieston's feet and the big substitute accepted the gift gladly

In the 52nd minute Langley made it 3—0.

Johnson pulled one back with half an hour left, but five minutes later Walker struck again.

Dalglish made the score more respectable with an 81st minute header but there was to be no frantic late fightback by England's top team.

Young Chelsea — even without skipper Ray Wilkins and man-mountain centre half Droy—had run Liverpool ragged.

Man of the Match: Clive Walker (Chelsea).

CHELSEA — Bonetti; Wilkins (G). Sparrow, Britton Harris, Wicks Garner Lewington, Langley Cooke Walker Sub: Finnieston.

LIVERPOOL — Clemence Neal Jones Thompson Kennedy Hughes Dalglish Fairclough, Highway Johnson Callaghan Sub: Hansen

REF.—P. Partridge (Cockfield).

Menacing Mac

SHEFFIELD UTD 0, ARSENAL 5

By KEITH MEADOWS

ARSENAL manager Terry Neill complained after this FA Cup demolition: "We didn't play all that well after the first twenty minutes."

On behalf of shattered Sheffield the only possible response is " For that small relief, much thanks!"

The true picture emerges from the comments of Malcolm Macdonald who celebrated his twenty-eighth birthday with a two goal show of deadly marksmanship and then said

" We annihilated them in the first quarter and it was all over

" What should have been a ninety minute spectacular was reduced to a lesson. They failed through sheer efficiency on our part."

It took the Gunners just eighteen minutes to blast a four-goal salvo which exposed Bramall Lane's defensive armoury and turned giant-killing dreams into a red faced mockery

Chance

As United's caretaker boss, Cec Coldwell, conceded " Arsenal proved they are one of the best sides in the country and we just didn't have an answer

" Even the chances we had were only token efforts."

One of those efforts was from the penalty spot, but Arsenal were already three up by that fifteenth

minute and Coldwell's reference was a polite way of describing the bad Hamilton spot-kick which 'keeper Jennings saved with his legs.

Take away a miss by Calvert and a Hamson shot which hit Nelson with a gaping net at either side of him and all United were left to rue was a Woodward humdinger which brought the best out of Jennings.

But the damage had been done long before that as Arsenal ruthlessly punished a square and slow rearguard.

The heartache and backache of United keeper Brown started when Rix floated over an eighth-minute free kick and O'Leary nodded the ball home unhampered.

Two minutes later Rice and Price set up Super-

mac for the sort of head-down goal-dash which he relishes and goal No. 2 was tucked low and hard into the net before United realised their own disarray.

Colquhoun kept Arsenal on the slaughter trail by mis-heading a Rice free-kick and as the ball dropped behind him Stapleton headed it over the stranded Brown.

Then Nelson crossed for Macdonald to rise majestically and bullet a header into the roof of the overworked net.

The disallowing of a Price effort for offside simply delayed the final blow as did Brown's one moment of glory in foiling Macdonald of a hattrick with a splendid save

Clever

But it came inevitably in the 52nd minute as Supermac cleverly found Stapleton to plant home the fourth headed goal of an afternoon Sheffield will want to forget.

On the other hand, perhaps they would be better learning from it For the Gunners had plenty of lessons to teach them in proving that they are a side all the others will want to avoid in tomorrow's fourth round draw

Man of the match David Price (Arsenal)

SHEFF UTD.—Brown, Cutbush Calvert, Kenworthy, Colquhoun Flynn, Woodward Edwards, Stainrod, Hamson, Hamilton Sub: Speight

ARSENAL—Jennings; Rice Nelson Price O'Leary Young, Brady Sunderland Macdonald Stapleton. Rix Sub Walford.

REF—K Burns (Stourbridge)

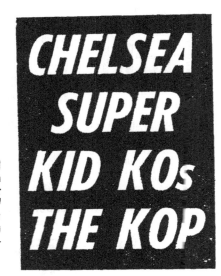

JUST ask Sheffield United's Jim Brown if Supermac has lost his goalscoring skills! Here, birthday boy Malcolm bullets a header past the helpless 'keeper

---

SOUTHEND BID TO TURN TIDE

DERBY 3, SOUTHEND 2

SOUTHEND gave swaggering Derby the fright of their lives with a storming fightback at the Baseball Ground.

The First Division outfit glided smoothly into a three-goal lead in less than an hour and the game looked over

But Southend never gave up fighting and two goals from the head of Derrick Parker kept the result in doubt until the final whistle.

Don Masson put the Rams in front after only five minutes turning in a hard low cross from Gerry Ryan.

Then Southend defender Dave Young put a ball through his own goal trying to clear an effort from Charlie George.

Derby hoping to give manager Tommy Docherty his third successive FA Cup Final kept up the pressure and George and

Gerry Daly both going close.

Ryan added the third goal when he raced through the Southend defence on to a neat through-ball from George to pick his spot.

But Southend came back and caught Derby napping on the hour Lanky centre forward Derrick Parker leapt high at the far post to head home signalling a frantic last-ditch flurry

But it was not until three minutes from time that Southend scored again, when Parker guided-in Mick Laverick's free-kick.

Man of the Match Charlie George (Derby).

DERBY — Middleton; Langan, Daniel, Daly Powell, Todd Curran, Rioch, Masson George Ryan. Sub: Nish

SOUTHEND — Rafter Moody Banks Laverick Yates Young, Morris, Pountney Parker Feli Hadley Sub: Abbott.

REF —G Courtney (Spennymoor)

TV SOCCER

CHELSEA v. LIVERPOOL
— London, Harlech, Southern, Westward, Channel, Ulster.

EVERTON v. A. VILLA
— ATV, Granada.

SHEFF. UTD. v. ARSENAL — Yorkshire.

PETERBOROUGH v. NEWCASTLE — Anglia.

MIDDLESBROUGH v COVENTRY
— Tyne-Tees,

LUTON 1, OLDHAM 1   By PAT GARROW

IT was as if Steve Taylor had decided to teach Luton a lesson. They failed to mention him in the programme.

The £80,000 buy from Bolton gave Oldham a Tuesday night replay with a 74th minute volley with a trapped nerve in his right ankle.

But manager Harry Haslam, who signed a new contract with Luton last night was unconcerned. I have no complaints. In many ways I welcome the replay. I've a lot of young players and it will mean more experience for them," he said.

Having just sold de-

fender Buckley and with Paul Futcher still recovering from a road crash, Luton lost skipper West, who was stretchered off after fifty-five minutes with a trapped nerve in his right ankle.

Haslam said he wouldn't know the extent of the damage until the swelling had gone down. But West said " I'll not be playing on Tuesday."

Six minutes from the end, Oldham nearly got a winner when Valentine burst in from the right and his shot cracked off the far angle of the bar with the 'keeper helpless.

Man of the Match Fuccillo (Luton).

reports and BEST pictures

CRACKER!

WE'RE ON OUR WAY TO WEMBLEY

Bowles rocks Stones

QPR 4, WEALDSTONE 0: By TERRY SMITH

ONE flash of inspired brilliance from Stan Bowles made sure that FA Cup disaster wasn't added to Rangers' growing list of worries.

Rangers' 1—0 lead wasn't looking too secure when Bowles, in his new midfield role, came to life in the 49th minute.

He skated past 4 opponents and laid the ball back for Leighton James to score his second goal for Rangers.

That was the end of Wealdstone. But the Southern Leaguers were perhaps unlucky to go in at half-time a goal down.

Then a Bowles penalty in the 63rd minute and an Ernie Howe goal 10 minutes later gave Rangers a scoreline that flattered them.

Wealdstone had three players booked — Watson, Brinkman and Fursdon.

Wealdstone's unluckiest moment was in the 28th minute when Parkes dropped the ball under pressure. Keith Furphy's shot was blocked and finally scrambled clear for a corner.

Rangers had gone ahead in the 7th minute when 'keeper Lightfoot was late in going down to a Givens header.

Man of the Match Steve Brinkman (Wealdstone).

QPR — Parkes, Shanks, Gillard, Hollins, Howe Cunningham, Wallace, Leach, James, Bowles, Givens Sub: Williams.

WEALDSTONE — Lightfoot, Thomas, Fursdon, Watson, Perratt, Barwick, Ferry, Brinkman, Furphy, Duck Moss Sub: Griffiths.

REF—R Crabb (Exeter)

YOU could say young Walker was a bit popular at Chelsea yesterday!

S-KILLED

CARDIFF 0, IPSWICH 2

MICK Mills celebrated his 494th game in Ipswich colours—a new club record—with a moment of classic skill that was to alter the game.

With 50 minutes gone and Ipswich's task getting harder as the minutes ticked by, skipper Mills moved quietly across the Welsh penalty area.

No danger threatened, but with a feint and a flick performed with the speed of a cobra he sent Paul Mariner driving through to shoot past Healey.

Mariner proved the sinker of City's Cup hopes after 73 minutes, with an unhindered header from Brian Talbot's long cross.

But as Ipswich manager Bobby Robson observed "They were finished with half an hour to go. We were always in command.

"Cardiff gave us a hard match but we had internationals in our team and that was the difference."

But Cardiff nearly grabbed a shock lead in the early stages through striker Ray Bishop.

By PAT NEEDHAM

Slow

He was just too slow to seize on a clear-cut opening during Cardiff's first attack, but minutes later he burst through the Ipswich defence to force a brave save from Cooper

Ipswich replied with two headers on target by Dave Geddis and a Colin Viljoen free-kick which grazed the crossbar

But after this bright opening flurry neither side was able to settle into a pattern.

Man of the Match Mick Mills (Ipswich)

CARDIFF.—Healey Dwyer Pethard Campbell, Pontin, Larmour Giles, Sayer Went, Bishop, Atley Sub: Parkin

IPSWICH.—Cooper Mills Tibbott, Talbot Hunter Osman, Wark Viljoen, Mariner Geddis, Gates Sub: Parkin

REF.—J. Bent Hemel Hempstead.

Playgirl

"It's nice to be chaired off, but I wish they were our supporters!"

Silly Fulham

BURNLEY 1, FULHAM 0

PAUL FLETCHER'S 86th minute winner put Burnley into round four after a replay seemed certain — and a bitterly disappointed Fulham manager Bobby Campbell.

Campbell said afterwards: "We deserved to get a replay and to go out to a late goal like that was a real sickener.

"Some of our lads thought the winger who put over the cross was offside."

The decisive moment came after a surging run down the right wing by Scott The ball was fed through to Morley whose low cross was forced into the net by Fletcher

Fulham 'keeper Peyton said: "If Fletcher had hit the ball properly I would have saved it, but he mis-hit it and it just bobbled past me."

Peyton had been his team's hero during the first half

Burnley manager Harry Potts said: "We've been dine a few breaks and we got some today."

Man of the Match: Derek Scott (Burnley).

HARTLEPOOL 2, PALACE 1

FOR all their skills, classier Palace 2-1 down at the break, just couldn't find a way through Hartlepool's do-or-die defence in the second half.

Yet Palace must have thought they were sitting pretty when Chatterton got his seventh goal of the season to put them ahead in ten minutes from a gem of a cross by Swindlehurst.

But it took Hartlepool only four minutes to get on terms. Following Downing's free kick. Smith set up the chance for Newton to blast his shot under the diving Burns.

The clincher for Hartlepool came in 19 minutes, when Newton was on the spot again, to stroke Pockett's cross inside the post.

Palace threw everything they'd got into their second half bid for salvation. In the last minute Bourne had cruel luck with a shot which cannoned back off the underside of the bar to be scrambled away.

Man of the Match: Bob Newton (Hartlepool).

BANK ON SAINTS

GRIMSBY 0, SOUTHAMPTON 0

FORMER Grimsby manager Lawrie McMenemy must fancy his Southampton side's chances in Tuesday's replay at The Dell. Yet Grimsby shook the Saints with a great first-half display

Then leading scorers Terry Donovan and Gary Liddell had successive shots blocked as the Fourth Division side rocked Southampton back on their heels with speedy aggressive soccer.

Just before half-time Grimsby almost took the lead with the best effort of the game. Ian Turner brilliantly finger-tipped a goal-bound twenty-yarder from Mike Brolly over the top.

But if the Saints were lucky at the interval it was Grimsby who were made to struggle at the start of the second half as Southampton at last showed their class.

With the Grimsby defence at sixes and sevens after a collision. Saints skipper Alan Ball, a magnificent driving force, screwed a shot over from a narrow angle.

But the best chance fell to an unusually quiet Ted MacDougall midway through the second half

A careless back pass by Malcolm Partridge let in the former Scottish international striker, but Nigel Batch saved the day when he blocked the shot with his legs and fell on the ball.

Man of the Match: Alan Ball (Southampton).

TRIGGER HAPPY!

PHIL DRIVER produced the kind of wing play and crossing that bore more than a marked resemblance to the late Peter Houseman at his best.

A decade ago, Houseman, on Chelsea's left, set up the kind of service for Peter Osgood and Ian Hutchinson that saw the Blues win the FA Cup and the Cup Winners' Cup.

Driver, with Colin Lee, in the middle as his target man and Clive Walker alongside is set to trigger off a rebirth of the Blues.

Already manager Geoff Hurst believes his side is better than the one that missed promotion on goal difference last season.

And with Driver and Peter Rhoades-Brown on the left, Chelsea at last have an attack capable of getting goals.

Driver, who cost just £20,000, was put on the

Driver puts Chelsea on route to top

By NIGEL CLARKE

Chelsea 6
Newcastle 0

scrap-heap by Luton three years ago. He drifted into non-League football with Bedford, who are run by Trevor Gould, younger brother of Chelsea's assistant manager Bobby Gould.

Then he moved on to Wimbledon where Gould himself saw him, and Hurst says: "We are now reaping the reward for the work Bobby put in when he was at Hereford.

"He made himself ill watching hundreds of games. Driver came under his microscope and we watched him four times before we got him. Paying that kind of money doesn't put any pressure on him, the club or myself. It was the perfect situation."

Driver had a hand in three of the goals, and his best moment was a cheeky back-heel through the legs of full back Chris Withe and a run and brilliant swerving cross for Lee whose header hit the 'keeper. It was only part of the clever stuff in an afternoon of exhilarating entertainment.

Hat-trick

No less scintillating was Walker's effort for Gary Chivers, and Rhoades-Brown's work that gave Lee his hat-trick.

He won the ball in his own half, ran 60 yards, turned the full back inside out, then crossed inch-perfect to Lee's head.

Scorers: Lee 3, Walker, Fillery, Chivers.

IPSWICH EARN ROKER VOTE

By COLIN DIBALL : Sunderland 0, Ipswich 2

SUNDERLAND defender Shaun Elliott voted Paul Mariner the best centre forward in the country and Ipswich the number one side after this lesson from the new pretenders to Liverpool's throne.

Sunderland were not so far behind in class as they carved out five chances in a first half.

But they were eventually drained embarrassingly dry of ideas and hope by an Ipswich defence rated in a "different class" by Roker Park manager Ken Knighton.

It was Mariner, playing at only 70 per cent fitness, who produced a quality performance before collecting the calf injury that will rule him out of tomorrow's League Cup tie with Birmingham.

He laid on a goal for Arnold Muhren (43 minutes) and substitute Mick D'Avray netted Ipswich's second in the 66th minute.

DOUBLE JOY — Spurs scorers Hoddle and Archibald celebrate.
Picture: KENT GAVIN

THE ENTERTAINER

By HARRY MILLER

Tottenham 4, Coventry 1

GLENN HODDLE has his own ideas about what will bring football's missing fans back.

While club chairmen were preparing for their weekend seminar in Solihull, the midfield man was giving his answer to the game's troubles with action.

His two goals in the trouncing of Coventry were breathtaking. More important, they were sheer entertainment.

The added irony was this. There was not a television camera and hardly a hooligan in sight.

Mick Coop, Coventry's

Glenn's style can bring back missing fans

veteran full back, captured the mood perfectly when he said later: "Those Hoddle goals are what they will be talking about in the pubs."

Hoddle, 22, today, doesn't always mark back the way he might. His stamina is questionable and so is his level of consistency.

But for skill, Hoddle has no equal in the English game.

Hoddle's first goal, in the 26th minute, was a

superb chip on the angle. His second, in the 75th minute, was struck with venomous power left-footed from fully twenty yards.

Hoddle said: "I know gates are down, but I'm not sure the situation is as black as it's been painted.

"I'd agree, though, that players have got a responsibility to entertain . . . to give the fans something special."

Steve Archibald put Tottenham two up before Ray Gooding got a reward for Coventry's enterprise.

Archibald scored again before Hoddle rounded off his exceptional afternoon.

Walley misses the point as Palace falter

By PETER COOPER

Leeds 1 C. Palace 0

CARETAKER boss Ernie Walley talked a better game than Palace played.

"Once we found some aggression after half time we started getting somewhere," said Walley. "We deserved a point."

But that improvement, from which Ian Walsh chiselled out two shots, remained half-baked. Clive Allen and Vince Hilaire were hardly noticed.

Terry Connor hit Leeds' tenth-minute winner with a shot on the turn.

MICK HARFORD, a striker bought in a £25 "job lot", was the hero of LINCOLN'S 8-0 thrashing of NORTHAMPTON on Saturday.

First to lead the praise was four-goal Gordon Hobson, who took his tally to 13 for the season.

"Mick is so big and strong and has got so much skill he creates chances for me," said the 21-year-old Hobson.

Harford, who scored two himself, was one of four players signed from Sunderland's Langton Street Youth Club three years ago for £25.

Lincoln boss Colin Murphy said: "Our fans have not been so happy with our performances recently, but I think we gave them what they wanted."

● ● ●

PORTSMOUTH manager Frank Burrows leaves for Liverpool's Anfield fortress with a message for the fans: "Travel safely. Behave yourselves. And be assured we will do our best."

Pompey warmed up for tomorrow's League Cup tie with a 2-1 win at Oxford, but Burrows, a member of the Swindon side that beat Liverpool in 1970, was honest enough to admit: "Oxford were unlucky. They played well enough for a point."

CHARLTON striker Derek Hales scored in the 2-1 win over Blackpool and declared: "There's still a lot of life left in the old man."

ALDERSHOT'S 1-0 win over Doncaster was their first in seven matches and manager Tom McAnearney said: "We're still not doing the job. Far too many chances went astray."

Burnley's stylish Martin Dobson felt sorry for BRENTFORD after the 2—0 victory.

"I can't understand how they didn't get a penalty," said Dobson. "I pulled back their Tony Funnell, but the referee only gave obstruction and let us off lightly."

● ● ●

Steve Bruce, GILLINGHAM'S admired central defender, faces suspension at a disciplinary meeting on Thursday. But he went out in style, scoring his first goal of the season in the 2—0 win over Hull.

FULHAM players gave their own team-talk before the game at Chester. It worked as they won 1—0.

Ted Drake, 68-year-old director and caretaker-manager, said: "It's the players who have got to do the job and they should do the talking themselves."

Fulham hope to appoint a new manager to replace sacked Bobby Campbell within a few days.

SECOND DIVISION

Harold has eyes on a city job

By GRAHAM BAKER

Bristol City 2, Derby 2

HAROLD JARMAN, sacked after a 17-year career with Bristol Rovers, may be set to join neighbours City.

The former Gloucestershire cricketer saved Rovers from relegation during his short spell as manager last season, but was then demoted to assistant manager and eventually fired.

After watching City throw away another vital point by conceding two goals in the last four minutes on Saturday he had talks with manager Bob Houghton and coach Roy Hodgson.

Bristol City had both points in their grasp with two goals from Kevin Mabbutt (34 and 19 minutes) but Derby substitute Kevin Wilson (86 minutes) and Paul Emson (89 minutes) changed that.

Said Houghton: "We were so much on top that we got complacent."

TWO-GOAL IAIN THANKS RIVALS

By DAVID MOORE : Notts Co 2, Blackburn 0

IAIN McCULLOCH, the two-goal hero against Blackburn, revealed one unexpected reason why Notts County are now setting such an impressive pace at the top of the Second Division.

"We owe an awful lot to West Ham, even though they look like being our biggest rivals," said McCulloch.

"Confidence was sky high when we went to Upton Park at the end of August. The Hammers thrashed us 4-0, but taught us a lesson about the dangers of becoming too cocky."

McCulloch, an £80,000 signing from Kilmarnock, struck first in the 17th minute, heading in Tristan Benjamin's centre.

His second, five minutes later, was an absolute cracker — a volley into the far corner.

Blackburn were mastered on every front — effort, organisation plus individual ability.

"We were an absolute shambles during the first half," admitted Rovers player - manager Howard Kendall.

ALVIN AIMING FOR A CAP

By KEVIN MOSELEY

West Ham 2, Bolton 1

ENGLAND manager Ron Greenwood could do worse than take a close look at impressive central defender Alvin Martin, again a key figure as West Ham moved into second place in Division Two with this win.

An own goal by Bolton's Mike Walsh (39 mins.) and Geoff Pike (47) gave West Ham a 2—0 lead before Brian Kidd pulled one back nine minutes from the end.

TERRY'S STAYING

By TONY STENSON: QPR 1, WBA 1

RANGERS manager Terry Venables yesterday killed speculation about his future by signing a new contract.

Venables has decided to lead the unfashionable West London club through their European adventure next season, saying: "This side is capable of winning the League as well.

"The length of my contract hasn't been decided—it could be four years—but these are exciting times and I want to be part of them.

"There wasn't one overriding factor that made me stay but I couldn't ask players like Terry Fenwick to sign a new contract and not be around myself.

"I've been here over three years and the time might come that I need to move on but it isn't now."

So Tottenham will have to look elsewhere for a new manager because first choice Alex Ferguson of Aberdeen has already snubbed their approach.

But the carnival atmoshpere that followed

Rangers get a Euro-boost

the pre-match announcement about 41-year-old Venables was quickly dampened by relegation threatened Albion.

Rangers, already booked for the UEFA Cup but still chasing second place, needed a stunning Wayne Fereday goal eight minutes from time to earn a point. He lobbed the ball home from 20 yards to wipe out Garry

VENABLES: Exciting

Thompson's 72nd minute opener.

Earlier Steve Wicks and Albion forward Cyrille Regis clashed in an ugly midfield incident and had to be separated by referee Roger Milford—the man who two weeks earlier had destroyed Wilf Rostron's Watford FA Cup dream.

Walsh is on his way says Luton boss

By JACK STEGGLES

Luton 0, Stoke 1

LUTON manager David Pleat last night confirmed that his England international striker Paul Walsh will be leaving at the end of the season.

Liverpool are favourites to sign him for £800,000.

An announcement will be made today, and Walsh said: "I have not been told a thing—and think it's about time that I was."

Stoke boosted their chances of staying up with an Ian Painter goal after 4 minutes that looked blatantly offside.

Casualty complaint

WOODCOCK

By HARRY MILLER: Arsenal 3, West Ham 3

TONY WOODCOCK became the latest victim of an over-long English season as Arsenal's European dream faded.

He limped through the last half-hour of a Highbury thriller, but was unable to come off because Graham Rix had already departed with an achilles tendon strain.

Woodcock has a hamstring pull and said: "Four games in the nine days have done me in. It's too much.

"It wouldn't happen in any other country, but here you just keep going. You realise how ridiculous it is when you become a casualty yourself.

"This could be a two or three week job. I must be doubtful for the England matches against Scotland and Russia."

Woodcock was among the scorers again as Arsenal three times came from behind to grab a point.

STEVE'S WORLD DOUBLE

From Back Page

means he's banked nearly £170,000.

Davis, wearing a broad smile of success, said afterwards: "The champagne's on me when I get back to London.

"I never knew there could be pressure like this. It's the hardest battle I've ever had in my life. Commiserations to Jimmy, he did great in his first final. He played his brains out."

Between sessions, Davis went for a nap and that seemed to do the trick as he went from 13-11 to 15-11. Surely now White would cave in.

But no, the potting prince of Tooting came to life, wearing an evening suit loaned to him by Alex "Hurricane" Higgins.

Higgins stood to lose his record as the youngest world winner, but with tears in his eyes Higgins said: "I wanted that kid to win so badly—he's a genius. It would have been great for the game."

NEVIN'S BRIDGE OF JOY

By NIGEL CLARKE

ANTHEMS of acclaim rang joyously around Stamford Bridge yesterday as a crowd of nearly 30,000 celebrated Chelsea's return to the top of the Second Division.

Now the championship is just one match away and the Blues can claim it if they beat Grimsby at Blundell Park next Saturday.

The news that Sheffield Wednesday had only drawn at home to Manchester City set off the celebrations that saw thousands dance deliriously on the pitch at the final whistle.

Chelsea	3
Barnsley	1

Fifteen minutes from time, with the score 1-1, a loudspeaker announcement broadcast the latest news from Hillsborough.

The roar that greeted it sparked Chelsea into a frenzy of attacking football and within five minutes they had reclaimed the lead when Pat Nevin deflected in a shot from Dale Jasper.

In the hysteria that followed, hundreds were cleared off the pitch and referee Victor Callow from Solihull held up the game until the pitch was cleared.

Then in the last minute Nevin got the clincher to set off the knees-up that electrified this famous old stadium.

Until that loudspeaker announcement, Chelsea had struggled against a Barnsley side reduced to ten men.

They had skipper Mick McGuire sent off for a foul on Nigel Spackman, and he was followed by coach Eric Winstanley, who was banished from the dug-out for swearing at a linesman.

But Barnsley were outraged at that announcement. Manager Bobby Collins said: "I thought it was very unfair, definitely a little bit of gamesmanship."

David Speedie had given then a 36th minute lead with a brilliantly headed goal from Nevin's cross. But the party mood was dampened by David Geddis, who equalised on the hour.

The high spirits were not shared by Barnsley's McGuire, who said: "I played in the First Division at 18 and I'm 32 now. I'm on the PFA management committee and I've never been suspended, let alone sent off. I'm sad because the reaction of a couple of Chelsea players may have led to me being sent off."

CELEBRATING: Happy fans chair David Speedie.
Picture: MIKE MALONEY

RESULTS, SCORERS, SUMMARY

FIRST DIVISION

Home		Scorers	Away		Scorers	H-T	Att
Arsenal	3	Talbot, Woodcock, Mariner	West Ham	3	Whitton 2, Hilton	2-3	33,347
Aston Villa	0		Everton	2	Richardson, Sharp	0-0	16,792
Liverpool	5	Rush 4 (1 pen), Hansen	Coventry	0		2-0	33,393
Luton	0		Stoke	1	Painter	0-1	9,867
Man. Utd	1	Hughes	Ipswich	2	D'Avray, Sunderland	0-0	44,257
Norwich	1	Watson	Birminghm	1	Gayle	0-0	13,601
Nottm. F	5	Atkinson (o.g.), Hodge, Davenport 2, Bowyer	Watford	1	Johnston	3-0	13,732
Q.P.R.	1	Fereday	W.B.A.	1	Thompson	0-0	14,418
S'thampton	5	Puckett, Wallace 2, Armstrong 2	Tottenham	0		2-0	21,141
Sunderland	0		Notts. Co.	0			14,517
Wolves	1	Smith	Leicester	0		1-0	7,405

SECOND DIVISION

Home		Scorers	Away		Scorers	H-T	Att
Blackburn	1	Patterson	Cardiff	1	Lee	1-1	3,107
Brighton	3	Smillie, Nattrass (o.g), E Young	Middlesbro'	0		1-0	9,168
Cambridge	1	Cooke	Shrewsbury	0		1-0	2,208
Carlisle	2	Poskett 2	C. Palace	2	Giles, Barber	2-0	3,013
Charlton	3	Robinson, Lee, Parker (o.g.)	Fulham	4	Scott, Houghton, Carr, Davies	2-2	6,151
Chelsea	3	Speedie, Jasper, Nevin	Barnsley	1	Geddis	1-0	29,541
Huddrsfld.	2	Cooper, Carney (o.g.)	Newcastle	2	Beardsley, Mills	2-2	25,101
Oldham	2	Quinn, Hopkinson	Grimsby	1	Lund	1-1	4,156
Sheff. Wed.	0		Man. City	0		0-0	36,763
Swansea	2	Marustik (pen), Loveridge	Leeds	2	Wright, Lorimer	0-1	5,498

THIRD DIVISION

Home		Scorers	Away		Scorers	H-T	Att
Bolton	3	Chandler 2, Caldwell	Sheff. Utd	1	Edwards	2-0	9,036
Bradford C.	0		Lincoln	0			3,085
Exeter	0		Bournemth	2	Morrel, O'Driscoll	0 0	2,790
Newport	1	Lilygreen	Brentford	1	Roberts	0-1	2,154
Orient	1	Brooks (pen)	Oxford U	2	Aldridge, Vinter	0-1	5,695
Port Vale	1	Bright	Hull City	0		1-0	3,958
Rotherham	4	Birch, Simmons 2, Dungworth	Wigan A	1	Bruce	2-0	3,863
Scunthorpe	4	Cammack 2 (1 pen), Cowling, Green	Burnley	0		2-0	2,620
Southend	1	May	Plymouth	1	Chamberlain	0-1	3,540
Walsall	2	Brazier, O'Kelly	Preston	1	Kelly	2-0	3,273
Wimbledon	1	Gage	Gillingham	3	Bruce, Cascarino, Sitton	1-0	6,009

FOURTH DIVISION

Home		Scorers	Away		Scorers	H-T	Att
Blackpool	4	Britton 3, Stonehouse	Halifax	0		1-0	2,324
Chester	1	Zelem	Bristol C.	2	Morgan 2	0-1	3,900
Chesterfld	3	P Brown 2, Newton	Aldershot	1		1-0	1,991
Colchester	3	Bowen, Adcock, Larkin (o.g.)	Hereford	0		1-0	1,286
Crewe	1	Waller	Mansfield	3	Caldwell 3	0-3	1,810
Reading	1	White	Tranmere	0		0-0	6,989
Rochdale	1	Williams	Torquay	0		0-0	1,042
Stockport	0		Doncaster	2	Snodin, Moss	0-1	2,993
Swindon T	2	Barnard, Mayes	Peterboro.	0		1-0	1,876
York C	3	Byrne, Hood, Ford	Bury	0		2-0	8,023

KENT LEAGUE—Div 1: Darenth 1, Ramsgate 1; Herne Bay 4, Alma Swanley 0.

ESSEX SENIOR LEAGUE—Heybridge 2, Canvey 0; Witham 3, Wrenhoe 2.

EASTERN COUNTIES LEAGUE: Ely 2, Braintree 2; Felixstowe 3, March 1; Haverhill 0, Clacton 2; Histon 0, Gt Yarmouth 0; Lowestoft 3, Wisbech 2; Newmarket 2, Chatteris 2; Stowmarket 2, Bury 0; Tiptree 1, Gorleston 2.

MIDLAND COMBINATION: Cinderford 2, Knowle 2.

SUSSEX LEAGUE—Div 1: Peacehaven 1, Southwick 1; Whitehawk 7, Hailsham 0.

LONDON SPARTAN LEAGUE—Premier Div: Brimsdown Rovers 3, Bracknell 1.

Senior Div: Barkingside 2, Wandsworth 2.

STAFFS SENIOR CUP FINAL.—Second leg: Kidderminster 2, Halesowen 1 (4-2 on agg).

WEST MIDLANDS LEAGUE: Hednesford 0, Shifnal 0.

TABLES AND POOLS — Page 25

BOWLS

COUNTY MATCH: West Monmouth 121, Essex 109.

SNOOKER

EMBASSY WORLD PROFESSIONAL CHAMPIONSHIP (Sheffield)- **Final:** Steve Davis (Plumstead) bt Jimmy White (Tooting) 18-16. Today's frame scores: 6-127, 29- 62, 1-76, 88-56, 42-65, 29-68, 4-80, 43-67, 64-15, 82-43, 19-91, 73-40, 6-84, 22-72, 40-74, 59-55, 60-65, 77-40.

CRICKET

BRITANNIC ASSURANCE COUNTY CHAMPIONSHIP (Edgbaston): **Warwicks** 275 (G Lord 55) and 19-2. **Surrey** 247 (D Pauline 57, N Gifford 4-62). **Today:** 11.0-5.30 or 6.0.

UNDER-25 COMPETITION (Taunton): **Somerset** 112-8 lost to **Gloucs** 116 (A Wright 54) by 8 wkts.

RUGBY LEAGUE

SLALOM LAGER PREMIERSHIP: Semi-finals; Hull KR 21pts, St. Helens 16, Hull 12, Castleford 22.

SECOND DIVISION: Swinton 44, Cardiff 16.

SPEEDWAY

FOURTH TEST (Ipswich): **England** 36 (C Morton 9, R Knight 8, K Tatum 6). **US** 72 (S Moran 18, D Sigalos 15, J Cook 13, L King 11, B Schwartz 9.) US take winning 3-1 lead.

NATIONAL LEAGUE: Rye House 42 (B. Garrad 10, K. Gray 9), **Canterbury** 36 (J. Luckhurst 13, B. Kennett 10). **Silver Helmet:** Garrad (holder) beat Luckhurst. **Scunthorpe** 46 (J Parr 11), **Arena Essex** 32 (B Humphreys 11, B Barrett 10).

LEAGUE CUP: Wolves 40 (D Sigalos 11), **Sheffield** 38 (L Collins 13, S Moran 11). **Reading** 47 (P Jonsson 11, M Shirra 11), **Eastbourne** 31 (L King 13). **Poole** 40 (K Smith 11, N Middleditch 10, M Lee 9), **Oxford** 38 (M Taylor 9). **Wimbledon** 52 (M Simmons 12, J Davis 12), **Exeter** 26 (B Petersen 14).

GREYHOUNDS

CRAYFORD.—7.45: Queens Spectre 7-2 (1-3, £2.49). **8.00:** Hazelwood Rebel 7-2 (6-5, 92p). **8.15:** Thompson Hawk 1-2f (6-4, 39p). **8.31:** Black Steel 11-10f (4-5, £1.00). **8.47:** Woodlea Jet 5-1 (3-2, £1.67). **9.03:** Poultry Sun 2-1f (6-3, 76p). **9.19** Decoy Diamond 5-1 (3-2, £2.74). **9.36:** Oriental Express 5-1 (2-4, £1.67). **9.53:** Race void. **10.10:** Urgent 3-1 (4-6, £1.57). NR: Monalee Samson (2).

HARRINGAY.—7.45: Kesboro Kairos 5-1 (4-2, £2.03). **8.00:** Lightning Sky 7-2 (3-2, £1.81). **8.16:** Georginas Boy 13-8f (1-4, 98p). **8.31:** Gan On Goldie 2-1f (5-6, £2.70). **8.46:** Poor Display 13-2 (3-2, £3.18). **9.02** Airfield 9-4f (5-2, 97p). **9.17:** Charmed Lady 4-1 (2-6, £3.17). **9.33:** Daily Mirror Derby Trial: Game Bell 1-4f (6-1, 50p). NR: Best Paddy (5). **9.49:** Perdys Gay 5-2 (6-4, 65p). **10.05:** Miltons Piper 7-2 (3-6, £1.46).

SOUTHEND.—7.30: Navaho Joe 7-2 (6-4, £4.97). **7.45:** Glenview Red 6-1 (5-6, £1.62). **8.00:** Glowing Light 3-1 (6-1, 96p). **8.16:** M'Nings Marimba 5-4f (3-6, 51p). **8.33:** My Estimation 5-1 (1-6, £3.42). Jack The Tyler ran for Colsallon Again (5). **8.50:** Stephens Light 2-1 (3-6, £1.70). **9.07:** Tampa Cosmo 6-4jf (2-3, 42p). **9.24:** Knock Joy 2-1 (4-3, £1.29). **9.41:** Lacca Queen 3-1 (1-3, 74p). **9.58:** Glenview Red 5-2 (6-1, 74p).

WEMBLEY.—7.45: Lucky Tiger 10-11f (5-1, 43p). NR: Flying High (4). **8.01:** Good Night 7-4f (6-3, 77p). **8.18:** Crowned Kairos 20-1 (3-2, £10.56). **8.34:** Claddagh Cruiser 5-1 (4-5, £3.86). **8.50:** Tartan Sarah 4-11f (5-2, 25p). NRs: Disco Fun (1), Woodside Bell (3). **9.06:** Sound Slave 5-1, £2.51). NR: Dunboyne Sailor (4). **9.23:** Wild Surprise 11-10f (5-3, 29p). **9.40:** Loyal Toby 5-2 '(2-5, 80p). **9.57:** Weston Prelude ev f (3-4, 80p). **10.15:** Foilish Pleasure 11-10f (1-5, £1.00).

TOP DOG'S BEST

ROMFORD (10 races): 8.15 Fawn Kizzy, **8.46** Sabre Black **7.03** Sergunho. **SLOUGH (10): 7.30** Scragg Mercury, **9.08** Talking Machine (NAP), **10.00** Tell No One. **WALTHAMSTOW (10): 8.32** Night Action, **9.35** Some Height, **10.10** The Snow Jet.

TONIGHT'S GAMES

CANON LEAGUE
THIRD DIVISION

Bristol Rovers v Millwall (7.45) ....

FOURTH DIVISION

Darlington v Wrexham ....

FA YOUTH CUP, final, second leg: Stoke v Everton.

IONS!

shade as Blues lift crown

CHINA GO TO THE OLYMPICS

Spurs 1
Man Utd 1

By KEN MONTGOMERY

some eccentric refereeing from Michael Taylor.

Keith Burkinshaw, who is leaving Spurs after eight years as manager, said: "I would have liked my last League match here to have been a classic, but it was not to be. It was a hard, tight match, and the football was a little bit of a disappointment."

Atkinson agreed: "It was a bit fierce, but I thought our lads kept their heads very well.

"We've just got to strengthen our resolve for next season. We are a lot closer to Liverpool than we were this time a year ago."

They would have been even closer had young Mark Hughes had the luck he deserved with a 79th minute header that hit a post.

So it was no fabulous farewell for Burkinshaw, nor was it for Ray Wilkins, Italy-bound after his last match for United.

Neither will be using match reports in their scrapbooks.

Man of the match: Mark Hughes (United).

THOMAS sheds a tear

ROAMING Chelsea fans halted play for eight minutes as the Londoners clinched the Second Division championship at Blundell Park.

Referee Don Shaw led both teams off as the supporters spilled onto the pitch twenty minutes into the first half.

Many had climbed over the ten-foot-high spiked railings to escape the packed stand where they were penned.

During the enforced interval, Chelsea chairman Ken Bates went on to the pitch to plead with his fans to "Cool it."

Grimsby 0
Chelsea 1

By PHIL BRAUND

But there was no mass violence. The trouble appeared to have been caused by the late arrival of many of the 10,000 Chelsea fans.

Grimsby found the Blues too much to handle on the pitch too.

And it was leading scorer Kerry Dixon who led the way as Chelsea, still smarting from a bruising 3-2 defeat by Grimsby in December, went looking for those title points.

Dixon had already been denied twice by keeper Nigel Batch when he got the winner after the break.

Batch was powerless as

Dixon outjumped everybody to head home a Pat Nevin cross for his 34th goal of the season.

Grimsby buckled under the pressure and Nevin had the chance to wrap it up from the spot after David Speedie was sent crashing in the penalty area.

Nevin struck his kick low and hard but Batch diving at full stretch, tucked it round the post.

CHINA will definitely send a team to the Los Angeles Olympics, games officials said yesterday.

A letter accepting an invitation to attend the games was handed to Olympics official Charles Lee in Peking and the news was received yesterday morning by Games chief Peter Ueberroth.

"After several difficult days, this is a very positive gesture," said Mr Ueberroth.

All the same, the acceptance by China, long an ideological foe of the Soviet Union, was in doubt. Romania, another Communist country with policies independent of Moscow, has also said it will send a team.

The Chinese decision means that China and Nationalist-ruled Taiwan will compete against each other for the first time at an Olympice, ending a 35-year-old feud between Peking and Taipei over international sports representation.

To settle arguments over what names China and Taiwan, who both consider themselves legitimate rulers of the mainland, should use a compromise has been worked out through the International Olympic Committee.

China will be called China and Taiwan will be Chinese-Tapipei.

China is expected to send a team of more than 200 athletes

● Czechoslavaka yesterday joined the Soviet Union, Bulgaria, East Germany, Vietnam and Mongola in withdrawing from the games.

Coe legs it

★ SEBASTIAN COE made a successful return to the track at Wolverhampton yesterday. Coe, missing for ten months following a glandular illness, clocked 47.6 sec. in a 400 metres relay leg for his new club Haringey.

Coe, already selected for the Los Angeles Olympics 800 metres, said: "Now I want to work hard at getting some speed work in."

Faldo flying

★ NICK FALDO, the new golden boy of British golf, shot a stunning three-under-par 66 at Moortown, Leeds, yesterday to set up the prospect of a £repeat £15,660 jackpot.

The 66 gave 26-year-old Faldo a three-round total of 205 and a share of the lead with Yorkshireman Howard Clark (69) in the £100,000 Car Care tournament.

Texan bar

★ BETHNAL Green welterweight Sylvester Mittee stopped Texan Kenny Releford in the third round of their fight at Stoke-on-Trent yesterday. Referee Paul Thomas stepped in despite protests from the Texan and most of the crowd.

Cruyff quits

★ JOHAN CRUYFF, 37, the Dutch soccer super star, is retiring. He plays his last game for champions and Cup winners Feyenoord today after a glittering career in which he was European Footballer of the Year three times.

ON THE BOIL

on Wembley trail again

Watford 2
Arsenal 1

By ARTHUR HOPKINS

● Taylor confirmed that the rest of yesterday's team will carry Watford's banner for the first time beneath Wembley's twin towers against Everton. The other contender for the right back position is teenager Nigel Gibb, but Taylor feels the occasion might be too big for him.

● Watford lost their regular captain Wilf Rostron for the final when he was sent off against Southampton. This season Rice has made only a few first team appearances and has been performing such duties as coaching and managing occasionally the youth and reserve sides.

● Rice left 11 minutes from the end—with cramp. But his old club, Arsenal, had already been gunned down by Watford's Scottish scourges, Little Mo Johnston and George Reilly.

● In just 12 minutes, Johnston and Reilly scored goals that fractured

Arsenal's end-of-season composure

● Stewart Robson boomed the Gunners ahead after 14 minutes. Then Elton John's Wembley wonders realised this was the final dress rehearsal before Sturday's showdown.

● Man of the match: Nigel Callaghan (Watford).

RICE

IPSWICH 2
VILLA 1

BOBBY FERGUSON, whose Ipswich side finished with a flourish, still wants to sign Alan Sunderland, who has been on loan from Arsenal—but the club can't afford a fee.

He said: "It would have to be a free transfer. I won't be speaking to Don Howe again until I see whether Alan is on Arsenal's retained list."

Mich D'Avray confirmed his emergence from Paul Mariner's shadow with a stunning winner

The England Under-21 striker, a regular choice since Mariner's transfer to Arsenal, scored with a thumping header that Mer-

Howe holds key for Ferguson

By JOHN HALL

vyn Day could only palm into his own net. in the 75th minute.

Ipswich have been hanging on for dear life

Yet the writing had seemed to be on the wall for Tony Barton's side when revitalised Ipswich surged into a 23rd minute lead.

Trevor Putney's telling through ball caught the Villa defence square and

Eric Gates darted clear to rifle home his 16th goal of the season.

But the advantage was shortlived as Villa were gifted an equaliser six minutes later.

A mix-up between Paul Cooper and Steve McCall presented Peter Withe with the most inviting of chances

Man of the match Steve McMahon (Villa).

● WOW! We've had a sackful of letters after England boss Bobby Robson named his real England team in last week's Sports Mirror. We're still sifting through them all—so we'll print the pick of your letters next Sunday.

SHARP END

EVERTON striker Graeme Sharp is looking forward to a glorious Wembley finale to a frustrating season.

The 23-year-old Scot struck twice in yesterday's 3-1 win over QPR to take his tally to three in three games.

He said: "I've only got ten goals all season but I hope today's and the one last week will be enough to clinch my Cup Final place.

Everton struck in the

Everton 3,
QPR 1

By BILL THORNTON

38th minute through Adrian Heath, after a lovely one-two with Sharp.

Rangers awoke briefly from their stupor for Terry Fenwick to cross for Gary Micklewhite to head the equaliser 13 minutes after the break.

But Sharp's two late goals were decisive. The

first came in the 79th minute when Peter Reid carved a huge hole in the defence before releasing a pass that left Sharp with the happy task of slotting the ball past Peter Hucker.

His second, four minutes later, was a gem. Sharp controlled beautifully just inside the penalty area, then turned and hammered an angled shot past the stunned 'keeper.

Man of the Match—Andy Gray (Everton).

QUESTION OF SPORT

OUR mystery man this week was Everton's skipper the last time they appeared at Wembley in the FA Cup Final—a big defender who played for England in the 1970 World Cup in Mexico. Can you identify him? There are fivers for the first ten correct answers to reach us by Thursday, May 17. Send your entries to: Question of Sport, Sunday Mirror, Box 641, London, EC88 1SU.

DAVE MACKAY was our mystery man last week and fivers are on their way to:— A. Green, Bexleyheath; M. Shattock, Taunton; G. Harby, Derby; G. Sergeant, Norwich; J Thomas, Port Talbot; D. Fraser, Newcastle; Mrs. D. Hill,

Oxon; W. Levy, Islington; M. Dunn, Co. Durham; Miss J. Higgins, Birmingham.

Brazil ban

★ SPURS star Alan Brazil will not be freed to play for Manchester United against Celtic in Lou Macari's testimonial today. Departing Spurs boss Keith Burkinshaw's approval was overruled.

Spurs in the cold

By HARRY HARRIS

| Portsmouth | 1 |
| Tottenham | 0 |

TOTTENHAM crashed out of the Milk Cup last night after failing to score in five hours of full-blooded action against Second Division leaders Portsmouth.

While the glory belonged to Portsmouth and their proud manager Alan Ball, the gory details of the riot outside the Fratton Park ground overshadowed the triumph.

But inside the police were in control on the terraces as Portsmouth reached their first quarter-final since the League Cup was introduced 25 years ago.

Spurs are becoming a Jekyll and Hyde outfit, able to score five against Oxford on Saturday, yet drawing another blank against Portsmouth.

Unless there is a big League revival, an assault on the FA Cup looks to be the only realistic target as Spurs enter the New Year.

Centre-half Noel Blake inflicted the body blow to Spurs when he broke the deadlock after four-and-a-quarter hours of this marathon tie.

From winger Kevin O'Callaghan's corner, Blake was left surprisingly free to head in from 10 yards.

Alan Knight was unbeatable in all three matches, and not even his Sunday night car crash could shake the England under-21 keeper.

The Milk Cup

JOE SETS UP CHELSEA

By CHRIS JAMES

| Everton | 1 |
| Chelsea | 2 |

TEN-MAN Chelsea last night lined up a quarter-final Milk Cup derby against QPR at Loftus Road with this sensational triumph at Goodison.

Yet again a clash between these great rivals ended in controversy as Chelsea full-back Darren Wood was sent off with 24 minutes to go and the score 1-1 in this fourth round replay.

Chelsea were not content just to hang on. They stormed forward and their centre-half, big Scot Joe McLaughlin, stabbed in the winner from a Jerry Murphy corner after 74 minutes.

Wood was the third player to be sent off in the three games between the sides this season, following the dismissal of

Lions to sweat it out

MILLWALL will learn next week whether they will be forced to close their ground for up to a month.

A five-man committee met at the Den yesterday to investigate the violence that scarred the Lions' recent match with Leeds.

FA spokesman Glen

Neville Southall and Kevin Sheedy (both Everton) in the two encounters at Stamford Bridge.

England centre-forward Kerry Dixon set up Chelsea's triumph with a 61-second goal and although Everton equalised through Gary Lineker after eight minutes they could not penetrate the Londoners' defence again.

Tempers were always on a short fuse. Scottish international David Speedie was booked in the first half after a tackle on Adrian Heath and was lucky to stay on the field after a number of later niggling incidents.

Wood's dismissal for the first time in his career appeared harsh, however.

Kirton said yesterday: "Every club has received a new memo from the FA and Football League jointly which states clearly that action will be taken to protect the interests of the game."

He was already committed to the challenge on Pat van den Hauwe before the Welsh international nicked the ball out of his path.

Van den Hauwe later limped off to spend the night in hospital and was substituted by Ian Marshall.

But it was yet another tale of woe for Everton —right from the opening seconds.

For the fifth time this season they conceded an early goal as Dixon clinically scored his 20th goal of the season from an acute angle after he had been put through by Speedie.

Dixon's England teammate Lineker leapt high to head powerfully beyond Eddie Niedzwiecki from a Trevor Steven free-kick for his 16th goal of the season.

The football that followed was fast, frantic and fierce. Yet neither goalkeeper was overstretched as two uncompromising defences kept their opposing World Cup strikers at arms length.

Chelsea manager John Hollins said: "We did not play well, but we got the result and that is what matters in the end.

"We can play football, but sometimes you have to scrap. We got a very good start, but we sat back on it as though we had done it all."

DIXON: Put Chelsea ahead after 61 seconds

Kevin's a Rebel rouser

By TONY STENSON

Slough 2, Orient 3

NON-LEAGUE Slough, the team they call the Rebels, finally had their roar silenced last night.

But they made Fourth Division Orient claw and battle every inch of the way in a gripping FA Cup second round replay.

In the end, though, their stamina finally proved the vital factor, together with the tormenting menace of Orient winger Kevin Godfrey, maker of one goal and scorer of another.

Godfrey supplied the pass for Ian Juryeff to score after 13 minutes to put Orient ahead.

But the Vauxhall Opel League side hit back on the stroke of half-time with a stunning 20-yard free-kick from Keith White that 'keeper Peter Wells could only help in.

Dream

But with Tony White, the former Arsenal player, full of inspiration, Slough took over until Godfrey put Orient ahead again in the 63rd minute.

Paul Shinners then killed Slough's hopes of repeating their giant-killing act over Millwall two years ago when he headed in an Andy Sussex corner in the 71st minute.

There was still time for a nail-biting finish when Slough skipper Derek Harris drove in an 85th minute penalty. But the dream never happened and Orient went shakily through to meet Oldham in the next round.

Orient boss Frank Clarke said: "It was one hell of a battle and we were under far too much pressure for my peace of mind."

■LUTON are to spend over a million pounds on improving their Kenilworth Road ground, including the building of 28 plush executive boxes, even though they are hoping to move from the site within five years.

SUMMARY

MILK CUP
Fourth round replay
Everton .... (1) 1 Chelsea ...... (1) 2
Lineker   Dixon McLaughlin
Att: 26,373
(Chelsea away to Q.P.R.)
Second replay
Portsm'th ... (1) 1 Tottenham (0) 0
Blake   Att: 26,306
(Portsmouth away to Oxford)

FA CUP
Second round replays
Bury .... (1) 2 Tranmere ... (0) 1
Valentine Ross Anderson
(pen)   Att: 3,137
(Bury home to Barnsley in Third round)
Rochdale ..... (1) 2 Scunthorpe (1) 1
Taylor Moore   Broddle
Att: 5,066
(Rochdale away to Man Utd)
Slough .... (1) 2 Orient .... (1) 3
White Harris (pen) Juryeff Godfrey
Att: 4,000 Shinners
(Orient away to Oldham)
Torquay .... (1) 2 Newport ..... (0) 3
Walsh 2   Boyle P. Jones
Att: 1,937 James
(After extra time score at 90 mins 2-2. Newport away to Sunderland)
Walsall .... (0) 2 Port Vale .... (0) 1
Cross Hawker   Brown.
Att: 5,671
(Walsall home to Man City)
Wigan .... (2) 4 Runcorn ..... (0) 0
Methven Newell 2
Jones (og)   Att: 3,390
(Wigan home to Bournemouth)
Wrexham ...... (0) 0 Notts Cnty (1) 3
                                Clarke Waitt
Att: 2,645 McParland
(Notts Co away to Stoke)

FINE FARE
SCOTTISH PREMIER
Clydebank ... (1) 2 Aberdeen ... (0) 1
Larnach Dickson   Black
Att: 2,095
FOOTBALL COMBINATION: Chelsea 0, Norwich 2; QPR 3, Fulham 0; Swindon 3, C. Palace 2.
VAUXHALL OPEL LEAGUE.—Div One: Grays 2, Leystone and Ilford 2; Oxford City 4, Staines 2; St Albans 1, Wingate 1. **Div Two South:** Banstead Ath 2, Camberley 1; Woking 5, Hungerford 1; Egham 1, Southall 3.
ESSEX SENIOR CUP—Second Round: Billericay 3, Averley 2.
SUSSEX SENIOR CUP—Third Round: Southwick 2, Lewes 2.
ESSEX THAMESIDE TROPHY: Woodford T 0, Chelmsford City 1.

SNOOKER
HOFMEISTER WORLD DOUBLES CHAMPIONSHIP (Northampton)—**Quarter-finals:** S Davis (Romford), T Meo (Morden) bt N Foulds (Perivale), J Parrott (Liverpool) 5-3. C Thorburn (Can), W Thorne (Leicester) bt S Francisco, P Francisco (SA) 5-2.

TONIGHT'S GAMES
(7.30 unless stated)
UEFA CUP
Third Rnd, Second Leg
Neuchatel Xamax v Dundee Utd (7.0)_
(First Leg: Dundee Utd lead 2-1)
SCREEN SPORT SUPER CUP
Norwich v Man Utd _
FULL MEMBERS CUP
Northern Final, Second Leg
Man City v Hull _
(First Leg: Hull lead 1-0)
SCOTTISH CUP
First Round Replay
Cowdenbeath v Berwick _

★ THE GOALS AND DRAMA

JACKPOT

● SECOND in the table West Bromwich, who tackle top dogs Chelsea on Saturday, warmed up with a convincing 3-1 victory at struggling Oldham

● They outclassed their opponents, scoring twice in 16 minutes through Don Goodman and Robert Hopkins.

● Gary Robson added a third in the second half before Tony Philliskirk hit a consolation for Oldham.

Merry Kerry
lifts Chelsea

Chelsea 3, Ipswich 0

KERRY DIXON and Gordon Durie hit the jackpot again yesterday to take Chelsea to the top of the Second Division and strengthen their bid for promotion.

The lethal strike duo flattened an Ipswich side, who disgracefully ran up the white flag of surrender after dominating the opening 25 minutes.

Durie scored his eighth of the season to give Chelsea the lead after 27 minutes, while Dixon completed the scoring in the 74th minute — his 12th of the season.

The other goal came from teenager David Lee, but Chelsea owe just as big a debt to Ipswich keeper Craig Forrest, who put his team in trouble with two horrendous blunders.

Durie beat him at the near post with a cross shot from the right. Then Forrest failed to claim a header from Dixon and Lee took advantage to poke the ball over the line from close range.

Important

"They were two bad mistakes and my keeper won't need reminding of that," said Ipswich boss John Duncan. "Even so we still lacked the character to battle back."

"It's OK giving it a go when you are winning. But it's more important to do it when you are behind and the way we allowed those goals to floor us was a bitter disappointment.

"Even though we failed to make anything of the chances we created we still did well early on and Chelsea never caused us a problem.

"But once they scored the picture changed and we allowed them to get well on top. Chelsea have

By JACK STEGGLES

got power in every department and obviously have to be a good bet for promotion."

Ipswich's own hopes of regaining First Division status took a savage knock and in the end they were lucky to get off so lightly.

"I am delighted with the way we stuck at it after a slow start. There is a lot of pressure on the lads — for they are expected to do well all the time," said Chelsea manager Bobby Campbell.

"Dixon is buzzing again after signing a new four-year contract and Durie is something really special.

"I am using him as a central striker — and that is not his best position. I see him really coming into his own in a free role."

If Durie gets that role the rest of the Second Division had better watch out!

Sheridan off

LEEDS midfielder John Sheridan was sent off for his second bookable offence with 16 minutes left — but jaded Blackburn couldn't cash in.

Don Mackay's 'nearly men', who missed out on promotion in the play-offs last season, began Boxing Day as Second Division leaders, but even after Sheridan's departure they looked second-rate and were easily defeated 2-0.

DEADLY DUO: Kerry Dixon and Gordon Durie (inset) both struck to send Chelsea to the top of the Second Division

RICH PICKINGS!

RICHARD HILL hit four goals in an amazing 16-minute second half burst at Fellows Park yesterday to keep desperate Walsall rooted to the foot of the Second Division.

Hill, the former Watford and Northampton player, struck in the 54th, 58th, 61st and 70th minutes, with Martin Foyle notching his 10th of the season in the 73rd minute to complete the Oxford romp.

Walsall, beaten for the 11th successive time, started well and were on top in the first half.

Hill's sweet news
for Oxford braves

Walsall 1, Oxford 5

Willie Naughton put them in front in the 16th minute from a penalty after Jimmy Phillips had pushed Trevor Christie.

But it was a different tale in the second half as Walsall fell apart.

David Bardsley was in

great form and with Hill dominant, Oxford tore the home team to shreds.

The pressure is now on Walsall boss Tommy Coakley. He received a reprieve from the sack only a week ago, but will be lucky to survive this latest setback. However, he insisted last night: "I will not resign."

HILL: Four goals

STEVE'S SHAKER

Watford 1, Portsmouth 0

WATFORD'S players, shaken by a bomb scare on Christmas night, steadied themselves to win this Second Division promotion clash yesterday.

Manager Steve Harrison and his players had to leave the local Hilton National Hotel in a hurry at 11 o'clock at night.

"They were hammering on our doors, telling us that we had two minutes to get out of the hotel," said Harrison.

"We rushed downstairs, and half the players were standing outside in their underpants. "Eventually they cleared out our gear and we decided to go to our homes instead."

For Harrison, 36 yesterday, the victory over Pompey was a perfect birthday present. His £150,000 signing from

Crystal Palace, Neil Redfearn, scored his first goal since his move six weeks ago.

Redfearn nipped in front of Portsmouth defender Clive Whitehead to volley in Kenny Jackett's cross in the 63rd minute.

Untidy

It was the one brilliant moment in a dour, untidy game.

"It was always going to be tight, but we maintained our concentration and I never felt we were going to lose," said Harrison.

Watford's £325,000 Christmas Eve signing from Aston Villa, Garry Thompson, was booked in the 31st minute for a foul in a game littered by 50 free kicks.

Bright ones!

Brighton 3, C. Palace 1

STRUGGLERS Brighton saw the light as they raced to their first win for five matches.

Goals from Kevin Bremner, Gary Chivers and Garry Nelson in front of the Goldstone's biggest crowd of the season, 13,515, ensured that Brighton kept with tradition in this derby match.

Palace, without a win on Sussex soil for 25 years, were unable to break the hoodoo and the usually deadly Ian Wright and Mark Bright were off target.

BLUE HEAVEN: Jubilant Dave Beasant (left), Joe McLaughlan and Tony Dorigo are in top form as they celebrate Chelsea's first-class return   *PICTURE: PAUL WEBB*

Plymouth 0 Palace 2

By ALAN LAKE

MARK Bright scored two match-winning goals for high riding Palace — and then admitted they were both mis-hits.

Bright struck after 12 minutes when his miscued shot from a smart John Salako pass bobbled into the net.

Then in the 54th minute he appeared to lob the ball skilfully over the advancing Rhys Wilmot and into the net.

But he confessed: "It just went off the top of my boot. I didn't aim the shot or even see the goalkeeper coming off his line."

Honest Mark's goals brought his season's tally to 24 and boosted Palace's promotion surge.

They have now won eight of their last nine games and looked in a different class to struggling Plymouth.

Palace's display was marred by the sending off of defender John Pemberton in the 76th minute for his second bookable offence.

Bright and Ian Wright were also booked and referee Keith Burge had to speak to manager Steve Coppell and coach Stan Ternent after a police officer had complained to a linesman.

Bright finish

Chelsea Champs

Super John's a hero again

CHELSEA won the Second Division championship more with a whimper than a bang — but they are determined to get back to the big time in style.

"Now we want to try to get 100 points and 100 goals," said boss Bobby Campbell.

"The lads have been fantastic this season. They have worked hard and done everything that I've asked them to.

"'To go up is an achievement, but to win the championship is something special.

"We've got some quality players at the club who have done the first part of their job.

"Now we've got to do it again in Division One."

Fittingly, it was Chelsea's longest-serving player who grabbed the goal that made sure of the title.

John Bumstead had a testimonial last season and was a member of the last Chelsea side to win the Second Division title in 1984.

But the highlight of his career came after 54 minutes yesterday when he controlled a cross from Kerry Dixon, turned inside the six yard box, and fired his shot passed Mervyn Day.

Chelsea 1 Leeds 0

By ROY DALLEY

"John typifies the spirit at the club," added Campbell. "I am delighted that our unsung hero got the goal."

Bumstead's only other goal this season was against Leeds at Elland Road last September.

"That was a complete fluke," he admitted. "The ball just hit my heel and went past Mervyn Day. I always seem to score against him.

"I've had a few chances in our last few games but, instead of shooting I have passed to someone else. This time I had a crack myself."

Chelsea beat Leeds 5-0 to clinch promotion five years ago.

But, with the Yorkshiremen clinging to a slim hope of a play-off spot, this game was always going to be tight.

Watford 2 Leicester 1

By IAN CRUSE

ROOKIE striker Dean Holdsworth came off the Watford bench to head a goal precious to his side's promotion hopes.

Sent on after 52 minutes to replace another young striker — newcomer Liburd Henry — Holdsworth took just eight minutes to make his mark.

From a Rod Thomas cross, Holdsworth rose unchallenged to head past a despairing Martin Hodge.

Victory was no more than Watford deserved. But the pressure told in some scrappy play.

Watford manager Steve Harrison tried to keep calm, insisting: "We are not even thinking of promotion or the play-offs. We just want to keep taking points."

His team seemingly got off to a dream start when Glyn Hodges curled home a free-kick which referee Mike Reed ruled should have been indirect.

But eight minutes later they were in front when Paul Wilkinson drove home his 20th goal of the season after a Nigel Gibbs long throw.

DEAN'S DAZZLER

Though Gibbs and Thomas both went close as Watford piled on the pressure, visiting skipper Mike Newell slid in an equaliser four minutes before the interval.

But then on came Holdsworth to deliver the goods.

The delighted scorer said: "We want to go straight up and will be going all out to catch Manchester City."

Ipswich 2, West Brom Albion 1

IPSWICH's play-off hopes stayed high with this win. But already manager John Duncan is worrying about the next game.

"We got the victory we wanted today, but if we fail next Saturday our promotion hopes are gone," he said.

Ipswich were on top early on, but Mich D'Avray, David Linighan and Ian Redford failed to turn their advantage into goals.

It was two minutes after the break when Tony Humes headed in from just inside the box.

Albion's Stacey North skied his clearance, Redford gave Humes the

By GRAHAM MILLER

chance and the header went in off the post.

The match was sealed on the hour when David Lowe's shot was fisted over by Albion defender Arthur Albiston.

John Wark scored from the penalty spot.

Albion came back two minutes from time through Colin West.

It was a miserable return home for former Town favourite Brian Talbot, now in charge of Albion.

His motivation and experience were the qualities lacking in the Albion side. And Ipswich were happy to cash in.

THREE 'N EASY

PAUL SIMPSON ended Bournemouth's play-off hopes with a hat-trick at the Manor Ground.

And the former Manchester City star should have scored six against the bemused Bournemouth defence.

It was a nightmare match for reserve goal-

Oxford Utd 3 Bournemouth 1

By PETER DRURY

keeper John Smeulders, who was picking the ball out of his net after only 13 minutes.

And ten minutes before the break Simpson scored his second.

Bournemouth stormed

back into the game in the second-half, with Luther Blissett and Bobby Barnes causing Oxford problems.

Trevor Aylott gave the Cherries hope on the hour heading home an Ian Bishop free kick.

But despite the Bournemouth pressure, Simpson completed his hat-trick in injury time.

Portsmouth 1, Bradford 2

POMPEY slumped to their fifth home defeat of the season in front of their lowest League gate for seven years — 6,909.

Paul Jewell's 83rd minute strike sunk John Gregory's injury and suspension-hit side after Warren Aspinall had silenced the boo boys with a 50th minute equaliser.

A bitterly disappointed Gregory said: "We had a good spell just after half-time, but you don't win by playing for 20 minutes."

Bradford went ahead after 40 minutes through a Leigh Palin scorcher.

Aspinall then missed a sitter after rounding the keeper. But he saved face by heading in Steve Wigley's cross.

Brighton 0, Swindon 2

BRIGHTON'S second defeat in 16 home League games boosted Swindon's hopes of making the promotion play-offs.

Steve Foley broke the deadlock in the 60th minute for Swindon when he scored the first of his double with a neat shot following a long clearance by Ross MacLaren.

A chance for the Seagulls came when Paul Wood blasted a fierce drive, but keeper Fraser Digby dived brilliantly to push it on to a post.

In the 76th minute Steve White set up Foley for his 10th goal of the season and clinch Swindon's seventh victory in 41 League visits to Brighton.

Hans up

GOALKEEPER Hans Segers saved the day for Wimbledon when he blocked a penalty by Neil Ruddock.

Even Dons' winger Dennis Wise bet the hulking defender a fiver that he would miss.

And when Hans Segers beat the out the kick, a delighted Wise grabbed Ruddock and shook him by the hand.

The Dutchman has now saved four out of five penalties awarded against Wimbledon this season.

Anxious Saints never really looked like winning any other way and Wimbledon were quite happy with the draw.

Dons' boss Bobby Gould was not happy with Eric Young though. He went to the dressing room to clear some grit from his lenses and gulped down the team's sandwiches while he was there!

HOPE?

N'castle 0, Luton 0

● LUTON boss Ray Harford refused to give in as his side failed to ease their relegation woes.

● Hatters have gone ten League games without a win but with three of their four remaining games at Kenilworth Road, Harford said: "We can win all three. We are not finished yet."

CHAMPIONS
● GOALKEEPER Dave Beasant, who dived into a puddle in exultation after Chelsea's win, also celebrated in more traditional manner.

'Now I want to
BLUE

WHILE a case of champagne was quickly polished off in a dressing room celebration that confirmed Chelsea as champions, chairman Ken Bates talked about his dream for the future.

It is to overhaul Arsenal and Tottenham and become London's premier club.

He said: "It is a dream, a lovely dream, and not one just for me to get excited about. It would be something really special too for those guys out there in the Shed."

Bates knows that first he must aquire Stamford Bridge as the club's home, and remove once and for all the threat that the Bridge will be bulldozed into obscurity.

Bates said: "If we get the ground, we are on the way to making Chelsea London's top club.

Sick

"So far all we have done is promise so much and deliver nothing.

Our lack of achievements are quite disgraceful. Take away the success in the 1970's that I'm sick of hearing about and we haven't done much in our 84-year history.

"Both Arsenal and Spurs are younger clubs, and look what they have in terms of success.

"But if we could put up the kind of ground that the Government, and now society seems to want from football clubs we could be in there doing something about the balance of power.

"We are the only West End club in the country. We are just one mile from Harrods with the Kings Road outside.

"We could be the most glamorous club in the country."

And Bates believes he will win his battle with the developers. He goes on:

"I think we will get control of the ground. I just hope the landlords, Marler, come to their senses before long."

Leeds, impeccably behaved on and off the pitch, were never in with a chance and Chel-

sea were always going to win.

They clinched it when John Bumstead, the old Bridge warhorse who has been at the club 15 years, got the vital goal in the 54th minute.

It was only his second of the season. His first was at Elland Road in a 2-0 Chelsea win that stopped them going bottom of the Second Division back in September.

Records

Bumstead said: "This time last year I wasn't sure whether I'd ever play for Chelsea again.

"I was haggling over a contract, and a couple of clubs were looking at me.

"Now suddenly I've fought my way back to get the goal that wins

BATES: Excited

COPPELL

Plymouth 0, Crystal Palace 2

STEVE Coppell, boss of promotion-chasing Crystal Palace, was ordered back into the dug-out by a senior policeman who thought he was inciting the fans.

Coppell leapt out of the Home Park dug-out when his right back John Pemberton was sent off for swearing at a linesman 12 minutes from time.

He was immediately told to go back to the touchline by Superintendent Bob Stone, who was in charge of crowd control.

A policeman was then stationed a yard away.

The superintendent said this was to prevent Coppell from returning to the touchline and further inciting a section of the crowd.

Stone also asked match referee Keith Burge to have a word with the furious Coppell.

"I was not concerned about touchline coaching," he said.

"I wanted the referee to ask Coppell and others to sit down for the rest of the game. I was anxious

COPPELL: Angry

Steve in hot water

about all the banter inciting the crowd," said Stone.

And referee Burge said: "Coppell was getting a little excited and the police wanted me to calm him down.

"I had a word with him and there was no problem after that. That's the end of it as far as I am concerned"

Coppell said afterwards: "I have been told by the police that I was talking too much, so I am not saying anything else.

"But I do know that Pemberton's sending off will cost my team dearly

make Chelsea the capital's best'

HEAVEN

GOING UP IN STYLE

Marot makes merry

By JACK STEGGLES

VERONIQUE Marot, who would rather be English than French, produced a record-breaking victory in the ADT London Marathon.

Then she handed another snub to the international selectors.

"Don't choose me for the Commonwealth Games," said the 33-year-old who refused to run in the Olympics.

She won in a British record 2hrs, 25mins, 56secs.

Kenya's Douglas Wakiihuri won the mens race in 2:09.03, with Tony Milovsorov the leading Briton, sixth in 2:09.54.

Speedy Steve

By TONY STENSON

STEPHEN HENDRY last night continued his high-speed charge for the world snooker title.

In eight quick-fire frames at Sheffield he shot to a 6-2 lead over Willie Thorne.

Hendry is convincing his fans that he will become the youngest-ever world champion.

Bates has a dream

Chelsea the championship. It's a good feeling."

Bumstead remembers the 1984 Blues side that went into the First Division and adds:

"We are a lot more experienced, more of a team, resilient and tough."

But at the end the celebrations were low-key, apart from goal keeper Dave Beasant throwing himself full length in a massive puddle just one inch deep.

Chelsea are back. And this time Bates will make certain they stay.

But the Blues, having already reached a record number of points, are going for two more targets — 100 goals and 100 points — to really go up in style.

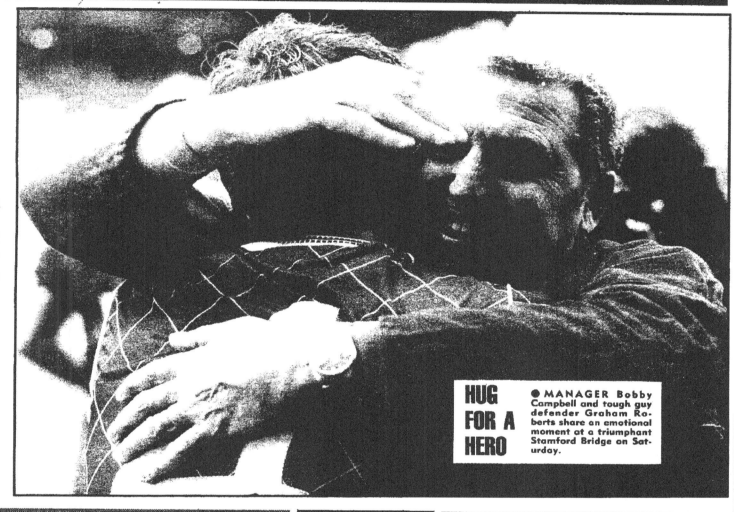

HUG FOR A HERO

● MANAGER Bobby Campbell and tough guy defender Graham Roberts share an emotional moment at a triumphant Stamford Bridge on Saturday.

COPS IT!

at a vital stage of the season"

In-form Palace are now six points behind second placed Manchester. City with two games in hand and could even now overtake them to win promotion outright to join Chelsea in the First Division next season. They play at Maine Road next Monday.

Cross

Palace grabbed their eighth win in nine matches, thanks to goals from leading scorer Mark Bright at the start of each half.

His goals brought this season's tally to 24, although they were hardly his most impressive strikes.

The first, in the 12th minute, was a mis-hit shot and the second was an attempted cross.

Bright admitted: "I did not see the keeper was out of his goal and the ball came off the top of my foot."

By DAVE HORRIDGE
Coventry 0, Q.P.R. 3

● TREVOR FRANCIS'S new-look Rangers team will be battling at the top end of the First Division next season.

● That is the view of former Merseyside rivals Peter Reid and Nigel Spackman, who engineered a win that removed any worries about relegation.

● Said Reid: "Paul Parker has the quality to ensure we don't concede many goals.

● "He was up against David Speedie, who can be a bit of a handful. But I thought he was superb and showed he is certainly good enough to play for England."

● And Spackman said: "David Seaman is pushing for an England place in goal."

● Colin Clarke looked one of the best front men in the country.

● After Justin Channing gave Rangers an early lead, Clarke stepped in with two more that enabled them to cruise through.

Trev's toppers

● Said Spackman: "This was the best team performance in the two months I have been here.

● "Rangers have some good young players and now Peter and I are providing the experience. Next season we could be a good side."

● Reid is equally optimistic, claiming: "The next step is to get a team that will be challenging for honours."

● Both players believe Francis has two potential England men on which to base Rangers' bid for the top.

EASY TREAT

By JACK STEGGLES
Charlton 1, Man Utd 0

CHARLTON took a giant step nearer First Division safety against a United side who were a disgrace to the name of a great club.

For much of the match United did not seem interested.

Their indifference staggered Tommy Caton. "We were allowed to dominate the game. And you just don't expect that sort of thing from Manchester United," he said.

Even manager Alex Ferguson admitted they were lucky to get away with just a one-goal defeat.

And Fergie had no complaints about the penalty from which Mark Reid scored the decisive goal for a Charlton side, once again looking likely to win their fight against relegation.

He also thought Paul Mortimer was unlucky to have a "goal" disallowed for a foul on Mike Duxbury.

SUNDAY SCOREBOARD

Hants v Somerset

SOUTHAMPTON.— Hants (4pts) bt Som by 5 wkts.

SOMERSET

Cook b Connor	2
Roebuck c Jefferies b Connor	6
Hardy c Nicholas b James	1
Tavare not out	120
Bartlett c Terry b Cowley	32
Marks run out	31
Rose lbw b Jefferies	0
Burns run out	6
Mallender run out	0
Jones not out	0
Extras (lb16, w2, nb4)	22

Total: (8 wkts - 40 overs) 220
Fall: 1-13, 2-16, 3-19, 4-109, 5-183, 6-183, 7-206, 8-217.
Bowling: James 8-3-10-1; Connor 8-3-28-2; Andrew 6-0-35-0; Jefferies 8-0-59-1; Nicholas 3-0-24-0; Cowley 7-0-48-1.

HAMPSHIRE

Nicholas c Burns b Mallender	57
Terry c Burns b Rose	45
R Smith c Russell b Rose	14
C Smith not out	41
Scott b Jones	31
Jefferies run out	4
Parks not out	2
Extras (lb16, nb1, nb1)	5

Total (5 wkts - 39.2 overs) 221
Fall: 1-100, 2-120, 3-120, 4-189, 5-219.
Bowling: Mallender 8-0-33-1; Foster 8-0-48-0; Rose 8-0-29-2; Jones 7.2-0-53-1; Marks 8-0-55-0.

Surrey v Gloucs

THE OVAL.— Surrey (4pts) bt Gloucs on faster scoring rate.

SURREY

Clinton c Athey b Alleyne	23
Robinson b Pooley	10
Stewart c Russell b Pooley	8
Ward c Graveney b Greene	57
Sadiq b Lawrence	34
Greig not out	9
Extras (lb16, nb1, w14)	31

Total (5 wkts - 38 overs) 164
GLOUCS.— 81 (19.1ov; Murphy 4-22, Feltham 3-23).

NO PLAY YESTERDAY.— (Matches abandoned: 2pts each): Derby; Derbys v Northants; Grace Road; Leics v Glam; Trent Bridge: Notts v Worcs; Edgbaston: Warwicks v Lancs.

Kent v Essex

CANTERBURY.— Essex (4pts) bt Kent by 6 wkts.

KENT

Hinks lbw b Foster	7
Benson b Topley	13
Taylor b Topley	27
C Cowdrey b Gooch	28
G Cowdrey b Lever	5
Ward c Prichard b Pringle	22
Marsh c Prichard b Gooch	6
Ellison c Gooch b Foster	5
Kelleher lbw b Pringle	4
Igglesden b Foster	2
Alleyne not out	1
Extras (lb9, nb2)	11

Total (40 overs) 135
Fall: 1-7, 2-43, 3-82, 4-90, 5-92, 6-116, 7-125, 8-132, 9-132, 10-135.
Bowling: Lever 8-1-16-1; Foster 8-0-25-3; Pringle 8-1-28-2; Topley 8-0-24-2; Gooch 8-0-33-2.

ESSEX

Gooch c Benson b Igglesden	34
Hardie b Alleyne	31
Prichard lbw b alleyne	5
Waugh not out	40
Pringle c Marsh b Ellison	10
Stephenson not out	0
Extras (lb8, w4, nb3)	15

Total (4 wkts - 35.4 overs) 136
Fall: 1-54, 2-64, 3-94, 4-132.
Bowling: Igglesden 8-2-21-1; Kelleher 8-0-24-0; Alleyne 8-0-35-2; Ellison 5.4-1-22-1; C Cowdrey 6-0-26-0.

Middx v Yorks

LORD'S.— Middx (4pts) bt Yorks on faster scoring rate.

YORKS.— 170-9 (40ov; Metcalfe 76, Robinson 55; Emburey 3-37).
Bowling: Cowans 8-2-16-0; Fraser 8-0-28-1; Carr 6-0-26-1; Hughes 8-0-51-2; Emburey 8-0-37-3; Sykes 2-1-7-1.

MIDDLESEX

Carr c Blakey b Jarvis	23
Downton c Bairstow b Byas	16
Gatting not out	81
Ramprakash not out	29
Extras (b2, lb6, w5)	13

Total (2 wkts - 33.1 overs) 162
Fall: 1-31, 2-55.
Bowling: Pickles 7-0-49-0; S Hartley 7-0-23-0; Jarvis 7.1-0-38-1; Byas 5-0-18-1; Carrick 5-0-16-0; Booth 3-0-10-0.

LO

■ **THE GOAL-DEN BOYS:** Roberto Di Matteo and Eddie Newton get a hug from Dennis Wise as they show off the trophy

By DAVID BARNES
at Wembley

CHELSEA (1) 2
Di Matteo 1, Newton 83
BORO (0) 0
Attendance: 79, 160

ROBERTO Di Matteo grabbed the royal blue flag of Chelsea and flew it as high as their anthem demands.

He knows as well as the rest of this rich cosmopolitan gathering that Wembley has seen far more compelling matches in its time.

But never an FA Cup Final with a quicker goal as the one Di Matteo struck to give Chelsea the lead after just 43 seconds.

Nor one that made Mark Hughes the first man this century to acquire four winners medals.

And not too many with the level of personal triumph achieved by unsung hero Eddie Newton who scored the second goal just seven minutes from time.

Newton, out of action almost all of last year through injury, felt his days at Stamford Bridge were numbered when Di Matteo signed for a club record £4.9m fee.

Now they shared together Chelsea's most delirious domestic achievement since the Blues won the FA Cup for the first and only previous time 27 years ago.

Their exploits left Middlesbrough manager Bryan Robson, who has had so much glory himself at Wembley, empty-handed and full of all-consuming despair.

Hope

If Boro had a hope, then it lay with Fabrizio Ravanelli, scorer of 31 goals this season, lasting the 90 minutes. But his troublesome thigh forced him out of the action midway through the first half.

Robson's plight was to be pitied, but I have witnessed nothing more moving at this stadium than Concetta Di Matteo, Roberto's lovely blind sister. LISTENING to the sounds of her brother's success in the stand.

Her father, relating events at her shoulder, will not have known his son's opening goal beat by just two seconds one registered by Wor Jackie Milburn against Manchester City 42 years ago.

Di Matteo's shooting power was destructive but Boro suffered also from the rapier-like artistry of his passing.

There was not a rival to get within tackling distance of him for the Man of the Match Trophy. No, not even Gianfranco Zola. Footballer of the Year, maybe, but he was a man searching for his genius here.

Nor Juninho, the Brazilian waif who has wept buckets of tears during a nightmare finale to a season that started with such blazing promise.

Juninho's heart has appeared to be impossibly large within his tiny frame while he has battled to rescue something from the dregs of a broken season.

He did his best to leave Boro with the FA Cup as an enduring memory of his quicksilver talents. And he

Pictures: KENT GAVIN AND BRENDAN MONKS

Blue what a scorcher!

■ THE CUP THAT CHEERS: The Chelsea players celebrate their Wembley final triumph

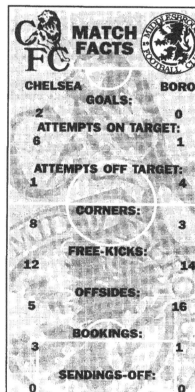

MATCH FACTS

	CHELSEA	BORO
GOALS:	2	0
ATTEMPTS ON TARGET:	6	1
ATTEMPTS OFF TARGET:	1	4
CORNERS:	8	3
FREE-KICKS:	12	14
OFFSIDES:	5	16
BOOKINGS:	3	1
SENDINGS-OFF:	0	0

certainly troubled Chelsea. Di Matteo could easily have been sent off rather than just booked when he brought the Brazilian down in the 55th minute.

You can imagine how Boro must have felt losing the Coca-Cola Cup Final and dropping out of the Premiership through three docked points.

But to go down to the fastest goal in any of the previous 115 versions of this showpiece was something else again.

It was a strike the speed and violence of which stunned the senses.

Robbie Mustoe, overawed by the occasion, was mercifully withdrawn from Boro's midfield after just 28 minutes. Sadly his first touch allowed Dennis Wise to slip the ball to Di Matteo.

Running straight at the heart of Boro's defence, Di Matteo made almost 50 yards before belting a 25-yarder over keeper Ben Roberts and in off the underside of the bar.

Di Matteo had approached the final deep within the shadows of men like Zola and Juninho.

Both were considered to carry the greater menace in their boots.

But, perhaps inspired by the majestic figure of his manager Ruud Gullit striding on to the Wembley turf, Di Matteo was imperious.

One deft pass with the outside of his foot gave Scott Minto a chance to add to the lead on nine minutes.

Minto forced the ball beyond the challenge of Roberts. Skipper Nigel Pearson slipped in the act of clearing and Phil Stamp whacked the ball

away from the empty net. Di Matteo's ruthless passing cut Boro to shreds once again halfway through the first half.

This time Romanian Dan Petrescu hoisted a lob over Roberts and was deprived by a courageous header from Pearson inches from the upright.

Boro lost Ravanelli within seconds of the incident. They must have sent him out to play with all fingers crossed and a prayer on their lips.

For Ravanelli pulled up short after a challenge from keeper Frode Grodas signalled the end of his Cup Final and, surely, his career with Middlesbrough.

Tedious

He was replaced by Danish striker Mikkel Beck, but much of the passion and creative instincts vanished with him.

Gullit, tired of the tedious rhythms that invaded the game, strode to the touchline to demand that his team raise the tempo.

Zola almost responded with a thumping 30-yard free kick. But young Roberts, third choice keeper at start of the season, plunged sharply to his left to produce a save to treasure.

And soon afterwards only a linesman's flag for offside robbed Gianluca Festa of an equaliser.

Festa was furious to see his powerful header from Stamp's cross ruled out, but TV replays showed the decision to be correct.

Zola then played a crucial part in

Chelsea's second goal as the clock wound down.

Petrescu lifted the ball beyond the far post. It would have run harmlessly out of play but for a clever back-heel from Zola that left Newton with a simple tap-in.

Zola had produced a piece of pure magic in the 71st minute when he evaded three challengers, turned inside, hurdled two more and fired a shot that Roberts saved partly with his face.

Yet Chelsea fans still howled for the presence of Gianluca Vialli for whom they have such affection.

Vialli had asked Gullit to give him five minutes so he could carry the memory of Wembley into a fast approaching retirement.

Gullit, apparently unmoved in the relentless quest for success, softened his heart and introduced him in place of Zola.

Concetta Di Matteo will not have understood the crescendo of booing Boro fans directed at FA chiefs Keith Wiseman and Graham Kelly before the start.

Nor their deafening clamour for those lost three points that have doomed them to relegation.

But she will always feel the full warmth of her brother's enchanting date with destiny.

Surely no one in the seats around her can have observed her sightless joy without having tears in their own eyes.

I'm off!

From Back Page

the deep sorrow of the Middlesbrough fans who have been left disappointed again."

It was a stunning 43 second strike from Roberto Di Matteo, a cracker from 30 yards, that left Boro reeling. A second from Eddie Newton in the final minutes sealed their fate and completed a disastrous season featuring relegation and double Cup failure.

But, we can reveal, chairman Steve Gibson will tomorrow give Bryan Robson £20 million to replace Juninho, Fabrizio Ravanelli and Emerson. A Boro insider told us: "Steve is determined to bounce back.

"He will also give the lawyers a blank cheque to take the legal fight to recover the docked three points. He hopes it will mean the Premiership has to include Boro as a 21st side next August."

Manager Bryan Robson said: "It's bad enough being beaten in one cup final let alone two. The lads are very disappointed.

"But getting to a major final, let alone two, is an achievement for a club like Boro, who have never won anything."

The duel was no jewel

By BRIAN McNALLY

THEY billed the 116th FA Cup Final as a showdown between the Sardinian Sorcerer and the Samba Superstar.

But it was another Latin legend, Roberto Di Matteo, who stole all the headlines with his history-making strike after just 43 seconds.

The mutual admiration between Chelsea's Italian imp Gianfranco Zola and Middlesbrough's brilliant Brazilian Juninho was shown when they emerged from the tunnel embracing each other.

But the expected personal duel didn't really happen.

Juninho was easily the more industrious performer in the first 45 minutes as he worked tirelessly to lift Boro after their first minute bombshell.

But far too much of his work was done outside the danger area and, apart from a poorly-struck second half free-kick, the little Brazilian never looked like scoring.

Zola by contrast was largely anonymous for most of the first half, but was denied on the stroke of half-time by Boro keeper Ben Roberts.

The Italian international lashed in a right-foot free-kick from 25 yards that was sneaking in until Roberts got down to turn it around his post.

Zola's skills came more to the fore in the second half as Boro seemed to tire and he again forced Roberts into a save in the 71st minute after he had danced past three despairing Boro tackles.

But his piece de resistance came seven minutes from time when he unselfishly flicked a Di Matteo cross into the path of Eddie Newton for Chelsea's second goal.

And at the final whistle the camaraderie between the two was evident as Zola sought out his Boro rival to immediately offer his commiserations.

ZOLA v JUNINHO

POSSESSION
First Touch: Zola 5minutes 21sec. Juninho 32sec.
Last Touch: Zola 83m (Substituted 88m) Juninho 87m.
Total Time: Zola 1m 38sec. Juninho 1m 50sec.

PASSES
TOTAL: Zola 44, Juninho 64.
Completed Zola 33, Juninho 46.
Astray: Zola 11, Juninho 18.

TACKLES
Total: Zola 3, Juninho 2.
Successful: Zola 1, Juninho 2.
Unsuccessful: Zola 2, Juninho 1.

SHOTS
Total: Zola 2 Juninho 3.
On Target: Zola 2, Juninho 0.
Off Target: Zola 2, Juninho 1.

FREE KICKS
Total: Zola 4, Juninho 4.
For: Zola 0, Juninho 3.
Against: Zola 0 Juninho 1.

CHELSEA......2

MATT FINISH: Roberto Di Matteo celebrates Chelsea's stunning opener with Scott Minto, Dennis Wise, Zola and Eddie Newton

LORD Attenborough defined perfectly the Ruud Gullit magic formula that has transformed Chelsea's Jurassic football into a slick Continental-style.

Chelsea's life vice-present remained in the royal box as long as any of the Blues faithful to enjoy the longest ever FA Cup Final celebration after the quickest Wembley Cup Final goal on record.

And after seeing Chelsea clinch their first trophy in just over a quarter of a century, he said: "Ruud has performed a magical job, marrying the continental style and flair of Di Matteo and Zola to the wonderful commitment and desire of English football.

"That has produced a great team."

In this, the Foreigners' Final, there was a distinct difference between Bryan Robson's collection of authentic world-class stars and Gullit's successfully integrated team of overseas captures.

Perhaps it's not the time to have a pop at Robson but to praise Gullit — who has broken the mould to become the first foreign coach to win a trophy in English football.

Mistakes

But by his own admission, Robson said: "I made mistakes, because we got relegated.

"When I come to assess this season to find out where it went wrong I will not want to make those mistakes again."

Unfortunately, the errors are irreversible. Emerson, a disgraceful, loose cannon in midfield, will be on his way along with the whingeing Fabrizio Ravanelli. But the greatest loss will be the genuine talent of Juninho.

In contrast, Luca Vialli, with just two minutes' contribution when the game was won, looked happy enough and it might even have been long enough to persuade him to stay!

Gullit reflected on his first season as a coach and the potential for more success at The Bridge.

He said: "As a coach you must

HIGH DI

BIG MATCH ANALYSIS

CHELSEA

FRODE GRODAS: Had only one shot to deal with all afternoon. Fearless Frode spread himself well to block sub Steve Vickers' 80th-minute effort. Otherwise untroubled for the easiest clean sheet of his career...................................6

FRANK SINCLAIR: Fiercely committed as ever, as Gianluca Festa will testify after claiming he'd been elbowed in the face in one angry first-half flashpoint. Looked

as though he'd been playing right-back all his life............................7
FRANK LEBOEUF: Nothing to worry about once Fabrizio Ravanelli hobbled off, except for a Mikkel Beck back-header that slithered through his legs at the near post. Festa spared his blushes by scuffing the chance. Booked for fouling Juninho..............................6
STEVE CLARKE: Rarely tested, but one expertly-timed tackle on Phil Stamp inside his own area in the first half was a class piece of defending. Chelsea were stretched

for once but Clarke stayed ice cool. Solid as they come...................7
SCOTT MINTO: Came up with the perfect answer to doubts over his Chelsea future. Aggressive in the tackle and adventurous going forward. Relished the occasion and was on top of his game.............7
DAN PETRESCU: No wonder his old Sheffield Wednesday boss David Pleat describes him as the best attacking wing-back in the game. Denied by Nigel Pearson's headed goalline clearance, and was a threat throughout............7

ROBERTO DI MATTEO: Scored the quickest Cup Final goal this century. The game then suffered a slow death, but that wasn't his fault. Smooth link player who always spelled danger...........................7
EDDIE NEWTON: Went largely unnoticed until timing a run into the box with Robson-style perfection, stealing in for a close-range finish............................7
DENNIS WISE: Was walking tall from the moment he released Di Matteo for that dramatic early opener. Sure touch about his work

in a dominant Chelsea midfield. Never wasted a ball..................7
MARK HUGHES: If you're going into a match with only one out-and-out striker, there's no one better. The old war horse has never battled harder.......................8
GIANFRANCO ZOLA: Not at his best but still a handful. Had Ber Roberts at full stretch with free kick and set up second goal. Milked it when Gianluca Vialli replaced him in 89th minute.........................7
SUBS NOT USED: Myers, Hitchcock.

JOHN EDWARDS

MIDDLESBRO..0

RUUD DI-LIGHT: Gullit congratulates goal hero Di Matteo

TRUE BLUE: Chelsea players celebrate holding the FA Cup aloft at Wembley

improve and I'd like my players to improve. What is important is they now know the feeling of winning and want to keep it going.

"I just did what I had to do. I knew that winning this Cup meant a lot to the club. It is also a boost qualifying for Europe, and our players are now famous around the world.

"This team didn't know its limits. If anything I have taught them how to be winners. My next aim is to win more."

With three new foreign acquisitions already completed as he planned ahead before the Final, Gullit's aim is to win his favourite trophy, the one with the "big ears"...the European Cup.

Impact

Can Chelsea be champions? Gullit said: "I certainly want to do better. We have made mistakes, all of us, but it still has been a very good season. We have played very well against the big teams and played some good football, but you don't win the Championship or qualify for the Champions' League unless you also beat the small teams."

Gullit will strive for greater League consistency having created a continental passing team capable of making an impact in

HARRY HARRIS Wembley verdict

Europe. For one of football's legends — World Footballer of the Year, European Cup winning star for AC Milan and captain of Holland's European championship winning team — his first FA Cup Final moved him.

He said: "There was a lot of noise and it was a great day out. I'm a little bit more proud as a coach than maybe I have been as a player, because I had a hand in the tactics and shaped this team.

"I'm really proud of this day, I feel I've grown up as a person.

"It's a great day, a great year and it went very fast."

Gullit stood back admiring each of his players as they climbed the famous Wembley steps to receive the FA Cup and their medals having already individually acclaimed them with personal hugs and kisses...even a cuddle for

Vialli. But as Dennis Wise lifted the Cup and each player in turn was handed the famous trophy, Gullit had to be reminded by FA official Adrian Titcombe that he had to collect his medal.

Gullit sprinted across the pitch and up the steps.

The first foreign coach privileged to receive the cherished winners medal, said: "My other medals are in a box, I didn't have time to unpack them, but after a while they will all have their places."

Gullit doesn't have a trophy cabinet or pictures of his glorious successes adorning the walls.

"No pictures to do with football, because my home is another environment, and I'm not that vain."

Clearly Gullit, who arrived in England two years ago, will eventually fully unpack because there's

no sign of his wanting to leave. "I'm happy to stay at Chelsea, I'm not thinking about leaving."

Gullit not only extended his players' after-match stay on the Wembley pitch for an unprecedented sing-song, he also summoned his chairman Ken Bates to join in.

Gullit explained: "He deserved it because all the time he's under pressure. He wants the best for Chelsea and people don't realise it. He was very proud of us.

"As well as Mr Bates, we also have to thank Matthew Harding, who is still with us spiritually."

When Di Matteo struck that marvellous dipping 30 yarder after just 43 seconds, Chelsea seemed certain to fulfil their destiny since Harding's tragic helicopter death and the miraculous recovery to beat Liverpool 4-2 on the road to Wembley.

That opening strike was also indicative of Middlesbrough's failings. When Wise won possession and his pass found Di Matteo in the centre circle, Robson's midfield was on the missing list.

Emerson seemed to be daydreaming, no doubt preoccupied about the flights back to Rio, as Di Matteo was allowed the freedom to burst forward unchallenged.

With the defence backing off,

captain Nigel Pearson preoccupied with Mark Hughes, the Italian's wickedly dipping shot whipped over Ben Roberts.

That goal gave Di Matteo the confidence to strike up a Man of the Match performance.

After nine minutes his precision pass could easily have given Scott Minto a goal, but his scrambled shot was half stopped as it went through the keeper's legs and didn't have enough pace to cross the line.

There were two turning points for Boro. First, after 20 minutes, when Juninho's glorious pass gave Ravanelli first sight of goal.

But the first time he had to break into a full stride his hamstring gave way a split second after Frank Sinclair's telling tackle. Without their 31-goal striker, Boro looked tame in attack after Mikkel Beck replaced him.

Doubts

Juninho looked their only hope, although just before the interval Gianluca Festa headed into the corner from Phil Stamp's cross but was caught marginally offside.

Gianfranco Zola had made his first telling contribution with a 30-yard free kick tipped round the post. But the irrepressible Italian helped create Chelsea's second goal seven minutes from the end to ease the doubts of their fans.

Eddie Newton began the move, Dan Petrescu's delicate chip to the far post seemed beyond Zola, but his delightful back-flick was finished off from close range by Newton.

The Chelsea fans chanted for Vialli and after 88 minutes and 33 seconds he came on for Zola, who departed the final a hero and paid homage to Vialli. It was a touching moment.

How popular Robson will remain at the Riverside depends on events next season in the Nationwide League. He has the haunted look of a loser as a manager that he never had as a player.

Pictures: KENT GAVIN, BRADLEY ORMESHER

HIGH!

BIG MATCH ANALYSIS

BORO

BEN ROBERTS: Tough start with the opening goal, but couldn't be faulted otherwise. Handled like a veteran and should be proud of his Wembley debut............................7

CLAYTON BLACKMORE: Been there and done it with Manchester United and it showed. Never flustered, whether trying to keep Chelsea in check or adding polished input to Boro's attacking ideas.........6

NIGEL PEARSON: Out of the same inspirational Captain Marvel mould as Robson. Flying fearless header from under his own bar said all about his approach. Deserved better than a loser's medal............8

GIANLUCA FESTA: Desperately unlucky with a far-post header ruled out for offside. Moved to midfield when Ravanelli hobbled off but lost none of his effectiveness.......7

CURTIS FLEMING: Another nervy Wembley performance. Nothing went right for him.

Knew it wasn't his day when the ball got stuck between his legs and bobbled out for a corner with no one near..........5

ROBBIE MUSTOE: Forced Boro to make a second early change when placed by STEVE VICKERS (28 mins), who defended stoutly and hit Boro's best chance against the keeper's legs......................6

PHIL STAMP: Looked overwhelmed. Pinpoint cross for Festa's disallowed header but otherwise made little impact down the right.....................5

EMERSON: Bobby Robson describes him as a "monster", but he didn't frighten Chelsea. Forget the planned end-of-season talks, Bryan, just flog him to the highest bidder. A complete waste of space.....5

CRAIG HIGNETT: Big disappointment. Bright, lively and full of clever touches in recent weeks but never got going on the big day. A sad figure when replaced by VLADIMIR KINDER in the 75th minute...............5

JUNINHO: Has been a one-man band lately but couldn't

hit the high notes at Wembley. Still the main inspiration. Deserved better than to finish once more with head bowed in despair............................7

FABRIZIO RAVANELLI: Sadly bold gamble backfired as he stretched for Juninho through-ball and pulled up in agony in 22nd minute. Replaced by MIKKEL BECK (24 mins) who made little impression.........5

REFEREE: Stephen Lodge (Barnsley): Over-fussy at times but kept a firm grip.............6

JOHN EDWARDS

Paul's badly out of time

GAZZA: Losing start

By MIKE WALTERS

WHILE the rest of us put our clocks forward yesterday, Paul Gascoigne spent 57 minutes trying desperately to turn his back.

To the good old days, when he swaggered around Wembley as if he owned the place – and when he wore a pair of false breasts on open-topped buses, nobody cared because the world laughed with him.

And in a sense, his mission was successful as Boro came unstuck against a familiar nemesis.

But sadly, just as he disfigured a Wembley showpiece seven years ago with recklessness bordering on dementia, the new patron saint of Teesside was lucky to escape with only a yellow card for his antics.

In 1991, of course, Gazza left the fray on a stretcher after a violent cameo in which he tested Gary Parker's ribcage for durability and Gary Charles' kneecap for sturdiness.

To most observers, Gascoigne has never been quite the same animal since then, and his genius has been only a sporadic feature where it was once his staple diet.

It would be stretching the point to claim that Boro's £3.45m debutant was consumed by malevolence from the moment he made his grand entrance after 63 minutes.

GASCOIGNE makes an instant impact, tangling with Wise.

BORO'S new man then went head-to-head with Zola.

Purge

But if lesser mortals had clattered into Mark Hughes, clobbered Gianfranco Zola without due care and attention and hacked Dennis Wise down from behind, their fate might have been more severe than a booking.

Certainly it would not be tolerated in the World Cup, where referees will be required to purge rash tackles.

Yet an unflattering collection of fouls, not to mention giving the ball away seconds before Chelsea broke the deadlock, was ultimately the sum total of Gascoigne's contribution to another barren day out at Wembley for Boro. True, there was the odd long-range pass sprayed across the hallowed turf with the effortless precision of a gifted artiste.

But in equal measure, he was caught in possession or too slow to capitalise on it.

And by the end, as Boro came quietly, Gascoigne was no more than a dispirited, peripheral figure.

Poor old Boro. Most clubs regard Wembley as a joyous outing designed to raise the spirits.

But three times in 11 months, they have infiltrated the home of legends merely to have their hearts broken.

And with only one full game under his belt since November, Gascoigne was barely in any condition to fulfil the red-and-white hordes' Messianic expectations.

REF Jones' quickly loses patience and flashes the card.

A HELPING hand for old rival Wise after another clash.

DEJECTION at the end for Gazza, Robson and Pearson

CHELSEA WISE

DOUBLE WINNER: Chelsea skipper and man-of-the-match Dennis Wise with a young admirer

Chelsea	2
Middlesbrough	0

(after extra time)
HARRY HARRIS at Wembley

ROBERTO DI MATTEO took 106 minutes instead of a Wembley record of 42 seconds but, fundamentally, the Coca-Cola Cup script was identical to that of the FA Cup final last May.

There was one fascinating and significant difference. Luca Vialli was the Chelsea manager instead of Ruud Gullit.

Gullit left Vialli on the bench for the FA Cup final but now he had the power to pick himself. He didn't even make the substitutes!

Instead Vialli took over Wembley, breaking with tradition.

Vialli, in his dapper Armani suit, led out the team ahead of captain Dennis Wise, while his opposite number Bryan Robson took the more mundane route around the old dog track.

Perhaps nobody explained to Vialli that this wasn't England's premier final. The managers, in their best suits, were not required to lead out their team.

More likely Wise, Vialli's new friend and unlikely bedfellow, had planned an exceptional day for the Italian.

For it was Vialli who led his team up the Wembley steps to collect the old League Cup, another traditional honour for the skipper. The bald headed player-coach kissed it with uninhibited delight.

Success

After just ten weeks after being plucked from the dressing room to succeed the dreadlocked Gullit, Vialli has become a virtual overnight success in Cup football.

While failing in the League in a season when Manchester United could have been caught, Vialli overcame Arsenal in the second leg of the Coca-Cola Cup after just five days in charge.

Now the most inexperienced coach in world football has won his first trophy.

Clearly the Chelsea fans will recognise the foundations laid by Glenn Hoddle, plus the first trophy in more than a quarter of a century delivered by Gullit.

Now a team that used to be mocked for their absence of silverware will have to build a larger trophy cabinet.

The next stop is the Cup-Winners' Cup in Vicenza on Thursday. And didn't the Chelsea fans let the country know that they are the only team left in Europe!

Not even the emergence from

Wembley made to measure for Luca

FROM BACK PAGE

him, but the players are all in this together and we respect the way he goes about his job."

Vialli, visibly moved by his players' gesture, said: "I was very happy to raise the trophy because I knew, when Dennis asked me, the request came from his heart.

"Of course, there's a great sense of satisfaction for me because it means the players care about their player-

manager. That means you know you are being appreciated. We have a great team spirit now. The players don't care only about themselves and everyone just wants to see Chelsea win."

Asked why he omitted himself from the Blues' line-up altogether, Vialli replied: "As you can imagine, I wanted to be involved as a player very badly, but this job takes something out of you   I'm talking

about physical and mental energy, stress.

"I didn't play myself because I knew Sparky (Mark Hughes) was up to it, and so was Franco Zola.

"I thought we deserved to win the game before extra time and I was totally confident in the way we were playing.

"I knew a goal would come sooner or later   I just asked the lads to be more ruthless and cynical in extra time." Vialli has banned his players from

excessive celebration ahead of Thursday night's European Cup-Winners' Cup semi-final first leg against Vicenza in Italy, when Chelsea carry the blue flag on to the continent as British football's lone survivors.

And he reserved a special pat on the back for predecessor Ruud Gullit, adding "He deserves some credit because he took us to the semi-finals. I think he will be a very happy man tonight."

GUYS DO IT AGAIN

Boro's new Wembley heartache

the bench just after the hour of Paul Gascoigne, on his long-awaited return to English football, could prevent this from becoming another blue day.

Franco Zola and Mark Hughes led an attack that looked full of goals, and only an outstanding goalkeeping display from Mark Schwarzer forced the final into extra-time. The crossbar played its part, too, denying Zola.

But Zola has returned to his peak just in time to help Chelsea collect more trophies and medals, playing a key role in both yesterday's goals.

In contrast Gazza's contribution was a booking just six minutes after his 64th-minute arrival. It was for a wild challenge on Zola.

They finished brow-to-brow, and even though Gazza, with his usual bravado, signalled that he had Zola in his back pocket, the little Italian was one of Chelsea's several contenders for man-of-the-match.

Perfect

Hughes battled fearlessly, again taking his usual quota of bumps and bruises. He came out for the second half with his left hand strapped and was finally taken off eight minutes from the end of normal time.

His most stunning contribution was a 21st-minute half-volley, somehow defying the laws of nature as the ball was slightly behind him.

Then Hughes, making his tenth Cup Final appearance, made perfect contact from Graeme Le Saux's cross, only for a one-handed reaction save from Schwarzer to stop him.

A couple of minutes later Zola's tricky feet gave him the space a perfect cross. Hughes did everything right with a header down but the Aussie keeper scooped it around the post.

After an early flourish by the club that lost both Cup Finals last season, Chelsea were in total control, creating numerous chances. The only menace came from Paul Merson's willingness to stretch Le Saux at every opportunity in the opening half.

It was a tough old battle, with Di Matteo's elbow catching Neil Maddison full on the chin after 15 minutes.

And when former Chelsea player Andy Townsend clattered into Wise in the 52nd

FRANKLY BRILLIANT: Sinclair outjumps Gianluca Festa to put Chelsea ahead. Pic: BRADLEY ORMESHER

minute, it loosened a couple of the captain's lower front teeth.

Gascoigne joined in some of the reckless challenges. Wise was shown the yellow card for a high lunge on Gazza. And when Gazza brought down Wise 13 minutes into extra-time from behind, he was fortunate to escape a red card.

It was not the welcome back that Gazza anticipated.

He started on the bench to Robson's left, waving and smiling to his friends in the crowd, but before half-time the cameras caught him yawning.

Once he has caught up with his sleep and is back in full training on Teesside, there will be other opportunities for Gazza to impress Hoddle.

But there was little on his Boro debut to warrant all the fuss as we wait for his international return.

"Boro cooking on Gazza" was one of the banners hailing his £3.45million transfer from Rangers.

But while he was on a low heat in terms of performance, there was still that uncontrollable side to his nature that threatened to reach boiling point.

The Boro fans gave him an incredible welcome but nothing was going to spoil Vialli's day in his quest to fulfil his prophe-

cy of becoming a Chelsea legend.

Five minutes into extra-time a Gazza-inspired move broke down. Frank Sinclair found himself in a forward position, starting a move that culminated in a goal that he will treasure for his entire career.

Sinclair provided possession for Zola and, as usual, he didn't waste it with a simple but effective pass to Wise in a wide position.

Wise almost overran it but his determination ensured that he delivered the cross inches before the ball ran out of play.

Fists

When the ball by-passed substitute Tor Andre Flo, Sinclair roared in with a powerful downward header that Schwarzer got his hand to but could not stop.

Vialli had sat for so long on the bench as the succession of near-misses, mostly a variety of long-range shots, whistled past the woodwork. Now he leaped from the bench, shaking his fists.

At the very outset of the second period of extra-time, the diminutive Zola soared for a header. The ball fell to the feet of Wise, whose pass to Flo provided yet another scoring attempt, but the Norwegian's

shot was saved. The danger did not pass because, from Zola's clever near-post corner, the white boots of Di Matteo got to the near-post first.

He was not going to miss with his side-foot effort from such close range. It was his ninth goal of a productive season from midfield.

In the very last minute, in yet another attack, Zola pulled up clutching his groin area, which is a huge worry with Chelsea's date in Europe so close.

Zola was reduced to walking pace but he wasn't going to come off.

Within seconds he joined the on-pitch celebrations that were reminiscent of the Cup Final success of just ten months ago.

Chelsea have now won the League Cup for the first time at Wembley. If they deliver the Cup-Winners' Cup from the final in Stockholm on May 13, that will be more silverware in the space of a year than Peter Osgood and his glamour boys of the Seventies could ever deliver.

These are heady days at Chelsea. Not long ago Gullit was bringing the glory to the club. Now it is Vialli.

Perhaps his reward will be the sack as well!

JUBILANT Sinclair salutes his gem. Pic: CHRIS TURVEY

Generous Gazza gives up his gong

HIGNETT with medal

By JOHN EDWARDS

PAUL GASCOIGNE picked up his first medal as a Middlesbrough player yesterday – and gave it away five minutes later.

The England midfielder received his Coca-Cola Cup losers' medal from Home Secretary Jack Straw, then sensationally went up to team-mate Craig Hignett and told him: "Here, it is yours."

A stunned Hignett initially protested that Gazza should keep it but was finally persuaded to accept his team-mate's offer.

"It was a fantastic gesture," said

the Scouse midfielder, denied a place on the bench and certain to quit Teesside this summer after rejecting a final contract offer from manager Bryan Robson.

"It has got to be one of the most unselfish acts I have ever come across in football.

"He just came up to me on the pitch and put it in my hand. I don't mind admitting that it brought a tear to my eye. I didn't

really want to take it off him, but he insisted."

Gazza, a 64th-minute replacement for Hamilton Ricard, was among the substitutes at his own request, according to Robson.

He said the £3.45million signing made an eve-of-final plea not to be picked from the start.

"Gazza told me he didn't feel right mentally to be chosen in the starting eleven," added Robson.

"He was concerned that it might upset some of his team-mates after they had done the

work to get to Wembley. In fact, the other lads have been good as gold and wanted him to play. But he said the only fair thing would be to put him on the bench.

"I had to consider that he's not quite 100 per cent fit and putting him on as the game opened up might be our best ploy."

Robbo reflected on further Wembley torment after being sunk by extra-time goals from Frank Sinclair and Roberto Di Matteo and admitted: "Chelsea were dominant after going ahead, but we matched them up to then."

SUITS YOU, LUCA

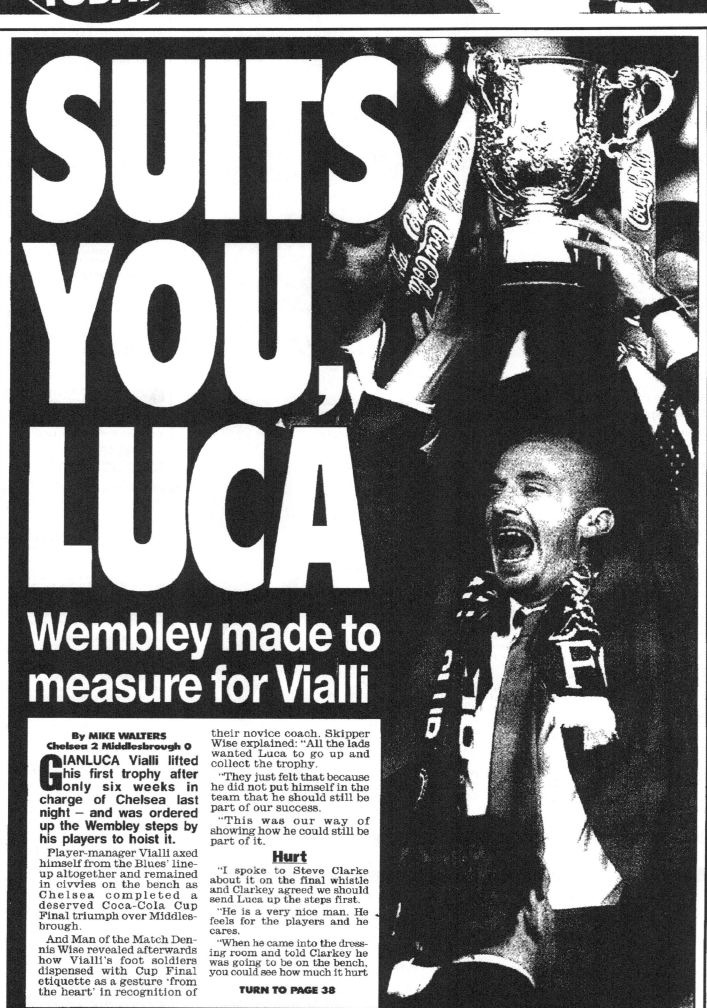

Wembley made to measure for Vialli

By MIKE WALTERS
Chelsea 2 Middlesbrough 0

GIANLUCA Vialli lifted his first trophy after only six weeks in charge of Chelsea last night – and was ordered up the Wembley steps by his players to hoist it.

Player-manager Vialli axed himself from the Blues' line-up altogether and remained in civvies on the bench as Chelsea completed a deserved Coca-Cola Cup Final triumph over Middlesbrough.

And Man of the Match Dennis Wise revealed afterwards how Vialli's foot soldiers dispensed with Cup Final etiquette as a gesture 'from the heart' in recognition of

their novice coach. Skipper Wise explained: "All the lads wanted Luca to go up and collect the trophy.

"They just felt that because he did not put himself in the team that he should still be part of our success.

"This was our way of showing how he could still be part of it.

Hurt

"I spoke to Steve Clarke about it on the final whistle and Clarkey agreed we should send Luca up the steps first.

"He is a very nice man. He feels for the players and he cares.

"When he came into the dressing room and told Clarkey he was going to be on the bench, you could see how much it hurt

TURN TO PAGE 38

Holli heroes lift England blues

From CHRIS LANDER

ENGLAND stormed to a thrilling 16-run win against the West Indies yesterday-to further enhance the captaincy claims of one-day leader Adam Hollioake.

Holli's heroes smashed 293-5 in their 50 overs thanks to man-of-the-match Nick Knight's superb 122.

The West Indies looked favourites to make their target when Brian Lara was racing to a century. But Hollioake's kid brother Ben came to England's rescue by running out the Windies skipper.

Mark Ealham kept his cool to take two late wickets – and maintain Hollioake's 100 per cent one-day record as captain.

FULL STORY – Page 37

SMART ALEC: Stewart joy

Published by MGN Ltd. at One Canada Square, Canary Wharf, London, E14 5AP (0171 293 3000) and printed by Mirror Colour Print Ltd. at Watford — Registered as a newspaper at the Post Office — **Serial No. 30,410** ©MGN, Ltd., 1997 Monday, March 30, 1998

NEWSPAPERS SUPPORT RECYCLING

MR ONE-DERFUL: Gianfranco Zola turns away in delight after crashing home a memorable 71st-minute winner in Stockholm last night

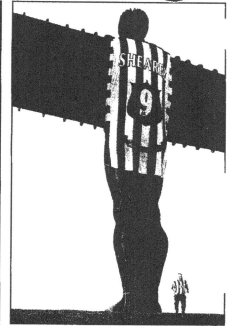

ANGEL of the North is kitted out with No.9 shirt

Shearer is avenging final angel

By JOHN DILLON

ALAN SHEARER is ready to spread his wings and become Newcastle's avenging angel in the FA Cup final.

Newcastle fans are convinced that Saturday's Wembley showdown with Arsenal is a heaven-sent opportunity for the England skipper to end their 43-year wait for a major domestic honour.

Now that his halo is back in place after being cleared by the FA, they can see Arsenal's dream of the double being dashed by divine intervention from their goal-scoring idol.

And to prove it, eight of them shelled out £1,000 between them to have a Newcastle replica jersey fitted on to the Angel of the North statue on the outskirts of the city.

The 29ft x17ft nylon shirt – with Shearer and a number 9 emblazoned across the back – was tailor-made for the 65ft-high iron construction.

It was eye-catching evidence that the £15million marksman has put all his recent controversy behind him and turned from villain to angel.

Mood

And last night he vowed to play the role to perfection at Wembley and lead Newcastle to their first FA Cup final triumph since the Jackie Milburn era in the mid-50s.

Shearer insists he is worry-free as well as injury-free after being cleared of allegations that he deliberately kicked Leicester midfielder Neil Lennon in the face.

And he revealed that he is in the mood to make Arsenal pay as they bid to add the FA Cup to the Premiership title they won 11 days ago.

"This will be my first major final, and I am determined to enjoy it to the full," he said. "I am feeling strong and fit and mentally far fresher than I normally would at this stage of the season.

"Our Cup form has been good, so let's hope that continues. We are up against a great team with a really strong spine. Seaman, Keown, Adams, Vieira and Petit provide an incredibly solid foundation.

"But we want to bring the Cup home to Tyneside for our fans. They have been tremendous, and hopefully the pubs of Newcastle will be hosting a giant celebration on Saturday night."

ZOLA POWERS BLUES TO GLORY

From MIKE WALTERS

GIANFRANCO ZOLA took Chelsea into the European record books with an astonishing – and dramatic – entrance as substitute here last night.

Within seconds of his introduction to this noisy and pulsating Cup Winners' Cup final, the little Italian struck a priceless winner to trigger wild scenes of delirium in the Swedish capital.

The Blues' backroom staff were off the bench performing an uncontrolled war dance in celebration when Zola — who started on the bench because of injury — broke the deadlock in the 71st minute.

• And player-manager Gianluca Vialli's dream of meeting his former club Juventus in August's Super Cup Final in Monaco is alive and well.

But even Vialli, in his ninth major European final, could not

	Chelsea	1
	VFB Stuttgart	0

have envisaged the instant impact Zola would make on a night blue-blooded Londoners will remember for the rest of their lives.

An emotional Vialli said: "This is just the beginning. We are now good enough to challenge for the Premier League championship.

"I feel very sorry for the players who were left on the bench, but this has been a wonderful evening and now we are all going to go on holiday

"We had to be patient and wait for our chances and this was worth waiting for in the end. I am a very happy man."

The only disappointment on a glory, glory night though was the shock dismissal of Dan Petrescu six minutes from time. The Romanian star was dismissed by Italian referee Stefano Braschi for a dangerous late tackle on Munat Yakin, and left the pitch close to tears.

Chelsea, bidding to become the first club to win the Cup Winners' Cup twice, were roared on by an amazing 18,000-strong contingent from West London.

Vialli's heroes were dealt a cruel blow before a ball was kicked, when England full-back Graeme Le Saux was ruled out with an ankle injury.

Handed

But the men to whom Vialli handed the 11 most precious blue shirts in the club's history wore them with pride and distinction, especially in the face of some outrageous provocation.

Frank Leboeuf collected a set of stud-marks on his right shoulder after a poor challenge from Stuttgart's skipper Fredi Bobic, which amazingly went uncensored.

And Leboeuf's defensive partner Michael Duberry was no more

impressed with the flailing arm from the same player which gave him a first half nose-bleed.

But with 19 minutes to go, however, came Zola's dramatic entrance and there can never have been a more inspired switch than Vialli's decision to bring on his Italian compatriot at the expense of Tore Andre Flo.

Zola had barely been on the pitch 20 seconds when skipper Dennis Wise sent him darting through a yawning gap in Stuttgart's defence to launch an unstoppable rising drive beyond Austrian keeper Franz Wohlfahrt.

Zola's amazing strike left sacked boss Ruud Gullit on course to pick up £500,000 on wages and bonuses SINCE his shock departure from Stamford Bridge in February.

Sad Stuttgart ended the game with ten men when Gerhard Poschner was sent off for foul and abusive language in the dying seconds.

Published by MGN Ltd. at One Canada Square, Canary Wharf, London, E14 5AP (0171-293 3000) and printed by Mirror Colour Print Ltd. at Oldham. Registered as a newspaper at the Post Office. Serial No. 3C447 ©MGN. Ltd., 1997 Thursday, May 14, 1998

ZOLA MAKES THE

STUART PEARCE: Mission

It's win or burst for Psycho

By JOHN EDWARDS

WARNING to Douglas Hall and Freddy Shepherd: If you brave the wrath of Newcastle fans at Wembley on Saturday and live to tell the tale, don't start thinking you are over the worst.

The true test of nerve could follow later, if Newcastle lose and you bump into Stuart Pearce.

If that should happen, remember one thing. Do not, on any account, smile or try to lighten the mood with any high jinks or banter.

A group of Nottingham Forest directors were guilty of that seven years ago and were given a volley as venomous as anything that has left Pearce's sledge-hammer boot.

If the FA had a Scowl of Excellence, "Psycho" would be its prize pupil. Particularly when he is forced to take second-best on board.

Joke

The very word "defeat" triggers a rage. He revealed he tore into Forest's directors for daring to enjoy themselves just hours after losing to Spurs in extra-time at Wembley seven years ago.

The 36-year-old Newcastle defender said: "I could see some of the directors having a laugh and a joke.

"I approached one of them and gave him a real rocket. I was so angry, I tore into him and said: 'We've just lost the FA Cup final – what is there to laugh and joke about'.

"I was just annoyed that it didn't seem to have hurt them. They were part of the club and should have felt it as keenly as the players and supporters.

"I'm determined there will be no repeat on Saturday, but I accept that we are up against a team who are just as committed about winning.

"I'm sure the Arsenal lads will be when it comes to hating being on the losing side. Just look at Tony Adams, for example – I don't expect to see him smiling if he has to settle for a loser's medal."

Villa thriller

JOHN GREGORY and his Aston Villa players were in fiesta mood last night after qualifying for Europe.

Chelsea's victory over Stuttgart means Villa take the spare place in next season's UEFA Cup.

Gregory, who is holidaying with the Villa team in Majorca, said: "Right now, I'm Stamford Bridge's biggest fan."

CAPTAIN'S COURAGEOUS: Chelsea skipper Dennis Wise getting stuck into Gerhard Poschner of Stuttgart in the Cup Winners' Cup final

Chelsea	1
VfB Stuttgart	0

GIANFRANCO ZOLA plundered a remarkable goal to win the European Cup Winners' Cup for Chelsea here last night.

The £4.5 million Italian striker was on the pitch for only 18 seconds before his breakthrough strike.

Zola was surprisingly left on the bench by his compatriot, manager Gianluca Vialli. But after a barren 70 minutes Zola came on for Tore Andre Flo.

Zola's first touch was to try to beat a defender.

But when he was tackled Dennis Wise released a first-time pass and no-one could catch Zola as he tore into the box.

His second touch was to crack a first-time shot into the top corner.

Chelsea, England's only hope in Europe, were out to restore pride in the stadium where turnip Graham Taylor met his downfall.

Holders

Unfortunately, the FA Cup holders were given a cabbage patch of a pitch, hardly helpful to their multi-talented team.

England's World Cup dreams were shattered four years ago in this Rasunda Stadium here in Stockholm and Chelsea knew it would certainly raise English morale to beat a German team.

The Premiership side gratefully accept the challenge, even though Chelsea can hardly be described as an English team.

In fact the two squads contained players of 22 different nationalities.

And there were only three Englishmen in Chelsea's starting Wise, Michael Duberry and Danny Granville, who was deputising for the injured Graeme Le Saux.

And, despite all the adverse comments about young talent stagnating because of too many foreign imports, young Granville, a humble £30,000 purchase from Cambridge enjoyed a distinguished final.

Ed De Goey, so often Chelsea's hero in Europe this season, pulled off a vital save at a crucial time. The German team had threatened to rip Chelsea's fragile defence wide open and achieved just that far too early for comfort in this final.

The temperamental Krassimir Balakov was able to master the atrocious conditions in the Rasunda Stadium with crafty footwork that sent him past two defenders in the 18th minute.

D-DAY LOOMS FOR BERGKAMP

DENNIS Bergkamp's battle to play in Saturday's Wembley showpiece reaches crunch time this morning.

He faces a gruelling fitness test at Arsenal's training ground to determine whether he has shaken off a hamstring injury.

Coach Arsene Wenger is insisting that Dutch international striker Bergkamp remains a doubt for the FA Cup final clash with Newcastle when Arsenal hope to complete the second League and Cup double in their history.

Bergkamp has made it clear

By JOHN DILLON

he will not consider playing unless he is satisfied that he is in the best possible shape for the game. But inside Highbury there is growing optimism that he will pass today's test.

Wenger said: "Dennis has started running again and so far he seems OK.

"But he is still doubtful to play, although I would say his chances have gone up from 30 per cent to 40 per cent."

Bergkamp himself was slightly more hopeful. He said:

"It's getting better but there is still some way to go. I'd say at the moment it's 50-50.

"With a hamstring, it has to be 100 per cent because I don't want to let myself or the team down.

"This is a game you dream of so you want to do everything you can to play in it. However, I don't want to be stupid. I want to be sensible."

Bergkamp was prevented from kicking a ball for 24 hours after he resumed running exercises on Tuesday.

Bergkamp has scored 22 goals for Arsenal this season and

received two Footballer of the Year Awards for his key role in driving the Gunners towards their first championship victory since 1991.

He pulled a hamstring in Arsenal's clash with Derby at Highbury a fortnight ago.

That meant he missed the last three games of the season including the home match against Everton when the Gunners clinched the title.

Surprisingly, after such a long, intense season, Bergkamp is the only fitness worry in the Arsenal camp.

DENNIS BERGKAMP: Improving

PERFECT ENTRY

GERMANY FALLING: Substitute Gianfranco Zola fires the 71st minute goal which won the European Cup Winners' Cup for Chelsea last night

IT ALIAN JOB: Roberto Di Matteo tussles with Balakov

No-one mentioned the you-know what

Harry HARRIS
in Stockholm

And as the path to goal opened up, the Dutch keeper was perfectly positioned to parry the shot.

Both sides came to the final with reputations for attacking football and bizarre defending — a cocktail that promised a glut of goals.

But on this bumpy surface only the highly technical players were capable of mastering the conditions.

Horror

Steve Clarke was guilty of a horror clearance that screwed off his boot across the pitch, giving the dangerous Fredi Bobic a gift of a chance.

But as De Goey came out to narrow the angle the potentially dangerous German centre forward fired his angled shot wide.

Michael Duberry suffered a whack in the face in a clash with Bobic as Chelsea tried to stamp their authority on a game where three-quarters of the ground was packed with their exuberant fans. Thousands had suffered nightmare journeys to Stockholm — many were diverted because of fog at Stansted — but they still got here in the hope of seeing an historic Chelsea victory.

It might have been an awful lot easier if Roberto Di Matteo, who seems to specialise in Cup final goals, had finished off the first chance of the game.

Then a flowing move involving skipper Dennis Wise and Dan Petrescu was rounded off with the final pass from Gustavo Poyet.

But for once the Italian was off target in front of goal — Di Matteo pulled his shot wide.

The Chelsea team were packed with the usual quota of players capable of scoring from a variety of positions.

The big surprise was that Vialli had opted for Flo to lead the attack alongside him, with fit-again Zola on the bench.

Zola was alongside Mark Hughes, but the Welshman's omission was rather more expected than Vialli's decision to leave out Zola.

The little Sardinian missed two weeks with a groin injury, pulling up in the Liverpool match at the Bridge.

And after specialist treatment back home in Italy he returned determined to play in the last match before Cesare Maldini names his final 22 for the World Cup. To be benched was a bitter blow for Zola.

Vialli received a couple of early favourable decisions from Italian referee Stefano Braschi but he wasn't too pleased when a free-kick went against him, and when he tumbled in the box after a challenge from Marco Haber.

Wise received a yellow card for an off-the-ball block on Balakov and the Bulgarian retaliated by stamping on the Chelsea captain, but he escaped a caution for his blatant retaliation.

Chance

When Poyet eventually found the space for a chance, the Uruguayan's volley was pushed out by keeper Franz Wohlfart.

Then, when Di Matteo's free-kick was cleared outside the box, Wise's venomous half-volley flashed just wide.

Wise shot looked to be on target when he struck the ball but it swerved nearly two feet wide.

Jonathan Akopoborie was booked for a blatant trip from behind on Frank Leboeuf as the Frenchman was surging forward.

It wouldn't have been a particularly pleasant half-time assessment in the Chelsea dressing-room and there was certainly more urgency right from the start of the second half.

There was a superb cross from Vialli and a corner as Poyet drifted into the box.

And Stuttgart found it difficult to find a way out in the 52nd minute until Wise cracked a shot from the edge of the box that just skimmed the outside of the post.

The Stuttgart coach Joachim Low made a early substitution, taking off Thomas Schneider and sending on Endress.

Chelsea were comfortably holding on to that precious Zola goal, but then six minutes from the end Petrescu was shown the red card.

It looked no more than a rash challenge but certainly nothing that warranted more than a booking.

Petrescu had to be led away as he was furious with the decision.

But it left Chelsea clinging on for the remaining few minutes. Stuttgart were also reduced to ten men when Gerhard Poschner received his second yellow card in injury time.

CHELSEA: De Goey, Petrescu, Leboeuf, Clarke, Poyet (Newton 80), Vialli, Wise, Duberry, Di Matteo, Granville, Flo (Zola 70).

VfB STUTTGART: Wohlfahrt, Berthold, Yakin, Hagner (Ristic 79), Haber (Georjevic 75), Balakov, Bobic, Schneider (Endress 55), Akpoborie, Soldo, Poschner.

Referee: S Braschi (Italy).

THEY took us for a waltz by the Danube in Bratislava and left us pining for the fjords in the teeth of an Arctic blizzard in Tromso.

Next they stunned Real Betis with Gianluca Vialli's brand of rioja-'n-roll football before producing a stunning comeback against Vicenza in the semi-finals in defiance of all logic.

And shortly before 7.40pm in one of Stockholm's dreariest suburbs, a young mascot led Dennis Wise into the climax of Chelsea's astonishing European odyssey.

It has been a long time coming. Some 27 years earlier, Ron "Chopper" Harris had cavorted round Athens with the Cup Winners' Cup, and now history demanded that Chelsea should leave their fingerprints on the trophy in another foreign field.

They were followed to the Swedish capital, home of Abba, Volvo and meatballs, by a veritable army of blue shirts.

Control

A fleet of 40 charter planes crossed the North Sea, one of the largest peace-time air lifts in history, to keep the blue flag flying over Scandinavia.

Virtually every vehicle with a pair of wings and an aeronautic MOT was commandeered and air traffic control worked overtime to give Operation Smorgasbord lift-off.

There will never be a shortage of applicants to get out of Luton fast but rarely has there been such a grateful exodus from the airport as when early fog finally lifted yesterday.

The result of this impressive exercise in migration was that, inside the Rasunda Stadium, Chelsea fans outnumbered Stuttgart by at least five to one.

Everywhere, apart from the top deck at one end, was blue.

Chelsea chairman Ken Bates was visibly moved by it all, and 75 minutes before kick-off the man with the grey beard could be spotted dancing in the aisles with his partner Susannah to the strains of a pop music abomination squeaked by Kylie Minogue.

If Rasunda rings a bell with most English fans, it will trigger a whole battery of alarm bells for ex-national manager Graham Taylor.

It was here, at the 1992 European Championship, that Taylor brought the curtain down on an evening with Gary Lineker and gave us 20 minutes with Alan Smith instead.

And on the same night as Lineker's unhappy farewell to the international stage, England were destroyed by the same Tomas Brolin as the roly-poly model last spotted sinking without trace in Crystal Palace's midfield.

Swedes were glad to see the back of English hooligans six years ago, and they were so fearful of more riotous behaviour that 1,000 police were assigned to keep the peace last night.

Initially, the £1m cost of this formidable force caused resentment among locals whose standard greeting for English accents was a nasal whine about the bill for the thick blue line.

In the event, all the Swedes had to contend with was a bawdy, tone-deaf recital by an 18,000-strong male voice choir in the city centre.

So if it wasn't exactly all quiet on the Scandinavian front, at least the occasion was not laced with as much spite or tribal rivalry as previous Anglo-German encounters.

In fact, Basil Fawlty will be delighted to hear that, as the last bottles of over-priced and violently frothy local brew were taking root, nobody mentioned the you-know-what.

For that, and clearance for take-off from every available airstrip in the Home Counties, may Ken Bates be truly thankful.

BLUES UP CAS BIS TO £6m

From HARRY HARRIS in Stockholm

PIERLUIGI Casiraghi last night announced he's coming to Chelsea in a £6million deal.

The World Cup centre forward has negotiated his release from Lazio even though he's still under contract and the Serie A club wanted to keep him.

I understand that a high-level Chelsea delegation have already agreed personal terms with Casiraghi.

The only stumbling block has been Lazio's insistence on a £7m fee, while Chelsea had offered nearly half as much.

The two clubs are close to a compromise with a fee close to £6m.

Casiraghi's arrival at Stamford Bridge along with Brian Laudrup from Rangers, leaves little chance for 34-year-old Mark Hughes, who will soon have talks over his future.

Hughes cost £1.5m when he arrived from Manchester United three years ago and Chelsea will want their money back.

With Luca Vialli wanting to build up his squad, the new player-manager doesn't want to lose Hughes and the club could hold him to the remaining one year of his contract.

But Hughes' recent form is an indication of how he believes he has staked his claim for a first-team place. With two more forwards recruited, the Welshman now knows it's time to move on.

Not only that, but Laudrup and Casiraghi will be close to earning £100,000 a week between them and Hughes has fallen way behind in the pay league at Stamford Bridge.

Unless Chelsea offer Hughes a new two-year contract they will be keeping an unhappy star.

PIERLUIGI CASIRAGHI: Deal agreed

TOUGH TIE: Roy Hodgson faces a trip to France

French fears for Hodgson

ENGLAND'S European challengers avoided the big clubs at yesterday's draw in Monaco.

Unlike Manchester United — who face daunting Champions' League trips to Bayern Munich and Barcelona — Liverpool, Blackburn, Aston Villa and Leeds all appear to have straightforward UEFA Cup games.

Liverpool travel to Slovakia to play Kosice, the same side United hammered last season in their first match, while Blackburn will host French team Olympique Lyon. Aston Villa will take on Norway's Stromsgodset at home in their opening clash, while Leeds play Maritimo of Portugal.

But Liverpool's joint manager Roy Evans admitted that the draw worried him and immediately warned his men not to underestimate Kosice.

"Don't let anybody tell you this isn't a hard tie — this club has the monopoly on the best players in Slovakia," he said.

Honest

"And as with all teams from Eastern Europe, they will be very, very difficult to beat."

Blackburn manager Roy Hodgson, who led Inter Milan to the 1997 final before losing out on penalties to Schalke, holds Lyon in high regard.

"It's an interesting one and, to be honest, it would have been tough whoever we'd have got," he said.

"There are pluses in the fact that our opponents are from a league we know well, and we will have no problems in terms of travel or accommodation.

"I know a bit about them and none of us need reminding that France

KINGS OF EUROPE: Skipper Dennis Wise proudly shows off the European Super Cup after Chelsea's triumph over Real Madrid

By MARK McGUINNESS

are the world champions and so football in France is in the ascendancy."

Leeds boss George Graham was delighted with their UEFA Cup tie, but disappointed at having to play the first leg at home.

Graham will be able to call upon the experience of Jimmy Floyd Hasselbaink and Bruno Ribeiro, both of whom he plucked from Portuguese football.

In the Cup Winners' Cup, holders Chelsea have a chance to impress against Helsingborg of Sweden at Stamford Bridge, while Ruud Gullit's Newcastle will play Yugoslavian team Partizan Belgrade at St James' Park first.

"We're pleased with the draw. At least it's a part of the world where we know that everything will be well organised," said Chelsea managing director Colin Hutchinson.

Of the Scottish UEFA Cup entrants, Celtic will travel to Portugal to play Vitoria Guimares, while Rangers are off to Beitar Jerusalem. Hearts host Mallorca of Spain in the Cup Winners' Cup.

CUP-WINNERS CUP
First leg: Thursday, Sept 17
Second leg: Thursday, Oct 1

Rudar (Slovenia) v Varteks Varazdin (Croatia), Panionios Athens (Greece) v Haka Valkeakoski (Finland), Ried (Austria) v MTK Budapest (Hungary), Levski Sofia (Bulgaria) v FC Copenhagen (Denmark), Heerenveen (Netherlands) v Amica Wronki (Poland), HEARTS (Scotland) v Mallorca (Spain), CHELSEA (England) v Helsingborg (Sweden). MSV Duisburg (Germany) v Genk (Belgium),

Besiktas (Turkey) v Spartak Trnava (Slovakia), Rapid Bucharest (Romania) v Valerenga (Norway), Apollon Limassol (Cyprus) v Jablonec (Czech Republic), NEWCASTLE UNITED (England) v Partizan Belgrade (Yugoslavia), Lazio (Italy) v Lausanne Sports (Switzerland), Paris St Germain (France) v Maccabi Haifa (Israel), Metalurgs Liepaja (Latvia) v Braga (Portugal), CSKA Kiev (Ukraine) v Loko Moscow (Russia).

UEFA CUP
Matches to be played over two legs on Sep 15 and Sep 29. First team drawn plays first leg at home.

GROUP A
Sparta Prague (Czech Republic) v Real Sociedad (Spain), Dynamo Moscow (Russia) v Skonto (Latvia), Blackburn (England) v Lyon (France), Fenerbahce (Turkey) v Parma (Italy).

GROUP B
Vitoria Guimaraes (Portugal) v Celtic (Scotland), Stuttgart (Germany) v Feyenoord (Netherlands), Arges (Romania) v Celta Vigo (Spain), Silkeborg (Denmark) v Roma (Italy).

GROUP C
Lodz (Poland) v Monaco (France), Anderlecht (Belgium) v Grasshopper (Switzerland), Liteks (Bulgaria) v Grazer AK (Austria), Fiorentina (Italy) v Hadjuk Split (Croatia).

GROUP D
Kosice (Slovakia) v Liverpool (England), Sporting Club (Portugal) v Bologna (Italy), Maribor (Slovenia) v Wisla Krakow (Poland), Vejle (Denmark) v Real Betis (Spain).

GROUP E
ASTON VILLA (England) v Stromsgod-

set (Norway), Slavia Prague (Czech Republic) v Schalke (Germany), Servette (Switzerland) v CSKA Sofia (Bulgaria), Crvena Zvezda (Yugoslavia) v Metz (France).

GROUP F
Bordeaux (France) v Rapid Vienna (Austria), Athletico Madrid (Spain) v Obilic (Yugoslavia), Beitar Jerusalem (Israel) v Rangers (Scotland), Leeds (England) v Maritimo (Portugal).

GROUP G
Udinese (Italy) v Bayer Leverkusen (Germany), Steaua Bucharest (Romania) v Valencia (Spain), Willem II (Netherlands) v Dynamo Tbilisi (Georgia), Anorthosis (Cyprus) v FC Zurich (Switzerland).

GROUP H
Ujpesti (Hungary) v Club Bruges (Belgium), Vitesse (Netherlands) v AEK Athens (Greece), Werder Bremen (Germany) v Brann (Norway), Sigma Olomouc (Czech Republic) v Marseille (France).

STAN IN LAST CHANCE SALOON

STAN COLLYMORE is back in Premiership action today with just 90 minutes to save his Aston Villa career.

This stark warning for Stan the Man was spelled out last night by Villa boss John Gregory, after he picked Collymore to start a game for the first time since February.

By DAVID MOORE

Gregory, appalled by the summer incident when Villa's record £7million buy kicked and punched former girlfriend Ulrika Jonsson in Paris, said: "Stanley Victor Collymore has finally run out of options.

"Stan faces Sheffield

Wednesday at Hillsborough now he is free from injuries with one match to do the business and produce the goods.

"I want to see evidence from Stan that I don't need to step up my search for a new striker costing eight, ten or £12 million pounds to replace him.

"He must work his socks

off in a genuine bid to recapture the brilliant form which once made him so exciting at Nottingham Forest and Liverpool.

"I will require that same level of effort on a permanent basis, not merely when it suits Stan to turn on the style. If Stan continues to be a failure he has nowhere to go."

HEADACHE: Collymore

Harry HARRIS

Chelsea 1 Real Madrid 0

CHELSEA collected their fourth major cup in a sensational 16 months last night.

As the fans paid homage to manager Gianluca Vialli, no one can forget that the first trophy, the vital breakthrough, was delivered when Ruud Gullit was in charge.

How Newcastle would love Gullit to build the same sort of success story.

English football conquered Europe in the Super Cup — well, at least there were three Englishmen in the Chelsea line-up!

And it was the only Uruguayan among all the different nationalities on show who sealed the first one-off Super Cup final.

Gustavo Poyet was named man of the match for his telling contribution just 20 minutes after coming on as a substitute for Roberto Di Matteo.

Ironically the matchwinner was conjured up by Gianfranco Zola when he was about to be taken off.

The tiny Italian came off the bench to score the winner within seconds against Stuttgart in Stockholm that brought the Cup Winners' Cup to Stamford Bridge last season to add to the Coca-Cola Cup and Gullit's contribution — the club's first trophy in over a quarter of a century — the FA Cup in May last year.

Fortunate

Since then there's been no stopping Chelsea in any cup competition, so they are truly the Super Cup kings of Europe.

The league, though, is another matter.

Real Madrid are still rightfully the top club in Europe as the Champions' League holders, and in the Premiership the Stamford Bridge club have still to justify their potential as genuine challengers.

In fact, Vialli has managed one point less than Kenny Dalglish!

After last night's game Vialli singled out World Cup winner Frank Leboeuf for his "outstanding performance."

The Chelsea boss said: "I don't normally single out individual players but I'm going to make an exception as we have won a cup."

Vialli admitted that his side had been somewhat fortunate when the referee delayed Brian Laudrup's introduction from the bench for his debut to replace Zola.

He said: "We were ready to make a change and put Brian Laudrup on for Zola but the referee didn't see that the substitution was ready to be made.

"We didn't perform as well as we could have done, but we are making progress."

For all those rebel mercenaries here in Monte Carlo gambling on the future shape of European football the match in the Stade Louis II

POYET'S THE SUPER HERO

TOP OF THE WORLD: Gustavo Poyet is hugged by Pierluigi Casiraghi and Albert Ferrer after his late winner clinched the Super Cup

should have been a reminder of the true traditions of European football. Paraded before the tie were the European Cup and Cup Winners' Cup as well as the Super Cup.

These are the true prizes of the European game and no-one should dismantle the true standards of the European game for no other motives than avarice.

The greedy men

POY JOY: Gustavo Poyet hails his goal

of the Super League breakaway contingent were here to lobby their case but it was obvious that their mouthpiece Media Partners are simply a front for those who would destroy these traditions for an extra shilling, let alone the £2billion dangled in front of them.

With 20 of the players who were on show in France at the World Cup more was expected of this confrontation between the Spanish champions and the club from along the Kings Road.

Vialli opted to leave out Poyet, with captain Dennis Wise able to play despite being banned at the moment in the Premiership.

Leboeuf held the defence together and was my man of the match, making one vital tackle on Raul after the young Spanish striker eluded Michael Duberry.

From a Zola cross Celestine Babayaro miscued from six yards and then Real came close to the opener just after half an hour when Roberto Carlos lined up for one of his famous long-range free kicks.

Sneakily Fernando Hierro took just two strides and

whipped the free kick over Graeme Le Saux at the far end of the wall and the shot swerved five yards before striking the inside of a post.

Leboeuf curled a shot from outside the area just wide of the goal and Pierluigi Casiraghi headed over.

Vialli sent on Poyet and Laudrup stood on the touchline awaiting his first appearance for the club as Chelsea created the breakthrough.

Routine

Casiraghi headed on and Poyet opened up the defence for Zola. His shot was blocked but he regained possession and teed it perfectly for Poyet to shoot into the far corner from just inside the box.

Chelsea embarked on yet another of their goal-scoring celebration routines, all the players standing on one leg in a circle.

As Real pressed for an equaliser Duberry pulled back substitute Fernando Morientes, who went down screaming for a penalty while coach Guus Hiddink tore off his jacket in frustration.

By contrast, Vialli went home cloaked in glory.

Italy boot out Chelsea men

NEW Italian boss Dino Zoff has dumped a trio of Chelsea stars.

His first squad since taking over from Cesare Maldini, for the European Championship clash with Wales at Anfield on September 5, failed to include Roberto Di Matteo, Pierluigi Casiraghi and Gianfranco Zola.

Di Matteo and Casiraghi have been placed on stand-by.

The squad has been met with surprise in Italy, with AC Milan defender Alessandro Costacurta and goalkeeper Gianluca Pagliuca axed from the France 98 squad.

CF FC	**MATCH STATS**	CF FC
CHELSEA v REAL MADRID		
1	GOALS	0
6	SHOTS ON TARGET	2
10	SHOTS OFF TARGET	5
4	BLOCKED SHOTS	2
4	CORNERS	3
15	FOULS CONCEDED	16
3	OFFSIDES	2
0	RED CARDS	0
2	YELLOW CARDS	2

GAZZA'S GOT A LONG WAY TO GO

By DAVE ALEXANDER

PAUL Gascoigne will not be fit enough for an England return for at least two months.

Middlesbrough number two Viv Anderson claimed yesterday that Gascoigne needs ten games to reach top condition.

It means the £3.45million midfielder will be ruled out of England's two European Championship qualifiers against

Bulgaria and Luxembourg next month. But Anderson predicted Gazza will then be back to his best. "You could say he needs ten games on the bounce, playing at his maximum," he said.

"Then you will see the old Gazza, I'm certain of that.

"The more games he gets, the fitter, stronger and better he'll be. Then the real Gazza will emerge again because he's got

so much ability." The Middlesbrough maverick was left out of the England squad for next week's qualifier in Sweden and Anderson added: "We didn't expect him to be in.

"I don't know if he wants to play for England again after what has happened — you'll have to ask him.

"We don't talk about things like that here, but I can tell you

he's not lost any of his appetite for the game in any way.

"You should see him in training, he loves it. He's in love with football and it rubs off on the rest of the players."

Gascoigne's fitness will be thoroughly tested today as Boro revert to a 4-3-3 formation against Derby. "He will have to work, but that's all right, he'll do it," said Anderson.

IN THE COLD: Gascoigne

ROB'S DI MAN

VILLA RATINGS
Compiled by GARY FITZGERALD

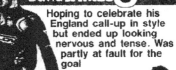

David JAMES 6
Hoping to celebrate his England call-up in style but ended up looking nervous and tense. Was partly at fault for the goal

Gareth BARRY 7
Booked early on for a bad foul on Melchiot and was kept over-busy by Messrs Zola and Co. Little chance to show his fluent attacking style.

Gareth SOUTHGATE 7
Not one of his happiest Wembley moments but he tried hard to keep Villa from tumbling apart. Unlucky to be in way for winning goal.

Ugo EHIOGU 7
Found it hard going after the break after dominating the powerful Chelsea strike-force in the first half

Alan WRIGHT 7
Another genuine and steady display by the little defender who did a good job in keeping Poyet quiet – pity for him Zola was around!

George BOATENG 8
Ran, tackled and hassled his rivals throughout the game. A determined display from a player who was clearly in the mood for the job.

Ian TAYLOR 6
Disappeared from the action after a shining start. A lot was resting on his shoulders to help Villa control the midfield but he failed.

Paul MERSON 6
Villa needed a massive display from Merse but the former England and Arsenal man could not produce – a big let-down for Villa fans.

Mark DELANEY 7
Raced up and down the flank when given the chance but couldn't cause enough damage in the forward areas to make a difference.

Dion DUBLIN 6
One of his quietest games on the big stage and was kept under lock and key by the awesome Marcel Desailly. Hardly had a shot on target.

Benito CARBONI 6
Substituted for the second time at Wembley this season after a tepid display – at least this time he didn't throw a tantrum. The bucket of water was safe!

SUBSTITUTES
Joachim for Carbone (87)
Stone for Taylor (87)
Manager:
John Gregory (rating: 6)

ROBERTO GLEE MATTEO: The Wembley matchwinner gets a hug from Frank Leboeuf while Chelsea skipper Dennis Wise rises to the occasion

FOR WEMBLEY

VILLA 0		CHELSEA 1
14	Fouls committed	17
2	Yellow cards	3
0	Red cards	0
2	Offside	5
3	Corners	2
5	Shots on target	3
6	Shots off target	2

PAUL HETHERINGTON

CHELSEA'S season was saved by Roberto Di Matteo, the Italian with a liking for Wembley goals.

Di Matteo hooked the ball into the net in the 73rd minute after Villa keeper David James failed to deal with Gianfranco Zola's free kick.

James, hoping to make England's Euro 2000 squad, pushed the ball against team mate Gareth Southgate, and it dropped invitingly for Di Matteo.

It meant the Chelsea midfielder, already the holder of the record for the fastest FA Cup Final goal, will also go into the record books for a second reason.

He will now be remembered as the player who scored the last Cup Final goal before the rebuilding of Wembley.

His strike gave Chelsea a deserved victory and a place in next season's UEFA Cup.

Otherwise, for Gianluca Vialli's side, it would have been the ignominy of trying to qualify for Europe through the ridiculed InterToto Cup.

The last time Chelsea played in the FA Cup Final — three years ago against Middlesbrough — Di Matteo scored after just 43 seconds.

But by the 43rd minute yesterday, they had produced only one decent attempt on goal.

And Merson saw a dipping 25-yard effort just clear the bar.

That was after 10 minutes when Dennis Wise, the only Englishman in Chelsea's starting line-up, hit a fine right foot drive from the edge of the box which rocked Villa keeper James back on his heels.

Vialli's side, who had scored 17 goals in their run to Wembley, failed in the opening half to pose a threat.

They seemed rattled by Villa's robust approach and picked up two cautions.

ASTON KILLER: Gareth Southgate is left floundering as Di Matteo reacts the quickest to score the game's only goal

Dutch full-back Mario Melchiot was booked for a foul on Gareth Barry and skipper Wise was cautioned for a late, nasty challenge on George Boateng.

It was the ninth yellow card of the season for Wise.

Villa, who had Barry cautioned in the 17th minute for a foul on Melchiot, had started the rough stuff with Boateng's third-minute foul on Wise.

But Villa were the more enterprising side in a low key first half.

Chelsea full-back Celestine Babayaro did well to prevent Boateng heading in a Paul Merson free kick, diverting the ball to safety.

And Merson also saw a dipping 25-yard effort just clear the bar.

But the opening half produced little to suggest "old" Wembley would be given a fitting send-off before being rebuilt.

Thankfully, the second half was an improvement — it certainly needed to be.

Ian Taylor glanced a header wide for Villa after Alan Wright had picked him out with a fine cross from the left, and then Southgate headed over from Merson's deep corner.

But Chelsea, who had Gustavo Poyet cautioned after a clash with Boateng, finally stirred themselves and were out of luck on two occasions in quick succession.

George Weah, preferred from the start to spearhead Chelsea's attack in place of Tore Andre Flo, shot inches wide in the 49th minute after moving menacingly on to Zola's pass.

And four minutes later Chelsea controversially had a goal disallowed.

James failed to hold Di Matteo's shot and Wise was on hand to poach what appeared to be a breakthrough goal, only for

Chelsea's celebrations to be cut short by an offside decision against Weah. Zola then created two chances for Weah, who shot over from six yards on the first occasion and was denied by James on the second as the Villa keeper flew off his line to block the ball.

But Chelsea's growing pressure was rewarded with Di Matteo's 73rd-minute winner.

It was a lead, though, which very nearly did not last long.

After Chelsea keeper Ed De Goey had failed to gather the ball, Benito Carbone should have equalised.

But the little Italian, in possibly his last Villa appearance after rejecting a new contract, shot weakly with his left foot and Leboeuf cleared off the line.

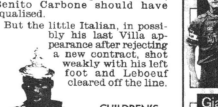

CHILDREN'S PARTY: Company for Weah and Leboeuf

CHILD'S PLAY FOR SKIPPER WISE

From Back Page

to that hospital's children's ward.

Wise, who has won the FA Cup three times, once with Wimbledon and twice with Chelsea, said: "All of the players said we would do it. Frank and Gus both followed me with their kids.

"I thought it would be something very special to remember and make a great picture. My wife Claire passed me my son. I nearly dropped him, but I can assure you the FA Cup would have gone first.

"He had some cotton wool in his ears to protect him from the noise, but one had fallen out. However, he enjoyed himself. I thought I might never get another chance to do something like that because I am getting on a bit."

Leboeuf had his eight-year-old son Hugo and daughter Jade with him, and the Frenchman said: "A steward said I was breaking the rules, but I told him I was French and it did not matter. Winning the FA Cup is also for our families

"This is the best feeling in the world, because I have never won the Premiership, but that is what we will try and do next year."

"We are now in the UEFA Cup which was also very important because a club this size should be in Europe."

Chelsea boss Gianluca Vialli picked out his defenders as the key players, and shrugged off his decision to leave £10million Chris Sutton out of the squad.

Matchwinner Di Matteo said: "It is such a pity they are pulling this down because I love it here. I always seem to have a bit of luck when I play here.

"We were the better side, but we defended for our lives. We have taken a lot of stick this year but it was a great way to finish the season. There were players other than Chris Sutton left out and they were all disappointed."

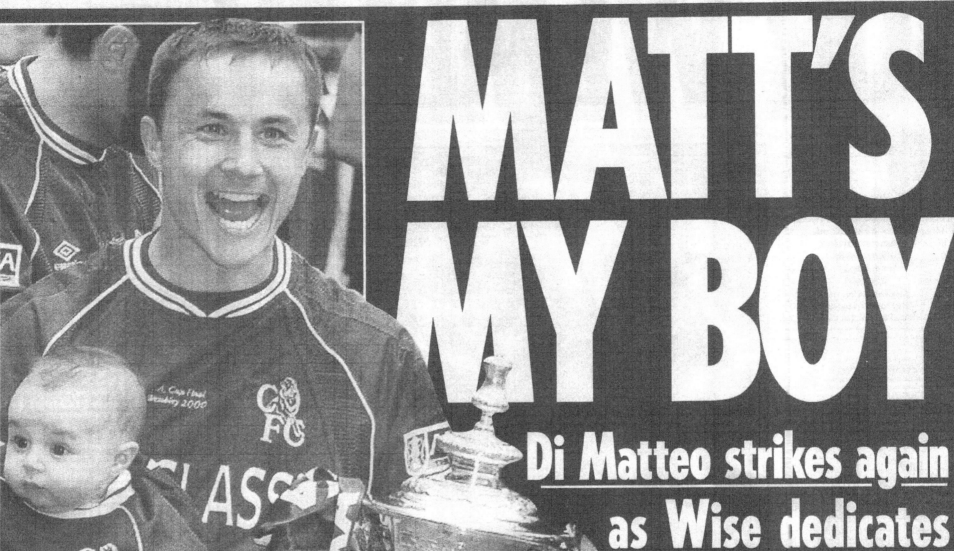

MATT'S MY BOY

Di Matteo strikes again as Wise dedicates Cup to son Henry

IT'S CHILD'S PLAY: Dennis Wise and son Henry lead the Blues' celebrations

VILLA 0 CHELSEA 1

By DANNY FULLBROOK

CHELSEA lifted the last FA Cup at old Wembley — and turned it into a family affair.

Skipper Dennis Wise led the way by picking up the trophy with his five-month old son Henry in his arms.

And he was followed up the steps by Frank Leboeuf and Gus Poyet who both had their kids with them.

Roberto Di Matteo, whose goal won it, dedicated the victory to his girlfriend — but his other big love affair is with Wembley Stadium itself.

The Italian scored the fastest goal in FA Cup history three years ago after 43 seconds when the Blues beat Middlesbrough 2-0, and he grabbed a goal a year later against Boro in the League Cup final.

Now his name will go in the history books again for scoring the last FA Cup goal before Wembley is rebuilt.

Wise's son Henry was the first baby of the Millennium to be born at London's Chelsea and Westminster hospital, and the Blues stars are donating all their player pool money

◀ **Turn to Page 87**

FA CUP 2000

Five-page special on the last Wembley: Pages 83-87

Published by MGN Ltd. (0207-293 3000) and printed by Mirror Colour Print Ltd. Registered at the Post Office as a newspaper.   **Serial No. 1831** ©MGN Ltd. 2000. ■ ■ ■ ■ ■ ■ ■ ■ ■ ■ **YO**

Red buys the Blues

SOAPER-STARS: Beckham and Henman

BECKSMANIA v HENMANIA

By JOHN CROSS

TIM HENMAN has already seen off two of Britain's favourite soap operas and today plans to upstage another... David Beckham's move to Real Madrid

British No.1 Henman faces Frenchman Sebastien Grosjean in the Wimbledon quarter-finals just over an hour after Beckham is unveiled as a Real Madrid player in front of a predicted worldwide TV audience of two billion.

Henman got the highest sporting viewing figures of the year with an incredible 12.7million for his thrilling fourth-round win over David Nalbandian and the roller-coaster victory delayed screening of EastEnders and sent the ratings of Coronation Street plummeting.

"I managed to keep EastEnders off for however long it was the other night," said Henman. "I suppose that's got to be a good sign." The staggering audience was half a million more than the 12.2m who tuned in for England's European Championship qualifier against Turkey in April and more than the 12.3m who watched the second leg of Manchester United's Champions League encounter

TURN TO PAGE 47

BATES SELLS CHELSEA TO A RUSSIAN FOR £140M

By JOHN CROSS

KEN BATES last night agreed an amazing £140million deal to sell Chelsea to a Russian billionaire.

Bates is ready to end his 20-year reign of power at Stamford Bridge after agreeing to sell his controlling 29.5 per cent stake to oil tycoon Roman Abramovich in a shock takeover of the club's parent company Chelsea Village.

Moscow-based Abramovich, 35, is the second richest billionaire in Russia, one of the most influential people in Russian politics and one of the most famous men in the city's history after making his fortune from aluminium and oil.

Enormous

Abramovich has promised to settle Chelsea's £90million debt, plough £50million into the club and also give Bates an honorary role.

Bates said: "This is a great deal for Chelsea Village, the club and our fans.

"We have achieved an enormous amount over the past 21 years, building a fantastic new stadium and a talented team which is firmly established as one of the top clubs in Europe.

"In today's highly competitive football market, the club will benefit from a new owner - with deeper pockets to move Chelsea to the next level.

"I look forward to working with Roman Abramovich to achieve even greater

TURNS TO PAGE 43

ROMAN JOLLY DAY: Abramovich is the new supremo at Chelsea

Published by MGN Ltd. at One Canada Square, Canary Wharf, London, E14 5AP (020-7293 3000) and printed by Mirror Colour Print Ltd. at Watford and Oldham. Registered as a newspaper at the Post Office. **Serial No. 31,849** ©MGN Ltd. **Wednesday, July 2, 2003** ■ ■ ■ ■ ■ ■ ■ ■ ■ ■ ■ **SL** Austria 2.50 EUR, Belgium 1.60 EUR, France 2.00 EUR, Germany 1.85 EUR, Greece 1.80EUR, Italy 1.70 EUR, Netherlands 1.80 EUR, Portugal 1.70 EUR (continent) 341Esc, Spain 1.75EUR, Malta 50 cents, Turkey 3,000,000Lire and Cyprus £1

9 770956 805837

CARLING CUP FINAL 2005: LIVERPOOL 2

THE FIRST

HOW THEY RATED: LIVERPOOL

Jerzy DUDEK 7

KEPT his side in the match during normal time with several impressive saves. Took a nasty knock but, with all the subs used he, had to carry on. Paid for his errors in extra-time

7 Steve FINNAN
ALWAYS looked calm under pressure from the normally dangerous Duff, and made several telling tackles. However, he had very few chances to venture forward himself.

Jamie CARRAGHER 8

UNFUSSY as always, the England star had outstanding game at the heart of a defence that was forced deep for long periods. Never shirked a challenge

7 Sami HYYPIA

HIS suspect pace on turn cost him an early booking against Drogba, but held his nerve under heavy Chelsea pressure. Missed a long throw which allowed Drogba to score.

Djimi TRAORE 6

FOUND life in Cardiff surprisingly easy, his discomfort on ball never exposed as opposition remained narrow. Taken off in favour of Biscan.

6 Luis GARCIA

STARTED very brightly but faded as Chelsea gradually took control of the midfield. Not afraid to try a few tricks, but they never quite came off for the little Spaniard.

Steven GERRARD 7

DIDN'T deserve to score the cruel own goal that robbed his side of victory. Showed he can do the defensive donkey-work, but was unable to power forward on a regular basis.

7 Dietmar HAMANN

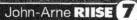
THE GERMAN was sound in the Liverpool engine room. His positional play was as immaculate as ever, and he even found time to test Cech with a rare venomous shot.

John-Arne RIISE 7

ILLUMINATED the match with a brilliant early goal that was dispatched with incredible technique. As Chelsea pushed forward he became more confined to defensive duties.

6 Harry KEWELL

FOUND it difficult to get on the ball, but did a good job tracking back – a task he normally treats with disdain. After his long injury lay-off he tired, and was replaced by Nunez.

Fernando MORIENTES 6

SHOWED strength in build-up to opening goal, but spent rest of his afternoon closing down defenders. Was eventually withdrawn, with Baros taking over the lone striker's role.

SUBSTITUTES Nunez (57 mins, 6) Outlet in attack. Biscan (67mins, 5) Uncomplicated. Baros (74 mins, 5) Head down as usual.

GLITTERING PRIZE: Drogba and Cole enjoy life in the spotlight as Chelsea lift their first trophy for Abramovich
Pictures: CHRIS TURVEY & BRADLEY ORMESHER

NOT JUST AN AVERAGE JOSE: OLIVER HOLT, PAGE 49

CHELSEA 3 (after extra time) from the Millennium Stadium

OF MANY

Mourinho men light the blue touch paper to winning dynasty

BELTER: Triumphant Blues skipper John Terry

THEY SAY the first one is the hardest. Nothing could have been harder than that.

But as Roman Abramovich watched on in wide-eyed wonder under the Millennium Stadium roof, Chelsea looked like a team that knows the glory story has only now started to be written.

Forget that it took a fluke own goal by Steven Gerrard to draw them level 11 minutes from the end, ignore the reality that the extra-time strikes from Didier Drogba and Mateja Kezman could not have been more ugly.

When you break your duck, it changes everything in an instant.

And after staring down the barrel of a devastating third cup defeat in the space of eight days to emerge in joyous relief with the Carling Cup in their grasp, Chelsea and Jose Mourinho know the pressure has been lifted.

Unreal

The fact that Mourinho could only see the scrambled efforts from Drogba and Kezman through a television screen only added to the bizarre Chelsea story.

But everything that has happened since Abramovich appeared out of nowhere to save a club on the verge of financial ruin has seemed outlandish and unreal.

Last night was just the latest episode and while Liverpool were left talking about what might have been, they must also concede that they were the agents of their own downfall.

Scoring inside 45 seconds, as Fernando Morientes crossed for John Arne Riise to thunder past Petr Cech, could have been the springboard for Rafael Benitez's side.

Instead, their response was as paranoid as Mourinho's subsequent rant at the world. Benitez sent out a team designed

Martin Lipton
CHIEF FOOTBALL WRITER

to contain and frustrate, the red shirts swarming around the ball, denying Chelsea any space. Lacking Arjen Robben's drive and galvanising energy, Chelsea were plodding, dominating possession but struggling to do much with it.

The chances that came were missed, Frank Lampard firing a free-kick at Jerzy Dudek, Drogba poking wide after being released by Joe Cole's angled ball, while Lampard's looping header was hacked off the line by Luis Garcia.

It had been one-way traffic, although Gerrard had decent penalty claims after a tangle with William Gallas but Mourinho made the decisive swap, with Eidur Gudjohnsen's arrival in place of the lightweight Jiri Jarosik at the interval much needed.

Now Chelsea were relentless,

LIVERPOOL		C
39%	POSSESSION	61%
5	SHOTS ON TARGET	9
5	SHOTS OFF TARGET	10
2	OFFSIDES	6
2	CORNERS	8
24	FOULS	17
4	YELLOW CARDS	4
0	RED CARDS	0
	ATTENDANCE: 78,000	
	MAN OF THE MATCH: Terry	

even if it appeared that Liverpool, with Sami Hyypia and Jamie Carragher so resolute, would not buckle. Dudek made a superb save to thwart Gudjohnsen's header from a teasing Cole cross, regathering his feet to block Gallas, who then saw his hooked centre cleared from under the bar by Hyypia.

The more Chelsea pressed, the more liable were they to the counter. Twice Liverpool engineered a clinching position, twice they failed to complete the task. Didi Hamann, who started and then finished a thrilling move, was foiled by Cech's fine stop.

But Gerrard, three yards out after substitutes Milan Baros and Antonio Nunez had combined, had no such excuse as he slid wide.

DROG'S DAY: Chelsea get their noses in front thanks to Drogba's instinctive finish

If Gerrard felt bad then, he was mortified four minutes later.

Drogba did not even leave the deck when Ferreira floated the ball in but the skipper ended up fighting with Carragher and Riise to get his head to the ball, the touch leaving Dudek flat-footed as it scraped in off the post.

Mourinho's celebratory taunting of the Liverpool fans behind him saw him banished to the TV room inside the tunnel but on the pitch Chelsea were now in charge.

The goal, though, would not come, Duff squandering a great chance and Lampard firing over and as extra-time began, Drogba saw his header from Duff's cross bounce off the woodwork.

Glorious

With both managers having played all their cards, the tiredness was showing. Igor Biscan missed a glorious chance to put Liverpool ahead when he headed over from six yards.

But when it mattered, Chelsea had the greater determination. Drogba struck first, two minutes into the second period, shielding Glen Johnson's long throw and forcing in his 12th goal since his £23m arrival from Marseilles.

Then Gudjohnsen drilled back through a crowd of bodies when Dudek palmed and as the ball squirmed loose, Kezman made enough contact to force over the line.

There was no need for goal-line technology as the flag was up.

Liverpool replied instantly, Gerrard's free-kick causing rare indecision from both Terry and Cech, with Nunez taking advantage to nod home.

But Chelsea were never going to let the game go. This was their day. This was the real beginning. The bubble has not burst, it has been inflated anew. And now they will not believe anybody, or anything, can stop them.

HAIL THE GENI

Super-Frank pounces to put Chelsea in Paradise

BOLTON 0
CHELSEA 2
Lampard 60, 76

simon MULLOCK

JOSE MOURINHO said Chelsea would be crowned champions at Bolton on the last day of April – and so the Chosen One's prophecy came to pass.

Two second-half goals from Frank Lampard finally tamed a Bolton side that were themselves handed a glimpse of the Champions League Promised Land by results at Craven Cottage and Anfield before the evening kick off.

But how the Blues were forced to rely on all their reserves of will and tenacity by Sam Allardyce's men before Lampard's class finally got the chance to shine through.

The home side hit Chelsea with the kind of hurricane that would have

VERDICT

A performance that illustrated Chelsea's season. Forced to rely on their survival instinct for long periods, they came through to clinch the title thanks to courage and class.

ATTENDANCE: 27,653

flattened lesser teams, particularly during a first half when Mourinho's men looked spent in both body and mind.

But with captain John Terry refusing to go off despite being able to see out of only one eye after a collision with Kevin Davies, and Petr Cech defying Bolton with some stunning saves, it soon became clear that this was to be the night when Chelsea claimed their place in history.

Then Lampard struck after 60 and 76 minutes to send 4,000 travelling fans into a Blue Heaven.

There was no trophy presentation at the end and Mourinho also ordered a Champagne celebration in the dressing room to be brought to an end

before the corks had even come bouncing back down off the ceiling with his thoughts already turning to Tuesday's Champions League semifinal return with Liverpool.

The Portuguese did promise to join Roman Abramovich on the pitch to accept the cheers of those supporters lucky enough to witness the club's first title triumph in 50 years.

But as the Russian billionaire was parading arm in arm with Terry and Lampard like a giddy schoolboy, his manager was sneaking out of the

Reebok and into the back of a waiting car to return to the team's hotel in Preston for a low-key dinner.

It was ironic that after shooting from the lip for the entire campaign, Mourinho left it to his players to do his talking – both on and off the pitch.

And it was fitting too that it was Lampard and Terry, the English heart of the Londoners' multi-cultural team, who were able to articulate the spirit that runs through the squad that Jose built.

Terry, swollen with both pain and

pride, said: "This is just the best feeling ever. We have worked so hard all season. We had a glass of Champagne in the dressing room and maybe we will have another half a glass at the hotel.

"But hopefully we can beat Liverpool to reach the Champions League Final on Tuesday night and really let our hair down with a few beers."

Lampard has now hit 18 goals during his emergence as the best attacking midfielder in the Premiership. But none has been as

controversial as the opener which will go down in Stamford Bridge legend.

Bolton were upset when Steve Dunn booked El Hadji Diouf for a foul on Geremi. But that soon turned into anger when Jiri Jarosik appeared to barge over Fernando Heirro as they challenged for Geremi's subsequent free-kick into the box.

The ball squirmed to Lampard and he cut inside Vincent Candela to bludgeon a shot past Jussi Jaaskelainen to spark Chelsea hysteria.

It needed a sensational Cech save

E OF THE LAMP

SIX OF THE BEST

Chelsea 1 Man Utd 0
Aug 15

Jose Mourinho (below) gets his reign off to a winning start with a win over one of his biggest rivals for the title, Sir Alex Ferguson.

Eidur Gudjohnsen puts Chelsea ahead after 15 minutes and, while Mourinho's side rarely look likely to get a second, United appear equally unlikely to equalise as the home defence put up what is to become a typically efficient display.

Chelsea 4 Blackburn 0
Oct 23

Chelsea bounce back in style from their first defeat under Mourinho, a 1-0 reverse at Manchester City.

Not only do the Blues return to winning form, they do so handsomely, scoring more than twice for the first time in the Premiership this season. Eidur Gudjohnsen leads the way with a hat-trick and Damien Duff hits the fourth against his old club.

Arsenal 2 Chelsea 2
Dec 12

Chelsea go behind twice against their deadly London rivals, one of the two big threats to their title dreams.

Thierry Henry gets both Arsenal's goals – the second a controversial quickly taken free-kick – but the visitors dig deep and equalise through John Terry (above) and Eidur Gudjohnsen in one of the most entertaining games of the Premiership season.

Liverpool 0 Chelsea 1
Jan 1

Mourinho's men take a firm grip on the title with a run of eight consecutive wins without conceding a goal – and the third of them is a narrow success at Anfield.

Liverpool dominate but Joe Cole fires home from 20 yards 10 minutes from time to clinch the sort of win that title-winning sides are made of.

Everton 0 Chelsea 1
Feb 12

Another banana-skin is deftly avoided as Champions League-chasing Everton are sunk at home.

James Beattie is sent off early on for butting William Gallas and Chelsea get a priceless winning goal midway through the second half from Eidur Gudjohnsen (above).

Chelsea 3 Fulham 1
Apr 23

By now Chelsea's pursuers are needing snookers but after two successive draws, the Blues' title momentum looks like stalling.

And when Collins John equalises for Fulham, the nerves are jangling at the Bridge until Arjen Robben, back from injury, sets up Frank Lampard for the goal that puts Chelsea in front again and Eidur Gudjohnsen completes a valuable victory.

MAN OF THE MATCH

FRANK LAMPARD Having emerged as the best attacking midfielder in the Premiership, it was fitting that he should secure the title.

BOLTON		CHELSEA
4	Shots on target	4
8	Shots off target	3
1	Shots blocked	3
7	Corners	3
20	Fouls conceded	17
3	Offsides	1
4	Yellow cards	3
0	Red cards	0

RATINGS

BOLTON: Jaaskelainen 6, Candela 6, Ben Haim 6, N'Gotty 6, Gardner 6, Hierro 6, Stelios 6 (Pedersen 6), Speed 7, Okocha 6 (Nolan 6), Diouf 7, Davies 7.

CHELSEA: Cech 8, Geremi 6, Carvalho 7, Terry 8, Gallas 6, Tiago 6, LAMPARD 9, Makelele 7 (Smertin 5), Jarosik 6, Gudjohnsen 6 (Cole 6); Drogba 6 (Huth 6).

MANAGERS: Allardyce 7; Mourinho 8

REFEREE: S Dunn 5

Chelsea's biggest-ever win at Bolton was their 5-2 victory at Burnden Park on New Year's Day 1955 – on their way to their last Championship.

FRANK'S A BUNCH: Lampard cracks the first of his two title-clinching goals at Bolton

---

to prevent an almost immediate equaliser, the keeper showing razor-sharp reflexes when Ricardo Carvalho's header was destined for the top corner of his own goal.

Then came Lampard's second 14 minutes from time, a powerful charge from the halfway line on to Claude Makelele's break-out pass and a clever shimmy to ground Jaaskelainen for another assured finish.

Lampard said: "The first goal was massive for us because we were below par. But it was the second one that really killed Bolton off."

Bolton would have relished the visit of the champions-elect in any circumstances.

But the occasion was spiced up even further by Everton's loss at Fulham and Liverpool's failure to beat Middlesbrough – results which meant Allardyce could once

again cast much more than just an envious glance towards the Champions League.

Certainly some of their early football, particularly from Diouf, made a mockery of the claim that Allardyce's side are nothing more than a bunch of kick-and-rush merchants.

But Chelsea came through unscathed – apart from a black eye for Terry caused by Davies' stray elbow – and showed why they are now worthy champions of England.

GAMES TO PLAY

BOLTON

May 7: Portsmouth (a)
May 15: Everton (h)

CHELSEA

May 7: Charlton (h)
May 10: Man Utd (a)
May 15: Newcastle (a)

THE SPECIAL ONES: SKIPPER

POWER MAN: Abramovich and Kenyon

KENYON'S PLAN FOR MOUR JOY

By DAVID MCDONNELL

CHELSEA chief executive Peter Kenyon believes Jose Mourinho has put Arsene Wenger and Sir Alex Ferguson in the shade with his achievements this season – and warned there is more to come.

Mourinho has added the Premiership title to an already impressive list of trophy successes, with Chelsea's 2-0 victory at Bolton giving them an unassailable 14-point cushion over Arsenal.

Gunners manager Wenger and Manchester United boss Ferguson have been left languishing in Mourinho's wake, and the 'special one' could yet go on to Champions League glory again if he can do for Chelsea what he did with Porto last season.

For Kenyon, it is clear that aside from the money billionaire owner Roman Abramovich has pumped into the club, the reason for Chelsea's dominance this season is Mourinho.

FERGUSON: Loser

"He is quite exceptional and was from the first time we met him and talked about what we wanted to achieve at Chelsea," said Kenyon.

WENGER: Second

"Obviously, he came with unbelievable credentials in terms of having won the UEFA Cup, European Cup and Portuguese League.

"I think he is the best manager in the Premiership. It's hard to argue with that, and

MOURINHO: Tops

I think he has to be one of the best managers in the world.

"He is certainly the best manager Chelsea could have had in order to achieve our plans in terms of success over the next several years."

That is why Kenyon is determined to tie Mourinho to a longer deal than the three-year contract he signed when he first moved to Stamford Bridge last summer.

Kenyon wants Mourinho to build a Chelsea dynasty over the next decade, adding: "He has a three-year contract, but right from the outset we spoke about him being here for the next 10 years. We would like him to stay for 10 years, and we've said that all along. We've said that to him and we will have those discussions with Jose."

TOP OF THE HEAP... BOTTOM OF THE PILE: Skipper John Terry and Frank Lampard are buried beneath their celebrating colleagues at Bolton
Pictures BRADLEY ORMESHER

HANDS UP WHO'S WON THE TITLE: Chelsea players hail their fans after the victory at the Reebok Stadium

Oliver Holt
CHIEF SPORTS WRITER

OUTSIDE the Reebok Stadium, Didier Drogba and Joe Cole had hoisted themselves out of the skylight in the Chelsea team coach so they could dance on the roof and drink in the cheers of fans beside themselves with joy.

A gleaming black Porsche idled behind the bus, blue Chelsea scarves draped around its wing mirrors, a sleek symbol of the new force that has swept aside the rest of the Premiership this season.

As the coach waited to take the newly-crowned champions off towards the M61, the club captain was inside the stadium, up on the third floor, still doing his job.

John Terry was gripping a transparent little plastic bag tightly to his side as he talked about the emotions that were washing over him in his finest hour.

At first, it seemed maybe there was ice inside the blue bundle to soothe yet another bruise or gash on the battered body of this indestructible colossus of a man.

But it was his shirt from the game, a memento he will treasure for ever. Some of his team-mates had thrown theirs into the crowd after the final whistle.

Others had changed into T-shirts with "Champions" written on them. Terry had kept his on his back until he disappeared into the dressing room.

"I've kept my shirt from every game this season and thankfully we've gone and won it," Terry said. "I've kept every shirt and every captain's armband.

"I'll put them in one big frame. I dreamed of being able to do that when I first started collecting them in the opening four or five games."

Somebody pointed out it was going to have be an awfully large frame on an awfully large wall to accommodate all 35 of those blue shirts. Terry laughed. "I'll overlap them a bit to fit them all in," he said.

Like his brother-in-arms Frank Lampard, Terry played in every single game of Chelsea's inexorable march on their first championship for 50 years.

Even when others were urging Jose Mourinho to give him a rest, Terry played on and played like a giant. If his defending has been commanding and assured, it has also been beyond brave.

It has already emerged that the Chelsea skipper has been playing through pain for some time now because of a foot injury that would have forced others out long ago.

Saturday was no different. Many had thought he would be rested before tomorrow's titanic clash with Liverpool but he was there at the heart of the defence as always.

He won everything in the air, rising head and shoulders above the Bolton forwards to clear danger when it threatened.

He was felled towards the end of the first half by what looked like an elbow from Kevin Davies but turned

LEADS THE WAY FOR CHAMPS

This is just the start for Blues .. Terry will bet his shirts on it

SACRIFICES ARE ALL WORTH IT NOW, SAYS COLOSSUS JOHN

out to be a finger in the eye. It was enough to give him double vision at half-time because the eye had swelled so badly. Again, others would have come off. Terry came out for the second half.

"After 10 or 15 minutes, it went away and I was perfectly fine," he said, as if he had been trying to stifle a sneeze.

Terry alluded to the physical ordeal his body has been through this season when he spoke after the game of the sacrifices he and his team-mates had made this season.

They have surrendered any notion of normal life to devote themselves to being winners and following the strictures laid down by Mourinho.

They have not strayed from the path. They have not lost their discipline, not

even once. The intensity of their focus has been almost frightening. They are a truly a team to admire.

"It feels very emotional," Terry said. "I just want to break down and cry really. I probably will when I get back to my hotel room on my own, when I sit back and watch it on TV.

"There was a time when Manchester United went 18 or 19 games unbeaten when I thought it might be starting to look a bit shaky, but we kept bouncing back.

"We've got the title by bringing in players and management who had the taste for it. With the youth and hunger from the other lads it was a great mix.

"The manager hates conceding a goal even in training. When you are training with that

intensity and at your best every day, you take it out into the games.

"Now we've got the first one, we've got to keep doing it year after year. If we can keep the squad together and keep the manager here for a few years we've got a very good chance."

Terry left then and took his place on the team bus. The biggest cheer of all came when he and Lampard thrust their heads out of the skylight and took the plaudits of the crowd.

An hour earlier, the same two players had remained out on the pitch, unable to tear themselves away from the fans.

They even walked backwards all the way to the tunnel as if they could not bear to turn away from a day they have waited their whole lives to celebrate.

Lampard wore a T-shirt stained dark blue with champagne. Terry wore the last of the shirts destined for that awfully big frame.

PREMIERSHIP TABLE

	P	W	D	L	F	A	Pts
Chelsea (C)	35	27	7	1	67	13	88
Arsenal	34	22	8	4	74	33	74
Man Utd	35	21	10	4	54	21	73
Everton	35	17	7	11	41	36	58
Liverpool	36	16	7	13	49	37	55
Bolton	36	15	9	12	45	41	54
Tottenham	36	14	9	13	47	40	51
Middlesbro	36	13	12	11	51	45	51
Man City	36	12	12	12	44	37	48
Aston Villa	36	12	11	13	43	48	47
Charlton	36	12	9	15	40	55	45
Birmingham	36	10	12	14	38	44	42
Blackburn	36	9	14	13	31	40	41
Newcastle	35	9	13	13	43	53	40
Fulham	35	10	8	17	42	56	38
Portsmouth	36	10	8	18	42	56	38
South'mptn	36	6	13	17	42	62	31
Crystal Pal	36	7	10	19	37	58	31
West Brom	35	5	15	15	33	58	30
Norwich	36	6	12	18	41	71	30

GUDJOHNSEN: Big game

TITLE JOY PROOF WE ARE BEST

FROM BACK PAGE

the final of the FA Cup. But the best team wins the league and we have done that.

"You look at Arsenal who lost at Bolton and Manchester United who drew, but we went up there and won. It's time for the others to take a look and know that we are definitely the best."

Mourinho, for once, took a back seat as his players celebrated, leaving the Reebok Stadium party early to return to the team's hotel near Preston.

But Lampard and his exultant team-mates believe that the buzz of lifting the league will give them the extra impetus they need tomorrow night.

Lampard added: "We wanted to win it at Bolton. We know what to expect at Anfield but what better way to go there than off the back of winning the league and the carrot of the cup final ahead. We're going there

HOW MANY WILL THEY WIN BY?

WITH THE Premiership title secured, William Hill have opened a book on how many points Chelsea will win it by and make 8-11 points their 11/8 favourite. They also offer 12-15pts – 13/8; 4-7pts – 4/1; 16 or more pts –13/2; 0-3pts – 16/1.

Hills make Arsenal 1/5 to finish second, Manchester United 10/3.

They have made Chelsea 10/11 favourites to retain the title next season and offer 11/4 Arsenal, Man U; 20 Liverpool; 66 Everton, Spurs; 100 Man C, Newcastle; 150 A.Villa.

as champions. We believe in ourselves and know that we can win at Anfield.

"The manager and some of the players have won things abroad. But people like myself, John Terry and Eidur Gudjohnson are not going to be happy with a second-rate performance at Anfield.

"We know that being champions here is the most important thing because you are the most consistent in the league. But we're in the semi-final of the Champions League and now that is the most important thing for us."

And skipper Terry promised there would be no hints of tiredness as Chelsea bid to become the first London club ever to reach the biggest game in European football.

Terry said: "When we get there and see our fans and their fans, any little bit of tiredness we feel will go out the window. It's such a big night.

"Last year, we got knocked out at this stage of the competition. It's one of the worst feelings I've ever experienced and I don't want to go through that again."

ROARING SUCCESS: John Terry

Mirror Sport
mirrorsport@mgn.co.uk

★ THE SPECIAL ONES: Chelsea heroes who have made history ★

TRIBUTE TO THE CHAMPIONS
SPECIAL ON THE NEW KINGS OF FOOTBALL

INSIDE: Don't miss your 20 page Mania pull-out

WE'RE OUT OF YOUR LEAGUE

Lampard's title taunt at Gunners and United

By MARTIN LIPTON
Chief Football Writer

FRANK LAMPARD last night taunted Arsenal and Manchester United as he claimed that Chelsea had shown just why they are the finest team in the land.

Lampard's double at Bolton sealed the Blues' first title in 50 years and set them up perfectly for tomorrow's Champions League semi-final second leg at Anfield.

And England ace Lamps was adamant that Jose Mourinho's men had proved why they are streets ahead of their closest rivals in the Premiership and that it was time for United and the Gunners to accept their change in status.

Lampard said: "We've proved that the best team wins the league.

"There have been some harsh words spoken about us not being entertaining and that the best two teams in the Premier League are in

TURN TO PAGE 51

DELAY: Ferdinand

FERGUSON RIO FEAR

By JOHN CROSS
Charlton 0 Man Utd 4

SIR Alex Ferguson last night admitted he is frightened of turning Rio Ferdinand's contract dispute into a "monster" after the England defender was jeered by his own fans yesterday.

Manchester United star Ferdinand, who has two years of his £70,000-a-week deal left, is stalling on a new £100,000-a-week offer as agent Pini Zahavi is holding out for more.

It has angered Sir Alex Ferguson and yesterday the United fans turned on him and chanted: "Rio, Rio sign the deal" and then taunted him with cries of "Chelsea's rent boy." Ferguson had

TURN TO PAGE 49

FRUSTRATED: Curbishley

CURBS IN QUIT HINT

By JOHN CROSS

CHARLTON manager Alan Curbishley last night admitted he was considering his future after his side's dismal 4-0 home defeat to Manchester United.

Angry Curbishley claimed his side's efforts "were not good enough" and revealed there was pressure for changes to be made in the summer.

Asked whether he would be considering his position, Curbishley said: "I do feel like that. I am a bit down, the players let me down. I expect more from them.

"One or two have been telling me to turn things around and let's hope we can do it."

FULL STORY: SEE MANIA, Page 2

BIG NOISE: Frank Lampard is proud to be a cheerleader for Chelsea's achievements Picture: BRADLEY ORMESHER

Published by MGN Ltd. at One Canada Square, Canary Wharf, London, E14 5AP (020-7293 3000) and printed by Trinity Mirror Printing Ltd. at Watford and Oldham. Registered as a newspaper at the Post Office. Serial No. 32,410 ©MGN Ltd. Monday, May 2, 2005 ■■■■■■■■■■■ ★★★ Austria 2.50 EUR, Belgium 1.60 EUR, France 2.00 EUR, Germany 1.85 EUR, Greece 1.80EUR, Italy 1.70 EUR, Netherlands 1.80 EUR, Portugal 1.70 EUR (continent) 341Esc, Spain 1.70EUR, Malta 53 cents, Turkey: 3,400,000 TL & 3.40 YTL, Cyprus £1.05, Denmark 20DK

NEWSPAPERS SUPPORT RECYCLING
Recycled paper made up 75.5% of the raw material for UK newspapers in 2004

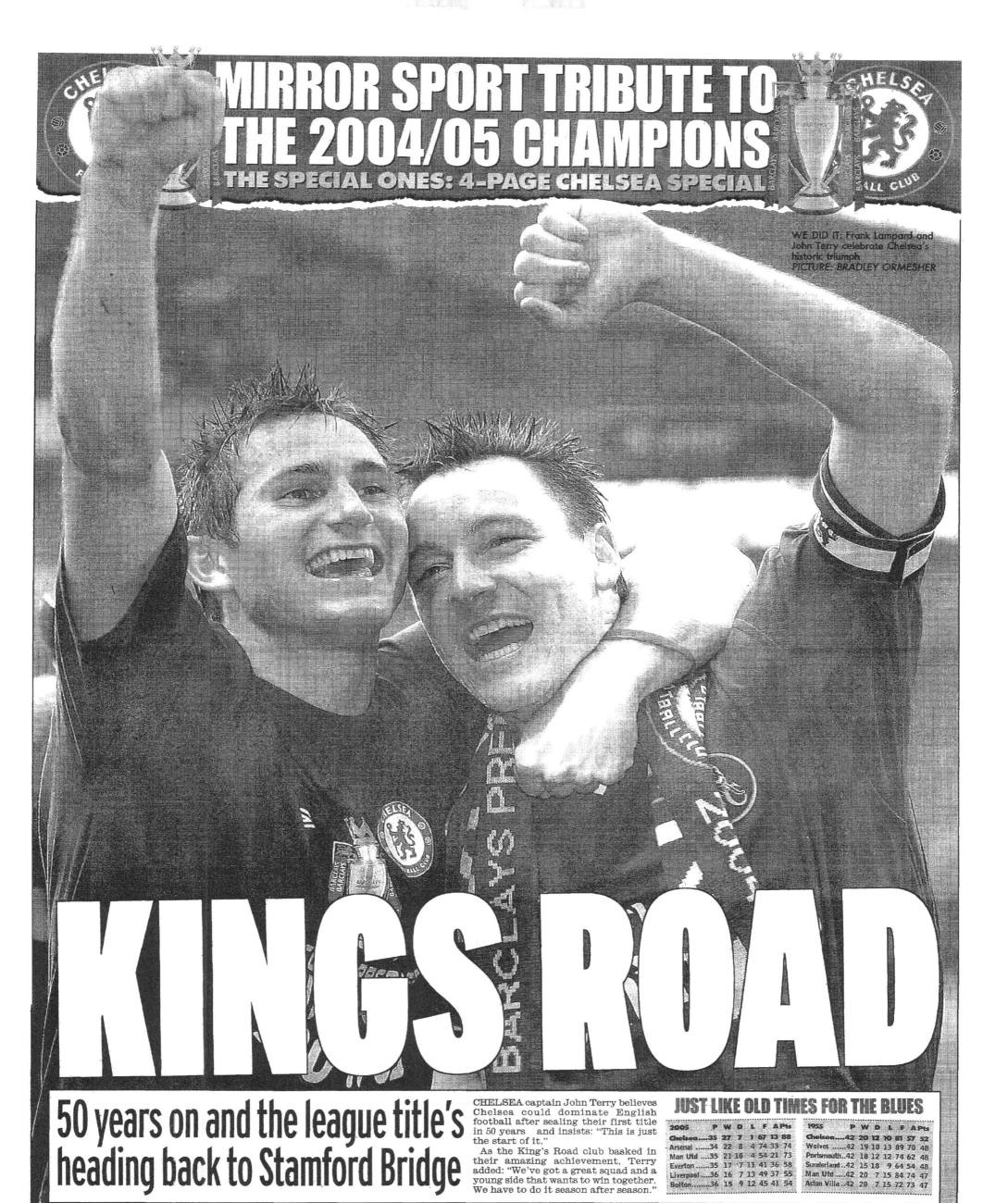

MIRROR SPORT TRIBUTE TO THE 2004/05 CHAMPIONS

THE SPECIAL ONES: 4-PAGE CHELSEA SPECIAL

WE DID IT: Frank Lampard and John Terry celebrate Chelsea's historic triumph
PICTURE: BRADLEY ORMESHER

KINGS ROAD

50 years on and the league title's heading back to Stamford Bridge

CHELSEA captain John Terry believes Chelsea could dominate English football after sealing their first title in 50 years and insists: "This is just the start of it."

As the King's Road club basked in their amazing achievement, Terry added: "We've got a great squad and a young side that wants to win together. We have to do it season after season."

JUST LIKE OLD TIMES FOR THE BLUES

2005	P	W	D	L	F	A	Pts
Chelsea	35	27	7	1	67	13	88
Arsenal	34	22	8	4	74	33	74
Man Utd	35	21	10	4	54	21	73
Everton	35	17	7	11	41	36	58
Liverpool	36	16	7	13	49	37	55
Bolton	36	15	9	12	45	41	54

1955	P	W	D	L	F	A	Pts
Chelsea	42	20	12	10	81	57	52
Wolves	42	19	10	13	89	70	48
Portsmouth	42	18	12	12	74	62	48
Sunderland	42	15	18	9	64	54	48
Man Utd	42	20	7	15	84	74	47
Aston Villa	42	20	7	15	72	73	47

QUICK OFF THE MAK: Makelele pokes in the rebound after his penalty was saved.

Two down, three to go as Jose demands Mour

CLAUDE MAKELELE stood in a small office near the changing rooms clutching the match ball and trying to explain why there was something missing.

On the other side of the wall, Jose Mourinho had given up trying to hide the fact his happiness had already been invaded by a wistful kind of melancholy.

Saturday at Stamford Bridge was party time but the champagne the Chelsea players swilled couldn't quite banish the bitter taste in their mouths.

They wanted to look back and savour their first title for 50 years but this new Chelsea is not a beast that sleeps after the kill.

Mourinho is a restless animal and Tuesday's Champions League defeat to Liverpool meant his team's hunger had not been sated.

"We have to fight to defend the two trophies we have got and we have to fight to get the other three," Mourinho said.

"Of course we won't get all five but we have to fight for all five and see what happens.

"In the middle of my sadness, I can feel happy for Liverpool, for Rafa, for the players.

"But a team who is 35 points behind Chelsea is not better than Chelsea." For much of the afternoon, Mourinho did a better job of disguising his pain.

A predictably lack-lustre affair was settled by a controversial last-minute penalty won when Frank Lampard was tripped, apparently outside the box.

Sentiment decreed that Makelele, who has not scored a goal for four years, should take the kick. Stephan Andersen dived to his right to push it away but Makelele scrambled home the rebound to spark wild celebrations that went on long after the match.

The club paid homage to its past by feting the surviving members of the side that last won the league title in 1955.

The old men in their best suits walked stiffly towards the half way line so that John Terry could present them with a replica of the league trophy they won half a century ago.

Through some oversight, the authorities had never actually given them the cup all those years ago and now these men in their 70s and 80s clamoured around it like the bold lads they once were.

The captain of that team, Roy Bentley, and the left back, Stan Willemse, had even carried the Premiership trophy out to the podium where it was to be presented to Terry.

Some of the unsung heroes among the backroom staff were granted a rare moment in the limelight when they marched one by one on to the pitch before the presentation ceremony.

An honour guard of eight Chelsea Pensioners had formed a corridor for Terry, Frank Lampard and the rest as they went to collect their medals.

And as the modern day players cavorted and danced, Bentley and his team chatted with the Pensioners and beamed when Mourinho shook each and every one of them warmly by the hand.

It was almost a perfect end to what has been pretty much a perfect season.

But when the players and the staff had finished drenching each other in champagne, Makelele came out to talk about the one element of nagging emptiness he couldn't quite suppress.

"If sometimes I appear to be too hard on this team when I speak about it," Makelele said, "it is not because I am not happy. It is because I am ambitious.

"I always want to improve and do things better next time. It's not a negative thing. If this young squad can stay the same, it can take over from Real Madrid and AC Milan."

Mourinho likes that kind of attitude. "This is the nature of my staff," he said.

"I have chosen them for their mentality, what I have created in them and what they have by themselves."

Chelsea 1 Charlton 0

By OLIVER HOLT
CHIEF SPORTS WRITER

Chelsea		Charlton
POSSESSION	59%	POSSESSION 41%
SHOTS ON	5	SHOTS ON 3
SHOTS OFF	9	SHOTS OFF 3
OFFSIDES	2	OFFSIDES 1
CORNERS	7	CORNERS 5
FOULS	0	FOULS 14
YELLOWS	0	YELLOWS 0
REDS	0	REDS 0

MAN OF THE MATCH: Cole
ATTENDANCE: 42,065

CHELSEA
Cudicini
Johnson Carvalho Galias
Geremi Makelele Terry Cole
Tiago Lampard
Lisbie Gudjohnsen
Hughes Kishishev Murphy
Konchesky Holland Johansson
Fortune el Karkouri Young

CHARLTON

SWING WHEN YOU'RE WINNING: Joe Cole clambers on to the bar while John Terry and Frank Lampard enjoy the party. Right: Jose hoists the trophy

Email us at mirrorsport@mgn.co.uk and text us after the caption's match at... AT 87222

GLORY OF THE BLUES: Chelsea players celebrate and owner Roman Abramovich, chief executive Peter Kenyon and Jose Mourinho pose with the trophy. Right: Gudjohnsen's close shave

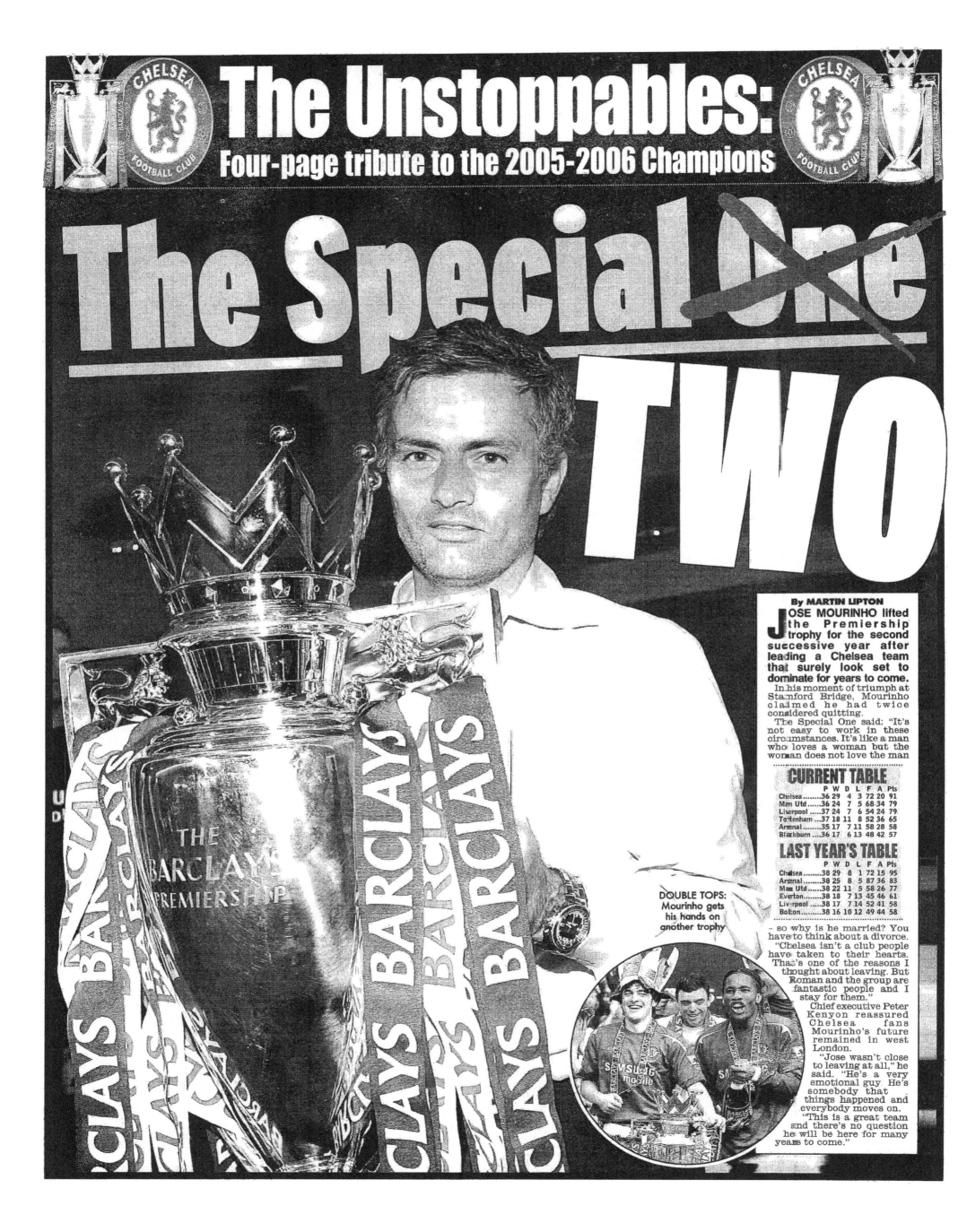

The Special ~~One~~ TWO

By MARTIN LIPTON

JOSE MOURINHO lifted the Premiership trophy for the second successive year after leading a Chelsea team that surely look set to dominate for years to come.

In his moment of triumph at Stamford Bridge, Mourinho claimed he had twice considered quitting.

The Special One said: "It's not easy to work in these circumstances. It's like a man who loves a woman but the woman does not love the man

CURRENT TABLE

	P	W	D	L	F	A	Pts
Chelsea	36	29	4	3	72	20	91
Man Utd	36	24	7	5	68	34	79
Liverpool	37	24	7	6	54	24	79
Tottenham	37	18	11	8	52	36	65
Arsenal	35	17	7	11	58	28	58
Blackburn	36	17	6	13	48	42	57

LAST YEAR'S TABLE

	P	W	D	L	F	A	Pts
Chelsea	38	29	8	1	72	15	95
Arsenal	38	25	8	5	87	36	83
Man Utd	38	22	11	5	58	26	77
Everton	38	18	7	13	45	46	61
Liverpool	38	17	7	14	52	41	58
Bolton	38	16	10	12	49	44	58

DOUBLE TOPS: Mourinho gets his hands on another trophy

- so why is he married? You have to think about a divorce. "Chelsea isn't a club people have taken to their hearts. That's one of the reasons I thought about leaving. But Roman and the group are fantastic people and I stay for them."

Chief executive Peter Kenyon reassured Chelsea fans Mourinho's future remained in west London.

"Jose wasn't close to leaving at all," he said. "He's a very emotional guy. He's somebody that things happened and everybody moves on.

"This is a great team and there's no question he will be here for many years to come."

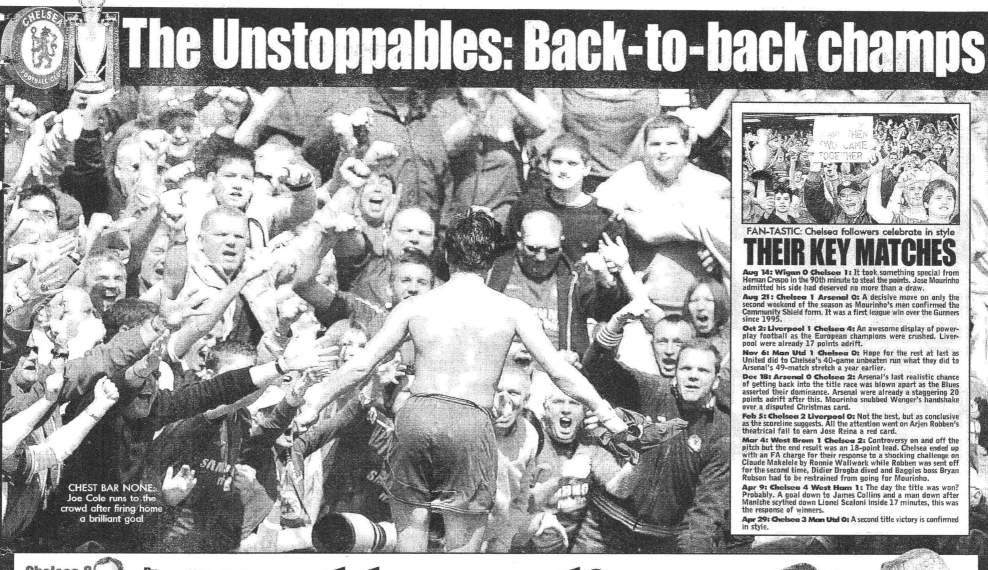

CHEST BAR NONE: Joe Cole runs to the crowd after firing home a brilliant goal

FAN-TASTIC: Chelsea followers celebrate in style

THEIR KEY MATCHES

Aug 14: Wigan 0 Chelsea 1: It took something special from Hernan Crespo in the 90th minute to steal the points. Jose Mourinho admitted his side had deserved no more than a draw.

Aug 21: Chelsea 1 Arsenal 0: A decisive move on only the second weekend of the season as Mourinho's men confirmed the Community Shield form. It was a first league win over the Gunners since 1995.

Oct 2: Liverpool 1 Chelsea 4: An awesome display of power-play football as the European champions were crushed. Liverpool were already 17 points adrift.

Nov 6: Man Utd 1 Chelsea 0: Hope for the rest at last as United did to Chelsea's 40-game unbeaten run what they did to Arsenal's 49-match stretch a year earlier.

Dec 18: Arsenal 0 Chelsea 2: Arsenal's last realistic chance of getting back into the title race was blown apart as the Blues asserted their dominance. Arsenal were already a staggering 20 points adrift after this. Mourinho snubbed Wenger's handshake over a disputed Christmas card.

Feb 5: Chelsea 2 Liverpool 0: Not the best, but as conclusive as the scoreline suggests. All the attention went on Arjen Robben's theatrical fall to earn Jose Reina a red card.

Mar 4: West Brom 1 Chelsea 2: Controversy on and off the pitch but the end result was an 18-point lead. Chelsea ended up with an FA charge for their response to a shocking challenge on Claude Makelele by Ronnie Wallwork while Robben was sent off for the second time, Didier Drogba dived and Baggies boss Bryan Robson had to be restrained from going for Mourinho.

Apr 9: Chelsea 4 West Ham 1: The day the title was won? Probably. A goal down to James Collins and a man down after Maniche scythed down Lionel Scaloni inside 17 minutes, this was the response of winners.

Apr 29: Chelsea 3 Man Utd 0: A second title victory is confirmed in style.

Chelsea 3 Man Utd 0
By MARTIN LIPTON
CHIEF FOOTBALL WRITER

My three lions made two titles says Mourinho

KIDSTUFF: Frank Lampard cradles daughter Luna as Chelsea celebrate

JOSE MOURINHO wore his Portugal scarf as he saluted Stamford Bridge – but it was the Three Lions at the heart of his Chelsea team that made him purr.

After Mourinho's men crushed Manchester United to make a mockery of Old Trafford claims that the gap is closing, the Blues boss hailed the trio who encapsulate the spirit of his team.

In John Terry, Frank Lampard and Joe Cole, Mourinho was blessed to inherit three exceptional players.

Back-to-back titles are the ultimate reward and it was no surprise that all three were central to the action as United were put to the Stamford Bridge sword.

And for Mourinho, it was time to hail the English gladiators who have helped make his team an unstoppable Premiership force. Mourinho said: "The next jump for JT is for people to look at him as the big player he really is. And for me he is the best central defender in the world. I could not have inherited a better leader of my side."

Or, as he demonstrated by the tackle on Cristiano Ronaldo that brought the corner from which William Gallas put the Blues in front, a better chief lieutenant than Lampard.

"Frank is a different kind of person," said Mourinho. "He is a fantastic JT shadow.

"Frank is not so emotional, but in the day-by-day squad life he's a fantastic shadow for the captain. I cannot separate them."

Perhaps, though, on a day when the fans were determined to enjoy the moment, it was only right that one of their favourites took centre stage.

Cole has been a key part of the success story all season, even if he does not always see eye to eye with the coach. As he pirouetted away from Nemanja Vidic and the flat-footed Rio Ferdinand before crashing home the killer second, all those problems were forgotten.

Cole admitted: "It's already my favourite goal ever. I still don't know exactly what I did, it was just something I did in the moment but I couldn't wait to see it on the telly.

"Maybe the game was a sign of how I have developed. Most of the match I was chasing Gary Neville back towards my own goal.

"But there are games when you have to realise that the ball isn't coming to you and so you have to make sure you're disciplined.

"Whenever something's not gone right I've always come back and worked hard, got my nut down. I'm not the sort of player to sulk or get upset. I just come back and try and do my best and it's always served me well.

"It's got me to where I am today, champion of the Premier League."

It is an attitude that has got Cole back into Mourinho's good books. "He has to play thinking about me and thinking about Chelsea, nothing else," Mourinho said.

"When he was chasing that status, that level, he was doing that.

"Then he stopped doing it. He lost and the team lost. He lost the status and the team lost a very important player. And now he is coming back to reality.

"He is the sort of player that you like and because you like him you want to help him. Joe can be even more consistent and an even better player."

Mourinho has already told his players they must do better next term, reinforcing the message that United, Arsenal and Liverpool will be even hungrier to rip the crown from their heads.

Sir Alex Ferguson's claims that his side were the better team were lost amid concerns over Wayne Rooney, who alongside Neville was the only player who could have played for the team in blue.

Indeed even now it appears that Mourinho's biggest threat next term will be the fixture list.

"Pre-season is a disgraceful situation," he said. "The players come from the World Cup and cannot have a proper holiday. Two weeks later they have to play in the Charity Shield.

Difficult

"I am telling you now in advance that next season the Charity Shield will not be a competition for us to win. It will simply be a training match.

"Between the Charity Shield and the first day of the Premiership we have international matches!

"So before my first game I have no players. Before the season starts I will be working with Cudicini and Diarra, just two players.

"The next Premiership is a very very difficult situation and Chelsea is most affected because we have more internationals than anyone."

BLUE DAY: Terry salutes the fans as the party starts

CHELSEA		MANCHESTER
53%	POSSESSION	47%
4	SHOTS ON TARGET	2
9	SHOTS OFF TARGET	5
3	OFFSIDES	0
2	CORNERS	3
18	FOULS	12
4	YELLOW CARDS	5
0	RED CARDS	0

ATTENDANCE: 42,219
MAN OF THE MATCH: Cole

TEAMS AND RATINGS

CHELSEA: Cech 8, Paulo Ferreira 7, Ricardo Carvalho 8, Terry 8, Gallas 8, Essien 7, Makelele 8, Lampard 8, Cole 9 (Crespo 76, 6), Robben 7 (Duff 67, 6), Drogba 8 (Maniche 86, 5)

MAN UTD: Van Der Sar 6, Neville 7, Ferdinand 5, Vidic 4, Silvestre 5, Ronaldo 4 (Van Nistelrooy 64, 6), O'Shea 7, Giggs 6 (Richardson 74, 5), Park 5, Rooney 8 (Evra, 81 mins, 5), Saha 5

Referee: MIKE DEAN

The Unstoppables: B

PLAYER-BY-PLAYER SEASON RATINGS

PETR CECH

9 Probably still best keeper in the country but slightly below the sensational standards he set in his first season in goal.

GAMES STARTED: 34 **CLEAN SHEETS:** 17

PAULO FERREIRA

6 Lost his place and at times lost his way. Certainly not as secure as he was last term and will have an anxious summer.

GAMES STARTED: 17 + 3 SUBS **GOALS:** 0

WILLIAM GALLAS

9 Model of determined consistency at the heart of the back line. Hard to pick a fault in his game. Will be missed if he does go.

GAMES STARTED: 31 + 1 SUBS **GOALS:** 5

JOHN TERRY

10 Captain Fantastic in every sense. A brilliant leader and brave as a lion too. Surely the best defender in England now.

GAMES STARTED: 36 **GOALS:** 4

ASIER DEL HORNO

6 Began well but failure to learn English and settle has angered Mourinho. Too many mistakes and regularly subbed by Jose.

GAMES STARTED: 24 **GOALS:** 1

MICHAEL ESSIEN

7 Superb for the first three months but never recovered from the storm surrounding his shocker on Didi Hamann.

GAMES STARTED: 27 + 4 SUBS **GOALS:** 2

CLAUDE MAKELELE

8 The man who gives the Blues poise and balance. Never flustered and always there in the middle to pick up the pieces.

GAMES STARTED: 29 + 2 SUBS **GOALS:** 0

FRANK LAMPARD

9 More up and down perhaps, but the peaks were higher and the troughs not too low. Sensational scoring contribution from midfield.

GAMES STARTED: 34 **GOALS:** 16

JOE COLE

9 Has now matured into the player we all hoped he would become. Not always in Jose's good books but a terrific campaign.

GAMES STARTED: 25 + 7 SUBS **GOALS:** 7

ARJEN ROBBEN

7 Another one who has dropped off from his first year at the Bridge. Sent off twice and should stay on his feet more.

GAMES STARTED: 20 + 7 SUBS **GOALS:** 6

DIDIER DROGBA

8 When he stands up you have to count him in. A beast of a man and at times unstoppable but let himself down too.

GAMES STARTED: 20 + 9 SUBS **GOALS:** 12

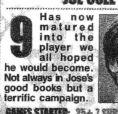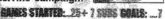

SINGING THE BLUES: The jubilant Chelsea players celebrate a second successive Premiership title – this time landing it in front of their home fans by seeing off closest rivals Man Utd

CARLTON COLE

5 Mourinho said Cole was his "bet" for the season. If so, then the bookies are laughing. Doubtful that the striker is.

GAMES PLAYED: 7 **SUBS GOALS:** 0

CARLO CUDICINI

6 He must love the atmosphere at Cobham – or the money. Too good to be a second-stringer but always ready to play.

GAMES STARTED: 2 + 1 SUBS **CLEAN SHEETS:** 2

MANICHE

4 At least we know he is not scared of a pie. Only real impact since January arrival was on Lionel Scaloni.

GAMES STARTED: 1 + 4 SUBS **GOALS:** 0

GLEN JOHNSON

4 Made his own bed and has to lie in it. He must know how badly he is wasting a natural ability. Surely no future at the club.

GAMES STARTED: 3 **GOALS:** 0

ROBERT HUTH

6 Mourinho's 4th-choice centre-back and only used against long-ball teams. Has not made the progress expected.

GAMES STARTED: 6 + 6 SUBS **GOALS:** 0

GEREMI

7 Mourinho's fill-in player, who has had more playing time than he anticipated. Limitations are obvious but his commitment clear.

GAMES STARTED: 7 + 7 SUBS **GOALS:** 2

HERNAN CRESPO

8 HAPPIER in London second time around and his movement has been outstanding. Sometimes his effort was less convincing.

GAMES STARTED: 19 + 10 SUBS **GOALS:** 10

DAMIEN DUFF

6 Started the campaign very well but faded badly after injury at Liverpool. Never the same again. Could be a summer casualty.

GAMES STARTED: 17 + 9 SUBS **GOALS:** 3

RICARDO CARVALHO

6 A Perfect end to the campaign against United but fell out with boss in August and never fell back in. Has disappointed.

GAMES STARTED: 28 + 2 SUBS **GOALS:** 1

EIDUR GUDJOHNSEN

7 Inconsistent season and not helped by the lack of real opportunities to show his scoring skills. Has become a squad man now.

GAMES STARTED: 15 + 10 SUBS **GOALS:** 2

SHAUN WRIGHT-PHILLIPS

6 Oh dear! The move was meant to be the winger's platform but he has struggled badly and must be regretting he joined.

GAMES STARTED: 5 + 16 SUBS **GOALS:** 0

CHELSEA RATINGS

PETR CECH

Made some excellent saves - a spectacular stop from Julio Baptista and a vital block from Abou Diaby. Commanding and impressive throughout. **7/10**

LASSANA DIARRA

Coped well as a makeshift right back even if his positioning and defending was suspect at times. But has done well enough to ensure he has a Chelsea future. **6/10**

JOHN TERRY

An awful afternoon for the England captain. Did not look fit to start with and ended up being carried off after a horrific collision with Diaby and hospitalised. **6/10**

RICARDO CARVALHO

Chelsea's best defender by a country mile. Was outstanding as he held the back four together while under pressure from Arsenal's pace and counter-attacks. **7/10**

WAYNE BRIDGE

Had a shocking first half when he got murdered by Walcott's pace. Improved after the break but needs to find some consistency as his performances are all over the place. **5/10**

CLAUDE MAKELELE

Substituted at half time, which said it all. Struggled to influence the game under pressure from Arsenal's midfield kids. The Chelsea veteran showed his age. **5/10**

FRANK LAMPARD

Hit a stunning 25-yard shot which hit the bar in the second half. Worked and ran himself into the ground as one of Chelsea's better players. **7/10**

MICHAEL BALLACK

Provided the pass for Drogba's equaliser but for a World Cup captain against kids it was another hugely disappointing game for Ballack, who just disappeared. **5/10**

MICHAEL ESSIEN

Lucky to stay on the pitch and escape with a booking for an over-the-top tackle which left stud marks on Baptista's chest. Slotted into defence after Terry went off. **7/10**

ANDRIY SHEVCHENKO

Best of Chelsea's forwards for his running and work rate. He is finding his feet in English football and improving with each game. But chances few and far between. **7/10**

DIDIER DROGBA

Quiet by his standards, but still ended up as Chelsea's match winner and man of the match. Used his pace and power for the first and then headed the clincher. **8/10**

SUBSTITUTES ARJEN ROBBEN (for Makelele, 46 mins): Threat throughout the second half. How he does not play more often is a mystery. Great cross for the winner..... **7**
JOHN OBI MIKEL (for Terry, 63 mins): Sent off for the second time this season. Got embroiled in bust-up.......**4**
SALOMON KALOU (for Shevchenko, in injury time).

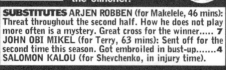

CARLING CUP FINAL, 2007
CHELSEA 2 ARSENAL 1

Martin Lipton
CHIEF FOOTBALL WRITER

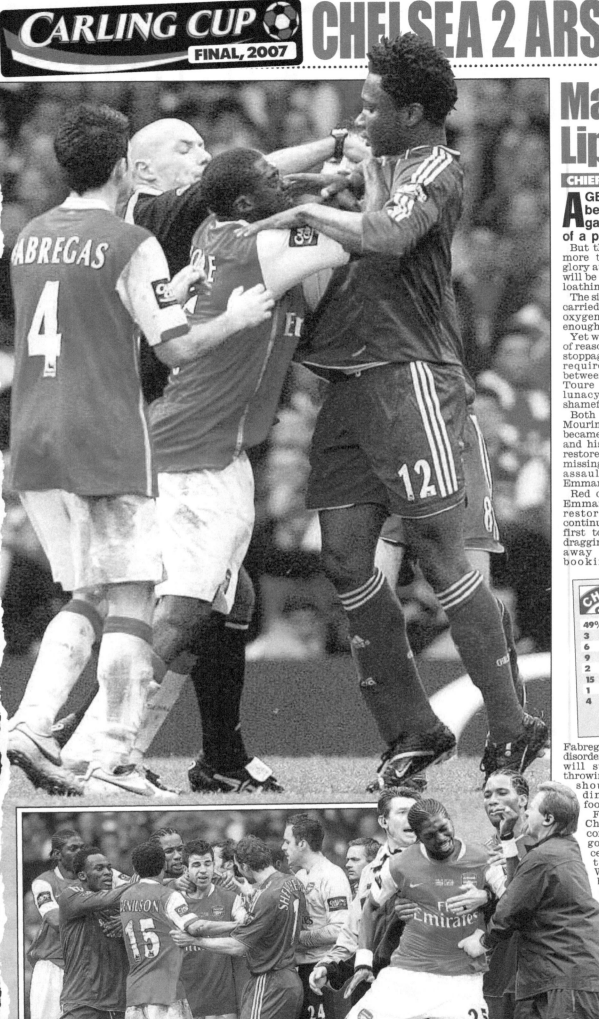

AGE FINALLY overcame beauty as Didier Drogba gave Chelsea the first leg of a possible Quadruple.

But the abiding memories, even more than Drogba's moment of glory at the last Cardiff Cup Final, will be the ugly images of fear and loathing that took centre stage.

The sickening sight of John Terry, carried off on a stretcher with an oxygen mask on his face, was enough to turn the stomach.

Yet when both sides lost all sense of reason and control deep into the stoppage time Terry's head injury required, as a brutal tear-up between John Obi Mikel and Kolo Toure sparked scenes of sheer lunacy, it degenerated into a shameful afternoon.

Both teams, the benches, Jose Mourinho and Arsene Wenger all became embroiled as Howard Webb and his officials tried in vain to restore order amid the mayhem, missing what appeared a shocking assault on Wayne Bridge by Emmanuel Eboue.

Red cards to Toure, Mikel and Emmanuel Adebayor failed to restore calm as the scuffles continued, physio Gary Lewin – the first to Terry's rescue earlier – dragging the enraged Togo striker away as Webb flinched, also booking Lampard and Cesc

CHELSEA		Arsenal
49%	POSSESSION	51%
3	SHOTS ON TARGET	6
6	SHOTS OFF TARGET	4
9	OFFSIDES	1
2	CORNERS	6
15	FOULS	12
1	RED CARDS	2
4	YELLOW CARDS	3

ATTENDANCE: 70,073
MAN OF THE MATCH: Drogba

Fabregas. But all the chaos and disorder, all the bile that spilled and will surely result in the FA throwing the book at both clubs, should not be allowed to diminish the enthralling football that preceded it.

For 60 minutes, until Chelsea's power-play took control, allowing Mourinho to go to the forefront of the celebrations to make his point to Roman Abramovich, Wenger's new kids on the block had been outstanding, a joy to watch.

If Arsenal were supposed to have been intimidated, somebody forgot to tell them before the game, as the six years per man extra experience of the Blues was simply blown away by their enthusiasm and commitment.

Inspired by Julio Baptista, elusive and electric, the red shirts asked questions Chelsea could not answer.

Only a desperate intervention by Terry, appearing out of nowhere to deny Jeremie Aliadiere from the Brazilian's cut-back along the six-yard line, kept the Gunners out.

A brilliant diving tip-over from Petr Cech prevented Baptista's rising drive from finding the top corner at the end of a thrilling move but within a minute the

RED MIST: Toure, Mikel (top) and Adebayor (right) all lose their heads

SOMEWHERE, IN THE MIDDLE OF ALL THE FIGHTING, A REALLY GOOD

FROM THE MILLENNIUM STADIUM

BEAUTY AND THE BEASTS

It all ends in chaos as Drogba sinks kids

0-1 Theo Walcott breaks his duck for Arsenal

1-1 Didier Drogba levels it up before half-time

2-1 Drogba beats Senderos to head the winner

Gunners were rightly ahead. For all the promise of Theo Walcott, he had still to really deliver. But all that changed as he played in Abou Diaby and went for the return as the French midfielder played a delightful angled ball into the box.

A touch took Walcott between Lassana Diarra and the otherwise impeccable Ricardo Carvalho, and the little whippet steadied himself and his nerves to steer past Cech.

It was Walcott's first for the Gunners, making him the second youngest scorer in League Cup Final history behind Manchester United's Norman Whiteside in 1983.

Whiteside too scored first only to finish on the losing side against Liverpool and history was to repeat itself, although only after Claude Makelele was lucky that Webb missed his clip on Baptista as the Brazilian went to ground in the box.

Chelsea were all over the place, a shapeless mess, lacking drive or invention. But then Drogba entered the equation on 20 minutes.

Poise

The African looked offside as Michael Ballack freed him on the right but the flag – correctly – stayed down and when Manuel Almunia committed himself too early, Drogba stroked home.

For a while, Arsenal rocked, but Fabregas and Diaby instilled poise when it was required, Walcott remained a threat and Carvalho was forced into overtime as he bailed out his colleagues as the desperate last man on three occasions.

It was no surprise when Robben came on at the break, Makelele making way. He immediately gave his side the thrust and dynamism they had lacked yet still it was Arsenal to the fore.

Diaby, found by Baptista's beautiful pass, was thwarted by Cech's dive and then Fabregas saw his shot sneak wide of the far post.

Then a moment of shared terror, the Arsenal players reacting as one with their opponents when Terry's bravery saw him caught in the face by Diaby's boot as he dived head-first to try to force the loose ball home from a Robben corner.

After six long minutes Terry departed for hospital and Chelsea gradually turned the screw.

Drogba was denied by Almunia before Lampard bent a stunner against the bar from 35 yards.

But the Ivorian was not to be denied and when Robben found space to bend the ball into the box, Drogba nodded his 28th goal of the season into the bottom corner.

Andriy Shevchenko smashed against the bar but the final act was the most crazy of an afternoon that defied belief as Toure's reaction to Mikel's tug exploded everything.

The final whistle brought more ill-grace from the Arsenal bench but frenzied joy to the men in Blue. For Mourinho, it is four trophies in three seasons, with more, he hopes, to come.

FOOTBALL MATCH THREATENED TO BREAK OUT OLIVER HOLT, PAGES 56 & 57

CHELSEA 1
DROGBA 116

CHELSEA RATINGS

petr CECH — 6

His courage has never been in question and once again he showed it with a brave second half dive at the feet of an onrushing Rooney. The best in the business.

paulo FERREIRA — 6

Handed the unenviable task of mastering compatriot Ronaldo for the first half and did a more than adequate job for a player whose defending has been questioned.

michael ESSIEN — 6

Once again Chelsea's man for all seasons. Drafted into central defence he produced two crucial tackles on Giggs and then Rooney to keep United at bay.

john TERRY — 6

Marshalled his troops in typical fashion although looked strangely vulnerable in the air against Rooney. Always on hand to make important tackles and interceptions.

wayne BRIDGE — 5

Never totally at ease against either Ronaldo or Giggs. A fully-fit Ashley Cole would have given Chelsea more attacking options as well as genuine pace at the back

johnobi MIKEL — 6

Became more assertive in the second half after a first 45 minutes when he seemed to be a victim of the occasion. More expansive as the nerves evaporated.

claude MAKELELE — 6

Mr Dependable yet again. Pace has never been his forte but he compensates with his uncanny radar-like sense to thrive in his seek-and-destroy role.

frank LAMPARD — 6

Has had better games. After a season of 100 per cent commitment, there is a price to pay and he seems to lack the dynamism he showed at the start of the season.

shaun WRIGHT-PHILLIPS 6

In fits and starts he looks the player that tempted Chelsea to part with £23m, but still to find consistent streak that may bring him back into England reckoning.

joe COLE — 6

Often looked Chelsea's most dangerous player in the first half. But Chelsea needed more penetration and pace, hence his replacement with Robben.

didier DROGBA — 6

He may be lethal when given the chance but struggled against Vidic and Ferdinand. To be fair, he lacked support and for most of the game had to forage alone up front.

SUBSTITUTES
Arjen Robben 6 – replaced Joe Cole at half time.
Salomon Kalou 6 – replaced Shaun Wright-Phillips at start of extra time.
Ashley Cole 5 – replaced Arjen Robben in second period of extra time.

JOSE MOURINHO
Organised his team to be as effective as usual and there was always the chance of a breakaway with dangermen like Drogba around.

WONDER
Didier late strike puts United to the sword

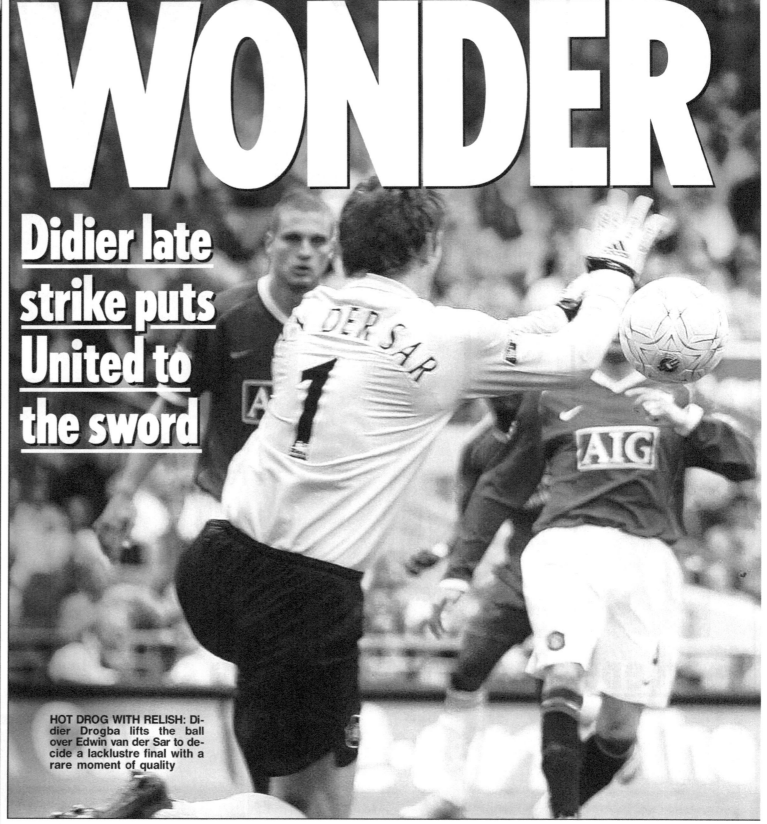

HOT DROG WITH RELISH: Didier Drogba lifts the ball over Edwin van der Sar to decide a lacklustre final with a rare moment of quality

FA CUP legends were everywhere as Wembley reopened its doors to the competition which made it famous – and now Didier Drogba can walk tall amongst them.

From Denis Law and Ron Harris to Mark Hughes, Peter Schmeichel and Marcel Desailly, Red and Blue heroes of the past came to pay tribute to their memories before Drogba served notice that the drama of the old tin pot will continue well into the future.

It took 115 minutes to finally separate the two teams who have gone at it hammer and tongs in the Premiership all season, but when the opportunity arose, Drogba seized it with the kind of ruthlessness that has brought him 32 previous goals this season.

An interchange of passes with

SIMON MULLOCK
AT WEMBLEY

Frank Lampard, after John Obi Mikel had found the Ivory Coast striker lurking 20 yards out, carved United wide open for the first time all afternoon.

And when keeper Edwin Van der Sar ventured from his line, Drogba showed tenacity and technique to lift the ball over the United keeper and so complete Jose Mourinho's haul of domestic trophies.

True, the game never came close to the kind of classic confrontation that would have truly graced football's magnificent new £750m home.

But that mattered little to the hordes in Blue as they saw their team take some comfort from a season which saw them lose their Premiership crown to United and falter in Europe.

Only time will tell

REF WATCH
STEVE BENNETT
Most of his decisions were the right ones, although he did break up a United attack to book Makelele and that did the champions no favours.

whether Mourinho will now survive the summer after a season of rifts, rows and rucks with billionaire owner Roman Abramovich.

It was fitting that the name of sponsors e.on was everywhere to be seen - given that it feels that long since Roberto Di Matteo scored the goal that claimed the Cup for Chelsea in the last final played here before the Twin Towers were reduced to rubble.

The oldest competition of them all was supposed to have thrown up the final that every neutral football fan wanted.

Premiership champions against runners-up, north taking on south, Red versus Blue.

But for much of the afternoon this was the Sweet FA Cup.

United clinched the title with a brand of attacking play that made Alex Ferguson's men the must-

watch team of the season. Yet the United manager brought with him a tactical plan that seemed hell-bent on playing Chelsea at their own cautious game, with Wayne Rooney asked to do an impression of the lonely Drogba and Cristiano Ronaldo ordered to opt for discipline instead of daring.

There was a decent early chance for Chelsea when Wes Brown's poor header fell to Shaun Wright-Phillips 12 yards out, but his miskicked effort seemed to set the tone.

At the other end, Paul Scholes also failed to connect properly with the kind of long-range volley that has become his trademark.

In fact, it was 22 minutes before Drogba finally came up with the first genuine threat of the game.

The Premiership's top marksman made the most of the decoy runs made by Wright-Phillips, Joe Cole and Frank Lampard to let rip with a 25-yard drive that swerved, dipped and beat Van der Sar only to skid a foot wide. Then Rooney's

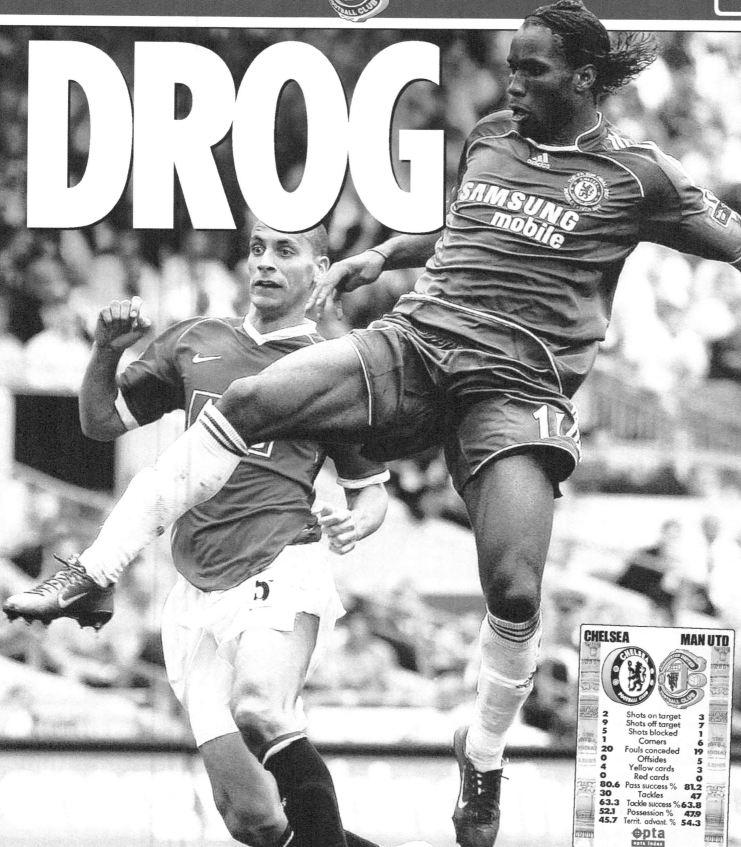

DROG

MAN UTD RATINGS

edwin VAN DER SAR 6
Rarely tested. Hardly looked in any bother anlooked comfortable enough against Joe Cole but the arrival of Robben gave him different problems and for periods

wes BROWN 6
Looked comfortable enough against Joe Cole but arrival of Robben gave him different problems and for periods looked uneasy against the Dutchman's sheer pace.

rio FERDINAND 7
Imperious. Not only the outstanding defender but also the most influential player. Hardly put a foot wrong with his immaculate passing, tackling and aerial power.

nemanja VIDIC 6
Managed to subdue Drogba and has formed one of the most solid partnerships in the Premiership with Ferdinand. Never shirks a challenge on or off the floor.

gabriel HEINZE 6
Sir Alex calls him his "warrior" and it was easy to see why. Defends as though his life defends on it and supports the attack when he can.

michael CARRICK 6
Struggled to make a real impact. His passing options were always limited by the crowded midfield zone in which he was forced to operate.

darren FLETCHER 6
Worked manfully in a highly congested midfield but was unable to open up a highly organised Chelsea quartet. Put in an honest shift.

paul SCHOLES 6
Buzzed around and occasionally penetrated the organised Chelsea resistance but unable to put his personality on the game as he frequently does to such kept

ryan GIGGS 6
Kept going until the end and showed real and true professionalism. The searing pace may no longer be there but the attitude is still first class.

cristiano RONALDO 5
Not in Footballer of the Year form. Could never impose himself on the game as he has so often this season and was frustrated at the lack of space afforded to him.

wayne ROONEY 6
Not one of his better days. He rarely produces his best in a lone front role and did much better when United were able to get men in support.

SUBSTITUTES

Alan Smith 6 – replaced Darren Fletcher after two minutes of extra time.
John O'Shea 5 – replaced Michael Carrick just before Chelsea's winner.
Ole Gunnar Solskjaer 4 – came on with O'Shea, replacing Ryan Giggs

ALEX FERGUSON

May have been guilty of selecting too conservative a line-up with Rooney up front on his own. With more support early on, United could well have won.

CHELSEA		MAN UTD
2	Shots on target	3
9	Shots off target	7
5	Shots blocked	1
1	Corners	6
20	Fouls conceded	19
0	Offsides	5
4	Yellow cards	3
0	Red cards	0
80.6	Pass success %	81.2
30	Tackles	47
63.3	Tackle success %	63.8
52.1	Possession %	47.9
45.7	Territ. advant. %	54.3

opta
opta index

determination to influence the game saw United's best chance of the first period go to waste.

With Chelsea's defence stepping up in a line, Ronaldo timed his run to perfection as Fletcher floated over a fine pass from the right, but Rooney instinctively made a dash for the ball and was instantly flagged offside.

Lampard had an angled shot easily gathered by Van der Sar and Wright-Phillips fired another effort high, wide and not so handsome as the match continued to flicker without fully igniting.

It was estmated that a billion people around the world had tuned in for the occasion.

In the United strongholds of Singapore they must have been going to bed in their droves at the break.

Goodness knows what the Surrey Reds and Sloane Ranger Blues who paid upwards of two grand a ticket to join the genuine loyalists must have thought.

At last the introduction of Ar-

jen Robben after the interval for Joe Cole - arguably Chelsea's best player of the first-half - livened things up, with the Blues carrying more threat and United looking to exploit the extra space.

Rooney went on the rampage

immediately after the restart and saw his 20-yard blast beaten away by Petr Cech.

Then Giggs was inches away from breaking the deadlock when he met Scholes' floated pass at the far post with a thumping volley that rose just too high.

Drogba went even closer after Scholes became the first player to be booked by referee Steve Bennett for a foul on Lampard 25 yards out.

The Chelsea striker's curling free-kick beat United's defensive wall and smacked the outside of Van der Sar's left-hand post, although the United keeper looked to have his goal well covered.

At least Rooney was now starting to rise to the occasion and one charge took him past Michael Essien and Terry only for Cech to plunge at the United striker's feet.

Extra time saw Ferguson introduce striker Alan Smith for midfielder Fletcher and Mourinho did the same when Salomon Kalou replaced Wright-Phillips.

Giggs claimed he had scored in

the 104th minute when Robben's woeful pass saw Rooney break down the right.

Rooney's cross was perfect for the sliding Giggs, but he could only fire his effort straight at Cech before his momentum took him into the Chelsea keeper.

Giggs insisted that Cech had carried the ball over his own goalline – but there was no linesman from Russia.

After Chelsea sub Robben limped off to be replaced by Ashley Cole in the second period of extra time, Cech once again showed no thought for his own safety when he once again saved bravely at the feet of Rooney.

Then, with penalties looming, Mourinho's favourite Drog emerged to bite United on their backside and the Cup was won.

THE FIRST NEW WEMBLEY FA CUP FINAL

HI HO SILVER LINING: Didier Drogba, whose goal won the first FA Cup Final at the new Wembley, leads the celebrations as Chelsea ease their title heartache

Revenge is sweet as Blues ease their title heartache

TOP DROGS

CHELSEA 2
Drogba 21, Lampard 72

FRANK FLIES

Lampard strike keeps up the cup tradition

BY SIMON MULLOCK
sport@sundaymirror.co.uk

IT was a sight that Evertonians prayed they would never see again – Frank Lampard dancing around a corner flag after breaking their hearts in the FA Cup.

Twenty-nine years after his father's iconic celebration in a semi-final replay against the Merseysiders at Elland Road, the Chelsea midfielder doffed his cap to history on the biggest stage of them all.

With 18 minutes of the 128th final remaining, Lampard slipped as he collected Nicolas Anelka's pass and skipped inside Phil Neville's challenge 25 yards out.

But he regained his balance to unleash a left-footed drive that carried too much power for Tim Howard as it flew through the American keeper's hands and into the top corner.

Then Lampard was off. There was his usual salute to the heavens to remember his

◀ OUT OF LUCK: Malouda

mother Pat, who died last year.

And next cam the famous tribute to Frank senior, who wouldn't have known whether to laugh or cry – but probably did both – as he watched from the stands.

So Wembley belonged to Chelsea once again. The Londoners won two of the last four finals to be played at the old stadium – including the last in 2000.

And now they've won two of the first three at the new £800m self-proclaimed Venue of Legends.

Yet for 20 minutes it was the House of Scouse.

Everton had waited 14 years for this occasion to come around again – and boy were they in a hurry.

Just 25 seconds had passed before their fans were hailing the fastest goal in FA Cup Final history.

Steven Pienaar looked suspiciously offside when he collected Leighton Baines' pass to cross from the left.

And when John Obi Mikel's weak clearing header was nodded back by Marouane Fellaini, it was Louis Saha who reacted first to beat Petr Cech with a thundering half-volley.

It beat Bob Chatt's strike for Aston Villa at Crystal Palace in 1895 by five seconds, while the Wembley record set by Chelsea's Roberto Di Matteo 102 years later had taken 42 seconds.

But the goal galvanised Guus Hiddink's side and encouraged Everton into a retreat that they couldn't halt.

And when right-back Tony Hibbert was booked for a trip on Florent Malouda eight minutes in, it was to be a pivotal moment.

Malouda and Ashley Cole attacked down the left at will, with Hibbert paralysed by the fear of seeing red.

The only surprise was that Chelsea didn't create their equaliser until the 21st minute.

Then Lampard's pass found Malouda once

0-1
Saha puts Everton ahead after 25 seconds

1-1
Drogba heads Chelsea level

again with time and space to exploit outside Hibbert.

And his delivery invited Didier Drogba to time his leap in front of Joleon Lescott to perfection and bury a textbook downward header beyond Howard.

Chelsea got lucky when referee Howard Webb failed to recognise the malice in Michael Essien's knee-high lunge at Fellaini.

But Cole should have cele-brated becoming the first player in 118 years to collect five cup winners' medals with a goal, but he shot too high after Hibbert had once again been embarrassed.

Moyes replaced the faltering full-back with Lars Jacobsen at the break and Everton finally regained some attacking momentum.

But Chelsea nearly got in again, Anelka lifting a shot too high for Chelsea after Lampard

had sent him clear on the hour.

Saha squandered a rare but glorious chance at the other end in the 67th minute when he arrived to meet Baines' cross but headed over from six yards.

Once Lampard had scored there was never any doubt that Hiddink's brief reign as manager was to end with Chelsea winning their fifth FA Cup.

Malouda should have finished it, but shot over from another Lampard pass. But he

was more accurate with a stunning 30-yard drive which bounced down off the crossbar and over the line.

Referee Webb was in no position to award a goal, but he was perfectly placed when Lampard was taken down by Pienaar only to wave away Chelsea's penalty appeals and book the midfielder for diving.

But it didn't matter – this was a day for the father and son called Frank Lampard.

2-1
Lampard cracks the cup winner

FIND OUT HOW THE TWO TEAMS

EVERTON 1
Saha 1

THE FLAG

STAT ATTACK

at WEMBLEY
ATT: 89,391

How they lined up

CHELSEA
Subs: Ballack (Essien)

Bosingwa   Cech   A.Cole
Alex   Terry
Essien   Mikel
Anelka   Lampard   Malouda
Saha   Drogba
Fellaini
Pienaar   Neville   Cahill   Osman
Lescott   Yobo
Baines   Howard   Hibbert

EVERTON
Subs: Vaughan (Saha), Jacobsen (Hibbert), Gosling (Osman)

Shots

8   off target   4

4   on target   2

Story of the game

5	Corners	1
15	Fouls Conceded	18
2	Offsides	3
2	Yellow	3
0	Red	0

Possession

61%   39%

MAN OF THE MATCH

8

ASHLEY COLE
Became the first player for 118 years to win a fifth FA Cup winner's medal – and marked the achievement with an outstanding exhibition of the left-back's art.

MANAGERS
GUUS HIDDINK

8

His impact on Chelsea has been clear, ending in silverware.

DAVID MOYES

7

Will have to wait to follow in the footsteps of Catterick and Kendall, but his time is sure to come.

REFEREE
HOWARD WEBB
missed clear penalty when Pienaar fouled Lampard   **5**

RATED AT WEMBLEY - PAGES 4&5

FA CUP POSTER SPECIAL

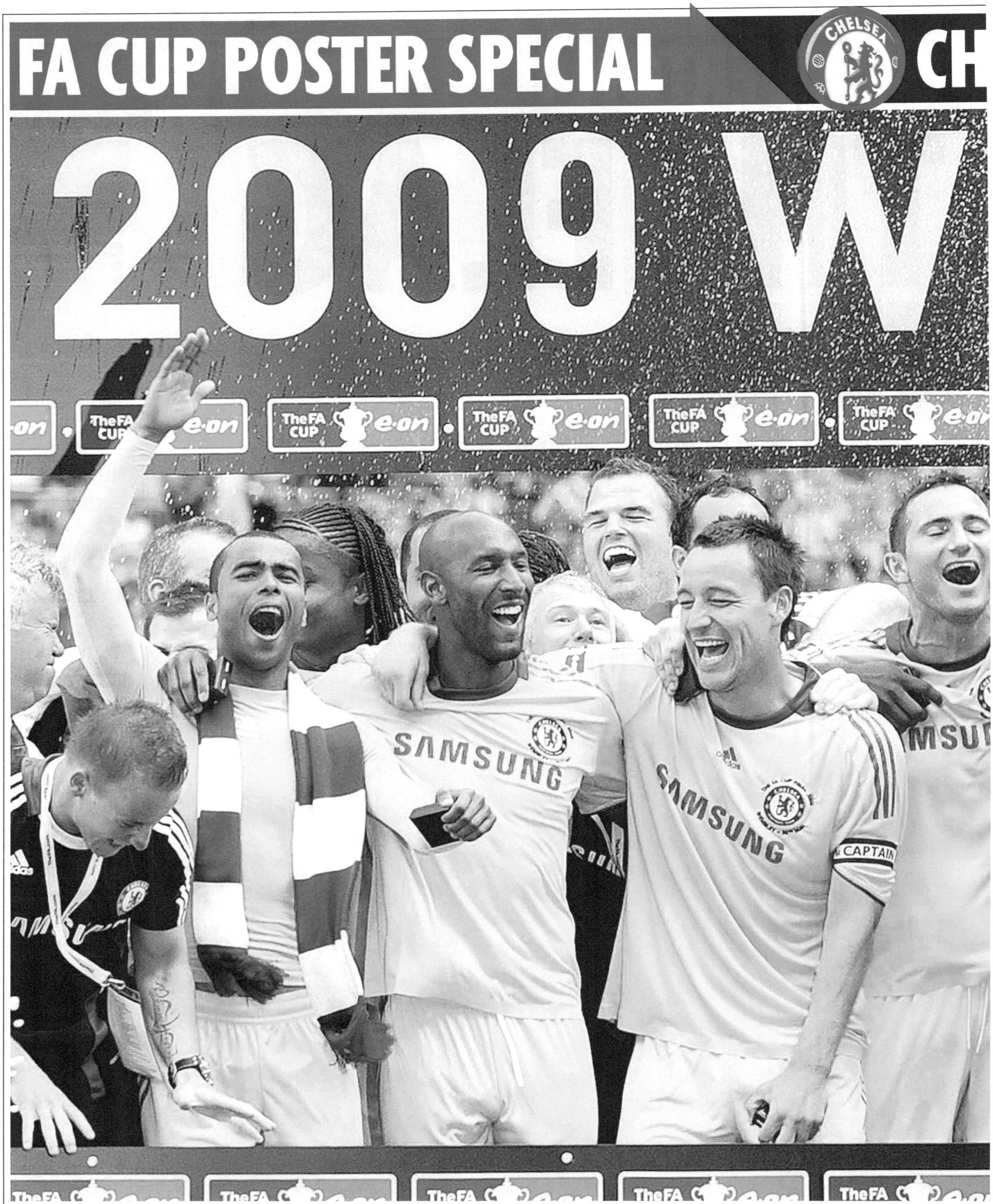

58 **M SPORT** | **Daily Mirror** MONDAY 10.05.2010

RELATED LINKS For more title-winning comment and reaction throughout the day today go to **mirrorfootball.co.uk/chelsea**

DM1ST

CHELSEA 8 WIGAN ATH 0 — BARCLAYS PREMIER LEAGUE — PREMIER

TRUE BLUE

▶ Most goals ▶ Top scorer ▶ Chelsea are worthy winners

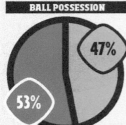

MATCH CENTRE
CHELSEA
WIGAN

BALL POSSESSION
47%
53%

FACE TO FACE
2 Corners 3
5 Offside 3
84% Pass completion 80%
18 Tackles 13
14 Fouls 10
2 Cards 2 1

SHOTS
7 off target 1
10 on target 2

£150,000 YOU THE MANAGER
FANTASY FOOTBALL 2009/10

MAN OF THE MATCH
(Worth an extra two Fantasy Football points)

Nicolas Anelka (CHELSEA) 8
Scored crucial opener and happy to be a part of Blues' big day

VILLAIN OF THE MATCH

Didier Drogba (CHELSEA) 6
Simply for his act of public selfishness

Mirror Football
For more reaction, pictures, interviews and comment on Chelsea's title triumph go to mirrorfootball.co.uk/

The title by NUMBERS

CHELSEA ended the season with **103** league goals, the first side to pass the century mark in the top flight since Spurs in 1963.

Their **8-0** win was their biggest ever in the league, beating the 9-2 win over Glossop in 1906.

Frank Lampard scored **27** goals, including 22 in the league. **10** were from the penalty spot.

Didier Drogba's hat-trick meant he finished top of the Premier League scoring charts with **29** goals.

Chelsea's **4th** top-flight title was their third in six years and first under Carlo Ancelotti.

Chelsea scored **7** three times – against Sunderland, Villa and Stoke – as well as yesterday's eight.

The Blues took the **2010** title with wins home and away against the other members of the 'big four' of Man Utd, Arsenal and Liverpool.

Chelsea will be going for their **1ST** Double in Saturday's FA Cup Final against Portsmouth.

BY **MARTIN LIPTON** Chief Football Writer m.lipton@mirror.co.uk

THAT'S how you win the title – in real style.

Not by scrambling over the line, edging your way point by point.

But by doing what you have done all season, having the courage of the manager's attacking convictions, ignoring the occasion and simply playing the game, setting another club record win to reinforce your mastery.

And while Carlo Ancelotti may need to win the Champions League, too, before he stops being judged by the standards of Jose Mourinho, this was the ideal way for the Italian to show what he has brought.

Sometimes the statistics tell you all you need to know.

So how about these: 103 goals in the season, the first time any side has broken the ton since Spurs in 1963. A hat-trick to clinch the

Golden Boot for Didier Drogba, even if the African behaved like a four-year-old when he was not allowed to take Chelsea's first penalty of the afternoon.

Frank Lampard making it 30 from midfield - yes 30 - for club and country.

Four points dropped at home all season to compete a run of seven wins out of eight since they stared into the abyss at Blackburn on March 21, six wins out of six against the Big Four.

As the joyful Blues fans bellowed: "That's why we're champions," even Sir Alex Ferguson and Manchester United cannot argue with that.

Chelsea's long wait since 2006 ended, fittingly, with a performance that was the embodiment of Ancelotti's vision, even if it took not one goal to quell the nerves cascading round Stamford Bridge, but two.

Indeed, even though Nicolas Anelka drilled home after just five minutes, from Chelsea's first attack, it was Wigan who

looked far more composed. But Roberto Martinez's men, nice on the ball but without any real punch, have a worse goal difference than Portsmouth and soon it was easy to see why.

Maynor Figueroa casually squandered possession, Salomon Kalou fed Drogba and as he slipped into Lampard's path, Gary Caldwell's response was to

> **Drogba won the Golden Boot, though he behaved like a four-year-old when not allowed to take a penalty**

grab a big handful of the midfielder's shirt and haul him to the ground.

An easy double decision for Martin Atkinson – a spot kick and a red card – but what followed from Drogba was pathetic.

Despite Ancelotti having made it clear on Friday that

Lampard was his penalty-taker, Drogba would not accept the situation, having to be calmed down by Florent Malouda and Kalou even as Lampard prepared to rifle into the bottom corner.

That was just the beginning of a 15-minute public tantrum by the striker, who showed no interest in playing, moaned constantly and even went over to Ancelotti to complain at the injustice.

No wonder Drogba was given the mother of all dressing downs at the break, emerging sheepishly to join the huddle before the restart and deciding he was one of a team and not a petulant little boy.

About time and it meant Drogba joined the celebrations that kicked off for real nine minutes into the second period. Kalou spotted Lampard's overlap and then slalomed past the last defender as he took the cut-back before sliding home.

And soon after, as Anelka met Branislav Ivanovic's cross with a textbook volley that again gave poor Mike Pollitt no chance, it became a question

of how many. The century was clocked up as Lampard teased in a cross that allowed Drogba to get that crucial strike to nudge him ahead of Wayne Rooney and when Mario Melchiot clipped Ashley Cole's heels, the African was given his spot-kick chance.

Drogba converted off the inside of the post completing his hat-trick as he stabbed home the rebound from Joe Cole's shot before the substitute, in perhaps his last appearance for the club, crossed for his namesake to hammer home the eighth.

This was Chelsea's day, Chelsea's season. Ancelotti deserves his tributes, too. This is his side. And boy do they look a good one.

CHELSEA: Cech 6, Ivanovic 7 (Belletti 59, 6), Alex 7, Terry 6, A Cole 6, Lampard 7, Ballack 6 (Matic 70, 5), Malouda 6, Kalou 7, J Cole 59, 7), Drogba 7, Anelka 8.

WIGAN: Pollitt 6, Boyce 6, Caldwell 4, Gohouri 5, Melchiot 6, Diame 7 (Scharner 72, 6), McCarthy 5, Figueroa 5, Watson 6 (Thomas 62, 5), N'Zogbia 6, Rodallega 5.

REF: M Atkinson. **ATT:** 41,383

▲ **PRIZE GUYS** Ancelotti (left) and his Chelsea stars go crazy PICTURES: KENT GAVIN

Oliver Holt's VERDICT PAGES 56 & 57

GAME BY GAME, PLAYER BY PLAYER.. HOW ANCELOTTI'S

LEAGUE TITLE PARTY FROM STAMFORD BRIDGE

CHAMPIONS

More flair..

▲ **COLE LOT TO CELEBRATE** Chelsea's Ashley Cole gets his hands on the trophy

GR-EIGHT FOR TERRY

FROM BACK PAGE

at the Stamford Bridge helm at the pinnacle of the English game.

This astonishing romp – with Didier Drogba's hat-trick earning him the Golden Boot, a double from Nicolas Anelka and further strikes from Frank Lampard, Salomon Kalou and Ashley Cole – took Chelsea to a best-ever 103 Premier League goals.

Terry said: "This feels magnificent. Over the last three years it's been really hard seeing Manchester United lift the title. I've been hurting inside and I promise you every one of us has sat there and watched it.

"Now it's their turn to sit there and watch us. We've got it back now and we need to do what United have done and maintain it for a few years."

Terry paid tribute to Ancelotti's "calmness" and the Chelsea manager, who joked that his victory toast had been spoiled by the poor quality of the wine on offer from the club, expressed his delight.

After taking to the microphone on the pitch to thank the "fantastic" players and fans, Ancelotti targeted an FA Cup win over Portsmouth to complete the Double as he roared: "Come on Chelsea!"

And the Italian then admitted: "I had a lot of help because I found a team and a club with fantastic organisation.

"So it was easy for me to do my best and, after the first year, I hope to stay here a long time and win a lot of titles."

And to cap a great day for him, the Chelsea fans sang his name out loud for the first time this season.

FINAL TABLE

	P	W	D	L	F	A	Pts
Chelsea	38	27	5	6	103	32	86
Man Utd	38	27	4	7	86	28	85
Arsenal	38	23	6	9	83	41	75
Tottenham	38	21	7	10	67	41	70
Man City	38	18	13	7	73	45	67
Aston Villa	38	17	13	8	52	39	64
Liverpool	38	18	9	11	61	35	63
Everton	38	16	13	9	60	49	61
Birmingham	38	13	11	14	38	47	50
Blackburn	38	13	11	14	41	55	50
Stoke	38	11	14	13	34	48	47
Fulham	38	12	10	16	39	46	46
Sunderland	38	11	11	16	48	56	44
Bolton	38	10	9	19	42	67	39
Wolves	38	9	11	18	32	56	38
Wigan	38	9	9	20	37	79	36
West Ham	38	8	11	19	47	66	35
Burnley (R)	38	8	6	24	42	82	30
Hull (R)	38	6	12	20	34	75	30
Portsm'th (R)	38	7	7	24	34	66	19

GOLDEN BOOT HOW IT ENDED

- DROGBA (Chelsea) 29
- ROONEY (Man Utd) 26
- BENT (Sunderland) 24
- TEVEZ (Man City) 23
- LAMPARD (Chelsea) 22
- DEFOE (Tottenham) 18
- TORRES (Liverpool) 18
- FABREGAS (Arsenal) 15
- ADEBAYOR (Man City) 14
- SAHA (Everton) 13
- AGBONLAHOR (A Villa) 13
- BERBATOV (Man Utd) 12

▲ **ROCK 'N GOAL STAR** Drogba gets the title party going

ACES WON THE TITLE IN STYLE ⚽ FOUR ~~GE~~ MANIA PULL-OUT

FA CUP FINAL

CHELSEA 1

Drogba 59

MASTER

Drogba the special one

CHELSEA RATINGS

PETR CECH 8
A memorable afternoon, beginning with his great instincts to deny Piquionne a golden chance. And though his did not have to be the best keeper in the world to stop Boateng's penalty, he still had to save it.

BRANISLAV IVANOVIC 6
His early marking of Boateng was important as Portsmouth looked to make an impression, but stayed strong throughout and was always quick to support the attack while rarely being out of position.

ALEX 6
More hits than misses, particularly with a number of strong headed clearances to break down Portsmouth's moves. Yet his late slip almost let in Dindane – had Terry not intervened to save his, and Chelsea's, skin.

JOHN TERRY 7
Close to breaking the deadlock in the first half when his header was placed wide of James and hit the bar. His touch 10 minutes from time, not that he knew much about it, was priceless as Dindane loomed.

ASHLEY COLE 7
Not a tough afternoon in defence and was electric in breaking forward. No wonder he was left furious when Kalou missed from close range after his excellent burst and cross set up the clear opening.

FRANK LAMPARD 6
Another landmark – the first man to put wide a penalty in an FA Cup final at Wembley. But it did not make a difference on a day when he made more of an impact in the early stages with two fine shots.

MICHAEL BALLACK 6
Always involved, until he was not allowed to be when the late tackle by Boateng might have rocked his World Cup dream. He was in agony as he limped off just as he was proving to be a key link.

FLORENT MALOUDA 5
By the outstanding standards of his season, he had a quiet afternoon. The odd cross and pass that led to a break but nothing to catch the eye, yet he would be excused it because of his overall form.

NICOLAS ANELKA 6
One shot was close, but he never really made himself a major threat. Always rapidly cutting in from the left, he was a danger, yet not one of his better games and taken off late to sum up a disappointing day.

DIDIER DROGBA 9
Boy, can he take a free-kick. After being denied by James' great save in the first-half, his match winner was all about amazing precision and power. As the wall moved, his placement was brilliant. A star show.

SALOMON KALOU 6
Had Chelsea lost, his nightmare would not have gone away after his sensational first-half miss when he hit the bar from Cole's cross. The ball came off his shin – but how he did not score was still a mystery.

SUBSTITUTES

44mins Juliano Belletti (for Ballack) Clumsy challenge gave away penalty 5; 71mins. Joe Cole (Kalou) A few good runs but not involved that much 6; 90mins. Daniel Sturridge (Anelka) No time to do anything 5.

MANAGER: CARLO ANCELOTTI

What an amazing start to his managerial reign in England with the double – and he will now build for a bid to win the Champions League next season. Tactics were right as Chelsea just played their normal game – fast flowing with so much going the way of Drogba, and it worked.

BY SIMON MULLOCK
sport@sundaymirror.co.uk

WHAT a way to banish the spectre of the Special One.

These may still be the players that Jose Mourinho first turned into champions – but rest assured this is now very much Carlo Ancelotti's team.

In his first season at Stamford Bridge, Ancelotti has delivered something that was beyond even Mourinho – a Premier League and FA Cup Double.

Didier Drogba's stunning 59th-minute free-kick enabled the Italian to get his hands on the oldest trophy of them all.

It was a devastating strike.

Enough to silence the incredible Portsmouth fans, who made this an occasion to savour, and the critics, who accuse Chelsea of having no history.

The Blues' place among the legends of the English game is now guaranteed after an achievement that has only been savoured by six other clubs.

For Pompey it was another day of heartbreak at the end of a season when everything apart from the heart has been ripped out of the club.

Avram Grant's men became the sixth club to be both relegated and beaten in the Cup Final.

Grant, of course, is the man that came within a penalty kick of making Chelsea the champions of Europe.

That John Terry slip in Moscow two years ago this week. It must seem like another lifetime for the Israeli.

A new challenge away from Fratton Park beckons for Grant, while Pompey's fans returned down the M3 contemplating life in the Championship and debts of £140million.

At the end, before Terry and Frank Lampard lifted the trophy in unison, both sets of supporters rose as one to acclaim Grant as he collected his medal. 'Carpe diem' they

say in Ancelotti's homeland. 'Seize the day'. And it seemed like Pompey would do just that after somehow surviving a first half which saw Chelsea strike the woodwork FIVE times.

When Aruna Dindane tore

past Juliano Belletti in the 55th minute and was then sent sprawling by the Chelsea substitute's desperate lunge, referee Chris Foy pointed immediately to the penalty spot.

Opportunity knocked for Pompey but, when Kevin-Prince Boateng fired his kick against the legs of Petr Cech, the door slammed shut.

Within minutes, Drogba

picked himself up after being fouled by the otherwise outstanding Aaron Mokoena 25 yards out.

And when David James took a slight step to his right as Drogba shaped to shoot, it was fatal.

Drogba's whipped effort beat the Pompey keeper's left hand by inches and bounced in off the foot of the post.

The Ivorian deserved his 37th goal of the season. In the

STAT ATTACK

at WEMBLEY
ATT: 88,335

How they lined up

● CHELSEA

Cech
Ivanovic   A Cole
Terry   Alex
Ballack   Malouda
Lampard   Kalou
Drogba   Anelka
Piquionne
Dindane   Diop
O'Hara   Boateng
Brown
Rocha   Mokoena
Mullins   Finnan
James

PORTSMOUTH ○

Shots

16   off target   4

4   on target   2

Story of the game

6	Corners	2
16	Fouls Conceded	15
0	Offsides	3
0	Yellow	2
0	Red	0

Possession

58%   42%

REFEREE
CHRIS FOY
Let game flow. No complaints about big calls 7

STAR MAN

PORTSMOUTH 0
BLASTER

DEMOLITION
Pompey's wall can't stop Drogba's opener

PORTSMOUTH RATINGS

DAVID JAMES   7
He made a stunning save to push Drogba's first-half free-kick onto the bar but had he not taken a step to the right in the second-half, he might have stopped Drogba's winner that inched past his left side.

STEVE FINNAN   7
Good positioning on a difficult afternoon when Chelsea broke quickly. Made a good block from Joe Cole and defended well. On his guard as Drogba and Kalou were always looking for breaks. Did well.

RICARDO ROCHA   6
A couple of good blocks but his day soured with a yellow card. He stayed strong, even though Chelsea's sweeping attacks meant there was little time to lose concentration as they had so many chances.

AARON MOKOENA   7
Threw himself in front of the ball twice to deny Drogba in the first-half and it was that spirit that seemed to galvanise Portsmouth into realising they had a chance of an upset which could have happened.

HAYDEN MULLINS   6
Left-back is not his normal position, yet he coped well on such a big stage. Attempted to join the midfield as much as he could but he defended well and kept Kalou at bay for periods as Chelsea broke.

MICHAEL BROWN   6
Never far away from being in the thick of the action, and it was his challenge that brought down Lampard for the penalty that the England star missed. Probably could have been more creative from his midfield role.

PAPE BOUBA DIOP   6
A poor game where he never really created as much as his side would have hoped, floating in and out of the action. He gave away a few too many free-kicks and did not have the best of days at Wembley.

KEVIN-PRINCE BOATENG   6
What if...? He will be asking himself that question for probably the rest of his life about his penalty that Cech saved. Why didn't he smash it? Had it gone in, the match could have been so different. What if...?

JAMIE O'HARA   8
Had a fine game, lively and always quick to set up a move. He saw a great deal of the ball and thrived on it, easily being Portsmouth's best player, and made some fine passes to set Piquionne on his way.

FREDERIC PIQUIONNE   7
As the ball headed to him he could do nothing but knock it towards the one part of the goal where Cech could show his best. He will long wonder how he missed that great chance – and will find no answers.

ARUNA DINDANE   6
Brought down for the penalty while on one of his fine runs that were crucial to Portsmouth's play. And was so near to touching the ball for an equaliser as Alex missed but Terry just knocked it out of his path.

SUBSTITUTES
73mins John Utaka (for Boateng) Slotted in well as Pompey chased 5; 81mins Nwankwo Kanu (Diop) No repeat of 2008 match-winning glory 5; 81mins Nadir Belhadj (Mullins) A change that had little effect 5.

MANAGER: AVRAM GRANT
His face normally tells the story and yesterday was no different. He knows his former club inside out and Pompey approached the match well, their outstanding 'all-for-one' spirit allowing them not to be overawed. Justified in being proud of the way his players performed.

---

latter stages of the first period, he had seen a free-kick clatter the crossbar off James' fingertips and another close-range effort strike the foot of the post.

At that moment Portsmouth must have believed they were going to produce one of the greatest upsets of them all.

In an emotional show of defiance before the tie, their fans in the East Stand turned one half of Wembley into a sea of waving flags. It harked back to the golden days of the FA Cup, the glittering silver vision that has always offered hope to the underdog.

This was top versus bottom; rich versus poor; champions against vanquished.

Lampard almost silenced the Pompey chimes inside four minutes with a snap shot on the run that curled wide.

And when he got another sight of goal – and a chance to score in successive finals – the outside of James' post intervened.

But Chelsea also had a let-off when Dindane stabbed instinctively at Boateng's volley inside Chelsea's six-yard box only to see Cech produce an incredible save.

The Blues went from the sublime to the ridiculous moments later when Florent Malouda somehow fired a shot against the underside of the bar. Then Terry rose between Ricardo Rocha and Boateng to meet Malouda's lofted free-kick only to see his header bounce off the bar.

Drogba twice struck the same overworked goal frame as the break approached. It seemed nothing would get past James.

But when Boateng fired over on the restart, and then blundered from the penalty spot, Drogba struck decisively.

Salomon Kalou and substitute Joe Cole should have made it comfortable.

And Pompey would have made Chelsea pay had Terry not inadvertently diverted substitute Nadir Belhadj's cross away from Dindane with the goal gaping.

Even Lampard was wasteful, shooting wide from the penalty spot in the 88th minute after being hauled down by Michael Brown.

▲ **YOU'RE THE MAN:** Blues players mob boss

CHELSEA 2
Ramires 11, Drogba 52

LIVERPOOL 1
Carroll 64

By SIMON MULLOCK
AT WEMBLEY

IT'S getting to the point where Roberto Di Matteo would have strong grounds for unfair dismissal if Roman Abramovich doesn't keep him as Chelsea manager.

The Italian was supposed to provide nothing more than a safe pair of hands until the end of the season, Abramovich deciding that having a man who was sacked by West Brom in temporary charge was a better option than Andre Villas-Boas.

But two months on, the Blues have won the FA Cup and have a Champions League Final still to come.

Goals by Ramires and Didier Drogba took the famous old trophy back to Stamford Bridge for the fourth time in six seasons and seventh time overall.

And if Di Matteo's men were impressive in the way they dominated Kenny Dalglish's side for more than three-quarters of the contest, the sheer defiance they showed after Andy Carroll's reply was just as telling.

Petr Cech's save to push Carroll's 82nd-minute header on to the crossbar will go down as one of the cup final's definitive moments.

Liverpool insisted that the ball had crossed the line – but television replays suggested that assistant referee Andrew Garratt's eyes had not failed him and the decision was correct.

And so, 14 years after he scored a goal that was once the fastest in FA Cup Final history, this was another day for Di Matteo to savour.

So what if he doesn't carry the kind of high-profile image that Abramovich had in mind when his patience

> ## 'We've been criticised this season but we've got a trophy'

with Villas-Boas snapped? And it would be tough to blame him for Chelsea's failure to claim a top-four finish in the Premier League.

In just a few weeks he has healed the dressing room divisions that were tearing the club apart.

The bouncing huddle of Chelsea players at the final whistle sent out the clearest of messages to the club's owner.

Di Matteo said: "I'm very happy for the players. We've been heavily criticised this season but we've got a trophy and we've got the chance for another.

"This group of players have made the club proud. It's been hard work, but we came through it."

Di Matteo has a close relationship with the FA Cup having twice scored goals in finals for Chelsea, beating Middlesbrough in 1997 and Aston Villa in 2000.

He added: "It's quite a unique situation to be able to win as a player and then as a coach. I feel honoured."

As a spectacle, this was the slowest of burners. But what a finale.

Chelsea assumed such control for the first hour that it seemed not whether they would win, but how many goals they would score.

But in the end it was Liverpool bemoaning how they had failed to force at least extra-time.

It was a classy touch to give Jimmy Armfield his first appearance in a FA Cup Final at the grand old age of 76, with the England and Blackpool legend presented to both teams as the guest of honour.

Then it was Chelsea who stepped up to the plate and their urgency was rewarded in the 11th minute.

Juan Mata, that matador of a midfielder, tempted Jose Enrique into believing he could intercept his threaded

pass towards Ramires. But Mata's precision was perfect and the Brazilian ran free to strike a low shot from just inside the box.

Even then Pepe Reina should have saved, but the Liverpool keeper plunged early to his right and could do nothing as the ball ricocheted off his wrist and into the net.

Craig Bellamy thought he had levelled but his close-range volley was blocked by Branislav Ivanovic's bulky Balkan thigh.

Liverpool used to visit Wembley so often that the old stadium was dubbed 'Anfield South' on Merseyside.

But the Reds have struggled on home soil this season.

And they looked set for hiding in the 52nd minute when Drogba continued his love affair with the Cup.

Frank Lampard's pass was weighted perfectly for the Ivorian as he pulled off the shoulder of Martin Skrtel and his low shot flew across Reina and into the corner.

Drogba ran to the Chelsea fans massed in the west end of the stadium to celebrate becoming the first man to score in four finals.

Dalglish quickly sent on Carroll for Jay Spearing and in the 64th minute the tide of the game turned.

Carroll conjured up the kind of finish that prompted Liverpool to pay £35million for him when he collected Downing's cross and turned past John Terry before bludgeoning a shot into the roof of the net.

Suddenly the Merseysiders were in the ascendancy.

And Carroll was certain he had levelled nine minutes from the end when he met Luis Suarez's far-post cross with a meaty header.

Cech seemed stranded but he somehow scrambled across his line before arching backwards to palm the ball on to the underside of the bar before Ivanovic cleared.

Liverpool were certain the ball was in, but their appeals were waved away.

It still took two crucial blocks by Terry and Ivanovic to deny Suarez and Carroll before Chelsea's celebrations could begin.

MATT
Masterful Di Matteo stakes his claim for the job

THE RAM RAIDER
Ramires fires home the opener past Pepe Reina

> ⊳ **MULLOCK'S VERDICT**
>
> **A FINAL that will be remembered for a rousing Liverpool rally, but Chelsea deserved their victory for having the match-winning quality at both ends of Wembley.**

Now read Andy Dunn's verdict from Wembley ▶Pages 4-5

SHINES

Killer stat

7

Chelsea have now won seven FA Cup finals, the same as Liverpool

AN ANDY REPLY

Carroll lashes in his 64th-minute goal to give the Kop hope

MATCH STATS

at WEMBLEY
ATT: 89,102

STORY OF THE GAME opta

CHELSEA		LIVERPOOL
5	SHOTS ON TARGET	4
7	SHOTS OFF TARGET	8
1	BLOCKED SHOTS	5
5	CORNERS	7
7	FOULS	8
3	OFFSIDES	4
79.4	PASSING SUCCESS%	85.2
20	TACKLES	17
85	TACKLES SUCCESS%	88.2
37.9	POSSESSION%	62.1
47.6	TERRITORIAL ADVANTAGE%	52.4

RED & YELLOW CARDS
Chelsea: Mikel ▢
Liverpool: Agger ▢ Suarez ▢

MAN OF THE MATCH
RAMIRES

MINUTES PLAYED	76
GOALS	1
ATTEMPTS ON TARGET (inc Goals)	1
ATTEMPTS OFF TARGET	0
TOTAL PASSES	26
PASS COMPLETION%	69.2
TOTAL TACKLES	2
TACKLES SUCCESS%	100
FOULS	0

REFEREE
PHIL DOWD
Insisted Carroll's effort didn't cross the line – and got it right. **7**

MATCH RATINGS
Compiled by Chris Hatherall

CHELSEA   LIVERPOOL

PETR CECH — **8**

Made excellent save from Suarez, and an incredible one at the death by pushing Carroll's close-range header onto the crossbar.

PEPE REINA — **5**

Allowed Ramires to score at his near post, which will have upset the Spaniard. But could do nothing about Drogba's strike, which flew past him.

JOSE BOSINGWA — **6**

He was doing well until cannoning a clearance off Downing to set up a goal for Carroll, which revived Liverpool.

GLEN JOHNSON — **5**

Failed to make the kind of impact going forward that Liverpool hoped for, and had to keep Cole at bay at the back instead.

BRANISLAV IVANOVIC — **7**
The solid defender, suspended for the Champions League Final, made his mark – and brilliantly cleared Bellamy's effort off the line.

DANIEL AGGER — **6**

Despite a harsh first half booking, he dealt with most things Chelsea threw at him – even when the Blues were in the ascendency.

JOHN TERRY — **6**

Looked solid enough until he was turned inside out by Carroll for Liverpool's strike. Recovered to make a crucial block to deny Carroll a second goal.

MARTIN SKRTEL — **6**

Did his best to keep Drogba at bay and put up a decent job in the air for most of the tie. But couldn't keep Drogba off the scoresheet.

ASHLEY COLE — **7**

His pace and energy down the flank were key early on – and neither Bellamy or Downing got the better of him all afternoon.

JOSE ENRIQUE — **5**

Uncharacteristically wobbly at times, which allowed Ramires to run all over him – that included the all-important first goal.

JOHN-OBI-MIKEL — **7**
Caretaker at the back who mopped up whenever needed. Did job quietly and without fuss, although booked for a late challenge.

JORDAN HENDERSON — **5**

Barely touched the ball in midfield as the game passed him by. Didn't look in the same class as Chelsea's men in the middle of the park.

FRANK LAMPARD — **7**
Looked comfortable and on top form by running the midfield and – just like in the semi-final – it was his pass that set up Drogba to score.

JAY SPEARING — **5**

Not a day for him to remember. He gave the ball away for Chelsea's opener and was hauled off in the second half – replaced by Carroll.

SALOMON KALOU — **6**

Di Matteo has shown a lot of faith in the winger ignored by former boss AVB. Although he didn't shine he certainly worked hard.

STEVEN GERRARD — **7**

Kept on driving Liverpool forward, and as usual he never gave up. But at times his team-mates just were not up to his level of quality.

JUAN MATA — **7**
The official man of the match was a constant menace – and Chelsea's most creative player. His pass set up Ramires for the opener.

CRAIG BELLAMY — **7**

His characteristic pace and effort was evident again at Wembley. Had a shot cleared off the line that would have made it 1-1.

RAMIRES — **8**

The once-derided Brazilian appears complete. His run and finish put the Blues ahead – with his pace and power wobbling Liverpool.

LUIS SUAREZ — **7**
Not one of his most influential games as he struggled to shrug off attentions of Mikel. Livened up late on to test Cech and spark Liverpool.

DIDIER DROGBA — **8**

He always scores at Wembley. His lethal left-foot finish made it 2-0 – and that was his eighth in eight games at the national stadium.

STEWART DOWNING — **7**

One of their better performers. Kept plugging away down the left flank and got his reward with an assist, but needs more end product.

CHELSEA SUBSTITUTES
Meireles for Ramires 76 – 6;
Slotted in to try and defend the lead.
Malouda for Mata – 6;
Late, tactical introduction.

LIVERPOOL SUBSTITUTES
Carroll for Spearing 55 – 7;
What an impact he made. He came on and thumped a goal then nearly got a second.
Kuyt (for Bellamy 78) – 6;
Too late to make a real impact.

Subs not used: Turnbull, Essien, Torres, Ferreira, Sturridge.

Subs not used: Rodriguez, Carragher, Doni, Shelvey, Kelly.

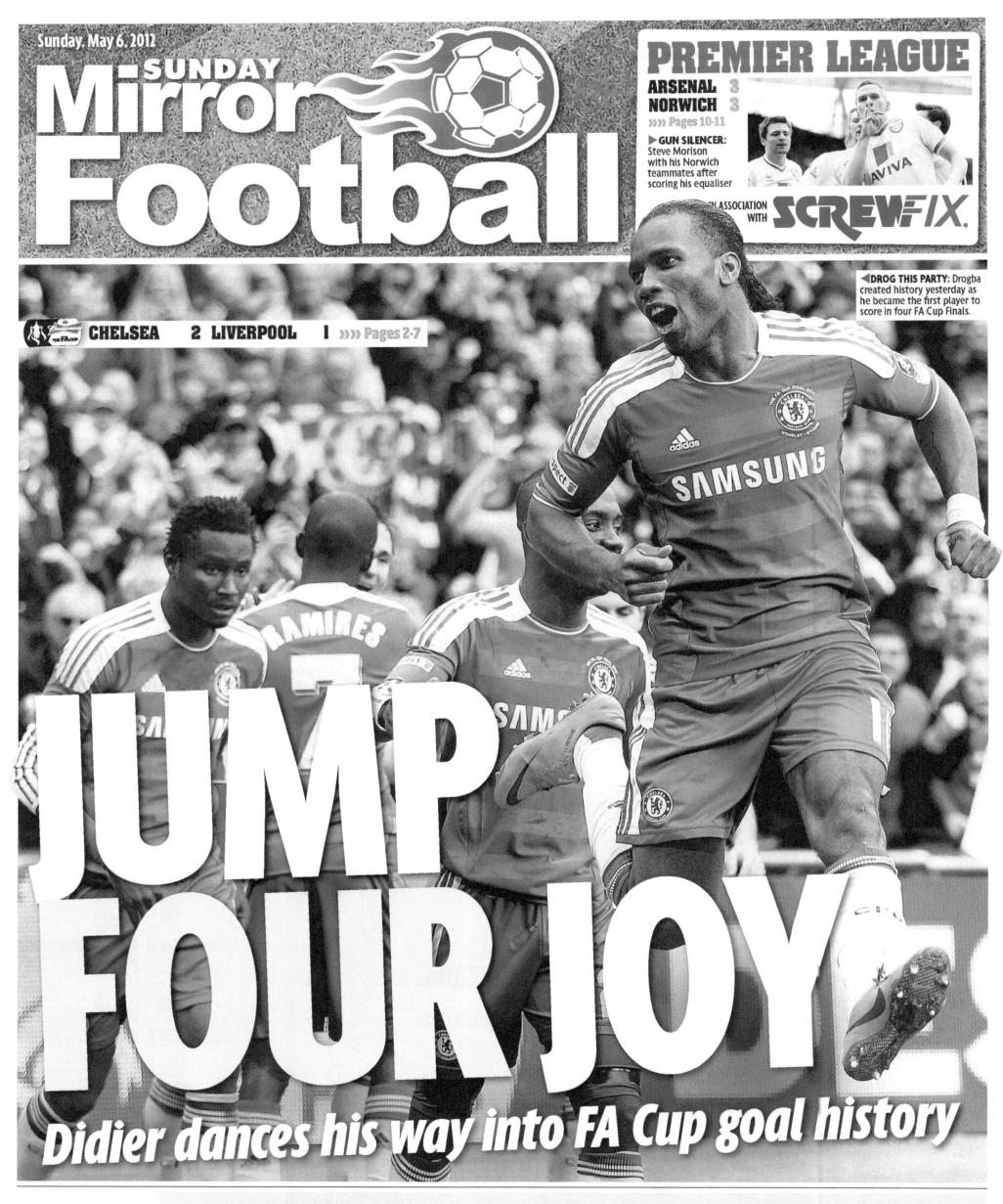

Sunday, May 6, 2012

SUNDAY Mirror Football

◄**DROG THIS PARTY:** Drogba created history yesterday as he became the first player to score in four FA Cup Finals.

THE FA CUP   CHELSEA **2** LIVERPOOL **1** »»» Pages 2-7

JUMP FOUR JOY

Didier dances his way into FA Cup goal history

BAYERN MUNICH 1 CHELSEA 1 »»» Pages 2-7
(1-1 at 90mins, Chelsea win 4-3 on penalties)

HERO OF DI HOUR

KEEPING THEM IN THE GAME: Cech dives to save Arjen Robben's spot-kick in extra-time

Classy Cech's penalty heroics help Roberto's braves to Munich glory

▲**BASTIAN BATTLE:** Didier Drogba (left) and John Obi Mikel join forces to halt the threat from Bayern ace Schweinsteiger

BLUES

Di Matteo's men are spot on to win Europe's biggest prize

B MUNICH 1
Muller 83

CHELSEA 1
Drogba 88
(aet. Chelsea win 4-3 on pens)

By SIMON MULLOCK
AT THE ALLIANZ ARENA

DIDIER DROGBA fired home the crucial shoot-out penalty to make Chelsea champions of Europe at last.

In a night of high drama at the Allianz Arena, Roberto Di Matteo's men looked to be heading for defeat after Thomas Muller had given Bayern the lead after 83 minutes.

But Drogba saved the day again with an equaliser two minutes from time.

With no further goals in extra time, the Blues proved that Germans can be beaten on penalties.

Petr Cech had already saved an Arjen Robben spot-kick in extra time.

Then he denied Ivica Olic and Bastian Schweinsteiger in the shoot-out.

Juan Mata missed for Di Matteo's men, but David Luiz, Frank Lampard and Ashley Cole all hit the target before Drogba wrote another chapter in the Stamford Bridge history books.

This was supposed to be a neutral venue. Try telling that to the 17,500 Chelsea fans in the south end of the Allianz Arena surrounded by a sea of Bayern red.

Chelsea's four suspended players tried to stay involved, John Terry, Raul Meireles, Branislav Ivanovic

and Ramires all suited and booted in the dug-out alongside Di Matteo.

Their disappointment must have been magnified by the sight of 22-year-old Ryan Bertrand starting a Champions League tie for the first timee.

After defying the odds to overcome Napoli and Barcelona, beating Bayern on their own soil would allow them to lay claim to the greatest European campaign of them all.

But from the moment Schweinsteiger's shot was deflected over by Gary Cahill's block, it was clear Di Matteo's plan was containment. Toni Kroos shot wide before Philipp

> *It seemed a matter of time before Bayern broke through*

Lahm's quick throw and Muller's speed of thought presented Mario Gomez with a sight of Cech's goal.

The striker hesitated and as the ball escaped from his control, Jose Bosingwa was fortunate not to put through his own goal.

When Cech diverted Robben's low strike on to the post with an ugly combination of boot and fist it seemed only a matter of time before Bayern broke through.

Mata finally came up with an effort on goal but his floated free-kick had the Bayern fans ducking.

At least the Blues were carrying some threat now and Salomon Kalou tested Manuel Neuer with a raking drive after Cole, Drogba and

Lampard had linked up. But Gomez would have scored if he had controlled Franck Ribery's miscued volley six yards from goal.

And the Bayern striker blundered again when he fooled Cahill but blazed over.

Only once has a team lifted the European Cup on enemy territory, Liverpool beating Roma on penalties in the Eternal City 28 years ago.

But it needed Cole's early intervention to prevent Robben's cross from finding Muller after the Dutchman had torn past Luiz.

Bayern had the ball in Cech's net in the 54th minute when Ribery fired home after Cole had blocked Robben's shot, but he was a yard offside.

Bayern boss Jupp Heynckes was growing increasingly agitated on the touchline.

But Cole, in particular, proved reports of his demise are premature and he came to the rescue again to block a Schweinsteiger rocket.

But Bayern finally broke through in the 83rd minute.

Kroos clipped a glorious cross to the far post and Muller leapt above Cole to score with a downward header that bounced over Cech's hand.

But the lead did not last long. After Di Matteo sent on Fernando Torres for Kalou, the never-say-die Blues levelled in the 88th minute.

Drogba rose above Jerome Boateng to meet Mata's corner and score with a bullet header that Neuer could only help into the roof of his net.

Bayern got a glorious chance to retake the lead when Ribery tumbled under Drogba's tackle and referee Pedro Proenca pointed to the spot.

Germans don't miss penalties – but it was Dutchman Robben who took it and he was foiled by a stunning Cech save.

KINGS OF EUROPE
Chelsea players go wild after Drogba scores the winning penalty

B MUNICH ✓ LAHM ✓ GOMEZ ✓ NEUER ✗ OLIC ✗ SCHWEINSTEIGER
CHELSEA ✗ MATA ✓ LUIZ ✓ LAMPARD ✓ COLE ✓ DROGBA

GALLING FOR GERMANS
▲ It's heartache for Bayern players as their dream of European glory is left in tatters

HEAVEN

MATCH RATINGS
Compiled by Richard Lewis

BAYERN MUNICH

MANUEL NEUER 6

Would have expected a busier night but apart from saving well from a free-kick by Mata, he didn't have much to do until Chelsea's late equaliser.

PHILIPP LAHM 6
Pushed forward when he could, but as Chelsea had rare moments breaking forward he was back in his position and had the pace to hold off his man.

JEROME BOATENG 6
Stayed powerful at the back and kept concentration because Chelsea had so few major openings – and when they did he had to be right on the ball.

ANATOLIY TYMOSCHUK 6
Facing the prospect of Drogba breaking forward could not have been much fun, especially late on. But he was in command for the counter attacks.

DIEGO CONTENTO 7
A player Chelsea might not have thought would be a key, but he caused trouble powering down the left and his cross almost saw Muller score.

BASTIAN SCHWEINSTEIGER 8
Booked after only two minutes for a needless handball, which hardly had an effect on the way he approached his play – brilliant passing and movement.

TONI KROOS 6
Attacked a great deal and Chelsea had to keep an eye on him for blindside runs on a night when Bayern had so much control that any man could have scored.

ARJEN ROBBEN 6
Extra time penalty saved. Hit the post after 21 minutes and was a constant threat against his old club. His pace when on the ball is so difficult to manage.

THOMAS MULLER 8
Thought he had grabbed a winner with his late strike – and nearly scored with a first-half volley when he was unmarked and shouldn't have been.

FRANCK RIBERY 6
Wheeled away celebrating, unaware his early second-half 'goal' had been disallowed. But his role in supplier to Robben caused trouble.

MARIO GOMEZ 6
He did the hard bit, brilliantly controlling the ball to beat Cahill as half-time beckoned, but to the disbelief of his team-mates he fired way over.

BAYERN MUNICH SUBSTITUTES
Daniel Van Buyten for Muller (86mins) – 6;
Eased into the flow of the game, but made no real impact.
Ivica Olic for Ribery (97mins) – 5;
Never had enough time to leave any mark on proceedings.

Subs not used: Butt, Rafinha, Usami, Pranjic, Petersen.

CHELSEA

PETR CECH 7

Has had a fabulous season and although he should have done better as Muller struck, he made up for it with his brilliant penalty save from Robben.

JOSE BOSINGWA 7
It was always going to be tough but he probably could not have imagined such a busy night. He held the line well as Bayern attacked in wave after wave.

GARY CAHILL 8
A race against time to make it after injury but lack of match fitness never showed. He looked strong, and needed to be with what Bayern had in store.

DAVID LUIZ 8
Outstanding with his tackles and his presence alike. Robben and Muller were such a threat, but Luiz was a tower of strength as the attacks kept flowing.

ASHLEY COLE 7
In the thick of the action from the start as he looked to break away, and knew his experience was so important as Chelsea's solid defence held strong.

JOHN OBI MIKEL 6
Busy chasing as Bayern had so much of the ball that he never had the chance to develop his own game, though showed good touches in patches.

FRANK LAMPARD 7
A quiet game in terms of distribution but as captain his role was immense. Always talking, always cajoling and always running to plug any gaps.

SALOMON KALOU 5
At least had the claim of a shooting chance for Chelsea as his drive forced Neuer into a smart save at his near post, but should have put more power into it.

JUAN MATA 5
Creative overall but failed to make anything of a dangerous free-kick. He kept looking to set Drogba off on runs that ended quickly.

RYAN BERTRAND 6
What a stage to make your debut in the Champions League and whatever nerves he had, he never showed them, confidently breaking forward with pace.

DIDIER DROGBA 9
Equalised with a header just when Chelsea were slipping to defeat. Gave away a penalty but became their all-time hero with the shoot-out winner.

CHELSEA SUBSTITUTES
Florent Malouda for Bertrand (73mins) – 6;
Slotted in well and proved an effective link in midfield.
Fernando Torres for Kalou (84mins) – 7;
Determined to impress. His fresh legs caused Bayern danger.

Subs not used: Turnbull, Ferreira, Essien, Romeu, Sturridge.

JUST CECH I'VE CLEARED IT
▲ Blues hero Petr Cech gets up highest to clear the danger from another Bayern attack

FRANCKLY YOU'RE OFFSIDE
▼ Petr Cech is relieved after Ribery has a goal disallowed for offside early in the second half

BLUE ROAD TO MUNICH

Chelsea's Champions League final route

2-0 David Luiz scored Chelsea's first in a Group E win over Bayer Leverkusen

Sept 13 Stamford Bridge

1-1 Genk fared better at home, but a goal from Ramires (left) earned a group point

Nov 1 Genk Arena

1-1 Frank Lampard put Chelsea ahead at Valencia in the second group game

Sept 28 Mestalla Stadium

3-0 Didier Drogba's second as a win over Valencia saw Chelsea top Group E

Dec 6 Stamford Bridge

5-0 Struggling Fernando Torres hit two in a romp against Genk

Oct 19 Stamford Bridge

1-2 Manuel Friedrich's last-gasp goal in Bayer Leverkusen's battling win

Nov 23 Bay Arena

A NOU HERO
Joy for Ramires (right) as his team-mates mob Fernando Torres who made it 2-2 in Barcelona

2-2 This Ramires chip gave 10-man Chelsea hope in the battle to knock out mighty Barcelona

April 24 Nou Camp

1-3 Last 16 disaster as Edinson Cavani scores and Napoli get a 3-1 lead

Feb 21 Stadio San Paolo

March 14 Stamford Bridge **4-1** Branislav Ivanovic's extra-time goal seals a memorable win over Napoli

1-0 Quarter-finals and this Salomon Kalou goal is enough for a fine win at Benfica

March 27 Estadio Da Luz

2-1 Raul Meireles calms nerves with this injury-time winner over Benfica

April 4 Stamford Bridge

1-0 Semi-finals and Chelsea stun Barcelona thanks to Didier Drogba's first-half goal

April 18 Stamford Bridge

UEFA CHAMPIONS LEAGUE

BLUE DID IT, BOYS!

2012 CHAMPIONS LEAGUE FINAL: BAYERN MUNICH 1 CHELSEA 1

1-1 AFTER EXTRA-TIME, CHELSEA WIN 4-3 ON PENALTIES

SUNDAY Mirror SPORT

www.sundaymirror.

BIG SAM SLAM!

SAM ALLARDYCE hit out at the West Ham fans who didn't believe in him as the club celebrated promotion back to the Premier League.

Ricardo Vaz Te fired the late winner at Wembley as they beat Blackpool 2-1.

But Allardyce said: "You get criticised everywhere. There is a small minority of West Ham fans who make themselves heard, but the majority are behind us."

Reaction: Pages 68-69   Report: Pullout

2012 CHAMPIONS LEAGUE FINAL: BAYERN MUNICH 1 CHELSEA 1

1-1 AFTER EXTRA-TIME, CHELSEA WIN 4-3 ON PENALTIES

DI KINGS OF EUROPE

Drogba scores winning penalty as Roberto pulls off a miracle

By SIMON MULLOCK
sport@sundaymirror.co.uk

CHELSEA are champions of Europe after Didier Drogba's shoot-out penalty handed owner Roman Abramovich his football dream.

Drogba, whose late header equalised Thomas Muller's opener in normal time, slotted home to spark amazing scenes at the Allianz Arena.

Frank Lampard, Chelsea's captain for the night, said: "Didier's our hero and without him we would not be here. We have waited so long for this moment. We showed spirit and we deserved that."

Skipper John Terry, who was suspended, helped lift the trophy which was passed to an ecstatic Abramovich.

REACTION: PAGES 70-71 & PULL-OUT

MUNICH MARVELS
Chelsea lift the Champions League trophy after their shoot-out win

RED ROBIN

Russians will offer Van Persie £300k-a-week

EXCLUSIVE
By STEVE STAMMERS

GUUS HIDDINK has been given a blank cheque to go and sign three world-class stars for Anzhi.

And Hiddink has put Arsenal's Robin van Persie (left) on his shopping list.

Anzhi owner Suleyman Kerimov, one of the richest **TURN TO PAGE 71**

TURN TO PAGE 71

▲ RUMOURS Wayne Rooney

ROON ARMY .. JUST BARMY

By SIMON BIRD

WAYNE ROONEY is at the centre of a bizarre transfer saga linking him with a move to Newcastle.

The unsettled Manchester United striker has already asked to leave Old Trafford.

Now a website – backed by Newcastle owner Mike Ashley – has claimed that the club have made a move for Rooney. Ashley founded Sports

TURN TO PAGE 67

DOUBLE DUTCH Champions League holders Chelsea are now Europa League winners

FOLLOW THAT, JOSE

▲ **SILVER SEND-OFF** Benitez lifts the Europa Cup last night

Ivan the Incredible gifts Rafa perfect send-off

From JOHN CROSS in Amsterdam
Branislav Ivanovic handed Rafa Benitez the perfect farewell gift in Amsterdam.

Hero Ivanovic rose deep into stoppage time to clinch Chelsea's second major European trophy within a year.

And Benitez, whose troubled interim period ends when Jose Mourinho returns on July 1, will now leave after another dramatic European triumph. A delighted Benitez said: "It was a great performance

TURN TO PAGE 71

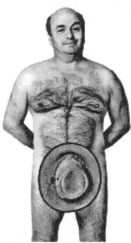

Published by MGN Ltd at One Canada Square, Canary Wharf, London, E14 5AP (020-7293 3000) and printed by Trinity Mirror Printing Ltd at Watford, Oldham, Teesside, Birmingham, Cardiff and Glasgow. Registered as a newspaper at the Post Office **Serial No. 34,725** ©MGN Ltd Thursday, May 16, 2013 ★★★ Austria €3.50, Belgium €2.00, Bulgaria 3.70 BLG, France €2.00, Germany €2.00, Greece €2.00, Italy €2.00, Netherlands €2.00, Portugal €2.00 (cont) 341 Esc, Spain €2.20, Malta €1.80/ML60 cents (inc VAT), Turkey YTL 5.00, Cyprus €1.80 (CYP£1.05), Denmark 20DK, Norway NKR22, Egypt EGP 10.00

RESULT!

with sports betting's top tipster **DEREK McGOVERN**
E-MAIL ME AT: betsguru@aol.com

Kiwis can get a draw... weather we like it or not

LOSING punters like to believe bookies have an intelligence system that would put the CIA to shame, but in reality it often wouldn't put C&A to shame.

Eighty per cent of the bets Hills have taken on the First Test at Lord's have gone on the draw, which suggests an awful lot of people have a strong idea what the weather will be like this week.

But still you can get 13-8 about a Lord's stalemate.

That's not very intelligent of the bookies. Normally I hate backing the draw, but all three Tests between the sides in New Zealand in March were drawn.

That included England's great escape in the Third Test, thanks to the last wicket stand by Matt Prior and Monty Panesar (below).

Another pointer is the fact that no matter how bad you thought the weather was yesterday, it's likely to be even worse over the next few days. Why do I say this? Because it always is.

I read somewhere that only four of the 12 Tests matches played at Lord's in May have finished without a result, but most of those Tests were pre-Ice Age.

The only thing that would amaze me more than Alastair Cook (above) & Co getting five days' play at Lord's is if I watched any of it.

First Test (Hills): 5-6 England, 12-1 New Zealand, 5-4 Draw

BET OF THE DAY OK I admit it, I like a drink. I always keep a whisky handy in case I see a snake, which I also keep handy. Get on the First Test at Lord's to finish drawn at 13-8.

Rob won't stay on for Thursday shifts

WIGAN must now prepare themselves for nine long months of Championship football – two months longer than they normally play it.

Their traditional late rally wasn't enough to keep them in the top flight and now the FA Cup winners face the double whammy of Doncaster and Bournemouth on a Tuesday night and, worse still, ITV4 on a Thursday night.

Wigan fans want their club to continue playing football to get out of the Championship – after all, it got them out of the Premier League.

But they may have to do it without boss Roberto Martinez, now just 5-4 to take over at Everton, who have been doing without it for years.

Wigan are 7-2 to bounce straight back into the Premier League but remember that the three teams who went down last season all failed to finish in the top six – and two of them failed to finish in the top 16.

Next Everton manager (Hills): 5-4 R Martinez, 20-1 N Lennon, 5-1 G Poyet, 7-1 A Stubbs, 12 M Mackay, 14-1 P Neville.

Inferno a surefire hit

DAN BROWN'S new book Inferno has come out – a big surprise to those who had no idea it was gay.

If you read Brown's Da Vinci Code you'll know what Inferno is about – about £10.99 too dear.

From the moment I picked it up my face wore expressions of alarm, disgust, and horror – one day I intend to read it.

I shouldn't criticise Brown because I took six years to complete my last book – I've always been a slow reader. The Da Vinci Code sold squillions as a hardback and paperback but also did well as an audio book – I put it down to word of mouth.

Hills quote just 1-2 for Inferno to sell more than a million hardback copies before the end of May.

ADDITIONAL REPORTING BY JOHN SHAW

EUROPA LEAGUE FINAL

From vitriol to victory.. Rafa bows out with respect he deserves

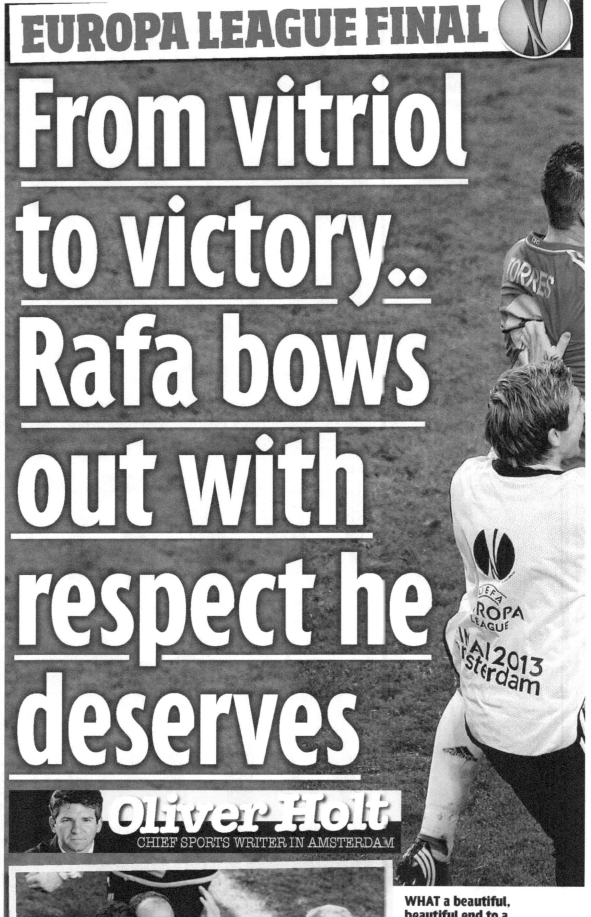

Oliver Holt
CHIEF SPORTS WRITER IN AMSTERDAM

WHAT a beautiful, beautiful end to a troubled, tortured relationship.

Rafa Benitez and Chelsea was supposed to be the marriage made in hell but it ended in a kind of forgiveness last night.

When Branislav Ivanovic headed the winner, the boss Chelsea never wanted turned to the bench and clenched his fist.

Then, when the final whistle confirmed victory, he walked calmly over to the stricken Benfica coach, Jorge Jesus, and shook his hand.

Finally, he went on to the pitch and found himself being enveloped in hugs by Chelsea players.

At the very last, after so much hostility, Benitez, the most unlikely hero of another dramatic English football season, was feeling the love.

It was not before time. A few

BENI'S FROM HEAVEN ▲ The Blues boss celebrates with his staff

BENFICA 1 CHELSEA 2 AMSTERDAM

TIME TO PARTY Chelsea players link arms for a victory huddle after the final whistle

▲ **TIME'S UP** Carragher plays last game on Sunday

CARRA'S KOP TITLE REGRET

By DAVID MADDOCK

JAMIE CARRAGHER admits he has one aching regret in his remarkable career – Liverpool's failure to win the Premier League.

The Reds legend will bow out on Sunday after his 737th and final senior appearance for the club he joined as a nine-year-old.

Carragher said: "If there is an 'I wish' moment after my last game, then it is I wish I'd won the Premier League.

"But there are no fancy reasons or excuses why we didn't do it during my time at Liverpool – we weren't good enough and that's it.

"A couple of times we went close, but there was always a team better than us."

The defender, 35, insisted he will make a clean break from the club. "I will miss it, especially the training ground," he said. "I've been going there every single day since I was nine and I'm going to miss it – but I won't be crying.

"But once I've gone I don't think I'll be going back. Once you're done, you're done.

"The people here don't really want you coming back, hanging around the place all the time."

RESULTS

FOOTBALL

UEFA EUROPA LEAGUE FINAL

Benfica	(0) 1	Chelsea	(0) 2
Cardozo 68 (pen)		Torres 59	
53,000		Ivanovic 90	

CLYDESDALE SPL

Kilmarnock	(0) 1	Hibernian	(1) 3
O'Hara 57		Robertson 10	
3,198		Doyle 86, 90	

	P	W	D	L	F	A	Pts
Celtic (C)	37	23	7	7	88	35	76
Motherwell	37	18	9	10	67	49	63
Inverness CT	37	13	15	9	64	59	54
St Johnstone	37	13	14	10	43	44	53
Ross County	37	12	14	11	46	48	50
Hibernian	37	12	12	13	48	52	48
Dundee Utd	37	11	14	12	51	58	47
Aberdeen	37	11	14	12	40	42	47
Kilmarnock	37	11	12	14	51	50	45
Hearts	37	11	10	16	39	48	43
St Mirren	37	8	14	15	44	59	38
Dundee (R)	37	7	9	21	28	65	30

**IRN-BRU FIRST DIVISION
PLAY-OFF FINAL, 1ST LEG**

Alloa	(2) 3	Dunf'mline	(0) 0
Tiffoney 27		2,765	
Elliot 45, Moon 90			

**IRN-BRU SECOND DIVISION
PLAY-OFF FINAL, 1ST LEG**

| East Fife | (0) 0 | Peterhead | (0) 0 |
| 826 | | | |

TENNIS

ITALIAN OPEN, Men's 2nd Round: M Granollers (Spa) bt **A Murray (GB)** 6-3 6-7 (ret), R Nadal (Spa) bt F Fognini (Ita) 6-1 6-3.

Women's 2nd Round: S Errani (Ita) bt C McHale (US) 7-5 5-7 6-2, R Vinci (Ita) bt N Burnett (Ita) 6-1 6-4, N Li (Chn) bt J Zheng (Chn) 6-3 6-1, A Morita (Jpn) bt U Radwanska (Pol) 6-3 6-1.

CYCLING

GIRO D'ITALIA, Stage 11 (Tarvisio - Vajont, 182km): 1 R Navardauskas (Lit/Garmin-Sharp) 4hr 23min 14sec. **Others:** 29 B Wiggins (GB/Sky) +5min 41sec. **Classification:** 1 V Nibali (Ita/Astana) 43hr 26min 27sec. **Others: 4 B Wiggins** (GB) +2min 5sec.

TODAY'S CRICKET

FIRST TEST (Lord's): England v New Zealand (11).

TODAY'S RUGBY LEAGUE

NORTHERN RAIL CUP, Quarter-final: Dewsbury v Halifax (7.30).

---

hours earlier, as they poured off the Metro train, Chelsea fans chanted the name of their manager. "Jose Mourinho," they yelled over and over again.

Some of it was for the benefit of the Benfica fans walking alongside them, fans who dislike any former manager of FC Porto.

But even on a night like last night, there were still plenty of Chelsea supporters keen to fast-forward to a time when Benitez is no longer part of the club.

Benitez remains, simply, the man who Chelsea fans wish wasn't there. They started off despising him. Now they can just about bring themselves to tolerate him.

There is little regret at his imminent departure.

Inside the Amsterdam ArenA, there was no acknowledgment of Benitez at all. His name was not sung, nor was he acclaimed in any of the flags or banners.

There was a sign that read "Thank you, Roman". Another

declared Frank Lampard an "Immortal".

And the banner which usually occupies a place behind the goal in the Matthew Harding Stand at Stamford Bridge recognising John Terry as "Captain, Leader, Legend" was there, too. But of Benitez, there was nothing.

In Chelsea's recent dysfunctional relationships with their own managers, the situation Benitez finds himself in is not wholly unusual.

Avram Grant was largely unloved when he took the team Mourinho had built to within a penalty kick of winning the 2008 Champions League final.

He was damned by the assumption that he was a stop-gap until a permanent manager could be found.

And labelling Benitez 'interim' when he took the job meant that he never stood a chance of winning over fans who

already disliked him from his time at Liverpool. Even his detractors would have to admit, though, that Benitez has never hidden during his time at Chelsea.

Last night was no different. He spent most of the first half out on the touchline, constantly cajoling and gesticulating. He put an arm

around David Luiz during a break in play, shouted instructions to Lampard and tried to impart tactical nuances to Juan Mata.

Benitez has done a fine job managing the club's fixture congestion. This was their 68th game of the season and Benitez has faced an increasingly difficult job juggling his resources.

And in the first half, Chelsea looked a tired side. They were comprehensively outplayed.

Even the detractors of Benitez accept that he is a clever tactician, though, and after Chelsea had withstood Benfica's pressure, they took the lead.

There was still no acclaim for Benitez when Fernando Torres went around Artur and clipped the ball into the open net.

But that has stopped mattering to the Chelsea boss, if it ever mattered in the first place. Benitez is a realist. He took

the Chelsea job because it was an opportunity to compete for trophies and titles. He achieved the first target that was set for him of qualifying Chelsea for next season's Champions League.

That is his gift to his old enemy, Mourinho, who is poised to take over at Stamford Bridge next month.

Last night, though, was a fourth major European final for Benitez and leading Chelsea here has burnished his reputation.

It has put him back in the spotlight and led to him being coveted once more by leading European teams.

The denouement will not do him any harm, either. Oscar Cardozo equalised for Benfica seven minutes after Torres's opener but Ivanovic's winner was a fairytale ending.

So there is no need to feel sympathy for Benitez any more. He has succeeded for Chelsea and Chelsea has succeeded for him.

OUR SPECIAL REQUEST ▲ Chelsea fans call for old boss Jose

THE EUROPA LEAGUE FINAL

UEFA EUROPA LEAGUE

BENFICA 1

BLUES LINE-UP AND RATINGS
COMPILED BY JOHN CROSS

Petr Cech
Will be thankful that Benfica's finishing was so erratic and made a sensational late save from Cardozo. **7**

Cesar Azpilicueta
Given all sorts of problems by Benfica's movement. Made one sensational last-gasp clearance, but his handball gifted Benfica equaliser. **6**

Branislav Ivanovic
Pick of Chelsea's under-siege defenders and was a worthy hero as he nicked a last-gasp winner. **7**

Gary Cahill
Nervous, short of confidence and shaky at back. Well below his usual commanding best, but crucially denied Cardozo at end. **6**

Ashley Cole
Terrific early block to stop Benfica going ahead, but got runaround like rest of the Chelsea defence. **6**

Frank Lampard
Swerving shot brilliantly saved by Benfica keeper Artur and smashed a late effort against bar as Chelsea chased winner. **8**

David Luiz
Handed thankless task of being midfield shield in front of Blues' overworked defence and did job well. **6**

Ramires
Defensively poor. Continually showed a lack of discipline, lost his man and was over run in midfield. Brazilian had a disappointing night. **5**

Juan Mata
Chelsea's main man this season, but could not find his rhythm. Threatened very rarely going forward. **6**

Oscar
The Brazilian was booked for pulling Enzo Perez's shirt. Maybe it was out of frustration as he struggled to impose himself on the game. **6**

Fernando Torres
Ruthless finish after holding off two defenders, rounding keeper and slotting in to fire Chelsea ahead. **6**

Substitutes
None.

BENFICA LINE-UP
Artur Morales, Almeida, Luisao, Garay (Jardel, 78), Melgarejo Perez (Ola John, 66), Matic, Rodrigo (Moreno Lima, 65), Gaitan, Cardozo, Salvio.

Ref: Bjorn Kuipers Att: 53,000

MY BLUE HEAVEN

After 68 games, Ivanovic seals Euro glory in the final minute

THE OLD ONE-TWO Fernando Torres puts Chelsea in front (left) and Ivanovic seals the victory

▲ **UP FOR IT** Chelsea's Ramires and Gary Cahill battle for a high ball

By MARTIN LIPTON
Chief Football Writer
reports from Amstedam
m.lipton@mirror.co.uk

IT HAS taken them 68 games in 12 countries, over eight competitions.

But right at the death, Chelsea tasted the sweet smell of success again last night, earned the right to another victory parade.

Not the one they wanted, of course. Indeed, being in Europe's secondary competition was the reason Roberto Di Matteo was replaced by Rafa Benitez in November.

In truth, they did not deserve it, second best for most of the game, relying on their sheer refusal to submit. Yet as Branislav Ivanovic's header looped through the Amsterdam air to nestle in the back of the Benfica net, with seconds left on the clock, none of that mattered.

Ivanovic, of course, missed last May's glory in Munich but on an evening which carried constant echoes of Chelsea's greatest triumph, the Serb ensured another trophy for the Blues, another for Benitez.

Extra-time had loomed, Oscar Cardozo's penalty cancelling out a piece of quality finishing that gave Fernando Torres his 20th competitive goal of the season.

But Ivanovic rose to convert Juan Mata's corner, crowning another astonishing Chelsea season which has defied logic and the odds.

Benitez, deprived of John Terry and Eden Hazard, was down to his last 11 fit players, his bench horribly weak.

And just as in Munich 12 months ago, when they pulled off a minor miracle against all the odds, Chelsea faced being overrun from the start.

Quite how Benfica failed to translate their possession and opportunities into tangible reward was hard to work out – other than a reluctance to actually pull the trigger.

Serbian Nemanja Matic, who went the other way when David Luiz came to Stamford Bridge in 2011, and his partner Enzo Perez dominated the Brazilian and stand-in skipper Frank Lampard in the middle.

Further up, Nicolas Gaitan orchestrated the attacking thrust which left the disoriented

OLIVER HOLT  FROM VITRIOL TO

CHELSEA 2

FROM THE AMSTERDAM ARENA

▲ **WINNER** Benitez continued his great Euro run of success

PERFECT SEND-OFF FOR RAFA

FROM BACK PAGE

in the second half, against a very good team.

"I'm really pleased for the players and everyone involved. We didn't have the legs in the first half, so we had to adapt.

"They players have worked so hard, all season. I am proud –it was not easy. I'm really pleased."

The game was heading to extra time before Ivanovic looped home a header from a corner in the third minute of added time.

Ivanovic said: "It's a great feeling. This team deserved this, because we have had a very difficult season and a lot of games.

"In the end, today was a very hard game and Benfica played very well. But we scored from set-pieces and work very hard preparing that part of our game. We deserve that trophy."

Fernando Torres put Chelsea in front on the hour only for Oscar Cardozo's penalty to level eight minutes later.

Frank Lampard, captain in the absence of injured John Terry, crashed a 35-yard shot off the bar three minutes from time before Ivanovic's late drama.

Lampard and Terry lifted the trophy together and Lampard then said: "It's been an amazing time for all of us involved."

Blues back line chasing shadows, while at the other end Torres was barely noticeable. Somehow, though, mainly due to Benfica's failings, Chelsea stayed on terms.

Time and again, Benfica passed up the chance to test Petr Cech, Gaitan's hasty scoop over the bar and two air-shots in front of goal by Rodrigo moments for regret.

When Mata got on the ball Chelsea appeared as if they might manufacture something, although even the Spanish matador showed frailties when he failed to play Oscar in on goal.

Too often, though, Chelsea played long, giving the ball away all over the park, lucky that Benfica lacked the courage of their own convictions when they saw the whites of Cech's eyes.

Lampard, by contrast, has never been afraid of a shot, demonstrated as he looked up and let fly from 25 yards, the late swerve sending Artur the wrong way before his left hand stretched out to flip just over.

A signal for the Blues? For a few minutes, even if their moments of threat were ended by the flag going up on three occasions as the Chelsea fans began to rise to their feet. But Benfica remained the more poised, Gary Cahill just doing enough to thwart Cardozo before the interval.

Benitez's lack of options was painfully clear. It was back to the old Chelsea virtues, the ones imbued into the club by the King across the water, Jose Mourinho, resilience, grit, determination and desire.

Those, though, are the enduring attributes, fostered in every new arrival, key clearances from Cahill then Cesar Azpilicueta at the start of the second period further evidence. When you are under the cosh, you need the breaks as well.

A Dutch linesman used hawk-like vision to decide Cardozo was fractionally – a matter of inches – offside when he nodded home Gaitan's cross. And just before the hour, seconds after Cech saved Gaitan's back-post header, Torres struck, out of absolutely nothing.

Cech's clearance was never meant to reach the Spaniard but it did, Torres suddenly finding himself isolated against Luisao, shrugging off the Brazilian and, in slow motion, rounding Artur to roll over the line. It was the sort of goal the old Torres scored, the one Chelsea paid £50million to bring to the Bridge, the one that has rarely been seen since, although slightly more regularly since Benitez took the helm.

Within seven minutes, though, Azpilicueta's arm was outstretched to block Eduardo Salvio's header and despite the protests Cardozo smashed home from the spot.

Torres, caught in a Luisao bear-hug, tumbled theatrically in the box, before Cech used his fingertips to make a terrific save from Cardozo's volley. And while the crossbar kept out a terrific Lampard drive, Ivanovic delivered the final twist.

BENFICA v CHELSEA

MAN OF THE MATCH

OSCAR CARDOZO
Scored a penalty, constant menace

58%	BALL POSSESSION	42%
3	SHOTS ON TARGET	5
7	SHOTS OFF TARGET	4
4	CORNERS	4
1	OFFSIDE	8
17	FOULS	18
2 0	CARDS	1 0

A GREAT VICTORY <<PAGES 68 & 69

▲ **BUNDLE OF JOY** David Luiz leads the celebrations

DM1ST

CHELSEA 2 TOTTENHAM 0
Terry 45, Walker og 56

Champagne pops for Jose again as Blues get taste for glory

THE THIRST OF MANY

CECH 7 — Surprise choice ahead of Courtois. Lucky to see Eriksen's free-kick hit the bar in the first half but little to do otherwise

IVANOVIC 8 — Unlucky to see early header go wide. Denied Chadli a late chance by wrong-footing the Belgian at the back post

AZPILICUETA 7 — Given a hard time by the direct running of Andros Townsend and Kyle Walker. But gave blood for the Chelsea cause.

TERRY

9 — Captain, leader, scorer. In right place at the right time yet again to put Chelsea ahead – and a great late tackle on Kane too

CAHILL 7 — Missed a great chance in first-half injury time to kill the game off with a free header from close range

RAMIRES 6 — Conceded possession continually during a difficult first half. Better in the second after Chelsea established control

ZOUMA 6 — Pushed into midfield with Matic suspended, but he was given the runaround at times by Spurs' Bentaleb and Mason

FABREGAS 6 — Didn't impose himself on the game in the manner that many people expected him to. Replaced

WILLIAN 7 — Sent in the cross which Tottenham failed to defend for Chelsea's goal. Booked for his foul on Rose

COSTA 8 — You get what you pay for - and with this striker that is quite a bit. Fortunate with the goal but his usual combative self

HAZARD 6 — Kept quiet during the first half by a combination of Walker and Mason. Glimpses of skill in the second half

SUBSTITUTES
Cuadrado (Willian 76) 5
Oscar (Fabregas 88) 5
Drogba (Costa 93) 5

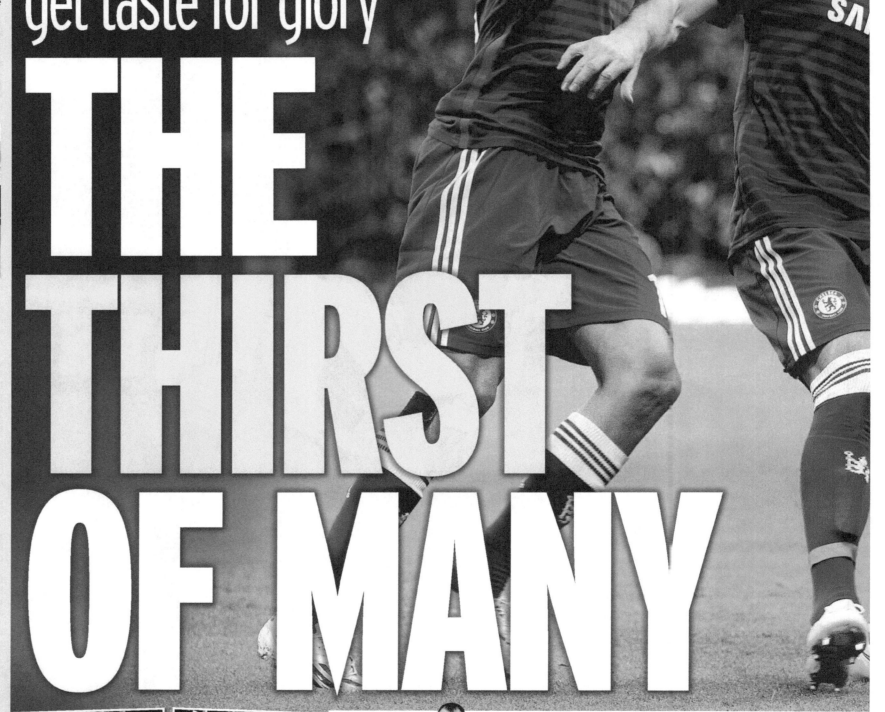

2015 Banned Matic donned kit to lift trophy...

2012 ...like Terry did in Champions League final

BY **DAVE KIDD** Chief Sports Writer

COLD and calculated in its planning, brutal in its execution, Jose Mourinho's first major trophy in three years was delivered with typical efficiency.

There was precious little beauty and no overwhelming sense of joy in Chelsea's performance as Tottenham's young innocents were skewered in the Wembley rain.

The capture of the Capital One Cup may have been celebrated extravagantly by Mourinho and his players but there are more important baubles to be won.

Manchester City's defeat at Liverpool means the Premier League title is in touching distance while Chelsea are likely to be England's lone standard bearers in the Champions League quarter-finals.

As Spurs flogged themselves in Florence during midweek Mourinho was feeding raw meat to Diego Costa and revving up a Routemaster to stick in front of Petr Cech. From the moment Costa eyeballed out Eric Dier in the opening minutes, this was brutes against boys.

Fired up by his manager's dark conspiracy theories after the three-match ban he earned in the semi-final against Liverpool, Costa was in Tottenham's faces from the word

go. And it was little surprise when he delivered the killer second goal shortly after half-time.

The opener had come from John Terry, who ended up in hospital with concussion after a kick in the head from Arsenal's Abou Diaby the last time Mourinho lifted this pot. Costa and Terry are Mourinho's type of players. Mourinho's type of men. It was fitting they should net the goals which earned the first silver of his second coming.

We had wondered whether Gary

DM1ST

CAPITAL ONE CUP FINAL FROM WEMBLEY STADIUM

2-0
Diego Costa's shot deflects off Walker and past Lloris

WINNERS Jose Mourinho and John Terry with the trophy

OLD SCHOOL Blues legends Drogba, Terry and Cech celebrate

JOSE'S NOT KIDDING

JOSE MOURINHO admitted to feeling the hunger of his first final before Chelsea beat Spurs to lift the Capital One Cup.

The Blues boss – who won the League Cup back in 2005 to kick off his first Chelsea winning spree – repeated the feat with victory at Wembley.

After being joined by owner Roman Abramovich in the dressing room, Mourinho – who has now won the trophy three times with Chelsea – said: "For me, it's important to feel that I'm a kid. Very important for me to feel I am a kid.

"Before the game, I had the same feelings as my first final however many years ago. It's important to feel the same happiness after the victory, and to feel like a kid at 52 years old.

"That for me is very important. I know I have a team to build, which is what we're doing.

"But it's difficult for me to live without titles, even with all the work to be stable that we are doing."

1-0
Terry (centre) celebrates with Costa & Cahill after scoring the opening goal
PICS: KENT GAVIN

TOTTENHAM
BY DARREN LEWIS

LLORIS
6 So unlucky to be beaten by two deflections on shots he otherwise would have saved easily

WALKER
6 Not his day. Snuffed out Hazard but was injured in first half and deflected Costa's effort into his own net

DIER
5 Stood up to the physical challenge from Costa but was booked – perhaps harshly – for his troubles

VERTONGHEN
5 Only needs to look at the way Terry and Cahill threw their bodies bravely into blocks to see how it should be done

ROSE
6 Made an important 66th-minute header to prevent Cesc Fabregas scoring a third at the back post

BENTALEB
6 Helped to overrun the midfield in the first half. Could have done better with his efforts on goal though

MASON
6 A mature midfield display packed with industry. Intelligent in possession but tracked back well to frustrate Hazard

CHADLI
5 Gave away the free-kick from which Chelsea scored. His decision-making was also poor throughout

ERIKSEN
6 Unlucky to see his ninth-minute free-kick hit the crossbar. Combative and creative but came up short

TOWNSEND
5 Demanded the ball at every opportunity. Not afraid to run at the Chelsea backline. But no real end product

KANE
5 Worked all day but just could not get any change out of John Terry who kept him quiet all game

SUBSTITUTES
Dembele (Townsend 62)   **5**
Lamela (Mason 71)   **6**
Soldado (Chadli 80)   **5**

MATCH STATS		
37%	**POSSESSION**	63%
3	**SHOTS ON TARGET**	2
6	**SHOTS OFF TARGET**	8
4	**CORNERS**	6
3	**OFFSIDE**	3
19	**FOULS**	15
3 0	**CARDS**	2 0

REFEREE: Anthony Taylor
ATTENDANCE: 89,294

Cahill or Kurt Zouma would play alongside Terry but Mourinho simply chose both, the vast young Frenchman employed as a midfield sentry guard.

Mourinho had brought 'parking the bus' into the English football lexicon after Spurs' goalless draw at the Bridge during his first reign – yet no manager is more adept at doing the

same. The last time he won a significant prize, Mourinho led Real Madrid to the Spanish title with 100 points, overcoming Pep Guardiola's Barcelona in 2012.

This was far more prosaic but it will doubtless instil this team with the same belief as the 2005 League Cup success had done for Mourinho's back-to-back title winners a decade ago.

Spurs had demolished Chelsea on New Year's Day in a 5-3 victory at White Hart Lane, with Harry Kane monstering Cahill.

Early on, the young English

striker attempted a Ricky Villa run, beating three players before Cesc Fabregas mowed him down.

Christian Eriksen shook the crossbar with a 30-yard free-kick and that was pretty much that from Kane and Spurs.

Costa (left) had a grab at Nabil Bentaleb's face. The Spurs midfielder went ballistic, Costa reacted as if butter were imperishable to flames.

Dier was then booked for a late challenge on Costa, who was firmly beneath Tottenham skin.

The breakthrough arrived two minutes before the break, Spurs unable to clear Willian's free-kick and Terry's shot deflected past

Hugo Lloris by Dier. Chelsea had the fresher legs and the more experienced heads, so they began the second half in upbeat mood, destination jugular.

An overhead kick from Cesc Fabregas forced a sprawling save from Lloris. And on 56 minutes, it was game over when Fabregas fed Costa on the left and the striker's shot cannoned off Kyle Walker's leg to beat Lloris at his near post.

Eden Hazard curled one just wide as Chelsea, fleetingly, threatened to run riot. Yet they brought down the shutters, efficient until the end, Terry and Zouma usually there with a crucial block.

Mourinho allowed himself one sentimental moment when Didier

Drogba arrived as a late sub for Costa – the veteran Ivorian may never play here again.

The Chelsea manager embraced Rui Faria before the final whistle then disappeared down the tunnel scowling and jabbing a finger towards the stands, presumably at his imagined conspirators.

He re-emerged a picture of happiness, wide smiles at the trophy presentation, then joining his players to caper on the sodden turf.

But he'll already have been thinking about West Ham on Wednesday. He's never satisfied, this man. Which is why he'll carry on winning.

david.kidd@trinitymirror.com

DMIST

CHELSEA 1 CRYSTAL PALACE 0

Hazard 45

RATINGS BY JOHN CROSS
mirror.co.uk/sport/football

CHELSEA — OUR RATING

Courtois 6
Made excellent late block to stop Zaha from equalising

Ivanovic *Booked* 6
Lost his cool after ding-dongs with Zaha and Mutch

Cahill 7
Steady display in the heart of Chelsea's defence

Terry *Booked* 7
Heroic block to stop Puncheon - typifies his whole season

Azpilicueta 7
Crazy that he didn't make PFA Team of the Year

Matic 6
Not one of his best games but got the job done

Fabregas *MOTM* 7
Some moments of real quality. Terrific season

Cuardrado 4
Was so bad that he got hooked at half-time

Willian 6
Worked hard, had a good season, subbed for Zouma

Hazard 6
Scored at the second attempt

Drogba 5
Fired a good chance wide. This was his farewell

SUBS
Mikel (Cuadrado 46) 6
Zouma (Willian 85) 6
Luis (Hazard 90) 6

62%	Possession	38%
7	Shots on target	1
8	Shots off target	4
3	Corners	6
1	Offside	2
12	Fouls	13

Ref: Kevin Friend Att: 41,566

C PALACE — OUR RATING

Speroni 5
Saved a penalty - but still blew it. Awful handling

Mariappa *Booked* 6
Silly trip on Hazard. Was solid

Dann *Booked* 7
Harsh yellow for silly foul on Cuadrado

Delaney 7
Palace's centre-halves were very strong and resolute

Ward 7
Palace's defence was strong end held firm

Ledley 6
Put in a shift in midfield up against Chelsea's quality

McArthur 6
Caught up in the Hazard diving row

Puncheon 5
Frustrating afternoon. Rare moments of quality

Mutch 5
Had a great battle with Ivanovic. Didn't win it

Zaha 7
Constantly troubled Chelsea's defence

Bolasie 6
Didn't threaten enough to justify a £60m asking price

SUBS
Kelly (Mariappa 60) 6
Murray (Mutch 60) 6
Sanogo (Puncheon 70) 6

ℹ In 95 Prem games at the Bridge, Mourinho has lost just one

PARTY

While Chelsea stars danced with joy, Jose snarled and snapped before stomping down the tunnel unhappy with the critics of his winners

BY JOHN CROSS
Chief Football Writer

JOSE MOURINHO is only interested in winning trophies not popularity contests.

He did not even join his players for the joyous blue ticker-tape celebrations on the pitch after Chelsea were finally crowned champions.

Instead, the Portuguese went to his son and then his wife and daughter who were sitting near the dugout before heading down the tunnel.

It almost felt like Mourinho was determined to miss his own parade as the Chelsea boss did not look to be in the mood to party with the rest of Stamford Bridge.

In fairness, his father has been ill and last week the manager flew back to Portugal to be at his bedside. But it was more than that. Mourinho clearly wasn't happy, rarely have we seen a title manager look so sullen and even seemed to turn on Chelsea's fans as at times it did seem rather quiet and flat.

He is all about winning and his demeanour at Stamford Bridge was almost a sense of disbelief at Chelsea not getting the credit they deserve. Forget style, thrills and spills. Enjoy the glory.

The Blues were the best team by far in the first half of the season, playing free-flowing football which entertained us all. And no one should blame them for the poor title race. Blame the rest.

The last few weeks of the season has been an uncomfortable stumble over the finishing line as the west Londoners have run out of gas.

Victory here even felt strangely unsatisfying as they had to rely on a moment of controversy to accomplish it.

PFA Player of the Year Eden Hazard won a penalty, had it saved and then headed in the rebound. But Palace were incensed and their travelling fans made it clear they felt Hazard had dived under James McArthur's 44th-minute challenge.

They chanted "cheat" at the Belgium international in amongst songs about the lack of atmosphere at Stamford Bridge during the game.

Mourinho seemed to love the Palace fans. At one point he turned to them, acknowledged their loud singing, then looked at the Matthew Harding stand before turning to the bench and said, "Nothing".

Just before half-time, the boss even mocked his own fans by pretending to fall asleep while he appeared to turn away in disgust and mouth obscenities during the second half when they started singing about Frank Lampard.

Mourinho has no time for

THE TITLE-WINNING GOAL

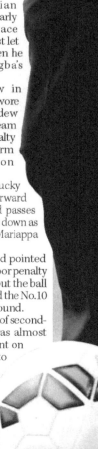

SPOT THE HERO Hazard's penalty is saved but he heads home the rebound for the title

sentiment, he is only interested in winning. And the fact not everyone appreciates Chelsea or understands his philosophy, seems to have really upset him.

But he has the medals to prove his brilliance. This is his third Premier League title from his two spells in west London and he has also won titles at Porto, Inter Milan and Real Madrid.

His teams just know how to win and never has that been more true than here as it was a forgettable game but they got the three points – and clinched the title.

The Blues offered little in the first half as twice Julian Speroni's poor handling nearly gifted chances. The Palace keeper's poor punch almost let in Nemanja Matic and then he spilled Didier Drogba's fierce free-kick.

The Eagles grew in confidence as the half wore on and boss Alan Pardew was convinced his team should have had a penalty when John Terry's arm blocked from Jason Puncheon.

But Chelsea got a lucky break. Hazard broke forward from the left, swapped passes with Willian, then went down as McArthur and Adrian Mariappa tried to block him off.

Referee Kevin Friend pointed to the spot, Hazard's poor penalty was saved by Speroni but the ball spun up into the air and the No.10 headed home the rebound.

Palace had a couple of second-half chances but it was almost inevitable Chelsea went on to grind out a 1-0 win to clinch the title.

But no one should dispute that they are worthy champions.

Mourinho certainly doesn't care how they won. Just as long as they did.

PREMIER LEAGUE

	P	W	D	L	F	A	Pts
(C) Chelsea	35	25	8	2	69	27	83
Man City	35	21	7	7	71	36	70
Arsenal	33	20	7	6	63	32	67
Man Utd	35	19	8	8	59	35	65
Liverpool	35	18	7	10	49	38	61
Tottenham	35	17	7	11	55	50	58
So'hampton	35	17	6	12	48	28	57
Swansea	35	15	8	12	43	44	53
West Ham	35	12	11	12	43	42	47
Stoke	35	13	8	14	39	44	47
Everton	35	11	11	13	46	46	44
Crystal Pal	35	11	9	15	42	48	42
West Brom	35	10	10	15	33	46	40
Aston Villa	35	9	8	18	29	50	35
Newcastle	35	9	8	18	36	60	35
Hull	34	8	10	16	32	45	34
Leicester	35	9	7	19	39	54	34
Sunderland	34	6	15	13	28	50	33
QPR	35	7	6	22	39	61	27
Burnley	35	5	11	19	26	53	26

POOPER

WE'RE TOP OF THE PILE Fabregas leaps on his team-mates as they celebrate their title success after the final whistle

HAPPY RETURNS Birthday boy Fabregas gets a title back in the Prem

A FAB BIRTHDAY GIFT AS CESC'S A WINNER AT LAST

BY **JOHN CROSS**

CESC FABREGAS toasted his first ever Premier League title – and admitted it was a moment he always dreamed of.

The Chelsea midfielder, who celebrates his 28th birthday today, had eight years at Arsenal but never finished on top. But Fabregas lifted the trophy in his first season at Stamford Bridge on his return to England.

He said: "I cannot believe it, I have fought very hard for this moment and it is here, I'm very proud. This is a top club, a top team and we are the champions."

Didier Drogba has won four league titles at Chelsea and claims this one is particularly satisfying. It may be his farewell as the veteran striker is out of contract this summer. Drogba, 37, said: "This one is sweet. With or without me, Chelsea will always be No.1. Chelsea is bigger than me and always will be."

Nemanja Matic added: "It is special to me.

"I played almost every game and I am very happy for the club, the fans and my team-mates.

"We still have three games left and

we are champions. It was very important to win because it is better to finish when you have the opportunity.

"When you see how many good teams play in this league, we are proud. This is why we play our football. We showed we have a winning mentality."

Ramires rocked by major scare

CHELSEA midfielder Ramires was rushed to hospital after complaining of a kidney problem.

Ramires was originally named in the starting line-up but complained of feeling very ill before kick-off and was replaced by Juan Cuadrado.

The Brazilian is expecting to stay in hospital as tests are carried out to try to diagnose the problem which was a serious concern to Chelsea's own medics.

Blues' boss Jose Mourinho broke off from the club's celebrations to go and visit Ramires in hospital.

Mourinho said: "He was feeling so bad we had to take him out of the dressing room."

BLUE IS THE COLOUR Boss Mourinho (left), captain Terry and owner Abramovich (both below) show their delight

TRIBUTE TO THE CHAMPS See our football pullout

TERRY: LAST 5 YEARS HURT

FROM BACK PAGE

is. I'm still here, still fighting.

"This is what I live for. I've been a ball-boy here, I've been a mascot here, I've painted the stadium, I've done everything.

"It has been five years since we've won it and it has really hurt.

"When you go four or five years, when you go game after game, trips away from the family and get nothing for it, it really hurts. We are going to enjoy today."

Chelsea boss Mourinho insisted his team were worthy champions – and aimed a bizarre snipe at some of the team's detractors. He said: "The

people who have a big face to say we don't deserve it are the ones who, in my country, say the dogs bark and the caravan goes by.

"We did everything the team needs to do. That's why we're champions. That's why we deserve it. Everybody knows that."

And Mourinho has vowed there will be no easing up in his team's last three games against West Brom, Liverpool and Sunderland.

He added: "I'm going to give the boys a few days off but when we're back we're going to try and get maximum points."

WE BLUE THEM AWAY AGAIN AT THE BRIDGE

CHELSEA owner Roman Abramovich (left) punches the air after seeing his Blues clinch their fourth Premier League crown since he took charge in 2003.

Striker Didier Drogba and skipper John Terry (below with Branislav Ivanovic) now have all four title-winning medals, but it was a first for new boys Loic Remy, Kurt Zouma and keeper Thibaut Courtois (above).

Cesc Fabregas was ecstatic to land his first Prem winner's medal (below) after failing to in eight seasons at Arsenal – and the Spaniard drapes himself in the Catalan flag as he joins in the dressing-room celebrations.

Champions 2014-15
Chelsea

CHELSEA 3   SUNDERLAND 1

Costa 37 pen, Remy 70, 88   Fletcher 26

BLUE IS THE COLOUR
Skipper John Terry leads the celebrations with the Premier League trophy yesterday

BY JOHN CROSS
Chief Football Writer

IT was as much leaving party as celebration for the champions.

Chelsea legends Didier Drogba, 37, and Petr Cech, 33, were given a wonderful send off as they bade farewell to Stamford Bridge during the post-match knees-up on the pitch.

Drogba's goodbye was bizarre as he was carried off shoulder high by team-mates after being substituted – to a standing ovation from the fans – after just half an hour.

It was the sort of thing you only usually see in testimonials. And, in truth, it did feel like a friendly at times as Sunderland's defending didn't exactly make life difficult for their hosts.

In fact, Dick Advocaat's men – already assured of survival – almost played their part in the celebrations as they stood aside and let Chelsea enjoy their coronation as Premier League winners.

Steven Fletcher, with his first goal in six months, briefly threatened to be a party pooper as he gave the Black Cats a 26th-minute lead. But an upset never looked likely.

Diego Costa, who came on for Drogba, equalised from the spot after Sunderland captain John O'Shea tripped Juan Cuadrado eight minutes before the break. Blues sub Loic Remy, who has been a bit-part player so often this season, showed he might have much to offer next term with two goals, albeit courtesy of some woeful defending.

The Frenchman's first came after 70 minutes when Sunderland keeper Vito Mannone should have stopped his 20-yard shot. His second was a tap-in two minutes from time after the visitors' defence went AWOL.

Chelsea boss Jose Mourinho paid a glowing tribute to Drogba – who started as

PLAYED EVERY MINUTE

3,420 minutes of 38 Premier League matches in 2014/15

John Terry (Chelsea)
Aaron Cresswell (West Ham)
Tom Heaton (Burnley)

captain – while fans chanted at Cech "we want you to stay" throughout the game.

Mourinho said: "The substitution was decided because he had a problem with his knee and, in normal conditions, he could not play for long. We left him on for half an hour.

"The captaincy was John's desire, to give him the armband. The players to bring him off the pitch? I think that was decided between them because they like him a lot.

"It's not just the fans, I also want Petr to stay. I didn't sing it, but I keep saying the same. He's a legend of this club, but he's a legend at 33. Thirty-three for a goalkeeper is a very young legend.

"When Thibaut Courtois was injured, Petr made decisive saves in matches for us. I'm not sure if we could be champions had Petr not been here for those seven matches, so his contribution was decisive."

Mourinho held up eight fingers during the post-match celebrations to represent the number of titles he has won at four different clubs. But he has already set his sights on even more.

"A lot, eh? I may run out of fingers in the future," said Mourinho, who threw his winners' medal to daughter Matilde in the crowd. "Let's go for a ninth and 10th.

"We had the players from 2005 here. It'd be a dream to be here in 2025 and be with the champions of 2005, 2015 and 2025. That would be fantastic, but my future doesn't matter. What matters is Chelsea's future."

Sunderland boss Dick Advocaat revealed he has been offered a three-year deal to stay but admitted the squad needs a major overhaul and says he will announce his decision quickly.

Advocaat said: "Wait and see. They offered me two or three years. But I have to be honest to myself and to everybody about what I want to do for the future."

j.cross@trinitymirror.com

TOP DROG IS FEELING THE LOVE

FROM FRONT PAGE
the Chelsea fans – who gave him a great send-off during the post-match celebrations – when Mourinho (left) held up eight fingers to signify the number of titles he has won.

Drogba, 37, who announced before kick-off he was leaving Chelsea, but wanted to carry on playing for one more year, was carried off shoulder-high by his team-mates.

Drogba, toasting his fourth Premier League title with the club, said: "You can't do better than winning the Champions League final, but today is also a special one. "

Drogba grabbed the microphone to tell the Chelsea fans: "You are the best fans in the world – I love you guys."

And he said being carried off by his team-mates was a memorable moment, adding: "JT just decided to carry me off. It was really emotional."

GA
THI
Chelsea players ca

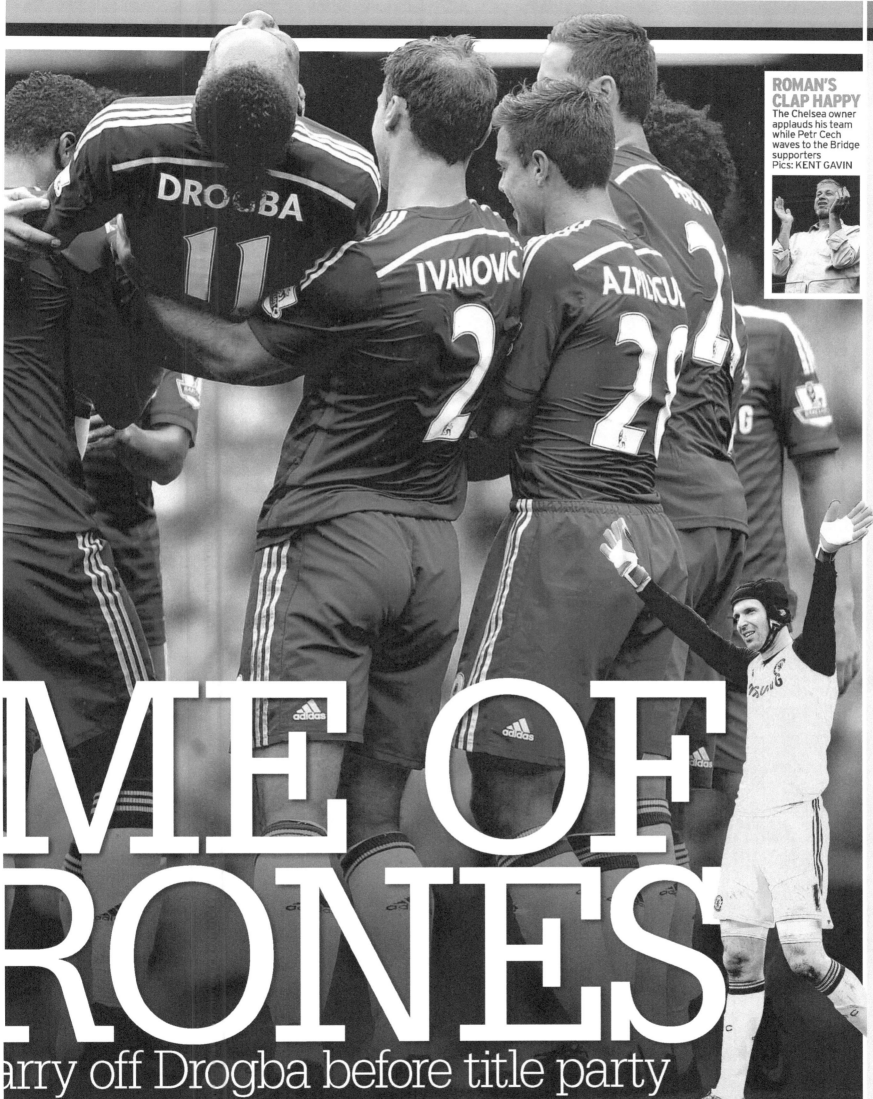

ROMAN'S CLAP HAPPY
The Chelsea owner applauds his team while Petr Cech waves to the Bridge supporters
Pics: KENT GAVIN

ME OF RONES

arry off Drogba before title party

CHELSEA
OUR RATING

Cech 7
The Chelsea fans chanted: "We want you to stay"

Ivanovic 6
Good going forward, sloppy at the back

Cahill 6
Nice and solid at the back for Chelsea

Terry 7
Couldn't get the goal for his best ever tally

Azpilicueta 7
Another excellent performance, rock solid

Mikel 6
Could be his last game. Not very memorable

Matic 6
Missed a sitter but supplied the third goal

Willian 7
Always works hard, good long range passing

Cuadrado 6
Booked. Won penalty, went off injured

Hazard 7
Miraculous recovery after having wisdom teeth out

Drogba 6
Carried off shoulder high - midway through first half

SUBS
Costa (Drogba 30) 6
Remy *MOTM* (Cuadrado 44) 8
Christensen (Mikel 78) 6

64%	Possession	36%
8	Shots on target	9
7	Shots off target	7
11	Corners	3
1	Offside	1
12	Fouls	8

Referee: Lee Mason Att: 41,620

SUNDERLAND
OUR RATING

Mannone 5
Shocking goalkeeping on Remy's first goal

Jones 5
Sunderland horribly exposed defensively

O'Shea 5
Clumsy and silly when he conceded penalty

Coates 5
Sunderland's defence parted for Remy to score

Van Aanholt 6
Got forward well, was exposed a few times

Rodwell 6
Booked. Couple of good passes, not much else

Larsson 6
Lucky to escape after pushing Ivanovic in the box

Johnson 6
Supplied the corner for Fletcher's opener

Defoe 6
Worked hard for the team in deeper role

Wickham 6
Dangerous when in possession going forward

Fletcher 6
Scored his first goal in seven months

SUBS
Giaccherini (Johnson 75) 6

DMLI

CHELSEA CHAMPIONS!

WEST BROM 0 CHELSEA 1
Batshuayi 82

HOW THE PREM WAS WON: BLUES SEASON... GAME BY GAME

AUGUST

15: Chelsea 2 (Hazard, Costa) West Ham 1 (Collins)

20: Watford 1 (Capoue) Chelsea 2 (Batshuayi, Costa,)

27: Chelsea 3 (Hazard, Willian, Moses) Burnley 0

SEPTEMBER

11: Swansea 2 (Sigurdsson, Fer) Chelsea 2 (Costa 2)

16: Chelsea 1 (Costa, top) Liverpool 2 (Lovren, Henderson)

24: Arsenal 3 (Sanchez, Walcott, Ozil) Chelsea 0

OCTOBER

1: Hull 0 Chelsea 2 (Willian, Costa)

15: Chelsea 3 (Costa, Hazard, Moses) Leicester 0

23: Chelsea 4 (Pedro, Cahill, Hazard, Kante) Manchester United 0

30: Southampton 0 Chelsea 2 (Hazard, Costa)

NOVEMBER

5: Chelsea 5 (Hazard 2, Alonso, Costa, Pedro) Everton 0

20: Middlesbrough 0 Chelsea 1 (Costa)

26: Chelsea 2 (Pedro, Moses) Tottenham 1 (Eriksen)

DECEMBER

3: Manchester City 1 (Cahill OG) Chelsea 3 (Costa, Willian, Hazard)

11: Chelsea 1 (Costa) West Brom 0

14: Sunderland 0 Chelsea 1 (Fabregas)

17: C Palace 0 Chelsea 1 (Costa)

26: Chelsea 3 (Pedro, Hazard, Cook OG) Bournemouth 0

31: Chelsea 4 (Cahill, Willian 2, Costa) Stoke 2 (Martins Indi, Crouch)

JANUARY

4: Spurs 2 (Alli 2) Chelsea 0

14: Leicester 0 Chelsea 3 (Alonso 2, Pedro)

22: Chelsea 2 (Costa, Cahill) Hull 0

31: Liverpool 1 (Wijnaldum) Chelsea 1 (Luiz)

FEBRUARY

4: Chelsea 3 (Alonso, Hazard, Fabregas) Arsenal 1 (Giroud)

12: Burnley 1 (Brady) Chelsea 1 (Pedro)

25: Chelsea 3 (Fabregas, Pedro, Costa) Swansea 1 (Llorente)

MARCH

6: West Ham 1 (Lanzini) Chelsea 2 (Hazard, Costa)

18: Stoke 1 (Walters) Chelsea 2 (Willian, Cahill)

APRIL

1: Chelsea 1 (Fabregas) C Palace 2 (Zaha, Benteke)

5: Chelsea 2 (Hazard 2) Manchester City 1 (Aguero)

8: Bournemouth 1 (King) Chelsea 3 (Smith, Hazard, Alonso)

16: Manchester United 2 (Rashford, Herrera) Chelsea 0

25: Chelsea 4 (Hazard, Cahill, Costa 2) Southampton 2 (Romeu, Bertrand)

30: Everton 0 Chelsea 3 (Pedro, Cahill, Willian)

MAY

8: Chelsea 3 (Costa, Alonso, above, Matic) Middlesbrough 0

12: West Brom 0 Chelsea 1 (Batshuayi)

ROMAN'S LEGIONS HAVE WON IT AGAIN

CHELSEA have now been crowned champions of England five times in 12 years – having just once in their previous 100-year history.

Ted Drake's legendary side topped the First Division in 1955 – but the Blues had to wait until Roman Abramovich (above) brought in Jose

Mourinho, who delivered the prize in his first season- 2004-05. He then repeated the trick the following season.

Carlo Ancelotti brought an end to three seasons of Manchester United dominance in 2010, but the Blues had to wait until 2015 for another title, under Mourinho again.

SINGING THE BLUES
Cesc Fabregas and Diego Costa lead the dressing room celebrations last night

BATMAN IS SUPER HERO

FROM BACK PAGE

my players. I have to say thanks for their commitment, their attitude and passion and their will to do something great this season.

"This win is for the players. They deserve this for their commitment through the season. We won this together. We fought a lot to win

this title. My players were fantastic in a club who supported us. I show my passion and my desire to stay with my players."

Substitute Batshuayi (left) was an unlikely hero as the £33million striker scored only his second Premier League goal and Conte admitted it has been tough for the

Belgium striker. Conte said: "I thought Hazard and Pedro were tired and we needed more energy. Michy paid me a lot with this change! It was great.

"It wasn't easy for me to arrive in England and try different habits, a different language and inherit players after a bad season."

All this in one year ..what a difference the manager makes

ANDY DUNN

Chief Sports Writer

ON the corresponding match weekend of the last Premier League season, Chelsea travelled to Sunderland and lost.

They lost 3-2 to a team that started the game in 18th position.

Seven of the Chelsea starters that day were in the team that sealed title formalities here.

John Terry was sent off in the dying moments of a defeat at the Stadium of Light that meant Chelsea had a tally of 48 points from 36 matches.

At the same stage of this season, not only are they champions courtesy of Michy Batshuayi's unlikely intervention, they are 39 points better off.

Amidst the celebrations, it is actually easy to forget how dramatic the transformation has been, not just in the statistics.

Easy to forget, with the sweet taste of success, the sourness that pained faces in the first half of last season.

Easy to forget, in the din of euphoria, the long grumble of discontent drifting from beneath the Bridge.

Easy to forget, amidst the beauty of emphatic triumph, the ordinariness of that title defence.

Easy to forget a transformation vividly personified in Eden Hazard, the only Footballer of the Year to go into hibernation for a season.

One campaign later, it has been non-stop squirrelling, relentless darting into nooks and crannies of danger. That his probing did not pay off here for him, before he hobbled off, was the night's biggest surprise.

There was, though, one brief cameo that was symptomatic of how this team toils for boss Antonio Conte (celebrating at the final whistle, below).

On one of West Brom's rare counter-attacking occasions, Hazard hared half the pitch to haul in James McClean, forcing a possession-surrendering error.

There has been a selflessness about Hazard that Jose Mourinho seemed to believe had disappeared.

It was a self-perpetuating belief. Jose got the unnecessary hump, Hazard reacted negatively.

It was an individual summation of the team's sudden slump under Mourinho.

Conte gives Hazard freedom of expression and is rewarded by a flair footballer tracking back

fifty yards. Not that he has to do that often. Not that Conte would want him to do it often.

This performance was full of the criss-crossing havoc he can cause, only without the end product.

That penchant for switching flanks with the ball is unrivalled in this league.

Apart from anything else, it has the propensity to draw fouls, a useful tool even when Michael Oliver was, contrary to West Brom protests, not at his strictest.

That no final benefit came from Hazard's shrewd scampering was down to an element of Chelsea over-confidence and over-elaboration.

When even ultra-cautious Conte, after the cruise against Middlesbrough, conceded the title was almost a given, there was always the slight threat of complacency.

Excusably, there was a swagger for much of this Chelsea performance that suggested they no longer thought if but when.

They were proved right.

The relatively unheralded component of this title triumph will inevitably be the defensive unit.

That they were resilient against the sometimes-celebrated Albion set-piece was a reflection of, amongst other things, how the second Chelsea edition of David Luiz is such a sturdier, stronger, more disciplined version than the first.

Yet, with Cesar Azpilicueta and Gary Cahill, this is a trio of defenders who each take full responsibility.

It would be wrong to call one a leader.

Like all effective defences, they work as a unit.

In their strength, they lead together.

They did not face a massive amount of hard labour at the Hawthorns but, the odd minor scare apart, never really looked like being breached and, for a long time, despite Hazard's relentless efforts, it was Chelsea's cutting edge that was lacking.

That was until Batshuayi stepped into the fray, one of the few Chelsea men with plenty to prove.

He might not have proved much but at least he found a small place in history, and not only were Chelsea champions – the transformation from a year ago was complete.

CHELSEA CHAMPIONS!  WEST BROM 0 CHELSEA 1

Batshuayi 82

RATINGS By JOHN CROSS
mirror.co.uk/sport/football

WEST BROMWICH

FOSTER 7
Fabulous save to deny Moses, a return to top form this season

DAWSON 6
Strong performance on right, all about defending but did that well

McAULEY 7
A true legend in these parts, always so committed

EVANS 7
Another rock-steady and strong display. Excellent centre-half

NYOM 6
Looks a big presence on the left of West Brom's defence, stood tall

McCLEAN Booked 6
Took out Moses twice, booked once and lucky to escape another

BRUNT 6
Good delivery with his terrific left foot, one or two moments

LIVERMORE 6
Strong and energetic in midfield but little chance to get forward

FLETCHER 7
Covered a lot of ground, always puts in the hard yards. Tenacious

FIELD Booked 6
The teenage midfielder got stuck in and West Brom fans love him

RONDON 6
Physical and strong, gave Luiz some hairy moments on the break

SUBS:
YACOB (Field 51) 6
CHADLI (McClean 59) 6
WILSON Booked (McAuley 64) 6

MOTM
CESC FABREGAS

CHELSEA

COURTOIS 6
Not much to do but made it look easy and comfortable again

AZPILICUETA 6
Another good display. Set up Batshuayi's late winner

LUIZ 7
Had ding-dong battle with Rondon – and came out on top every time

CAHILL 6
Has loved wearing the armband and must surely get it long-term

MOSES 7
Dangerous from right wing-back, caused McClean problems

MATIC 6
Patrolled midfield, looked to get a shot in and did simple things well

FABREGAS 8
Ran midfield for Chelsea. Has had such a strong influence on run-in

ALONSO 6
Got forward well and tucked in defensively. Shut down Brunt

PEDRO 7
Good darting runs from midfield, energetic and quick. Always busy

HAZARD 7
Class apart with the ball, always trying to make things happen

COSTA 7
Led the line well and was dangerous for Chelsea

SUBS:
WILLIAN (Hazard 75) 6
BATSHUAYI (Pedro 76) 7
ZOUMA (Moses 86)

WILD BLUE

Cahill: We proved our critics wrong ..WE ARE THE CHAMPIONS!

Jubilant Chelsea players are in party mood after completing a magnificent league title triumph

BY **JOHN CROSS**
Chief Football Writer

GARY CAHILL led Chelsea's wild title celebrations and roared: We have proved everyone wrong.

Blues boss Antonio Conte was seen as having no chance of winning the title in his first season, his team rank outsiders with the bookies at the start of the campaign.

But Cahill insisted they are deserved champions after winning the Premier League comfortably, and says they are the best team by far.

Centre-back Cahill, who has worn the captain's armband for much of the season, said: "You have to cherish these moments, you work so hard all season to be where we are. Consistently we have been the best team in the league. There is no better feeling in football.

"People have written us off as a team and individually and this has shut them up. We are champions. It's another one in the cabinet."

Chelsea star Eden Hazard admitted that partying with the delirious Blues supporters after the final whistle was particularly special, and paid a warm tribute to Conte.

Hazard said: "It's amazing to celebrate something with the fans, especially when the game was so difficult. We deserved a lot all season, and today we are so happy.

"He's a fantastic manager. He worked us a lot in training, and that was the key this season. So credit to him, and also the players.

"When we lost to Liverpool and Arsenal and then made an unbelievable run, winning 13 games. That's when we realised we could win the title. It's quite the same for me. It's always good.

"When you start the season, you want to win titles. Last season was difficult and we came back.

"This season we have a lot of new players, like Marcos Alonso, N'Golo Kante and Michy Batshuayi, and we did well. It's always good to win trophies, a good feeling."

Chelsea hero Batshuayi, who grabbed the 83rd-minute winner to clinch the title, said: "It's good. Everybody is happy.

"This is the best day for Chelsea. I want the trophy today.

"This is the best moment in my footballing life, for sure."

Chelsea defender John Terry, who has become a bit-part player this season, celebrated with his team-mates as he prepares to leave this summer.

Terry said: "These boys have been on the field doing it week-in, week-out.

"It's been a delight to sit and watch, a

WONDERS

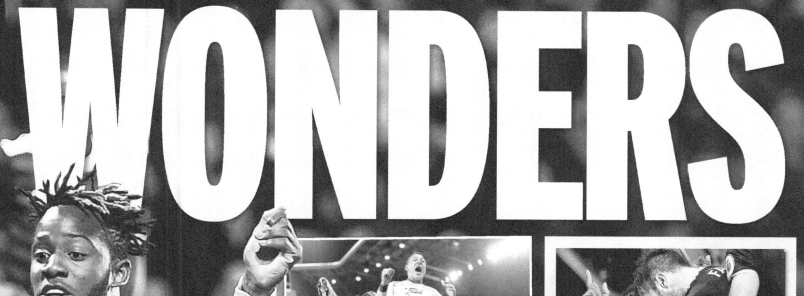

STRAIGHT OFF THE BAT
Blues substitute Batshuayi scrambles in the winner.. to get the title party started

UNLIKELY LAD
Blues substitute Batshuayi was the Chelsea goal hero

PREMIER LEAGUE THE HAWTHORNS

PARTY TIME FOR CHARMER CONTE

THEY ran onto the pitch to celebrate in front of the travelling Chelsea fans.

And right in the middle was Antonio Conte, determined to enjoy every moment.

"Antonio, Antonio," chanted the away end over and over in tribute to their party-loving manager who has led the club to a fifth Premier League title in his first season in charge.

The Chelsea squad milked it, taking it in turns to bounce title-winning hero after title-winning hero into the air.

There was John Terry doing TV interviews. The Chelsea legend will go out on a high.

But this was about a new era, a new way of winning under Conte, who has built a team which has been far better than the rest.

Tight in defence, inventive in midfield. The Italian has got the best out of Eden Hazard and Diego Costa and their goals and creativity, as well as N'Golo Kante's midfield tenacity, has been the key element in their success.

Conte's touchline histrionics were also a feature of the campaign and no one deserves the title more than the Chelsea boss.

He has been a breath of fresh air, mixing tactical nous with charm.

After the spats and divisions of last season, he has united the dressing room, made them look an unstoppable force again.

Last night's title-clinching win came from an unlikely source. Substitute Michy Batshuayi, a £33million flop since arriving last summer, got only his second Premier League goal this term – and wrote history with it.

Chelsea had dominated but failed to break down West Brom's stubborn resistance and were beginning to think they would have to leave the champagne on ice until at least Monday, when Watford visit Stamford Bridge.

But with eight minutes to go, and not long after coming on, Batshuayi slid in to turn home Cesar Azpilicueta's cross.

Cue wild celebrations.

FABREGAS TURNS THE AIR VERY BLUE

BY JOHN CROSS

CESC FABREGAS turned the air blue as Chelsea celebrated in front of millions of TV viewers.

Fabregas was being interviewed on Sky Sports as they celebrated on the pitch - and let out a swear word in excitement. The Chelsea midfielder shouted: "Football is f***ing unbelievable!"

Fabregas admitted he thought the chance to clinch the title at the Hawthorns would slip away.

He added: "I thought it was going to be one of those days. We had so many chances in the first half and then we got a bit nervous.

"The beauty of football, a player who didn't play a lot scores the winning goal for the championship."

different perspective. The togetherness was shown from day one."

Conte admitted that the turning point in Chelsea's whose season was when he went to a back three.

And his tactical switch paid dividends as they went on a 13-game winning run.

Conte said: "That decision changed our season. We had to find a new suit for our team. In my mind there was this option to play a 3-4-3 because I knew I had the players to do that.

"We were not lucky, we did a great job. It is a great season but now we can win the FA Cup.

"Every game I feel like I have played with my players!

"I show my passion and my will, my desire to stay with my players in every moment of the game. I stay with my players in positive and negative situations. We won this title together."

HOW THEY STAND

	P	W	D	L	F	A	GD	Pts
Chelsea (C)	36	28	3	5	76	29	47	87
Tottenham	35	23	8	4	71	23	48	77
Liverpool	36	20	10	6	71	42	29	70
Man City	35	20	9	6	70	37	33	69
Arsenal	35	20	6	9	68	42	26	66
Man Utd	35	17	14	4	51	27	24	65
Everton	37	17	10	10	61	41	20	61
West Brom	36	12	9	15	41	46	-5	45
Leicester	35	12	7	16	45	54	-9	43
S'hampton	35	11	9	15	39	46	-7	42
B'mouth	36	11	9	16	52	65	-13	42
West Ham	36	11	9	16	45	59	-14	42
Stoke	36	10	11	15	39	52	-13	41
Burnley	36	11	7	18	37	51	-14	40
Watford	36	11	7	18	37	59	-22	40
C Palace	36	11	5	20	46	61	-15	38
Swansea	36	10	5	21	41	69	-28	35
Hull	36	9	7	20	36	69	-33	34
Mid'bro (R)	36	5	13	18	26	48	-22	28
Sun'land (R)	35	6	6	23	28	60	-32	24

MATCH STATS

32%	POSSESSION	68%
2	SHOTS ON TARGET	5
2	SHOTS OFF TARGET	10
5	CORNERS	8
3	OFFSIDE	1
13	FOULS	8
3 **0**	CARDS	**0** 0

REF: Michael Oliver **ATT:** 25,367

DM1ST

CHELSEA 5
Willian 8, Hazard 61, Pedro 77, Batshuayi 90, 90

SUNDERLAND 1
Manquillo 3

RATINGS by DARREN LEWIS
mirror.co.uk/sport/football

CHELSEA

COURTOIS 7
Exposed for Sunderland's shock opener but composed otherwise

ALONSO 7
Hit the bar before the equaliser. Always a threat

AZPILICUETA 7
Solid and consistent either side of a few tricky moments

TERRY 6
Emotional cameo in order to milk the applause for his send-off

LUIZ 7
Not the easiest of rides against a relegated Sunderland side

MOSES 7
Totally composed as usual in all that he did

KANTE 7
Made everything tick in the middle - just as he usually does

FABREGAS 7
Couldn't quite get going against stubborn side but decent enough

HAZARD 9
Stunning second-half goal to cap a stunning season for him

WILLIAN 8
Hit the equaliser, almost set up a third for Batshuayi. Quality

COSTA Booked 7
An off-day for the Brazilian marksman. Was it his farewell?

SUBS: Batshuayi (Costa 62) **8**
Pedro (Hazard 71) **8**
Cahill (Terry 26) **7**

MOTM
EDEN HAZARD

SUNDERLAND

PICKFORD 5
Another couple of decent saves after good display at Arsenal

JONES Booked 4
Sent this way and that by Hazard in the first half

LESCOTT 4
Nightmare header from the star to allow Pedro in for 3-1

O'SHEA 4
Took a first-half whack in the face from Costa for his troubles

MANQUILLO 6
Smashed in a lovely early goal to leave the Bridge stunned

CATTERMOLE 5
Defiant in the middle as ever but just not good enough

RODWELL 4
Hung in there as Chelsea lost their way but soon outclassed

LARSSON 4
All the effort but lacked class as the hosts stepped it up

OVIEDO 4
Never able to land a blow with Chelsea just too good

JANUZAJ 4
Another who was just not good enough to make an impact

BORINI 4
Lots of running but no end product whatsoever

SUBS: Gooch (Januzaj 62) **4**
Gibson (Cattermole 88)

THANK YOU TERRY MUCH

Champs tribute to skipper JT.. now Blues can look to future

BY **DARREN LEWIS**

IN the end, the perfect day.

Bathed in sunshine, ticker-tape and afforded a guard of honour, John Terry received the emotional send-off his trophy-laden service for Chelsea over two decades had earned.

Then, the dawn of a new era under Antonio Conte.

Blues fans were losing a legend but gaining a serial winner who has left the Premier League trailing in his wake.

Soaked in Champagne, Conte lifted his first title since being tasked by the board last summer with restoring the club's glory days.

A move through the gears saw off Sunderland and made the Blues the first English team to record 30 wins in a Premier League season. Thibaut Courtois (right) clinched the Golden Gloves for the most clean sheets with 16 shut-outs.

Blur's Parklife provided the soundtrack as supporters partied in the stands, while the players, flanked by their wives and children, passed the Premier League trophy around.

Then, Terry was handed the microphone. He and Chelsea had been vilified for the substitution in the 26th minute (the number of his shirt) which had allowed Stamford Bridge to mark the end of his 22 years as a Blues player with their goodbyes.

Why though? Terry is Mr Chelsea. He has an affinity with the club's fans like no other player.

He has put his body on the line to earn 15 major trophies, including five titles, the Champions League and Europa League. He could lift a sixth FA Cup later this month.

This game was a dead rubber. Terry had agreed his exit with Conte. David Moyes had agreed for his Sunderland players to kick the ball into touch in order to form a guard of honour. Where was the problem?

Terry struggled to hold it together as he addressed the faithful. He fought back tears as he spoke of one of the most difficult days of his life.

He paid tribute to owner Roman Abramovich, who beamed a smile, waved and clapped maniacally as the fans joined in.

The tears welled up again as Terry thanked his wife and kids, then the supporters for "picking me up when I was down".

Rival fans and social media may have tut-tutted, but this was Chelsea's party. They were allowed to cry if they wanted to.

Earlier the goals had flowed

PREMIER LEAGUE STAMFORD BRIDGE

MATCH STATS

71%	POSSESSION	29%
8	SHOTS ON TARGET	3
12	SHOTS OFF TARGET	2
11	CORNERS	1
0	OFFSIDE	1
8	FOULS	15
1 0	CARDS	1 0

TALK OF THE TOWN
Terry with boss Conte after his speech to fans and above with his title-winning team-mates

with Sunderland taking a surprise third-minute lead. Javier Manquillo smashed in the opener after Seb Larsson's free-kick had been deflected to the right side of the box.

Willian drove an effort in from the right to equalise five minutes later. Eden Hazard smashed in a peach just after the hour, before Pedro came off the bench to score with 13 minutes left.

The Spaniard went on to make two more for fellow sub Michy Batshuayi at the death – all part of a perfect day.

LEGEND'S GOODBYE TO BRIDGE

FROM BACK PAGE

before Antonio Conte's men lifted their fifth Premier League title. Terry was handed a rare start for his final home appearance but Chelsea's No.26 was then taken off after just 26 minutes and given a guard of honour by team-mates.

He returned to the pitch to address the crowd during the trophy celebrations, thanking Blues owner Roman Abramovich (above) and his family.

A tearful Terry said: "Today is without doubt one of the most difficult of my life. You guys are the best supporters in the world. You've given me everything from the age of 14. Thank you will never, ever be enough." The defender, 36, has yet to decide whether to retire or join a new club.

FOOTBALL SPY

THE ORIGINAL GOSSIP COLUMN... LATEST NEWS... THE BIGGEST MOVES...

£20M GIBSON IN DEMAND

BY JOHN CROSS

LEICESTER and West Brom are trying to prise Ben Gibson away from Middlesbrough.

Both Midlands clubs have scouted him extensively and will lead the summer chase.

Stoke also hope to be in with a shout while Chelsea, Liverpool and Tottenham have looked at Gibson (right).

The £20million-rated central defender admitted: "I think every player in the world wants to play in the Premier League, everyone wants to play at the top level. I'm no different to that. What I would say is that no decision has been made regarding my future as of yet."

England boss Gareth Southgate is likely to involve Gibson, 24, in the end-of-season internationals against Scotland and France.

» DAVID OSPINA is in talks with Fenerbahce about a £5million move. Arsenal's No.2 keeper has become frustrated at a lack of chances playing second fiddle to Petr Cech, and the Turks are long-time admirers.

Ospina still has two years left on his current deal with the club but is determined to quit the Gunners this summer.

CRYSTAL PALACE ARE HAGGLING WITH MARSEILLE OVER THE PRICE FOR STEVE MANDANDA TO GO BACK TO FRANCE

CHELSEA 1 MANCHESTER UNITED 0
Hazard 22 (pen)

RATINGS
by Simon Mullock & Neil Moxley

CHELSEA

COURTOIS *Booked*
MotM Outstanding.
Stunning saves to deny
Jones and Rashford — **8**

AZPILICUETA
Another top display by
Mr Consistency, but
had to dig deep — **7**

CAHILL
Marshalled the men
around him when Blues
were under the cosh — **7**

RUDIGER
Rock at heart of the
Chelsea defence and
now a club cult hero — **7**

MOSES
Needed to defend
more than usual, but
was up to the task — **7**

FABREGAS
Great pass that led to
the first goal, but faded
after the break — **7**

KANTE
Covered every blade of
Wembley grass and
didn't waste a pass — **7**

BAKAYOKO
Did well in flashes in a
display that summed
up Frenchman's season — **6**

ALONSO
Should have put
Chelsea out of sight.
Struggled with pace — **6**

HAZARD
Put Chelsea ahead
from the spot after
being fouled by Jones — **8**

GIROUD
Linked well with Hazard
but lacked service in
the second half — **6**

SUBS: Morata (Giroud 86),
Willian (Hazard 90)

MAN UTD

DE GEA
Smart stops from
Hazard and Alonso.
Well beaten from spot — **6**

VALENCIA *Booked*
Lacked usual energy
going forward and was
troubled by Hazard — **6**

SMALLING
Dealt with Giroud's
aerial threat well, did
his job proficiently — **7**

JONES *Booked*
On his heels for the
decisive goal, not his
best afternoon — **5**

YOUNG
Provided a decent
outlet, but delivery
from wide was poor — **5**

MATIC
Mourinho's stand-out
player. On top of his
game from the first — **5**

HERRERA
Played out of position.
Battled gamely, but
was found wanting — **8**

POGBA
Should be dominating
big games, but still no
signs of him doing it — **6**

LINGARD
Provided energy, but
little else. Needed to
show more — **5**

RASHFORD
A big audition, but he's
not yet ready to lead
United attack — **5**

SANCHEZ
Strange afternoon.
Lacked his normal fizz.
Minimal threat — **5**

SUBS: Lukaku (Rashford 73)
6, Martial (Lingard 73) 5,
Mata (Jones 87)

FACTS
■ Chelsea have won their
eighth FA Cup and their first
since 2012, level with
Tottenham - only Man Utd
(12) and Arsenal (13) have
won more.
■ **Seven of the last 10 FA
Cup winners have been
London clubs (Chelsea 4,
Arsenal 3).**
■ Jose Mourinho has lost his
first cup final in charge of an
English club, after winning
each of the previous six (4 x
League Cup, 1 x FA Cup, 1x
Europa League).
■ Antonio Conte has
tasted success in a
domestic cup final for the
first time in three
attempts as a manager,
after losing with Juventus
vs Napoli in the 2012
Coppa Italia, and the 2017
FA Cup with Chelsea
against Arsenal.

VITAL STATS *opta*

CHELSEA		MAN UTD
3	Shots on Target	5
1	Shots off Target	9
2	Blocked Shots	4
5	Corners	9
11	Fouls	13
3	Offsides	1
1	Yellow Cards	2
0	Red Cards	0
74.1	Passing Success	87.9
22	Tackles	15
68.2	Tackles Won %	80
33.6	Possession	66.4
38.9	Territorial Adv %	61.1
305	Total Passes	586
5	Total Crosses	34
34.9	1st Half Poss	65.1
32.3	2nd Half Poss	67.7

REFEREE: Michael Oliver 7.
ATTENDANCE: 87,647

HERE COMES
Conte's Blues finally win silverware to end a

BY **SIMON MULLOCK**
at Wembley

SO Antonio Conte's final act
as Chelsea boss will be to
drink from the poisoned
chalice called the FA Cup.

Eden Hazard's 22nd-minute
penalty ensured the Italian's
reign came to an end with
another piece of silverware for
Roman Abramovich.

But it won't be enough to
save Conte from the sack.

And it was ironic that the
players who failed to be
consistent enough to deliver a
top-four finish, sent Conte on

his way with a performance
that bristled with character.

Conte and Mourinho shared
a hug at the final whistle when
they probably felt like
strangling each other.

Mourinho had wanted this
one badly – and on another day
United's second-half onslaught
would have realised at least an
equaliser.

But the Red Army had every
right to ask why their team
only woke up after sleeping
through the first 45 minutes.

With Romelu Lukaku only
making the bench, due to

injury, opportunity knocked for
Marcus Rashford. But he failed
to open the door.

When he scuffed a decent
chance just before the break, it
summed up a first half in which
he had Mourinho
shaking his head.

Not that the
Portuguese was
faultless. He
had a game
plan in which
Ander Herrera
s h a d o w e d
Hazard (right) to
make the contest

10 versus 10. It had worked
before. But this time, Conte
had planned for it by giving
Hazard the freedom to roam

Herrera ended up standing
next to United right-back
Antonio Valencia and
marking no one.

Hazard saw an
early angled
drive saved by
the feet of
David De Gea.
But he was
soon looking
into the whites of
the Spain keeper's

eyes again – and this time it
was decisive. The Belgian
sensed that Cesc Fabregas was
going to feed a first-time pass
down the right-hand channel
in the 21st minute and, when
Phil Jones's brilliant first touch took him clear.

It seemed Jones was running
in quicksand as he tried to
catch Chelsea's No.10.

And when he did close the
gap, he could only slide through
the back of Hazard's legs as he
shaped to shoot from deep
inside the United penalty area.

Chelsea felt the challenge

EMIRATES FA CUP FINAL FROM WEMBLEY

HEAD OFF: France star considers future after snub

WE BLUE 'EM AWAY Chelsea players and staff celebrate FA Cup victory after Hazard (right) clinched it with his penalty

THE PRIDE!
disappointing season in blaze of glory

Snub could see Martial quit United

BY **PHIL BLANCHE**

DAVID GINOLA believes Anthony Martial might be tempted to leave Manchester United after being left out of France's World Cup squad.

Martial missed out when Didier Deschamps named his 23-man squad for Russia on Thursday, being placed on the stand-by list, despite starting France's last friendly game.

The 22-year-old's omission comes after he was marginalised at United with the arrival of Alexis Sanchez in January and speculation over a summer move to Chelsea.

"The reason Anthony Martial is not in the squad is that you need to be a regular in your club before becoming a regular in your national team," said Ginola.

"Deschamps has so many options – strikers such as Kylian Mbappe and Antoine Griezmann, who have been consistently good for France.

"Players like Martial need to play and score goals for the confidence.

"If he is not a regular at Manchester United, he will probably search for another club."

Email axe for Collins

FROM BACK PAGE

his future before the end of the season. But Moyes couldn't give him any promises as the boss didn't know whether or not he'd be staying at the end of his own short-term contract.

Moyes was let go last week and the club decided to take the same option with cult hero Collins.

The Welshman was emailed the news just days before yesterday's deadline for Premier League clubs to submit their retained list of players for the top flight.

The Hammers insist "Ginge" knew it was unlikely he would get a new deal and the memo was written confirmation.

Manuel Pellegrini – the favourite to replace Moyes – left his club, Hebei China Fortune, last night.

---

warranted more than the yellow card shown to Jones.

But, once Conte had calmed himself down, Hazard brought a smile to his boss' face by sending De Gea the wrong way.

Paul Pogba headed over from close range and then fired wide from 25 yards.

But Alexis Sanchez's attempts to score directly from successive corners left Mourinho frustrated.

And so did the downward header that Jones planted wide just before the break.

United were a different beast

after the interval. Rashford let fly with a thunderbolt from just inside the box that was beaten away by Thibaut Courtois.

And perhaps Courtois deserved the huge slice of luck that broke his way just after the hour.

He produced a stunning fingertip save to divert Jones' header on to his left-hand post and although Sanchez guided the loose ball into the net, he had drifted an inch offside.

Marcos Alonso had the chance to finish the contest when he was put clear by

N'Golo Kante, but the Spaniard fired straight at De Gea.

Rashford saw another chance go begging when he broke clear, Courtois this time standing tall to defy the striker as he attempted a clipped finish.

Mourinho sent on Lukaku and Anthony Martial in a last desperate bid to break Chelsea's resistance.

The Portuguese probably feared the worst when Paul Pogba rose alone to meet Martial's corner only to direct his downward header wide.

He was right to.

CRUCIAL MOMENT: United's Jones takes out Hazard for Blues' penalty

DMLI

THE FULL ENGLISH 1

CHELSEA 4 ARSENAL 1
Giroud 49, Pedro 60, Hazard 65 pen, 72   Iwobi 68

RATINGS by DARREN LEWIS
mirror.co.uk/sport/football

CHELSEA

ARRIZABALAGA **6**
Flapped at Maitland-Niles' cross and lucky not to concede penalty

AZPILICUETA **8**
Good 16th-minute block to deny Sokratis on the left of the box

CHRISTENSEN **7**
Booked Not bad overall after Arsenal's early dominance

LUIZ **7**
Struggled in the first half against the pace of Maitland-Niles

EMERSON **8**
Poor in first half, but inch-perfect cross for Giroud's diving header

KANTE **8**
Wasn't he supposed to be unfit? Ran Arsenal's midfield ragged

JORGINHO **8**
Nice block to prevent Maitland-Niles cross reaching six-yard box

KOVACIC **7**
Neat and tidy in possession - but not potent going forward

PEDRO **8**
Booked Yellow card for diving, but grabbed Chelsea's second goal

GIROUD **8**
Blew two first-half chances, scored with third, teed up Hazard

HAZARD **9**
MOTM Involved in first two goals. Deserved his own double to seal win

SUBS: Willian (Pedro 71) 6 Barkley (Kovacic 76) 6 Zappacosta (Hazard 89)

ARSENAL

CECH **5**
Nightmare end to his career. Not the fairytale send-off he wanted

SOKRATIS **4**
Couldn't get his 32nd minute header on target. Was awful after

KOSCIELNY **3**
Slow for Giroud's opener. And slow to react for Pedro's goal

MONREAL **4**
Taken apart by Chelsea movement. Replaced in the second half

MAITLAND-NILES **5**
Dangerous in the first half. Clumsy after break bringing down Giroud

TORREIRA **5**
Super ball almost fed Lacazette. But unable to cope with Blues

XHAKA **5**
Unlucky to see his 27th-minute screamer skim the bar

KOLASINAC **4**
Kept finding good positions, but kept wasting possession

OZIL **3**
Went missing as the going got tough in the second half

LACAZETTE **5**
Just couldn't reach Aubameyang's 27th minute cross with head

AUBAMEYANG **5**
Should have done better from his ninth minute chance

SUBS: Guendouzi (Monreal 66) 5 Iwobi (Torreira 67) 6 Willock (Ozil 77) 6

WON MORE.

Hazard signs off with stunning display to seal Blues'

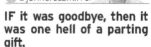

FROM **JOHN CROSS**
Chief Football Writer
@johncrossmirror

IF it was goodbye, then it was one hell of a parting gift.

Eden Hazard scored twice and made it clear he wants to leave Chelsea in his post-match TV interview even before lifting the trophy on a night Arsenal and UEFA will want to forget.

Hazard made it his night in a London derby played 3,000 miles from home, and delivered another match-winning performance and another piece of silverware for the Blues. He will be a loss to English football and not just to his club.

This was the 16th major trophy of Roman Abramovich's 16-year reign and, for once, Chelsea's billionaire Russian owner was in the Olympic Stadium in Baku to see it.

He, of course, was one of the lucky ones. Many fans of both clubs could not make the trip following UEFA's farcical decision to host a major final in Azerbaijan.

This should serve as a warning that without the fans, the lifeblood of the game, then football is nothing.

It was a derby with a European trophy at stake played out in a strange atmosphere with no passion and far too few real supporters.

The Unai Emery magic touch in the Europa League also ran out, his three previous successes at Sevilla counting for little with Arsenal looking unbalanced and woefully short of ideas and quality.

Their capitulation – conceding four goals in 23 minutes – was embarrassing. There are too many gaps in the team and another season out of the Champions League means less money for improvements.

Chelsea, on the other hand, disprove the football logic which says clubs need stability.

Their revolving-door policy with managers ensures there is never a dull moment. Maurizio Sarri looks to be heading for the exit despite winning a European trophy and finishing third in the Premier League.

They have high standards at Stamford Bridge, yet the uncertainty seems to bring the best out of the players.

Arsenal started better but Chelsea's collection of big-game players and serial winners rode it out to get the

MATCH STATS

50%	POSSESSION	50%
8	SHOTS ON TARGET	2
1	SHOTS OFF TARGET	9
7	CORNERS	5
1	OFFSIDE	3
14	FOULS	11
2 0	CARDS	0 0

REFEREE: Gianluca Rocchi

FOR THE ROAD

BAK IN THE OLD ROUTINE
It's party time as Chelsea's jubilant squad celebrate after cruising to victory in a one-sided Europa League final in Baku

1-0

2-0

3-0

3-1

4-1

16th trophy of Abramovich era

EDEN STARS IN CHELSEA ROUT

FROM BACK PAGE

is the perfect end. I want to say to the fans that I love them, they are part of my family and I will always support Chelsea.

"If it is a goodbye, thank you for these seven years.

"We will decide in a few days and the only target in my mind tonight was to win this final.

"I have made my decision already. I think it is a goodbye, but in football you never know.

"My dream was to play in the Premier League and I have done that for one of the biggest clubs so maybe now it is the time for a new challenge.

"It is up to the clubs. We will see in the next couple of days."

Chelsea boss Maurizio Sarri said he has known "for a long time" Hazard wanted to go and also revealed he will speak to the club about his own future.

Sarri said: "We deserved to win. Tomorrow I will begin to speak with my club.

"We need to know what the club can do for me, and what I can do better for the club.

"Then, after a couple of days, I will decide. I have a contract so, at the moment, we are talking about nothing."

Chelsea's thumping victory in front of Russian owner Roman Abramovich (above) was a devastating blow for Arsenal who missed out on a place in the Champions League.

Mesut Ozil was booed when he was substituted while others looked close to tears.

Boss Unai Emery said: "Maybe some players need to leave, to take a new way.

"I'm not very proud of not hitting our target, but very proud of our work.

"Other players will come in and help us get better."

job done. Arsenal can rightly complain about Henrikh Mkhitaryan not being in Baku, but others did not turn up either, most notably Mesut Ozil. He again went missing and was booed when substituted for Joe Willock in the second half.

The Gunners were the better team in the first half an hour. Alexandre Lacazette felt he should have had a penalty, Pierre-Emerick Aubameyang missed a big chance and Granit Xhaka sent a shot just over.

But Chelsea know how to win and after 49 minutes, as is often the case in football, a player was back to haunt his old club. Olivier Giroud's flying header beat Petr Cech but Chelsea's former Arsenal striker did not celebrate.

On the hour, they got a second. Mateo Kovacic started the move, Hazard found Pedro and although the Spanish winger scuffed his shot it still bobbled past Cech and into the far corner.

Ainsley Maitland-Niles' push on Giroud gifted Hazard a penalty which he slotted home.

Alex Iwobi came on as a substitute for the Gunners and smashed home a brilliant shot, but any hope of a comeback was short lived.

Hazard got his second of the night and Chelsea's fourth after 72 minutes when he guided in a half volley from Giroud's cross.

Hazard is a class act and will be missed but this was yet another big trophy.

Arsenal, meanwhile, have got out of the winning habit and Emery's biggest task is to bring that back to the Emirates.

DMIST

Pog for Oz say Reds

BY **DAVID McDONNELL**

MANCHESTER UNITED say Paul Pogba will travel to Australia on Sunday for the start of a pre-season tour.

Pogba, who admitted he wants to leave United, has yet to return to pre-season training with the squad.

Most of United's squad returned from their summer break on Monday, but Pogba was the most high-profile absentee.

He has been linked with a move to Real Madrid or return to Juventus, but he has still not returned to begin preparations for the new season.

But United are adamant he will fly to Perth with the rest of the squad.

The squad members were given time off, according to international schedules this summer.

Pogba made three appearances for France in June, which is why United boss Ole Gunnar Solskjaer allowed him extra time off, but his future is uncertain.

SUPPORT Joe Montemurro

Lionesses spark plan

FROM BACK PAGE

success, Arsenal will stage more of their women's games at their main stadium around Premier League fixtures as a way of improving attendances and the profile of the WSL.

The "double-header" idea of playing women's games before or after Premier League fixtures is being discussed at the top of the game to capitalise on the popularity of England's success in reaching the World Cup semi-final.

Arsenal manager Joe Montemurro said: "This will showcase some of the highest quality in women's football and it will enable more Arsenal supporters to see them in action."

CHELSEA FANS DELIGHT AS LEGEND

I'M MISTER

18 years ago Lamps had to prove he was good enough to be a star at the Bridge ...now he's ready to prove he can raise the standards of this most demanding club, insisting: I know what it takes to be a Blue

CLUB-BY-CLUB RECORD

Team	Mats	Gls
West Ham 1995-2001	187	39
Swansea City (loan) 1995-96	9	1
Chelsea 2001-14	648	211
Man City 2014-15	38	8
New York City FC 2015-16	31	15
Total	913	274

ENGLAND RECORD

England 1999-2014	106	29

HIS CHELSEA HONOURS

Premier League: 2004-05, 2005-06, 2009-10
FA Cup: 2006-07, 2008-09, 2009-10, 2011-12
League Cup: 2004-05, 2006-07
Community Shield: 2005, 2009
Champions League: 2011-12
Europa League: 2012-13

BY **JOHN CROSS**
Chief Football Writer
@johncrossmirror

FRANK LAMPARD arrived at Chelsea as a player 18 years ago with everything to prove.

Now he is putting himself under the same pressure after making a fairy-tale return as a manager.

There are no excuses or free passes because of Chelsea's transfer ban or the fact Eden Hazard has gone.

Lampard, 41, stressed he will not go on about his own past glories but, equally, says the standards are as high today as they were when he, Didier Drogba and co ruled Europe.

The former England midfielder, who won every major trophy in a glittering 13-year career at Stamford Bridge, claims no one needed to set him targets because he expects to be challenging from day one.

"Coming here 18 years ago was a challenge," said Lampard. "I remember driving home and had the radio on, and some were questioning whether I should be here for £11 million.

"I worked really hard to put that right as a player, and now I'm in a position where I have to work really hard to be successful as a manager here.

"The reality is that the owner has won 16 trophies in 16 years – huge success. He runs it as his own desire and his desire has always been for the best of the club. He has chosen me, hopefully on that premise.

"Maybe I am at fault for mentioning the Drogbas and so on. What you won't hear me saying, though, is that, in my era, we used to do this and we used to do that.

"I don't want to be going back in time to what we did before, or this is how Chelsea should be. The football world is moving on really quickly and I want to be open-minded, I want to be moving with it.

"We know about the transfer ban, and that Manchester City and Liverpool pulled away slightly last year. We have to be realistic about that, but we should never stop trying for Chelsea to be up there.

"I don't want to proclaim that we will do this and that, but my instinct was to come to this job and will always be that we have to be competitive and look to start the season looking to win.

"My job is now to push on and be successful." Lampard

CECH MATE Lampard was watched by technical adviser Petr Cech, director Marina Granovskaia and chairman Bruce Buck

was so polished in what he said that he even refused to say it was a "dream job" for fear of it becoming a headline.

There was never any chance of him proclaiming himself the "Special One", as Jose Mourinho did, but he wants to leave his own mark on the Blues and create his own history.

Lampard says he will speak to Chelsea owner Roman Abramovich in the next few days, as the squad head to Dublin to begin pre-season, but his first target is to demand the same pride and professionalism he had as a player.

"I don't have to give myself a name or a title, but I love this club and I want to do my best. If we are successful, then you can

LAMPARD IS BACK AT THE BRIDGE

CHELSEA!

THE YOUNG GUNS OUT TO IMPRESS LAMPARD

THE CLUB HE LOVES Lampard wants his players to feel the same way he does – and be honoured to be part of the team

	Starts	Sub	Gls
Ethan Ampadu, **18**, defender	7	5	0
Callum Hudson-Odoi, **18**, forward	18	16	9
Mason Mount, **20**, midfield	0	0	0
Tammy Abraham, **21**, striker	0	3	0
Fikayo Tomori, **21**, defender	0	1	0
Ruben Loftus-Cheek, **23**, midfielder	29	42	12

THREE PREMIER LEAGUE TITLES

ONE EUROPA LEAGUE CROWN

FOUR FA CUPS

'I DON'T EXPECT ANY FAVOURS'

ONE CHAMPIONS LEAGUE TROPHY

ask me at the end," he said. "It is not easy every year. Nobody can win the league year in, year out, and have complete success.

"But for me that desire hasn't changed so, when I do speak to the owner, I expect him to demand the same things I demand of myself and the team.

"The players have to drive that to a degree. But it will be a part of my message, that you have to 'feel' the club. You should feel very privileged to be here, play here... I will promote that daily.

"If you run out on the pitch, you have to feel that way – it enhances performances and training, puts a smile on your face every day, and that's what I want players to do."

The Blues are preparing for a

youth revolution under Lampard. England Under-21 midfielder Kasey Palmer, 22, has become the latest academy graduate to decide to stay at the Bridge next season.

And the likes of Ethan Ampadu, Mason Mount, Andreas Christensen and Callum Hudson-Odoi can expect to get more game time too.

Lampard added: "My eyes will always be open to young players, but they have to show they are good enough.

"I am not going to be doing young boys favours and putting them in."

FROM BACK PAGE on what I do here and what I do going forward."

Former Derby County boss Lampard, 41, confessed it was always his dream to return to Stamford Bridge from the moment he became a manager – but knows he is putting his whole reputation on the line.

He said: "I am quite bold. You have to be in football because the minute I stepped into management, I did what I want to do.

"This is no disrespect to Derby, a fantastic club for me. I was ambitious as a player, I wanted to manage at the top. The

opportunity to come here, having had my link here, this is an obvious club I would love to manage, simple as that.

"The minute I started management, I realised this could be the case. I knew if I did OK, I could get the job at Chelsea and risk it.

"I have belief in myself and try to be the best manager I can. I understand the risk, but would rather look at the upside.

"Can I go and do something similar to my playing career and have the same success (as a manager) that I had as a player?

"I am a realist and I don't want favours going into something. That is not the way I work."

PEREZ TARGETS EUROPE

BY JAMES NURSEY

AYOZE PEREZ is aiming for Europe with Leicester after completing a £30million switch from Newcastle.

The Spanish forward, who has penned a four-year deal, is also aiming to improve on his haul of 12 top-flight goals last term.

"Leicester want to keep growing and that's something I liked – the ambition of the club," said the 25-year-old. "We have to keep looking to get into the European positions. That's the ambition. And as a striker, I have to help the team as much as I can with goals."

Perez (above) says boss Brendan Rodgers was key in persuading him to join. "He's been a big part of the deal," he said. The Foxes have added full-back James Justin from Luton and want to make Youri Tielemans a permanent signing.

RAMS HAVE THEIR PHILL

BY JAMES NURSEY

PHILLIP COCU is jetting off to America to link up with Derby County's squad for pre-season training.

Cocu will be confirmed today as Frank Lampard's successor at the Championship Rams.

The ex-Holland midfielder (right) and former PSV Eindhoven boss, 48, is due to pen a long-term deal at Pride Park.

Derby's 26-man squad flew to Florida yesterday for a training camp and two friendlies. New boss Cocu was due to follow on after completing the paperwork for his new post.

SPURS WILL GO FLOR IT

BY DARREN LEWIS

TOTTENHAM could follow the record deal for Tanguy Ndombele by signing his former club's talent spotter.

Florian Maurice, who heads up Lyon's transfer committee, is believed to be unsettled after a reshuffle at the club. It has left Spurs considering adding Maurice (above) to their £65million Ndombele deal.

Ndombele was signed by Lyon from Amiens for £7m two years ago after a successful loan.

Former Spurs right-back Pascal Chimbonda, meanwhile, believes the club were right not to rival Manchester United's £50m purchase of Crystal Palace defender Aaron Wan-Bissaka.

He said: "He's still very far from becoming a proven player. Tottenham need to strengthen other parts and Wan-Bissaka would have taken a massive wedge out of the budget."

Weather

TODAY
A generally cloudy day with showers, rain later

Most of the UK will see a generally cloudy day with scattered showers and occasional brighter spells. Through the afternoon, a heavy band of rain will move into northern and western areas. A moderate southwesterly breeze.

---

10 MIN CROSSWORD

ACROSS
2 Feeling of resentment (6)
5 – Moore, GI Jane? (4)
6 Although (6)
7 Crop such as maize (4)
8 Tag (3)
11 Medicinal herb, – vera (4)
13 Short-sighted (6)
14 Kiln for drying hops (4)
15 Character created by Edgar Rice Burroughs (6)

DOWN
1 Roman emperor (4)
2 Huge mythical being (5)
3 Antlered animal (4)
4 Tempt (6)
7 Carry out (6)
9 Breakfast rasher (5)
10 Entrance to a room (4)
12 Remove from power (4)

FRIDAY'S SOLUTIONS ACROSS: 6 Heave, 7 Leo, 8 Ill at ease, 13 Deterrent, 18 Sun, 19 Elite. **DOWN:** 1 Thai, 2 Haul, 3 Wept, 4 Ulna, 5 Ooze, 9 Lie, 10 Awe, 11 Err, 12 Son, 13 Dose, 14 Tony, 15 Reel, 16 Eric, 17 T-rex.

Brought to you by CROSSWORD

CORONAVIRUS CRISIS:
GAME

ON
Horse-racing at Cheltenham

OFF
No games at the Emirates

» **Fears over clubs going to the wall and big job losses**

» **Large gatherings banned next week & work at home push**

BY **GRAHAM HISCOTT**
Head of Business and **BEN GLAZE**
Deputy Political Editor

THE mass suspension of football games and sport events has sparked fears of big job losses and clubs being driven to the wall.

All elite football in England was yesterday called off until April 3 in a bid to tackle the worsening outbreak of the coronavirus.

Wales's Six Nations match against Scotland today has been postponed as has tomorrow's Premiership Rugby Cup final between Sale and Harlequins.

Others sports, from cricket and golf to motor racing, have also either been ditched or delayed.

Next month's Virgin Money London Marathon was postponed until Sunday, October 4 and the Manchester marathon on April 5 was also called off.

It means thousands of fans could lose cash on travel tickets already booked to go to events.

But yesterday's Gold Cup at Cheltenham, which was attended by 60,00 people, still went ahead.

Later, sources said the Government will officially ban all mass gatherings across Britain from next weekend in the fight against the deadly virus – which has killed 11 people here. The number of confirmed cases yesterday leapt from 590 to 798.

Ministers yesterday pushed for more people to work from home.

The unprecedented delay of so many sports events could prove a crippling blow to clubs' finances, and the firms that rely on sports for their livelihood.

Swathes of businesses, from food stalls to pubs, hotels, coach firms, and printers will be hammered.

Others, including airlines, cinemas and restaurants, have either suffered a slump in sales or are braced for the worst as the virus spreads across the UK.

Dale Vince, chairman of League Two club Forest Green Rovers, feared the suspension will mean the rest of the season being axed.

He said: "It will blow a hole in our finances. It won't sink us but it may be more devastating for some of the other clubs to deal with."

Shrewsbury Town's chief executive Brian Caldwell warned it could cost the League One club between £200,000 and £250,000 in lost ticket sales. He said: "I look at some of the others in League One and Two who haven't paid their wages on time and it will have a devastating effect."

The Football Association, Premier League, EFL, Barclays FA Women's Super League and FA Women's Championship collectively agreed to postpone their games in England. UEFA has put off next week's Champions League and Europa League fixtures. England's March friendlies with Italy and Denmark are also off.

Top-flight clubs, benefitting from TV rights money will not be affected as badly.

Sky and BT Sports confirmed they would not be refunding customers as a result of the delays.

But both outfits revealed they would broadcast any postponed games when they are rescheduled. Which? consumer rights expert Adam French said fans with tickets for games will be entitled to refunds if they cannot make the new date.

But he added: "It could be harder to get a refund on any travel or accommodation booked for the match, unless it was purchased as part of a package."

The devolved government in Scotland has advised against gatherings of more than 500, meaning football will be played

---

UK LATEST
Cases (up 208):	**798**
Deaths (up 1):	**11**

WORLD LATEST
Cases:	**145,336**
Deaths:	**5,416**

SPORTS FIXTURES CANCELLED
CHANGER

WE ARE LIVERPOOL

Food & Drink

OFF Wales won't play Scotland

OFF No games at Anfield stadium

REDUCTION BA has warned staff

BA tells staff to prepare for job cuts, groundings

BY **GRAHAM HISCOTT**
Head of Business

BRITISH Airways yesterday told staff it expected to make job cuts and ground more planes, calling the crisis "worse than 9/11".

Unions fear redundancies at Edinburgh Airport which warned it could be facing "close to zero" passenger demand.

In a message titled "the survival of BA", chief executive Alex Cruz said: "Please do not underestimate the seriousness of this for our company."

He said BA, which has 45,000 staff, is under "immense pressure" and will "have to react fast and definitively in response to the worsening situation".

As a result, jobs would be lost "perhaps for a short period, perhaps longer term" and BA is in discussions with trade unions.

A BA spokeswoman declined to comment when asked how many jobs could go.

Meanwhile global stock markets staged a rally yesterday – a day after the worst crash for more than 30 years.

The FTSE 100 closed the day up 128.63 at 5366.1, with the 2.5% rise clawing back £32billion of the £160bn shed on Thursday.

Russ Mould, investment director at City firm AJ Bell, said: "That truly was a nightmare of a week for savers and investors."

Germany's Dax gained 0.8% and France's Cac had a 1.8% win.

---

behind closed doors from Monday. It is the first time there has been such a widespread suspension of sport since Princess Diana's funeral in 1997.

No10, which has faced criticism for its slow response to the virus crisis, announced mass gatherings such as sports events, gigs and conferences, will be banned.

A Whitehall source said the move will help free up emergency services rather than curb the virus spread.

The insider declined to say how many constituted a mass gathering but added: "Ministers are working with the Chief Scientific Adviser and Chief Medical Officer on our plan to

stop various types of public event. We are also talking to businesses and other bodies about the timing of moving towards much more widespread working from home.

"We are concerned about the burden large events put on public services, including the NHS and police, from dealing with coronavirus.

"We drafted emergency legislation to give the Government the powers to deal with coronavirus, including powers to stop mass gatherings and compensate organisations."

Public tours of Parliament will be banned and MPs were also urged not to invite guests into the building and

to axe official visits abroad. Trade body UK Hospitality warned coronavirus "could put millions of jobs at risk" in the sector. Chief executive Kate Nicholls said the numbers of people using pubs and restaurants fell 26% in the past 10 days. And hotel bookings for the next two months have crashed by 50%.

Kate added: "Some of the firms affected will not survive. I have been through economic crashes and

> **It will blow a hole in our finances. It may be more devastating for other clubs**
>
> **DALE VINCE** CHAIRMAN OF FOREST GREEN ROVERS

foot-and-mouth, but I have never seen anything like this in terms of its severity."

Sport Relief host Gary Lineker last night kicked off this year's event by declaring the UK is going through "unprecedented times". He promised "a chunk" of the money raised from the charity telethon will go to help victims of the coronavirus pandemic. Former rugby World Cup winner Mike Tindall yesterday called for calm as sporting events were being axed or delayed.

As he arrived at the Cheltenham festival, he said: "Do I feel cancelling everything is going to solve it, I'm not sure. Keep calm and carry on, that's what British do, don't they?"

graham.hiscott@mirror.co.uk
@Grahamhiscott

VOICE OF THE MIRROR: PAGE 10

- Football, rugby, and London Marathon are postponed
- BA warns of jobs losses and aircraft grounded

AT A GLANCE

- Large gatherings to be banned, home-working to be encouraged
- Experts predict that

coronavirus will now return every winter

- Trump declares national emergency as 150m could be infected in the US

BACK YEAR AFTER YEAR: PAGES 4&5   **WHAT'S OFF: SEE SPORT**

LAMPS QUALIFIES FOR THE BIG 'UN

Blues reach Champions League in Frank's first season

CHELSEA	2
Mount 45+1, Giroud 45+4	
WOLVES	0

BY **JOHN CROSS**

FRANK LAMPARD punched the air in delight - it was "mission accomplished" after his remarkable first season in Premier League management.

Chelsea clinched a place in the top four which, as Lampard (above) is quick to remind everyone, few gave the Blues a chance of doing last summer with the odds stacked against them.

Operating under a transfer ban, they had sold their best player, Eden Hazard, while rookie boss Lampard had been brought in to champion Chelsea's youth and bring through a new generation. Fitting then, that it was academy graduate Mason Mount who scored and provided an assist – in another man-of-the-match display – to prove you do not always have to break the bank to get star quality.

Mount was outstanding in a solid, mature and composed Chelsea performance, as they only needed a point to clinch a Champions League place, but never showed any nerves they would blow it on the final day.

Olivier Giroud starred again with his 14th goal of the season, his eighth in the Premier League. The 33-year-old's renaissance has come at exactly the right time ahead of the FA Cup final against former club Arsenal on Saturday. And if Chelsea can add some silverware to a place in the top four, then Lampard deserves to be mentioned in the Manager of the Year candidates for everything he has achieved.

Furthermore, the future already looks bright because new £53million signing Timo Werner was at Stamford Bridge (with Petr Cech, left) to watch his new club clinch a Champions League spot while they have also signed Hakim Ziyech from Ajax.

It also looks likely they will be after a new goalkeeper as Kepa Arrizabalaga was dropped for the final game of the season and the only problem now for Chelsea is getting back their money on a £71m outlay.

Stand-in Willy Caballero seemed far more secure, but it looked like a game too far for Wolves who, despite needing to win in their own pursuit of Europe, were out of ideas and below this season's standards.

Wanderers can still sneak in as they remain in the Europa League. If Chelsea win the FA Cup, then seventh will be enough, but finishing that high still deserves credit after a season which began 12 months ago with a Europa League qualifier.

Chelsea were in command from the moment they went ahead in first-half injury time.

Pedro Neto conceded a foul on Marcos Alonso on the edge of the box. Alonso looked as if he would take the free kick, and maybe that wrong-footed Wolves keeper Rui Patricio for what happened next.

Up stepped Mount to whip a superb, right-footed effort up and over the wall, and into the far corner to break the deadlock with a sensational strike.

Chelsea got their second three minutes later, even deeper as the Blues broke from deep as Christian Pulisic surged forward and was fouled, but referee Stuart Attwell played a brilliant advantage to allow Mount to take it up and play in Giroud.

Giroud used all his experience and strength to stretch and

TWO SMART
Mount put Chelsea ahead and Giroud sealed the victory

steer the ball into the net with his left foot to maintain a remarkable and impressive run of form with his seventh goal since the season resumed.

Chelsea were now in full control with Wolves' season slipping away. On came Adama Traore at half time for some extra pace, and that was quickly followed by a treble change with Joao Moutinho, Daniel Podence and Ruben Vinagre.

But Nuno Espirito Santo's men just could not find a way back into the contest, while it was Chelsea who looked more likely to score again but the job was already done.

63%	POSSESSION	37%
3	SHOTS ON TARGET	1
5	SHOTS OFF TARGET	1
623	TOTAL PASSES	367
84%	PASSING SUCCESS	70%
3	CORNERS	3
3	OFFSIDE	1
10	FOULS	16
0 2	CARDS	3 0

Referee
Stuart Attwell

'BLUES STARS DESERVE THIS'

FROM FRONT PAGE

as I would like to start singing my own praises, it's down to the players and what they have done.

"There have been outstanding contributions from the players. They've all come together for what we've achieved together as a group. It makes me very proud.

"We want to be challenging for the title, but you have to put

brackets around that and know that it takes time. But even the likes of Spurs and Arsenal spent north of £100million last summer, so the top four is big for us."

Lampard praised goalscorer Olivier Giroud (above, right) and Mason Mount. He added: "Oli has to take all the credit from January onwards and Mason can definitely get better because he is so young."

NUNO: LIKE A PRISON HERE

BY **JOHN CROSS**

WOLVES boss Nuno Espirito Santo still has loads on his plate – but he can't wait to escape and put his feet up for a spell.

Nuno (below) now faces a last-16 Europa League tie with Olympiacos on Thursday week as Wolves' marathon season goes into a final lap and protocols mean there is no time for a break.

He said: "We have a couple of days off. Unfortunately we have to stay here because of the quarantines. It's like a prison."

Nuno also praised his players for a "big achievement" despite defeat on the final day at Stamford Bridge.

They still finished seventh for a second year running and could get back into Europe via the Europa League and Chelsea doing them a favour by winning the FA Cup.

Nuno said: "It's a big achievement for the boys, to achieve more points. It's a big sign of improvement. But we have to keep going. This season has ups and downs. In the end, the boys worked really hard.

"This is how we want to continue.

"The proper analysis on how we did things this season and how we want to proceed has to come after there aren't any matches left.

"We worked OK until we conceded. The second half was harder, Chelsea pressed us, we were unable to go out and play and play."

Nuno was unhappy with referee Stuart Attwell and added: "Football is a game of contact. When two players jump for the ball and it's a foul then the players lose focus."

MATCH FACTS

■ Chelsea are unbeaten in all six of their Premier League home games against Wolves (W5 D1), last losing against them in the top-flight at Stamford Bridge in March 1979 (1-2).

■ Wolves have lost five of their six closing day matches in the Premier League, winning the other against Sunderland in 2009-10.

■ After just five wins at Stamford Bridge in their opening 13 Premier League games this season (D3 L5), Chelsea have ended the season with six successive home victories.

■ Wolves have lost their first Premier League game in London since March 2012 (0-5 v Fulham), with Chelsea ending their 10-game unbeaten run in the capital.

■ Wolves are the fourth different side to go through an entire Premier League campaign without any English goalscorers (excluding own goals), after Fulham (2001-02 and 2005-06), Arsenal (2006-07) and Stoke (2015-16).

■ Olivier Giroud has scored eight Premier League goals this season, his best tally since 2016-17 when he netted 12 for Arsenal.